The Fathers on the Sunday Gospels

Stephen Mark Holmes is a priest of the Diocese of Edinburgh in the Scottish Episcopal Church and a doctoral candidate in the Edinburgh University School of Divinity. He previously studied at the University of St Andrews, Corpus Christi College, Cambridge, and the Maryvale Institute, Birmingham, and has taught in Birmingham and Edinburgh. For eighteen years he was a Benedictine Monk at Pluscarden Abbey in the North of Scotland, where he was Novice Master, and he is now Assistant Priest at Old St Paul's Church, Edinburgh. He is the author of a number of books and articles on the Fathers of the Church and Church History.

The Fathers on the Sunday Gospels

Edited by

Stephen Mark Holmes

LITURGICAL PRESS

Collegeville, Minnesota

www.litpress.org

Copyright © Stephen Mark Holmes 2012

Originally published in the UK under the title
Celebrating Sundays
by the Canterbury Press of
13a Hellesdon Park Road
Norwich, Norfolk NR6 5DR

This edition published in the United States and Canada in 2012 by
Liturgical Press
Saint John's Abbey, P.O. Box 7500
Collegeville, MN 56321
www.litpress.org

Library of Congress Control Number: 2012949229

ISBN 978-0-8146-3510-0

ISBN 978-0-8146-3540-7 (ebook)

CONTENTS

Good Friday

Holy Saturday

EASTERTIDE

Easter Day Years A–C

Second Sunday of Easter

Third Sunday of Easter

Fourth Sunday of Easter

CONTENTS

INTRODUCTION

Sunday by Sunday throughout the globe, the vast majority of the world's Christians hear the same passages from the Gospels proclaimed and preached as they celebrate in Church. The two lectionaries (books of Bible passages to be read on particular days in the Christian year) which are behind this remarkable phenomenon are the product of the renaissance of Christian scholarship and the renewed desire for Christian unity which flourished in the twentieth century. They are the revised *Roman Lectionary* of 1969 and the *Revised Common Lectionary* of 1992. *The Fathers on the Sunday Gospels* provides commentaries on each of these Sunday Gospels from some of the greatest early Christian writers and preachers, the 'Fathers of the Church'. There are also some commentaries from later writers who wrote in the same style. The authors come from all parts of the ancient and medieval Christian world, including Britain and Ireland, and they wrote in Greek, Latin, Syriac and Anglo-Saxon. The writings of these Christians experienced in the life of the Spirit help us understand the central doctrines and stories of our faith – their often surprising insights will be of use to preachers, teachers and all who wish to go deeper in their understanding of the Gospel heard in Church. As most of the text of the four Gospels is read over the three years of the liturgical cycle, this book also provides a commentary from the early Church on the four Gospels.

Reading the Gospel in Church

The Fathers on the Sunday Gospels was compiled in Scotland, a country with a long and famous Christian history. Among the first books that have survived from Scotland are Gospel Books such as *Book of Kells*, which was probably at Iona Abbey, the tenth-century *Book of Deer* from Aberdeenshire and the *Gospels of St Margaret*, which belonged to Queen Margaret of Scotland (*c.*1045–93). These books are all related to worship, either used in the liturgy or, as in the case of Margaret's book, containing Gospel passages read in the liturgy for personal use. The original Gospels themselves were written in the first decades of Christianity primarily as liturgical texts to be proclaimed in the Christian assembly, and it is hard for us, with our private copies of the New Testament, to understand this. Before going on to speak about the Fathers, this introduction to *The Fathers on the Sunday Gospels* thus needs to begin by looking at how the Gospels are read in Church and by examining the history of the lectionaries which contain the Sunday Gospels.

From the beginning the Scriptures have been read in the Christian assembly and the Church gradually accepted writings from the first Christians, what we call the 'New Testament', as inspired in the same way as the Jewish Scriptures which Christians call the 'Old Testament'. The Gospels and the rest of the New Testament thus, under the guidance of the Holy Spirit, came to be recognized as Scripture because of their use in the worship of the Church. In the middle of the second century AD the Christian writer St Justin Martyr wrote of this liturgical use of the Gospels in his account of the Sunday Eucharist:

> The Apostles, in the memoirs composed by them which are called Gospels, have handed on to us what they were given; that Jesus took bread, and when he had given thanks, said, 'do this in remembrance of me, this is my body'; and likewise having taken the cup and given thanks, he said, 'This is my blood'; and he gave it to them alone ... On the day called Sunday, all who live in cities or in the country gather together to one place, and the memoirs of the apostles or the writings of the prophets are read, as long as time permits; then, when the reader has finished, the President teaches and exhorts us to imitate these good things. Then we all rise together and pray, and, when our prayer is ended, bread and wine and water are brought, and the president offers prayers and thanksgivings according to his ability. The people then assent, saying 'Amen', and there is a distribution to those who participate in that over which thanks have been given. (*First Apology*, 66–67)

The phrase 'as long as time permits' suggests that the sacred books were read in sequence, with the reading at one service taking up where the reading had ended at the last. This continuous reading (called *lectio continua* in Latin) later came to be replaced by lectionaries where certain readings were appointed to be read on certain days. This is a practice already found in Judaism and it seems to have been linked to the development of the liturgical year in the second century AD with certain readings seen as appropriate in certain seasons, such as Acts and Revelation being read between Easter and Pentecost and Genesis in Lent. In Christianity different lectionaries for the Eucharist developed in the different liturgical families of East and West and a standard one-year cycle of Sunday Gospel passages became common in the Latin West. After the Reformation, this one-year cycle continued to be used with certain variations in Anglican, Lutheran and Roman Catholic Churches while some Protestant Churches reverted to a form of *lectio continua*.

But what are the Gospels? The four Gospels, which contain the 'memoirs of the Apostles', tell us about the life and teaching of Jesus Christ. He is the revelation of God to humanity who, by the mystery of his cross and resurrection, enabled men and women to pass from death to life and become adopted as sons and daughters of God just as Jesus is the Son of God by nature. It is this mystery of Christ which we share in the sacraments of Baptism and the Eucharist, mentioned in the extract from Justin, where material things become the bearers of grace, a sign of the transformation of the universe in Christ Jesus. The Gospels thus proclaim the heart of the Christian message which is also performed in the sacraments and it is for this reason that the reading of the Gospel in Christian worship is often surrounded by ceremony, for example in many Churches the sacred text is sung and the Gospel-book is kissed, reverenced and accompanied by candles and incense. The Gospels are thus not primarily texts to be read by people in private, they are books to be read out loud in the Christian assembly, to be listened to and talked about so that we can hear Jesus speak and meditate together on his life and teaching in community. This is the teaching of the sixteenth-century Reformers as well as of the saints of all ages, and our personal meditation of the Gospels draws from and feeds into this communal listening.

All this means that the Gospels do not reach us today in a sealed packet from the first century AD, they are handed on to us by the Christian community in a continuous tradition of preaching, meditation and celebration which goes back to the days before the stories and teaching in the Gospels were written down. This is what is called 'tradition', which for Christians is not an idolatry of the past but rather the ongoing life of the Spirit in the Church. To read the Gospels outside this living tradition is to court the danger of turning them into dead historical documents – though, of course, we know that the Holy Spirit can make even the dry bones live. The passages in *The Fathers on the Sunday Gospels* help us read the Gospels within this Spirit-filled stream of sacred tradition.

We experience this tradition in different ways. One is the tradition of preaching, of reflecting on the sacred text, interpreting it and applying it to our lives. Another is the way in which the Gospel story is 'unpacked' and celebrated in the liturgical year, the way in which the Church moves from the expectation of Advent to the celebration of Christ's birth and revelation at Christmas and Epiphany, and then to the desert of Lent and the glory of Easter, Ascension and Pentecost. The liturgical year really is a 'year of the Lord's favour' (Luke 4.19) in which the sequence of Gospel passages read takes us on a sustained and systematic tour of the Christian gospel. The way that biblical studies have sometimes been taught in universities, with a close attention to words and language and the use of historical-critical analysis, is thus only part of the task of interpreting the Gospels. It is really only a preparation for engagement with the sacred text in the context of the prayer of the Christian assembly and the application of its teaching to our lives. Early and medieval Christian teachers often had a better grasp of this truth than we do today: as well as its literal and historical sense, Scripture has a spiritual sense which can transform our lives and lead us beyond ourselves to the mystery of Christ and the final destiny of the cosmos in God. We need to read holy Scripture, the word of God in human words, with the help of the same Holy Spirit who inspired it.

The recovery of this way of reading the Scriptures and the rediscovery of the ancient practice of spiritual reading (*lectio divina*) have been part of the great renewal of Christian life in the last century which produced the new ways of reading Scripture in the Church-assembly on which *The Fathers on the Sunday Gospels* is based. Some of the books recommended in the Further Reading section on page 299 can help lead us into this Christian way of interpreting the Bible, but what is this new way of reading the Bible in public in the Christian assembly?

Our Common Sunday Lectionary

Behind the readings in *The Fathers on the Sunday Gospels* is a series of Gospel passages read on Sundays over a three-year period which has an interesting history. The century from about 1870 saw a tremendous growth of Christianity throughout the world and a number of exciting developments in Christian scholarship which have continued to influence the Church. The liturgical movement, the renewal of biblical studies, the rediscovery of the Fathers of the Church and a renewed sense of the mystery of the Church all bore fruit in a new appreciation of Christian worship. Part of this involved reflection on the way the Bible was read in church and a desire to feed the Christian community with more of the sacred text than the very selective traditional one-year lectionaries could supply. The Second Vatican Council, an assembly of Roman Catholic bishops from all over the world which met in Rome between 1962 and 1965, was influenced by this renewal and decided that the biblical lectionary used at Mass should be reformed.

> The treasures of the Bible are to be opened up more lavishly so that a richer share in God's word may be provided for the faithful. In this way a more representative portion of the Holy Scriptures will be read to the people in the course of a prescribed number of years. (*Sacrosanctum Concilium* 51)

As was the practice in the early Church, the volumes of the Lectionary with their Bible readings were to be separated from the Sacramentary (the book of prayers used at Mass) with which they had been combined in the Middle Ages to form a book called the Missal.

A group of learned scholars under the leadership of the Benedictine monk Cyprian Vaggagini was formed to revise the Lectionary and they began by studying most of the eucharistic lectionaries that had survived from the history of the Church together with various suggestions that had been made for lectionary reform springing from the renewal of liturgical and biblical studies and catechetics. Most of the work of the group was done between 1964 and 1967. In 1967 a draft Lectionary was sent out to over 800 experts and their suggestions were collated and used to refine the draft. The final text of the new Lectionary, the *Ordo lectionum missae*, was approved by Pope Paul VI on 3 April 1969. It was to be used in the Roman Catholic Church from the first Sunday in Advent 1971 and was slightly revised in 1981. The Gospel readings of this new lectionary include about 60 per cent of the text of each of the four Gospels. The scriptural texts of the revised *Roman Lectionary* are found in the many Roman Catholic Missals that are on sale and also in separate lectionary volumes.

This new Roman Catholic Lectionary came to influence the lectionaries of other Churches who shared its liturgical inheritance from pre-Reformation Western Europe. The one-year Sunday Lectionary of the *Book of Common Prayer* of the Church of England largely followed the standard Western one-year cycle as used in the pre-Reformation Sarum (Salisbury) rite used in Britain and Ireland and this, or variants of it, was adopted by many Reformed Churches. Until the twentieth century, then, most Western Churches, apart from those which had opted for a *lectio continua*, had a similar series of Sunday Gospel readings. The Lutheran Churches had largely retained a modified version of the pre-Reformation Sunday Lectionary and in Germany the Protestant Churches from the nineteenth century have developed a series of cycles of biblical 'sermon texts' which run alongside it, as found in the *Evangelische Gottesdienstbuch* of 1999. Similar lectionaries are also used in some of the Scandinavian and Baltic Lutheran Churches which are in full communion with the British and Irish Anglican Churches.

Outside the Roman Catholic Church in the English-speaking world there have been two main movements of lectionary reform. First in 1967, before the publication of the revised *Roman Lectionary*, the liturgical scholars of the British Joint Liturgical Group (JLG) produced a two-year Sunday Lectionary, emphasizing themes in the set of readings for each Sunday, which was adopted by a number of Anglican, Methodist and Reformed Churches. The JLG also produced an experimental four-year Lectionary in 1990 with each year devoted to one of the four Gospels but this has not proved popular. Second, in North America a number of Anglican, Methodist and Reformed Churches adopted the 1969 Roman Lectionary, sometimes with variants, but there was a growing desire to have a common Lectionary. The liturgical scholars of the North American Consultation on Common Texts (CCT), which had been set up in the mid-1960s, met in 1978 to discuss this common Lectionary and formed the North American Committee on Calendar and Lectionary (NACCL), composed of Episcopalian, Lutheran, Methodist, Presbyterian and Roman Catholic scholars. In 1983 it offered the Churches of North America a three-year *Common Lectionary* based on the revised Roman Lectionary. They invited comments on this text and took these into account in revising the text in collaboration with the international English Language Liturgical Consultation (ELLC). The group responsible for the revision included Anglican, Congregationalist, Methodist, Presbyterian and Roman Catholic scholars from all over the English-speaking world. The result of this remarkable ecumenical and international collaboration was the 1992 *Revised Common Lectionary*.

The *Revised Common Lectionary* has subsequently been adopted by many English-speaking Protestant denominations such as the Church of Scotland and various Methodist, Lutheran and Reformed Churches. It has also been adopted by some Old Catholic Churches and is widely used throughout the Anglican Communion, for example by the Church of Ireland, Scottish Episcopal Church, Church in Wales, the Episcopal Church (USA) and the Anglican Churches of Canada, Australia, Aotearoa/New Zealand and Polynesia, Melanesia, the West Indies, Central Africa, and Southern Africa. In the Church of England the two-year Sunday Lectionary of the *Alternative Service Book 1980* was replaced in 2000 by an adapted version of the *Revised Common Lectionary* in *Common Wor-*

ship. We have thus now returned to a series of Sunday Gospel readings which are almost the same in most of the world's Christian Churches. *The Fathers on the Sunday Gospels* has been constructed so that its commentaries on the Sunday Gospels can be used by all these Churches, whether they follow the *Roman Lectionary*, the *Revised Common Lectionary* or the *Revised Common Lectionary* as modified by the Church of England, which will be referred to as the *Common Worship Lectionary* (CWL).

Wisdom from the early Church

The Fathers on the Sunday Gospels consists of passages from the writers of the early Church, the 'Fathers of the Church', together with some later writers, commenting on the Sunday Gospels of the lectionaries discussed above. Many of these come from the Fathers' sermons preached in church but such patristic commentaries ('patristic' is a word from the Latin for father, *pater*) were also read as part of the liturgy itself.

In the sixth century St Benedict wrote in the ninth chapter of his Holy Rule:

> Let the books which have divine authority, from both the Old and the New Testaments, be read at the night office of Vigils, as also the expositions of them which have been made by well-known orthodox and catholic Fathers.

Benedict seems to have been the first monastic writer to allow readings from non-biblical authors in the liturgy and they have never been allowed in the Roman liturgy at the Eucharist. What Benedict is speaking of are not any writings by the Fathers but specifically their commentaries on Scripture (in Latin *expositiones*). Benedict lived in a time of political and doctrinal turmoil and he was concerned that the authors read to his monks were sound and reliable expositors of the sacred text. This tradition has continued in the Western Church not only in monasteries but also among the clergy in general who were given readings from the Fathers in their daily prayer book, the Breviary. On Sundays for monks, nuns and clergy throughout the Western Church, and in the Roman Catholic Church up to the 1960s, the Third Nocturn (the third and final part of the night office of Mattins or Vigils, each part of which consists of psalms and readings) ended with the Gospel passage read at the Sunday Mass together with readings from the Fathers commenting on it. This is the direct inspiration for *The Fathers on the Sunday Gospels*. But who do we mean by the Fathers?

First it is necessary to correct a misconception. A friend who is a Roman Catholic priest once went to a meeting called by a fundamentalist body to protest about a visit by the Pope to Scotland. At the end he stood up to ask a question and identified himself as 'Father James'; a voice from the platform thundered, 'Call no man your father on earth, for you have one Father, who is in heaven, Matthew 23.9'; the priest replied quietly, 'What did you call your Daddy?' It is clear to anyone with a sound grasp of Scripture that Jesus' words in Matthew 23 on the uniqueness of the divine paternity do not prohibit Christians from calling a respected teacher, let alone one's male parent, 'father' because St Paul wrote to the Corinthians, 'Although you have countless guides in Christ, you do not have many fathers; for I became your father in Christ Jesus through the gospel' (1 Corinthians 4.15). One could compare the relationship of Mark to his teacher Peter in 1 Peter 5.13, where Peter writes of 'my son Mark', and also note the reference to the first generation of Christians as 'the fathers' in 2 Peter 3.4. Christian bishops and priests have thus frequently been called 'Father' (or, in certain churches in modern times, 'Mother') and it is from this use in ancient times that we start to get the idea of a body of well-known and authoritative teachers who were to be known as the 'Fathers of the Church'. These were at first only bishops, but later presbyters (priests), deacons and layfolk were added, as Augustine included among 'the Fathers' the priest St Jerome because of the excellence of his teaching (C. Julian. 1.7.34), and the deacon St Ephrem the Syrian and the layman Tertullian were also later recognized as Fathers.

In the Christian West, St John Damascene (c.676–749) and St Bede (672–735) are often said to be the last of the Fathers of the Church but Bernard of Clairvaux is also at times called the last of the Fathers and he and many other medieval monastic writers continued to write in the same patristic style. It is commonly said that the Eastern Orthodox Churches hold that the patristic age has not ended and later writers such as St Gregory Palamas (1296–1359) or even modern writers are considered as 'patristic'. The Reformers of the sixteenth century, both Catholic and Protestant, frequently appeal to the Fathers and the period saw a revival of patristic scholarship with new editions of their works being produced by Erasmus (1469–1536) and others. The use of the historic creeds by all the main Churches of the world is a sign that they all accord a special value to the Fathers of the Church, in whose era these creeds were drawn up, although among the Churches there are various views of the authority given the Fathers in interpreting Scripture and mediating tradition. John Calvin's 1559 French *Confession of Faith* has a high view of the Fathers:

We confess that which has been established by the ancient councils, and we detest all sects and heresies which were rejected by the holy doctors, such as St Hilary, St Athanasius, St Ambrose and St Cyril.

Anglicanism has traditionally given great respect to the writers of the early Church. Archbishop Cranmer appealed to the 'ancient Fathers' in his preface to the *Book of Common Prayer* and Queen Elizabeth I wrote to the Roman Catholic Princes of Europe concerning the Church of England as reformed in the sixteenth century:

There was no new faith propagated in England, no new religion set up but that which was commanded by Our Saviour, practiced by the Primitive Church and approved by the Fathers of the best antiquity.

At the Second Vatican Council the Roman Catholic Church likewise emphasized the important place of the Fathers in the handing on of divine revelation through history in the Church:

The tradition which comes from the Apostles develops in the Church with the help of the Holy Spirit, for there is a growth in understanding of the realities and the words which have been handed down ... For as the centuries succeed one another, the Church constantly moves forward toward the fullness of divine truth until the words of God reach their complete fulfilment in her. The words of the Holy Fathers witness to the presence of this living tradition, whose wealth is poured into the practice and life of the believing and praying Church. Through the same tradition the Church's full canon of the sacred books is known, and the sacred writings themselves are more profoundly understood and unceasingly made active in her; and thus God, who spoke of old, continues to speak with the bride of his beloved Son; and the Holy Spirit, through whom the living voice of the Gospel resounds in the Church and through her in the world, leads those who believe into all truth and makes the word of Christ dwell abundantly in them. (*Dei Verbum* 8)

The Fathers are thus truly ecumenical and *The Fathers on the Sunday Gospels* has endeavoured to have a balance between writers from the Greek Christian East, about 43 per cent, and the Latin Christian West, about 54 per cent, with 6 Eastern writers who wrote in Syriac. A couple of the readings were written in Anglo-Saxon and English. The most used Fathers are St Augustine from the West and SS John Chrysostom and Cyril of Alexandria from the East, who between them contribute almost half of the commentaries. The vast majority of writers quoted are from the patristic period but about 15 per cent are from later periods, although the only modern writer is Blessed John Henry Newman (1801–90) who was himself deeply influenced by the Fathers. Newman is commemorated in the calendars of both the Anglican and Roman Catholic Churches; the passage used in *The Fathers on the Sunday Gospels* is from one of his Anglican sermons and it is commenting on a reading only used by Roman Catholics. Greek writers of the second Christian millennium are included such as St Gregory Palamas (1296–1359) and St Nicholas Cabasilas (*c.*1322–after 1391), who are primarily venerated by the Greek Orthodox Churches although their teaching is known in the West. Some of the Syrian writers such as St Ephrem the Syrian are venerated by all Churches but others such as St Jacob of Serugh and St Philoxenus of Mabbug opposed the Council of Chalcedon (AD 451), which was accepted as orthodox by the Latin and Byzantine Churches. I have followed the custom of using the title 'Saint' as it is used in the writer's own Church. The incorporation of writers who have been criticized by one side or the other as schismatic or heretical is justified by the excellence and orthodoxy of their teaching, but also by the inclusion of Origen of Alexandria. Origen was one of the greatest theologians and exegetes of the early Church but, despite his holy death after persecution, he was never recognized as a saint and his adventurous theological and philosophical speculations led to him being posthumously condemned by Church Councils in the sixth century. His Scriptural commentaries were, however, read in the Divine Office in the West during the Middle Ages because they were deemed to be orthodox and of great value. The commentaries in *The Fathers on the Sunday Gospels* are thus offered to the whole Church as examples of the unity-in-diversity of our common tradition.

As well as the fact that they are called 'father', another problem some people might have with the Fathers is that they are men. Recent scholarship has done much to uncover the hidden voices of women in the early Church but the inescapable maleness of the Fathers remains. Some get round this by speaking of the 'Fathers and Mothers of the Church' and this is accurate, given the important role played by women in Christianity from its beginning. One thinks of Jesus' female disciples, and, just to take one example related to some of the writers in this book, St Macrina the Younger, sister of SS Basil of Caesarea and Gregory of Nyssa, whom we meet as a holy woman, community leader and highly educated Christian teacher in Gregory's *Life of Macrina* and *On the Soul and Resurrection*. But even from a woman of the intellectual calibre of Macrina we do not have sermons or commentaries on the Gospels. Most of the commentaries in *The Fathers on the Sunday Gospels* are from the first millennium of Christianity and all the suitable texts are by male writers. It might have been possible to have extracted certain texts by or related to female voices and to have added medieval texts such as passages from Julian of Norwich that reflect on the Gospels, but this could not avoid an impression of tokenism. One needs to step back from these questions and join the women and men who were the audience for most of these commentaries in engaging with the teaching of the Fathers as a way of understanding the Gospel message in our own time.

The patristic commentaries on the Gospels which were part of the Third Nocturn of the night office of Mattins or Vigils in the traditional Roman and monastic offices have not been retained in the 1970 revised Roman *Liturgy of the Hours*, although this does retain a daily non-scriptural reading. The reform of the Divine Office in the Church of England at the Reformation, which resulted in Mattins and Evensong found in the *Book of Common Prayer*, excluded non-scriptural readings but some Anglican religious communities restored them and more recently they come into general use in books such as *From the Fathers to the Churches* (1983), compiled by Brother Kenneth CGA, which largely used the new Roman daily patristic readings adapted for use with the *Alternative Service Book 1980*. Other similar volumes have been printed, most notably *Celebrating the Seasons* (1999) and *Celebrating the Saints* (2004), compiled by Robert Atwell and published by Canterbury Press, which have daily readings taken from throughout Christian history for the seasons and saints of the Christian calendar but do not provided commentaries on the Scripture readings of the liturgy. It is the provision of commentaries from the early Church on the Sunday Gospel readings from the *Revised Common Lectionary* and the *Roman Lectionary* that is the distinctive feature of *The Fathers on the Sunday Gospels*.

The genesis of *The Fathers on the Sunday Gospels* and acknowledgements

This book began when Abbot Hugh Gilbert OSB, now Roman Catholic Bishop of Aberdeen, asked me to revise the patristic readings for the night office of Vigils used at Pluscarden Abbey in the North of Scotland. The aim was to create a patristic Lectionary where the readings were closely related to the Bible text for the day and to ensure that most of the non-biblical readings were from the Fathers of the Church and not from later periods of Christian history. For the daily readings the monastic community uses the Roman two-year cycle of Bible readings and a series of patristic readings was constructed as a commentary on this which is available online on the website of the Durham University Centre for Catholic Studies as, *A Two-year Patristic Lectionary for the Divine Office*, edited by Stephen Mark Holmes, www.centreforcatholicstudies.co.uk/?page_id=765. *The Fathers on the Sunday Gospels* is based on the Third Nocturn commentaries on the Sunday Gospels from this Lectionary which are not on the Durham University website.

I thank Bishop Hugh Gilbert for his encouragement of this project and his support for the publication of *The Fathers on the Sunday Gospels*. His inspiring teaching as Novice Master and Abbot has influenced profoundly my understanding of Christian history and theology. I am grateful to the Benedictine community of Pluscarden where I learned to live the rhythm of the Christian year in the changing seasons of the Morayshire countryside. I would also like to thank Mrs Eileen Grant for her secretarial assistance in the production of the Pluscarden Lectionary. A number of the readings in this book were originally in the two volumes entitled, *Christ our Light: Patristic readings on Gospel themes, Volume 1, Advent to Pentecost* and *Volume 2, Ordinary Time*, edited by The Friends of Henry Ashworth and published in 1981 and 1985 by Exordium Books, but now out of print. I thank The Friends of Henry Ashworth for permission to use their translations and especially Dame Anne Field OSB of Stanbrook Abbey, Yorkshire. I also thank Sr Benedicta White OSB and the community of Stanbrook. The other readings are either translated directly from the original languages or adapted from old out-of-copyright translations. The suggestion that I publish this set of patristic commentaries on the Sunday Gospels came from Canon Dr Mark Harris and Fr Pip Blackledge, fellow presbyters of the Diocese of Edinburgh. I would also like to thank Canon Ian Paton of Old St Paul's Church, Edinburgh, Dr Sara Parvis of Edinburgh University and Professor Lewis Ayres of Durham University for advice in the preparation of this book, and Mrs Christine Smith of Canterbury Press for her encouragement and help in seeing this project through to completion. All responsibility for the final text and for any imperfections is mine. Finally I would like to thank Professor Jane Dawson of Edinburgh University for encouraging this project, and my wife Rachel for her invaluable love and support.

How to use this book

The Fathers on the Sunday Gospels provides a commentary by a writer from the early or medieval Church on the Gospel passages read every Sunday in the year in churches that use the *Roman Lectionary*, the *Revised Common Lectionary* or the *Common Worship Lectionary*. These readings may be used for private meditation by those who are preparing for Sunday worship in their church; by preachers as they prepare their sermons; for reading at Morning Prayer on Sundays in parishes and other communities such as monasteries; or simply by someone who wants to see what some of the most profound thinkers of the Christian tradition have said on a particular passage from the Gospels. The great advantage of these readings is that by mediating the Great Tradition they take us out of the limitations of our own time and can challenge our prejudices about what the gospel means. The Fathers are privileged witnesses to the great mysteries of the faith and I would dare to suggest that, although some of what they say is limited by their own culture, there can be no authentic renewal of Christianity where their teaching and example is ignored. As Pope John Paul II said in 1982, 'placing oneself in the school of the Fathers means learning to know Christ better and to know the human person better'.[1]

Stephen Mark Holmes
School of Divinity, University of Edinburgh
Feast of St Duthac of Tain, March 2012

---

1 Address to the professors and students of the Augustinianum, 8 May 1982, AAS 74 (1982), 798.

ABBREVIATIONS

Bareille	*Oeuvres complètes de Saint Jean Chrysostome, d'après toutes les éditions faites jusqu'à ce jour*, ed. and tr., J. Bareille, 21 vols (Paris, 1865–78)
CCSL	*Corpus Christianorum series Latina* (Turnhout, 1953–)
CSCO Script. Syri	*Corpus Scriptorum Christianorum Orientalium* (Leuven, 1903–), *Scriptores Syri*
CSCO Script. Arm.	*Corpus Scriptorum Christianorum Orientalium* (Leuven, 1903–), *Scriptores Armeniaci*
CSEL	*Corpus Scriptorum Ecclesiasticorum Latinorum* (Vienna, 1864–)
CWL	*Common Worship Lectionary*
Edit. Maurist.	*Sancti Aurelii Augustini Hipponensis episcopi Operum ... Opera et studio monachorum ordinis S. Benedicti è congregatione S. Mauri*, 13 vols (Paris, 1679–1705).
GCS	*Griechischen Christlichen Schriftsteller* (Berlin, 1891–)
Guéranger	Prosper Guéranger, *L'année liturgique*, 16 vols (Tours, 1904–20)
Jaeger	Werner Jaeger (ed.), *Gregorii Nysseni Opera*, (Leiden, 1921–)
PG	*Patrologia Graeca*, ed. J. P. Migne (Paris, 1857–58)
PL	*Patrologia Latina*, ed. J. P. Migne (Paris, 1844–45)
PLS	*Patrologiae Latinae Supplementum*, ed. A. Hamman (Paris, 1958–)
RCL	*Revised Common Lectionary* (1992)
RL	*Roman Lectionary* (1969, revised 1981)
SC	*Sources Chrétiennes* (Paris, 1942–)
Whitman	*The Christ of Cynewulf: A Poem in Three Parts* (Boston, 1900)

TABLE OF READINGS

The Fathers on the Sunday Gospels is designed for use with the 1969 *Roman Lectionary* (RL), the 1992 *Revised Common Lectionary* (RCL) and adaptations of this lectionary for use in Churches such as the Church of England (*Common Worship Lectionary* – CWL). Where there is divergence, the Roman titles for the Sunday readings are given first followed by the titles from the 1992 *Revised Common Lectionary*, but the names for the Sundays used in different Churches are not all noted. Where there are certain slight differences in the length of the Gospel passages used, the RCL additions are given in square brackets. The Church of England occasionally substitutes a different Gospel reading and these are noted and given their own patristic commentary.

Advent Sunday 1A	Matthew 24.37–44	St Paschasius Radbertus, *On Matthew* 2.24: PL 120, 799–800
Advent Sunday 1B	Mark 13.33–37 [24–37]	Godfrey of Admont, *Festal Homilies* 23: PL 174, 724–726
Advent Sunday 1C	Luke 21.25–28, 34–36 [25–36]	St Bernard, *Advent sermons* 4.1, 3–4: *Opera omnia*, Ed. Cist. 4 (1966) 182–5
Advent Sunday 2A	Matthew 3.1–12	St Augustine, *Sermon* 109.1: PL 38, 636
Advent Sunday 2B	Mark 1.1–8	Origen, *Homilies on Luke*, 22.1–4: SC 67, 300–2
Advent Sunday 2C	Luke 3.1–6	Origen, *Homilies on Luke* 21: PG 13, 1855–6
Advent Sunday 3A	Matthew 11.2–11	St Ambrose, *On Luke* 5.93–5, 99–102, 109: CCSL 14, 165–6, 167–8, 171–2
Advent Sunday 3B	John 1.6–8, 19–28	John Scotus Eriugena, *Homilies on the Prologue of John*, 13: SC 151, 275–7

Advent Sunday 3C	Luke 3.10–18 [7–18]	Origen, *Homilies on Luke* 26.3–5: SC 87, 340–2
Advent Sunday 4A	Matthew 1.18–24	Ven. Bede, *Homily 5 on the Vigil of the Nativity*: CCSL 122, 32–6
Advent Sunday 4B	Luke 1.26–38	Ven. Bede, *Homily 2 on Advent*: CCSL 122, 14–17
Advent Sunday 4C	Luke 1.39–45 [*or* 39–55]	Bd Guerric of Igny, *Advent Sermons*, 2.1–4: SC 166, 104–16
Christmas I (midnight)	Luke 2.1–14 [*or*, 1–20]	Theodotus of Ancyra, *Homily 1 on the Nativity of the Lord*: PG 77, 1360–1
Christmas II (dawn)	Luke 2.15–20 [1-20, *or* 8-20]	St Aelred, *Sermon 2 on the Birth of the Lord*: PL 195, 226–7, 1471–4
Christmas III (day)	John 1.1–18 [1–14]	St Basil the Great, *Homily 2 on the Holy Birth of the Lord*: PG 31, 1459–62
Holy Family/Christmas 1A	Matthew 2.13–15, 19–23 [13–23]	St John Chrysostom, *Homily on the Day of Christ's Birth*: PG 56, 392
Holy Family/Christmas 1B	Luke 2.22–40 *or* 2.39–40	St Cyril of Alexandria, *Homily 12*: PG 77, 1042, 1046, 1047, 1050
Holy Family/Christmas 1C	Luke 2.41–52	Origen, *Homilies on Luke* 18.2–5: GCS 9, 112–13
Mary, Mother of God, OR, The Naming and Circumcision of Jesus, OR, The Holy Name, Years A, B & C	Luke 2.16–21	Bd Guerric of Igny, *Sermon 1 on the Assumption of Mary*, 2–4: PL 185, 187–9
	Luke 2.16–21	St Basil of Seleucia, *Sermons*, 39.4, 5: PG 85, 438, 442, 446
	Luke 2.16–21	St Cyril of Alexandria, *Homilies on the Incarnation of the Word of God*, 15.1–3: PG 77, 1090–1
Christmas 2A	John 1.1–18 *or* 1.1–5, 9–14	St Leo the Great, *Sermon 6 on the Nativity of the Lord*, 2–3, 5: PL 54, 213–16
Christmas 2B	John 1.1–18 *or* 1.1–5, 9–14	Bd Guerric of Igny, *Sermon 5 on the Nativity of the Lord*, 1–2: SC 166, 223–6
Christmas 2C	John 1.1–18 *or* 1.1–5, 9–14	Julian of Vézelay, *Sermon 1 on the Nativity*: SC 192, 45, 52, 60

Epiphany A	Matthew 2.1–12	St Basil the Great, *Homily 2 on the Holy Birth of the Lord*: PG 31, 1472–6
Epiphany B	Matthew 2.1–12	St Odilo of Cluny, *Sermon 2 on the Epiphany of the Lord*: PL 142, 997–8
Epiphany C	Matthew 2.1–12	St Bruno of Segni, *Sermon 1 on the Epiphany of the Lord*: PL 165, 863–4
Baptism of the Lord A/ Epiphany 1A	Matthew 3.13–17	St Gregory the Wonderworker, *Homily 4 on the Holy Theophany*: PG 10, 1181, 1183
Baptism of the Lord B/ Epiphany 1B	Mark 1.7–11 [4–11]	St Gregory of Antioch, *Homily 2 on the Baptism of Christ* 5, 6, 9, 10: PG 88, 1876–7, 1880–4
Baptism of the Lord C/ Epiphany 1C	Luke 3.15–16, 21–22	St Hippolytus (attr.), *Sermon on the Holy Theophany*, 6–9: PG 10, 858–9
Ordinary Time 2A/ Epiphany 2A	John 1.29–34 [29–42]	St Cyril of Alexandria, *On John*, 2: PG 73, 191–4
Ordinary Time 2B (RL)	John 1.35–42	St Basil of Selucia, *Exhortatory Sermon*, 3–4: PG 28, 1104–6
Epiphany 2B (RCL)	John 1.43–51	St Augustine, *Tractates on John*, 7.16, 17, 20, 21
Ordinary Time 2C/ Epiphany 2C	John 2.1–12	St Maximus of Turin, *Homily* 23: PL 57, 274–6
Ordinary Time 3A/ Epiphany 3A	Matthew 4.12–23 or 4.12–17	St Gregory the Great, *Forty Gospel Homilies*, 1.5: PL 76, 1093–4
Ordinary Time 3B/ Epiphany 3B	Mark 1.14–20	St Caesarius of Arles, *Sermon* 144.1–4: CCSL 104, 593–5
Ordinary Time 3C/ Epiphany 3C	Luke 1.1–4; 4.14–21	Origen, *Homilies on Luke*, 32.2–6: SC 87, 386–392
Ordinary Time 4A/ Epiphany 4A	Matthew 5.1–12	St Chromatius of Aquileia, *Sermon 39*: SC 164, 216–20
Epiphany 4A (CWL)	John 2.1–11	See Ordinary Time 2C
Ordinary Time 4B/ Epiphany 4B	Mark 1.21–28	St John Chrysostom, *Homily 5 on Hebrews*: Bareille 20, 158
Ordinary Time 4C/ Epiphany 4C	Luke 4.21–30	St Cyril of Alexandria, *On Isaiah*, 5.5: PG 70, 1352–3
Epiphany 4C (CWL)	Luke 2.22–40	See the Presentation of Christ

Presentation of Christ A	Luke 2.22–40	St Cyril of Alexandria, *Sermon 4 on Luke*, 28–9
Presentation of Christ B	Luke 2.22–40	St Augustine, *Sermon 13 de Tempore*, from the old Roman Breviary
Presentation of Christ C	Luke 2.22–40	St Ambrose, *Sermons on Luke*
Ordinary Time 5A/ Epiphany 5A	Matthew 5.13–16 [13–20]	St John Chrysostom, *Baptismal Catecheses* 4.18–21, 26, 33: SC 50, 192–3, 196, 199
Ordinary Time 5B/ Epiphany 5B	Mark 1.29–39	St Peter Chrysologus, *Sermon 18*: PL 52, 246–9
Ordinary Time 5C/ Epiphany 5C	Luke 5.1–11	St Augustine, *Sermon 43.5–6*: PL 38, 256–7
Ordinary Time 6A/ Epiphany 6A	Matthew 5.17–37 [21–37]	St John Chrysostom, *Homily 2*: Bareille, 3, 655–6
Ordinary Time 6B/ Epiphany 6B	Mark 1.40–45	St Paschasius Radbertus, *On Matthew*, 5.8: PL 120, 341–2
Ordinary Time 6C/ Epiphany 6C	Luke 6.17, 20–26 [17–26]	St John Chrysostom, *Homily 12.4*: Bareille, 17, 480–1
Ordinary Time 7A/ Epiphany 7A	Matthew 5.38–48	St Cyprian, *On Jealousy and Envy*, 12–13: CSEL 3/1, 427–30
Ordinary Time 7B/ Epiphany 7B	Mark 2.1–12	St John Chrysostom, *Homilies on Matthew* 29.1: Bareille, 12, 87–9
Ordinary Time 7C/ Epiphany 7C	Luke 6.27–38	St Augustine, *On the Psalms* 60, 9: CCSL 39, 771
Ordinary Time 8A/ Epiphany 8A [Proper 3A]	Matthew 6.24–34	St John Chrysostom, *Baptismal Catecheses* 8.19–21, 23–5: SC 50, 257–60
Ordinary Time 8B/ Epiphany 8B [Proper 3B]	Mark 2.18–22 [13–22]	St Paschasius Radbertus, *On Matthew* 10.22: PL 120, 741–2
Epiphany 8B (CWL)	John 1.1–14	See readings for Advent 3B, Christmas III or Christmas 2 A–C
Ordinary Time 8C/ Epiphany 8C [Proper 3C]	Luke 6.39–45 [39–49]	St Cyril of Alexandria, *On Luke*, 6: PG 72, 602–3
Epiphany 8C (CWL)	Luke 8.22–25	See reading for Ordinary Time 12B

Ordinary Time 9A/ Epiphany 9A [Proper 4A]	Matthew 7.21–27	St Philoxenus of Mabbug, *Homily* 1: SC 44, 27–31
Epiphany 9A (alternative)	Matthew 17.1–9	See reading for Lent 2A
Ordinary Time 9B/ Epiphany 9B [Proper 4B]	Mark 2.23 – 3.6 *or* 2.23–28	Unknown Greek author, *Sermon* 6.1–2, 6: PG 86/1, 416, 421
Epiphany 9B (alternative)	Mark 9.2–9	See reading for Lent 2B
Ordinary Time 9C/ Epiphany 9C [Proper 4C]	Luke 7.1–10	St Augustine, *Sermon* 62.1, 3–4: PL 38, 414–16
Epiphany 9C (alternative)	Luke 9.28–36 [28–43]	See reading for Lent 2C
Ash Wednesday A–C	Matthew 6.1–6, 16–21	I. St John Chrysostom, *Oration 3 Against the Jews*: PG 48, 867–8
		II. St Peter Chrysologus, *Sermon* 43: PL 52:320, 322
		III. St Augustine, Sermon 205.1: PL 38, 1039–40
Ash Wednesday (CWL alternative)	John 8.1–11	See reading for Lent 5C (RL)
Lent Sunday 1A	Matthew 4.1–11	St Gregory Nazianzen, *Oration* 40.10: PG 36, 370–1
Lent Sunday 1B	Mark 1.12–15 [9–15]	John Justus Landsberg, *Sermons: Opera omnia* 1 [1888], 120
Lent Sunday 1C	Luke 4.1–13	Origen, *On the Song of Songs*, 3.13: GCS 8, 221, 19 – 223, 5
Lent Sunday 2A	Matthew 17.1–9	St Ephrem the Syrian, *Sermon 16 on the Transfiguration of the Lord*, 1, 3, 4
Lent 2A (RCL alternative)	John 3.1–17	St Cyril of Alexandria, *Commentary on John*, 2.3
Lent Sunday 2B	Mark 9.2–10	St Ambrose, *On Psalm 45*, 2: CSEL 64, pars 6, 330–1
Lent 2B (RCL alternative)	Mark 8.31–38	St Cyril of Alexandria, *Commentary on Luke*, 49–50.
Lent Sunday 2C	Luke 9.28b–36	St Cyril of Alexandria, *Homily 9 on the Transfiguration of the Lord*: PG 77, 1011–14

Holy Saturday A	Matthew 27.57–66	St Cyril of Alexandria, *On John*, 12.19: PG 74, 679–82
Holy Saturday B	Mark 15.42–47	Origen, *On Romans*, 5.10: PG 14, 1048–52
Holy Saturday C	Luke 23.50–56	St Augustine, *Sermons*, Mai 146: PLS 2, 1242–3
Easter Day A–C	John 20.1–9 [1–20]; Matthew 28.1–10; [Mark 16.1–8]; [Luke 24.1–12]	I. St John Chrysostom, *Easter Homily*, 10–11, 12: PG 88, 1859–66
		II. Bd. Guerric of Igny, *Sermon 3 On the Resurrection*, 1–2 (PL 185, 148–9)
		III. St Hippolytus (attr.), *Paschal Homily*: SC 27, 116–18, 184–90
Easter Sunday 2A	John 20.19–31	St Cyril of Alexandria, *On John*, 12: PG 74, 704–5
Easter Sunday 2B	John 20.19–31	St Gregory the Great, *Forty Gospel Homilies*, 26.1–2: PL 76, 1197–8
Easter Sunday 2C	John 20.19–31	St Augustine, *Sermon* 88.1–2: Edit. Maurist. 5, 469–70
Easter Sunday 3A	Luke 24.13–35	St Augustine, *Sermon* 234.1–2: Edit. Maurist. 5, 987–8
Easter Sunday 3B	Luke 24.35–48	St John Chrysostom, *Homily 4 on the beginning of Acts*, 6: PG 51, 106–7
Easter Sunday 3C	John 21.1–19 *or* 21.1–14	St Augustine, *Sermons, Guelferbytanus* 16.2–3: PLS 2, 580–1
Easter Sunday 4A	John 10.1–10	St Clement of Alexandria, *Paedagogus*, 9.83.3 – 85.a: SC 70, 258–61
Easter Sunday 4B	John 10.11–18	St Peter Chrysologus, *Sermon 6*: PL 52, 202–4
Easter Sunday 4C	John 10.27–30 [22–30]	St Cyril of Alexandria, *On John*, 7: PG 74, 20
Easter Sunday 5A	John 14.1–12	St Ambrose, *On Death as a Blessing*, 12.52–55: CSEL 32, 747–50
Easter Sunday 5B	John 15.1–8	St Augustine, *Tractates on John*, 80.1; 81.1, 3, 4: CCSL 36, 527, 530–1

Easter Sunday 5C	John 13.31–33a, 34–35 [31–35]	St Cyril of Alexandria, *On John*, 9: PG 74, 161–4
Easter Sunday 6A	John 14.15–21	St John Chrysostom, *Homilies on John*, 75.1: PG 59, 403–5
Easter Sunday 6B	John 15.9–17	St Thomas More, *A Treatise upon the Passion*, 1
Easter Sunday 6C	John 14.23–29	St Leo the Great, *Sermon 77.5*: CCSL 138A, 490–3
Ascension A	Matthew 28.16–20 [Luke 24.44–53]	St Leo the Great, *Sermon 74.1–2*: CCSL 138A, 455–7
Ascension B	Mark 16.15–20 [Luke 24.44–53]	St Augustine, *Homilies on 1 John*, 4.2–3: SC 75, 220–4
Ascension C	Luke 24.46–53 [44–53]	St Cyril of Alexandria, *On John*, 9: PG 74, 182–3
Easter Sunday 7A	John 17.1–11	St John Chrysostom, *Homily on 'Father, if it is possible …'*: PG 51, 34–5
Easter Sunday 7B	John 17.11b–19 [6–19]	St Cyril of Alexandria, *On John*, 11.9: PG 74, 516–17
Easter Sunday 7C	John 17.20–26	St Cyril of Alexandria, *On John*, 11.11: PG 74, 553–60
Pentecost Sunday A	John 20.19–23	St John Chrysostom, *Homilies on Pentecost*, 2.1: PG 50, 463–5
Pentecost Sunday A (RCL alternative)	John 7.37–39	St Augustine, *Tractates on John*, 32.6–8.
Pentecost Sunday B	Jn 15.26–27; 16.12–15 [4–15]	St Aelred of Rievaulx, *Sermons*: Talbot 1, 112–14
Pentecost Sunday C	John 14.15–16, 23b–26 [8–17, 25–27]	St Leo the Great, *Sermons*, 75.1–3: CCSL 138A, 465–9
Trinity Sunday A	John 3.16–18 [Trinity B]	St John Chrysostom, *Homilies on Genesis*, 27.1–2: PG 53, 241
Trinity Sunday B	Matthew 28.16–20 [Trinity A]	St Nicholas Cabasilas, *The Life in Christ*, 2: PG 150, 532–533
Trinity Sunday C	John 16.12–15	St Hilary of Poitiers, *On the Trinity*, 12.55–6: PL 10, 468–72
Corpus Christi A	John 6.51–59 [RCL A–C]	St Augustine, *Sermon 272*: Edit. Maurist. 5, 1103–4
Corpus Christi B	Mark 14.12–16	St John Chrysostom, *Homilies on Matthew*, 82.1: PG 58, 737–9

Corpus Christi C	Luke 9.11–17	St John Chrysostom, *Homilies on 1 Corinthians*, 24.4: PG 61, 204–205
Sacred Heart A (RL)	Matthew 11.25–30	St Bruno of Segni, *Sermon 1 on Good Friday*: PL 165, 1007–8
Sacred Heart B (RL)	John 19.31–37	St Augustine, *Sermon 213*, 8: Edit. Maurist. 5, 942
Sacred Heart C (RL)	Luke 15.3–7	St Ambrose, *Sermons on Psalm 118*, 22.3, 27–30: CSEL 62, 489, 502–4
Ordinary Time 6A (RL)	Matthew 5.17–37	See Ordinary Time before Lent
Ordinary Time 6B (RL)	Mark 1.40–45	See Ordinary Time before Lent
Ordinary Time 6C (RL)	Luke 6.17, 20–26	See Ordinary Time before Lent
Ordinary Time 7A (RL)	Matthew 5.38–48	See Ordinary Time before Lent
Ordinary Time 7B (RL)	Mark 2.1–12	See Ordinary Time before Lent
Ordinary Time 7C (RL)	Luke 6.27–38	See Ordinary Time before Lent
Ordinary Time 8A/ Proper 3A	Matthew 6.24–34	See Ordinary Time before Lent
Ordinary Time 8B/ Proper 3B	Mark 2.18–22 [13–22]	See Ordinary Time before Lent
Ordinary Time 8C/ Proper 3C	Luke 6.39–45 [39–49]	See Ordinary Time before Lent
Ordinary Time 9A/ Proper 4A	Matthew 7.21–27	See Ordinary Time before Lent
Ordinary Time 9B/ Proper 4B	Mark 2.23–3.6	See Ordinary Time before Lent
Ordinary Time 9C/ Proper 4C	Luke 7.1–10	See Ordinary Time before Lent
Ordinary Time 10A/ Proper 5A	Matthew 9.9–13 [& 18–36]	St Augustine, *On the Psalms 58*, 1.7: CCSL 39, 733–4
Ordinary Time 10B/ Proper 5B	Mark 3.20–35	Unknown Greek author, *Paschal Homilies*, 5.1–3: SC 187, 318–22
Ordinary Time 10C/ Proper 5C	Luke 7.11–17	St Augustine, *Sermon 98*, 1–3: PL 38, 591–2
Ordinary Time 11A/ Proper 6A	Matthew 9.36 – 10.8 [or 9.36 – 10.23]	St John Chrysostom, *Last Homilies*, 10.2–3: Bareille, 20, 562–4
Ordinary Time 11B/ Proper 6B	Mark 4.26–34	St John Chrysostom, Homily 7: PG 64, 21–6

Ordinary Time 11C/ Proper 6C	Luke 7.36 – 8.3 *or* 7.36–50	Anon Syrian writer: *Homily: Orient Syrien* 7 [1962], 180–1, 189, 193, 194
Ordinary Time 12A/ Proper 7A	Matthew 10.26–33 [24–39]	St Augustine, *On the Psalms* 69: CCSL 39.930–931
Ordinary Time 12B/ Proper 7B	Mark 4.35–41	St Augustine, *Sermon* 63, 1–3: PL 38, 424–425
Ordinary Time 12C (RL)	Luke 9.18–24	St Cyril of Alexandria, *Homily* 49: ed. R. M. Tonneau, CSCO Script. Syri 70, 110–15
Proper 7C (RCL)	Luke 8.26–39	St Jerome, *Life of Hilarion*, 1, 23–4
Ordinary Time 13A/ Proper 8A	Matthew 10.37–42	St Hilary of Poitiers, *On Matthew*, 10.25–7: S 254, 246–251
Ordinary Time 13B/ Proper 8B	Mark 5.21–43 *or* 5.21–24, 35–43	St Peter Chrysologus, *Sermon* 34: PL 52, 296–9
Ordinary Time 13C/ Proper 8C	Luke 9.51–62	St Hilary of Poitiers, *On Psalm* 39, 12: CSEL 22, 784–5
Ordinary Time 14A/ Proper 9A	Matthew 11.[16–19] 25–30	St John Chrysostom, *Sermon on St Bassus*: Bareille, 4, 509–10
Ordinary Time 14B/ Proper 9B	Mark 6.1–6 [1–13]	St Symeon the New Theologian, *Catecheses*, 3.19: SC 113, 165–9
Ordinary Time 14C/ Proper 9C	Luke 10.1–12, 17–20 *or* 10.1–9	St Augustine, *Sermon* 101, 1–2, 11: PL 38, 605–7, 610
Ordinary Time 15A/ Proper 10A	Matthew 13.1–23 *or* 13.1–9	St Gregory the Great, *Forty Gospel Homilies*, 1.15.1–2, 4
Ordinary Time 15B (RL)	Mark 6.7–13	St Theophylact of Ohrid, *On Mark*: PG 123, 548–9
Proper 10B (RCL)	Mark 6.14–29	St John Chrysostom, *Commentary on Matthew*, 48.2, 4, 8
Ordinary Time 15C/ Proper 10C	Luke 10.25–37	Origen, *Homilies on Luke's Gospel*, 34.3, 7–9: SC 87, 402–10
Ordinary Time 16A/ Proper 11A	Matthew 13.24–43 *or* 13.24–30	St Augustine, *Sermon* 73A
Ordinary Time 16B/ Proper 11B	Mark 6.30–34 [53–56]	Didymus the Blind, *On Zechariah*, 2.39–42: SC 84, 446–9

Ordinary Time 16C/ Proper 11C	Luke 10.38–42	St Gregory the Great, *Homilies on Ezekiel*, 2.2.7–11: SC 360, 105–13
Ordinary Time 17A/ Proper 12A	Matthew 13.[31–33] 44–52 *or* 13.44–46	Origen, *On Matthew*, 10.9–10: SC 162, 173–7
Ordinary Time 17B/ Proper 12B	John 6.1–15 [1–21]	St Augustine, *Tractates on John*, 24.1, 6, 7: CCSL 36, 244, 247–8
Ordinary Time 17C/ Proper 12C	Luke 11.1–13	Ven. Bede, *Homily 14*: CCSL 122, 272–3, 277–9
Ordinary Time 18A/ Proper 13A	Matthew 14.13–21	St Ephrem the Syrian, *Commentary on the Diatessaron*, 12.1.305: CSCO 145 Script. Arm., ii, 115–17
Ordinary Time 18B/ Proper 13B	John 6.24–35	St Theophylact of Ohrid, *On John*: PG 123, 1297–1301
Ordinary Time 18C/ Proper 13C	Luke 12.13–21	St Basil the Great, *Homélies sur la richesse* (1935), ed. Yves Courtonne, pp. 15–19
Ordinary Time 19A/ Proper 14A	Matthew 14.22–33	St Augustine, *Sermon 76*.1, 4, 5, 8, 9: PL 38, 479–83
Ordinary Time 19B/ Proper 14B	John 6.[35] 41–51	St Eutychius of Constantinople, *On Easter*, 2–3: PG 86/2, 2394–5
Ordinary Time 19C/ Proper 14C	Luke 12.32–48 [32–40]	St Gregory of Nyssa, *Homilies on the Song of Songs*, 11: Jaeger vi, 317–19
Ordinary Time 20A/ Proper 15A	Matthew 15.21–28 [10–28]	St John Chrysostom, *Homily on the words, 'That Christ be proclaimed'*, 12–13: Bareille 5, 595–6
Ordinary Time 20B/ Proper 15B	John 6.51–58	St Theophylact of Ohrid, *Commentary on John*: PG 123, 1309–12
Ordinary Time 20C/ Proper 15C	Luke 12.49–53	Denis the Carthusian, *Commentary on Luke*: Opera omnia, xii, 72–4
Ordinary Time 21A/ Proper 16A	Matthew 16.13–20	St John Chrysostom, *Homily on SS Peter and Elias*: PG 50, 727–8
Ordinary Time 21B/ Proper 16B	John 6.60–69 [56–69]	St Cyril of Alexandria, *On John*, 4.4: PG 73, 613–17

Ordinary Time 21C (RL)	Luke 13.22–30	Bd John Henry Newman, *Parochial & Plain Sermons*, v, 254–6, 267–9
Proper 16C (RCL)	Luke 13.10–17	Origen, *Against Celsus*, 8.54
Ordinary Time 22A/ Proper 17A	Matthew 16.21–27	St Augustine, *Sermon* 96, 1–4: PL 38, 584–6
Ordinary Time 22B/ Proper 17B	Mark 7.1–8, 14–15, 21–23	St Irenaeus, *Against Heresies*, 4.12.1–2: SC 100, 508–14
Ordinary Time 22C/ Proper 17C	Luke 14.1, 7–14	St Bruno of Segni, *Commentary on Luke*, 1.14: PL 165, 406–7
Ordinary Time 23A/ Proper 18A	Matthew 18.15–20	St John Chrysostom, *Catecheses*, 6.18–20: SC 50, 224–5
Ordinary Time 23B/ Proper 18B	Mark 7.31–37 [24–37]	Ven. Bede, *Homilies on the Gospels*, 2.6
Ordinary Time 23C/ Proper 18C	Luke 14.25–33	St John Cassian, *Conferences*, 3.6–7: SC 42, 145–7
Ordinary Time 24A/ Proper 19A	Matthew 18.21–35	St Augustine, *Sermon* 83.2, 4: PL 38, 515–16
Ordinary Time 24B/ Proper 19B	Mark 8.27–35 [27–38]	St Caesarius of Arles, *Sermon* 159, 1, 4–6: CCSL 104, 650, 652–4
Ordinary Time 24C/ Proper 19C	Luke 15.1–32 or 15.1–10 [15.1–10]	St Peter Chrysologus, *Homily* 168: PL 52, 639–41
Ordinary Time 25A/ Proper 20A	Matthew 20.1–16	St Augustine, *Sermon* 87.1, 4–6: PL 38, 530–33
Ordinary Time 25B/ Proper 20B	Mark 9.30–37	St Theophylact of Ohrid, *On Mark*: PG 123, 588–9
Ordinary Time 25C/ Proper 20C	Luke 16.1–13	St Gaudentius of Brescia, *Sermon* 18: PL 20, 973–5
Ordinary Time 26A/ Proper 21A	Matthew 21.28–32 [23–32]	St Clement of Alexandria, *Who is the rich person who shall be saved?*, 39–40: PG 9, 644–5
Ordinary Time 26B/ Proper 21B	Mark 9.38–43, 45, 47–8	St Symeon the New Theologian, *Catecheses*, 1.3: SC 96, 299–305
Ordinary Time 26C/ Proper 21C	Luke 16.19–31	St John Chrysostom, *Homily 2 on Lazarus*, 5: Bareille 2, 582–3
Ordinary Time 27A/ Proper 22A	Matthew 21.33–43 [33–46]	St Basil the Great, *Homilies on the Hexameron*, 5: SC 27, 304–7
Ordinary Time 27B/ Proper 22B	Mark 10.2–16	St Jacob of Serugh, *Homily on the Veil of Moses*: Guéranger, iii, 1023–5

Ordinary Time 27C/ Proper 22C	Luke 17.5–10	St Augustine, *Sermon* 115: PL 38, 655
Ordinary Time 28A/ Proper 23A	Matthew 22.1–14	St Augustine, *Sermon* 90, 1, 5–6: PL 38, 559, 561–3
Ordinary Time 28B/ Proper 23B	Mark 10.17–30	St Clement of Alexandria, *Who is the rich person who shall be saved?*, 4, 6, 8–10
Ordinary Time 28C/ Proper 23C	Luke 17.11–19	St Augustine, *Questions on the Gospels*, 2.40: CCSL 44B, 97–102
Ordinary Time 29A/ Proper 24A	Matthew 22.15–21	St Ambrose, *On Luke*, 9.34–6
Ordinary Time 29B/ Proper 24B	Mark 10.35–45	St John Chrysostom, *Homily 8 against the Anomoeans*: Bareille, 2, 253–4
Ordinary Time 29C/ Proper 24C	Luke 18.1–8	St Gregory of Nyssa, *Homily on the Lord's Prayer*: PG 44, 1119, 1123–6
Ordinary Time 30A/ Proper 25A	Matthew 22.34–40 [34–46]	St Augustine, *Sermons*, Mai 14.1–2: PLS 2, 449–50
Ordinary Time 30B/ Proper 25B	Mark 10.46–52	St Clement of Alexandria, *Protrepticus*, 11: SC 2, 181–183
Ordinary Time 30C/ Proper 25C	Luke 18.9–14	St Augustine, *Sermon* 115
Dedication Festival A (CWL)	Matthew 21.12–16	Origen, *Homilies on Joshua*, 9.1–2: SC 71, 144–6
Dedication Festival B (CWL)	John 10.22–29	St Augustine, *Sermon* 336.1, 6: PL 38, 1471–5
Dedication Festival C (CWL)	John 2.13–22	See reading for Lent 3B
Ordinary Time 31A/ Proper 26A	Matthew 23.1–12	St Paschasius Radbertus, *On Matthew*, 10.22: PL 120, 769–70
Proper 26A (CWL)	Matthew 24.1–14	St John Chrysostom, *Homilies on Matthew*, 75.1–2, 5.
Ordinary Time 31B/ Proper 26B	Mark 12.28–34	St Basil of Caesarea, *Asceticon*, Longer Responses 1–3 (abridged)
Ordinary Time 31C/ Proper 26C	Luke 19.1–10	St Philoxenus of Mabbug, *Homilies*, 4.78: SC 44, 96–97
All Saints' Day A (RCL & RL)	Matthew 5.1–12	St Augustine, *Explanation of the Sermon on the Mount*, 3.10.
All Saints' Day B (RCL)	John 11.32–44	See reading for Lent 5A

ADVENT

PREPARE a way for the Lord by living a good life and guard that way by good works. Let the Word of God move in you unhindered and give you a knowledge of his coming and of his mysteries. To him be glory and power for ever and ever, Amen.

Origen

I LOOK from afar, and behold I see the power of God coming, and a cloud covering the whole earth. Go out to meet him and say, 'tell us if you are the one who is to reign over the people of Israel'.

Matins responsory for the first Sunday of Advent, Aspiciens a longe

ALMIGHTY God, give us grace that we may cast away the works of darkness, and put upon us the armour of light, now in the time of this mortal life in which thy Son Jesus Christ came to visit us in great humility; that in the last day, when he shall come again in his glorious majesty to judge both the quick and the dead, we may rise to the life immortal; through him who liveth and reigneth with thee and the Holy Ghost, one God, now and for ever. Amen.

Collect for the first Sunday of Advent, Book of Common Prayer

O WISDOM, coming forth from the mouth of the Most High, reaching from one end to the other mightily, and sweetly ordering all things: Come and teach us the way of prudence.

Advent Magnificat antiphon, O Sapientia (Ecclesiasticus 24.3 and Wisdom 8.1)

'Now we give you thanks because you sent Jesus Christ to redeem us from sin and death and to make us inheritors of everlasting life; that when he shall come again in power and great triumph to judge the world, we may with joy behold his appearing and in confidence may stand before him.'[2] Advent is the season of preparation both for the coming of Christ in the flesh at Christmas and for his coming in glory at the end of time. In addition to these two comings of Christ in past and future, St Bernard and the Cistercian Fathers also speak of a present, intermediate, coming of Christ in grace to the waiting soul. Advent is a preparation for Christmas and in some ways it is like Lent which is a preparation for Easter. It shares with Lent certain distinctive marks in worship such as purple vestments and the omission of the *Gloria in excelsis* at the Eucharist, but the penitential character of Advent is much less marked and the dominant note is one of joyful expectation.

The name Advent is from the Latin '*adventus*' which means an approach, a coming or an arrival. It was a technical term for the official arrival or manifestation of a King or a God and has a similar meaning to the name of the feast of Epiphany, in Greek '*epiphaneia*', on the other side of Christmas. The celebration of the birth of Jesus at Christmas is the real *adventus Domini* ('coming of the Lord') but the season of Advent is a preparation for this. For over a thousand years Advent has marked the beginning of the Christian year for Western Christians.

Advent begins on the Sunday nearest the feast of St Andrew (30 November) and includes four Sundays. It seems to have had its remote origin in Spain and Gaul as a preparation for the feast of Epiphany with a penitential character like Lent. Our current Advent, however, has its direct roots in the Roman liturgy of the sixth century when it included six Sundays before Christmas, although by the seventh century these had been reduced to the current four. Advent is a distinctively Western Christian season but the Eastern Christian liturgies also have their own periods of preparation for the feast of the Nativity.

The Sunday Gospels of the three-year cycle of the *Revised Common Lectionary* and the *Roman Lectionary* are broadly the same and follow a thematic plan in which John the Baptist and the Blessed Virgin Mary have a central role: staying awake to wait for the Lord (Advent 1); John the Baptist and the message of repentance (Advent 2); John the Baptist and Jesus Christ (Advent 3); Mary, Mother of the Lord (Advent 4). It is interesting to note that these three series of Gospels present time in reverse, they start with the final consummation of all things at the end of history and move through events in Jesus' public ministry to stories of the months before Jesus' birth.

---

2 Advent short preface, *Common Worship*.

The liturgy is above history and sees all history in the light of the mystery of Christ as it exists in the heart of the Father, from Christ's eternal pre-existence to his final advent as Judge of the Universe. The mystery of Jesus' birth can only properly be understood in the light of all this. Apart from Origen's homilies on Luke, the commentaries on the Gospels in *The Fathers on the Sunday Gospels* are taken from Latin writers as Advent is a Western Christian season. Among them Bernard and Guerric represent the distinguished medieval Cistercian monastic tradition of Advent sermons.

The sequence of Advent Gospels in our contemporary lectionaries is a development of the traditional Roman series of Advent Gospels, which was in part preserved in the *Book of Common Prayer* (BCP) of the Church of England. The first Sunday (BCP Advent 2) had Luke 21.25–33 on the signs of the end times but without the call to watch and pray (21.34–36) found in the Gospel for Advent 1C in the modern lectionaries; the second Sunday (BCP Advent 3) had Matthew 11.2–10 on Jesus and John, as on Advent 3A; the third Sunday (BCP Advent 4) had John 1.19–28 on Jesus and John, now used on Advent 3B; the fourth Sunday had Luke 3.1–6 on the start of John's ministry, now used on Advent 2C. The focus on the Virgin Mary on the fourth Sunday is taken from the ancient Gospels for Wednesday (Luke 1.26–38, now used on Advent 4B) and Friday (Luke 1.39–47, now used on Advent 4C) in Ember Week in Advent (the Ember Saturday Gospel is Luke 3.1–6). Embertide is four series of Wednesdays, Fridays and Saturdays, corresponding to the four seasons. The name derives from the Anglo-Saxon word *ymbren* (a circuit or revolution) with reference to their place in the annual cycle of the year, or perhaps from their Latin title, *ieiunia quatuor temporum* (fast of the four times/seasons). They are periods of prayer and fasting and for centuries they have been the time for ordinations. The series of Gospels on the Sundays of Advent thus preserves all the riches of the traditional Catholic and Anglican liturgy.

As the season of Advent progresses the liturgy shifts its focus from the final coming of Christ to his first coming at Bethlehem and there is a distinct change on 17 December when the Great 'O' antiphons begin to be sung at Evensong, starting with O *Sapientia* (O Wisdom – the calendar of the BCP has this antiphon on 16 December, which was its date in the pre-Reformation English calendar of Salisbury). The usual modern liturgical colour of the season is purple but medieval colour sequences also indicate blue, red and black, and blue is used today in some churches. On the third Sunday of Advent, called Gaudete Sunday from the first word of the traditional entrance chant, *Gaudete in Domino semper* (rejoice in the Lord always …, Philippians 4.4–6), rose-pink vestments are sometimes used, following the Roman Missal of 1570.

First Sunday of Advent Year A: Matthew 24.37–44

A READING FROM THE COMMENTARY ON MATTHEW BY ST PASCHASIUS RADBERTUS

Watch, for you do not know the day nor the hour. Like many other Scriptural texts, this admonition is addressed to all of us, though it is formulated in such a way that it would seem to concern only Christ's immediate audience. We can all apply it to ourselves because the Last Day and the end of the world will come for each of us on the day we depart this present life. This means we must make sure we die in the state in which we wish to appear on the Day of Judgement. Bearing this in mind each of us should guard against being led astray and failing to keep watch, otherwise the day of the Lord's return may take us unawares. If the last day of our life finds us unprepared, then we shall be unprepared on that day also.

I do not for a moment believe the apostles expected the Lord to return in judgement during their own lifetime. All the same there can be no doubt that they took every care not to be drawn from the right path. They kept watch, observing the universal precepts their master had given to his disciples so as to be ready when he came again.

Consequently we must always be on the lookout for Christ's twofold coming, the one when we shall have to give an account of everything we have done, and the other when he comes day after day to stir our consciences. He comes to us now in order that his future coming may find us prepared. If my conscience is burdened with sin what good will it do me to know when the Day of Judgement will be? Unless the Lord comes to my soul beforehand and makes his home with me, unless Christ lives in me and speaks his word in my heart, it is useless for me to know if and when his coming will take place. Only if Christ is already living in me and I in him will it go well with me when he comes in judgement. If I have already died to the world and am able to say, *The world is crucified to me, and I to the world*, then, in a sense, his final coming is already present to me.

Consider also our Lord's warning: *Many will come in my name.* It is only the Anti-Christ and his members who, albeit falsely, claim the name of Christ, though they lack his works and his true doctrine and wisdom. You will never find the Lord in Scripture actually declaring, 'I am the Christ.' His teaching and miracles revealed it clearly enough, for the Father was at work in him. Louder than a thousand acclamations his teaching and mighty works proclaimed: 'I am the Christ.' And so whether or not you find him describing himself in so many words, the works of the

Father and his own message of love declared what he was, whereas the false Christs who possessed neither godly deeds nor holy doctrine loudly claimed to be what they were not.

St Paschasius Radbertus, *On Matthew*, 2.24: PL 120, 799–800

First Sunday of Advent Year B: Mark 13.33–37 [24–37]

A READING FROM A HOMILY BY GODFREY OF ADMONT

Take heed, watch, and pray, the Scripture says. By these words our Lord and Saviour admonished not only his disciples whom he was addressing in the flesh; by these same words he also made clear to us what we must do, and how we should keep watch. The three parts of this saying plainly show how all destined to be saved, who forget what lies behind them and desire to press on toward what lies ahead, can attain the summit of perfection which is their goal.

Those then who, moved to compunction by divine grace, have decided to renounce the world and its desires, must have their eyes open and take heed, according to the warning of the word of God at the beginning of the gospel reading. In other words, they must begin by distinguishing between what should be done and what should be avoided.

However, people intending to change their way of life will not reach perfection simply by knowing what is right. After learning how to live a good life they must also strive to be watchful by performing good works. Hence, after warning his disciples to take heed, the Lord fittingly adds, *Watch and pray*. The command to watch means that we must strive to put our understanding of what is right into practice. We must turn our backs on the lazy, indolent way of life into which we had fallen, and eagerly watch for anything that we can do.

But to those who thus keep watch by the zealous performance of good deeds, the Lord shows a yet higher way. He immediately adds the admonition: *and pray*. All the elect are commanded to pray, which means that their desires are to be for things eternal; their only motive in performing a good deed should be their hope of a reward in heaven. It would seem to be perseverance in this kind of prayer that the apostle Paul enjoins on his disciples when he tells them to *pray without ceasing*. We pray without ceasing if for performing a good deed we have not the slightest desire to receive the glory of earthly praise, but think longingly only of what is eternal.

Take heed, watch, and pray, our text says; meaning, *take heed* by understanding what is right; *watch* by doing what is good; and *pray* by desiring what is eternal. And the following words show clearly why they must be so very heedful, watchful, and prayerful. *You do not know*, the text says, *when the time will be*. So since we are ignorant of the time of this great visitation, we must be always watching and praying; that is to say, for the grace of so great a visitation we must prepare the innermost recesses of our hearts by vigilant effort.

Godfrey of Admont, *Festal Homilies*, 23: PL 174, 724–6

First Sunday of Advent Year C: Luke 21.25–28, 34–36 [25–36]

A READING FROM A SERMON BY ST BERNARD

It is surely right that you should celebrate our Lord's coming with all your hearts, and that the greatness of the consolation which his Advent brings us should fill you with joy. Indeed one can only be amazed at the depth of his self-abasement, and stirred up to new fervour by the immensity of his love. But you must not think of his first coming only, when he came to seek and save what was lost; remember that he will come again and take us to himself. It is my desire that you should be constantly meditating upon this twofold advent, continually turning over in your minds of all that he has done for us in the first, and all that he promises to do in the second.

It is time for judgement to begin at the house of God. But what will be the fate of those who do not obey the Gospel? What judgement will be reserved for those who will not submit to the judgement taking place now? In this present judgement the ruler of this world is being cast out, and those who seek to evade it must expect – indeed they must greatly fear – the judge who will cast them out along with him. However, if we are fully judged now, we may safely *await the Saviour who is to come, our Lord Jesus Christ, who will change our lowly bodies into the likeness of his glorious body*. Then the just will shine forth so that both learned and simple may see it; they will *shine like the sun in the kingdom of their Father*.

When our Saviour comes *he will change our lowly bodies into the likeness of his glorious body*, provided that our hearts have been changed and

7

made humble as his was. This is why he said: *Learn of me, for I am meek and humble of heart.* We may note from this text that humility is twofold: that is intellectual humility and a humility of one's whole disposition and attitude, here called the heart. By the first we recognize that we are nothing; we can learn this much of ourselves from our own weakness. The second enables us to trample the glory of the world under our feet, and this we learn from him who emptied himself, taking the form of a servant. When the people desired to make him a king, he fled from them; but when they wanted to make him undergo the shame and ignominy of the cross, he gave himself up to them of his own free will.

St Bernard, *Advent Sermons*, 4.1, 3–4: *Opera omnia,*
Ed. Cist., iv (1966), 182–5

Second Sunday of Advent Year A: Matthew 3.1–12

A READING FROM A SERMON BY ST AUGUSTINE

The gospel tells us that some people were rebuked by the Lord because, clever as they were at reading the face of the sky, they could not recognize the time for faith when the kingdom of heaven was at hand. It was the Jews who received this reprimand, but it has also come down to us. The Lord Jesus began his preaching of the gospel with the admonition: *Repent, for the kingdom of heaven is at hand.* His forerunner, John the Baptist, began his in the same way. *Repent*, he said, *for the kingdom of heaven is at hand.* Today, for those who will not repent at the approach of the kingdom of heaven, the reproof of the Lord Jesus is the same. As he points out himself, *You cannot expect to see the kingdom of heaven coming. The kingdom of heaven*, he says elsewhere, *is within you.*

Each of us would be wise therefore to take to heart the advice of his teacher, and not waste this present time. If it is now that our Saviour offers us his mercy; now, while he still spares the human race. Understand that it is in hope of our conversion that he spares us, for he desires no one's damnation. As for when the end of the world will be, that is God's concern. Now it is the time for faith. Whether any of us here present will see the end of the world I know not; very likely none of us will. Even so, the time is very near for each of us, for we are mortal. There are hazards all around us. We should be in less danger from them were we made of glass. What more fragile than a vessel of glass? And yet it can be kept safe and last indefinitely. Of course it is exposed to accidents, but it is not liable to old age and the suffering it brings. We therefore are the more frail and infirm. In our weakness we are haunted by fears of all the calamities that regularly befall the human race, and if no such calamity overtakes us, still, time marches on. We may evade the blows of fortune, but shall we evade death? We made escape perils from without, but shall we escape what comes from within us? Now, suddenly, we may be attacked by any malady. And if we are spared? Even so, old age comes at last, and nothing will delay it.

St Augustine, *Sermon* 109.1: PL 38, 636

Second Sunday of Advent Year B: Mark 1.1–8

A READING FROM A HOMILY ON LUKE BY ORIGEN

Let as examine the scriptural texts foretelling the coming of Christ. One such prophecy begins with a reference to John the Baptist. *The voice of one crying in the wilderness: Prepare the way of the Lord; make his paths straight.* What follows, however, applies directly to our Lord and Saviour, since it is by Jesus rather than by John that *every valley has been filled in.*

You have only to recall the kind of people you were before you put your faith in the Lord to see yourselves as deep valleys, as pits plunging precipitously into the lowest depths. But now that the Lord Jesus has come and has sent the Holy Spirit in his name, all your valleys have been filled in with good works and the Holy Spirit's fruits. Love no longer tolerates the presence of valleys in your lives; if peace, patience, and goodness find a home in you, not only will each of you cease to be a valley but you will actually begin to be a mountain of God.

Among the pagans we daily see this prophetic filling of every valley realized, just as among the people of Israel, now deprived of their former privileged status, we see the overthrowing of every mountain and hill. But *because of their offence, salvation has come to the pagans, to stir Israel to emulation.*

If you prefer you can visualize these fallen mountains and hills as the hostile powers that formerly raised themselves up in opposition to the human race. Such an interpretation is legitimate because, in order to fill in the kind of valleys we have been speaking of, the enemy powers – the mountains and hills – must be laid low.

Now let us turn to that part of the prophecy which also concerns the coming of Christ and see whether this too has been fulfilled. The text continues: *Every crooked way shall be straightened.* Each one of us was once crooked; if we are no longer so, it is entirely due to the grace of Christ. Through his coming to our souls all our crooked ways have been straightened out. If Christ did not come to your soul, of what use would his historical coming in the flesh be to you? Let us pray that each day we may experience his coming and be able to testify: *It is not I who now live, but Christ who lives in me.*

So then, by his coming Jesus my Lord has smoothed out your rough places and changed your disorderly ways into level paths, so that an even, unimpeded road may be constructed within you, clear enough for God the Father to walk along, and Christ the Lord may himself set up his dwelling in your hearts and say: *My Father and I will come to them and make our home in them.*

Origen, Homilies on Luke, 22.1–4: SC 67, 300–2

Second Sunday of Advent Year C: Luke 3.1–6

A READING FROM A HOMILY ON LUKE BY ORIGEN

The word of God was addressed to John, son of Zechariah, in the desert, and he went through all the Jordan valley. Where else could he go but through the Jordan valley, where there would be water at hand to baptize those wishing to amend their lives?

Now the word Jordan means descent or coming down. Coming down and rushing in full flood is the river of God, the Lord our Saviour, in whom we were baptized. This is the real, life-giving water, and the sins of those baptized in it are forgiven.

So come, catechumens, and amend your lives so that you may have your sins forgiven in baptism. In baptism the sins of those who cease to sin that are forgiven, but if anyone comes to be baptized while continuing to sin, that person's sins are not forgiven. This is why I urge you not to present yourselves for baptism without thinking very carefully, but to give some evidence that you really mean to change your way of living. Spend some time living a good life. Cleanse yourselves from all impurity and avoid every sin. Then, when you yourselves have begun to despise your sins, they will be forgiven you. You will be forgiven your sins if you renounce them.

The teaching of the Old Testament is the same. We read in the prophet Isaiah, *A voice cries out in the desert. Prepare the way for the Lord. Build him a straight highway.* What way shall we prepare for the Lord? A way by land? Could the Word of God travel such a road? Is it not rather a way within ourselves that we have to prepare for the Lord? Is it not a straight and level highway in our hearts that we are to make ready? Surely this is the way by which the Word of God enters, a way that exists in the spaciousness of the human body. The human heart is vast, broad, and capacious, if only it is pure. Would you like to know its length and breadth? See then what a vast amount of divine knowledge it can contain.

Solomon says: *He gave me knowledge of all that exists; he taught me about the structure of the universe and the properties of the elements, the beginning and the end of epochs and the periods between, the variations in the seasons and the succession of the months, the revolution of the year and the position of the stars, the natures of living things and the instincts of wild animals, the force of the winds and the thoughts of human beings, the various kinds of plants and the medicinal properties of roots.*

You must realize that the human heart is not small when it can contain all this. You ought to judge it not by its physical size but by its power to embrace such a vast amount of knowledge of the truth.

But so that I may convince you that the human heart is large by a simple example from daily life, let us consider this. Whatever city we may have passed through, we have in our minds. We remember its streets, walls, and buildings, what they were like and where they were situated. We have a mental picture of the roads we have travelled. In moments of quiet reflection our minds embrace the sea that we have crossed. So, as I said, the heart that can contain all this is not small!

Therefore, if what contains so much is not small, let a way be prepared in it for the Lord, a straight highway along which the Word and Wisdom of God may advance. Prepare a way for the Lord by living a good life and guard that way by good works. Let the Word of God move in you unhindered and give you a knowledge of his coming and of his mysteries. To him be glory and power for ever and ever, amen.

Origen, *Homilies on Luke*, 21: PG 13, 1855–6

Third Sunday of Advent Year A: Matthew 11.2–11

A READING FROM THE COMMENTARY ON LUKE BY ST AMBROSE

Calling two of his disciples, John sent them to Jesus saying: 'Are you the one who is to come, or must we look for another?'

It is no easy matter to understand these simple words. If we take them at their face value they conflict with what was said earlier. We find John declaring his ignorance of the one whom he had previously recognized on the Father's testimony. How is this possible? How could John recognize a man hitherto unknown to him, and later deny any acquaintance with him? Here is what he says: *I did not know him, but the one who commissioned me to baptize told me he would be the man upon whom I should see the Holy Spirit coming down from heaven.* John believed these words, and recognized the man thus revealed to him. Not only did he baptize him, he paid homage to him and proclaimed him as the one who was to come, announcing: *I have seen and have borne witness that this is God's chosen servant.* What are we to think then? Is it conceivable that a prophet of John's stature could be so far from the truth that after identifying Jesus as the one who takes away the sins of the world he still could not believe Jesus to be the Son of God?

Since the literal sense of this passage appears to be contradictory, let us look for its spiritual meaning. I have already told you that John represents the law which foreshadowed Christ. And so how fitting it was that the law should have been kept imprisoned materially in faithless hearts, deprived of the light of eternity! There it was to remain as if confined within a womb where, despite persistent birth-pangs, incomprehension barred its exit: it could not bear full witness to the Lord's saving plan without the confirmation of the Gospel. Because Christ is the fulfilment of the law, John sent his disciples to him to obtain further information. Knowing that it was impossible for anyone to possess the fullness of faith without hearing the Good News (for the faith that has its origin in the Old Testament is brought to completion in the New), our Lord answered the disciples' question not by giving them a verbal assurance of his identity, but by pointing to his actions. *Go,* he said, *and tell John what you have seen and heard. The blind see, the lame walk, the deaf hear, lepers are cleansed, the dead rise again, and the poor have the Gospel preached to them.*

Nevertheless these things are only minor proofs of the Lord's presence. The fullness of faith consists of recognizing the Lord when he is crucified, dead, and buried. This was why Jesus concluded by saying: *Blessed are those who are not scandalized by me.* It is indeed possible for the cross to prove a stumbling block even for the elect. But we have no greater testimony to Christ's divinity, nothing which more clearly shows him to be more than human, than his offering himself as the unique sacrifice for the whole world; this alone fully reveals him as the Lord. Moreover it was in this light that John pointed him out: *Behold the Lamb of God, who takes away the sins of the world.*

However, Christ's answer was addressed not to John's disciples but to all of us, in order that when we found his claim supported by facts we might come to believe in him.

St Ambrose, *Commentary on Luke*, 5.93–5, 99–102, 109: CCSL 14, 165–6, 167–8, 171–2

Third Sunday of Advent Year B: John 1.6–8, 19–28

A READING FROM A HOMILY ON JOHN BY JOHN SCOTUS ERIUGENA

Into the theological plan of his gospel John the Evangelist draws John the Baptist; deep calls to deep at the utterance of divine mysteries. We hear the Evangelist relating the story of the forerunner, the man whose gift it was to know the Word as he was in the beginning, speaking to us of the one who was commissioned to go ahead of the Word made flesh. *There was,* says the Evangelist, *not simply a messenger of God, but a man.* This he said in order to distinguish the man who shared only the humanity of the one he heralded from the Man who came after him, the Man who united godhead and manhood in his own Person. The Evangelist's intention was to differentiate between the fleeting voice and the eternally unchanging Word. The one, he would suggest, was the morning star appearing at the dawning of the kingdom of heaven, while the other was the Sun of Justice coming in its wake. He distinguished the witness from the one to whom he testified, the messenger from him who sent him, the lamp burning in the night from the brilliant lights that filled the whole world, the light that dispelled the darkness of death and sin from the entire human race.

So then, the Lord's forerunner was a man, not a god; whereas the Lord whom he preceded was both man and God. The forerunner was a man destined to be divinized by God's grace, whereas the one he preceded was God by nature, who, through his desire to save and redeem us, lowered himself in order to assume our human nature.

A man was sent. By whom? By the divine Word, whose forerunner he was. To go before the Lord was his mission. Lifting up his voice, this man called out: *The voice of one crying in the wilderness!* It was the herald preparing the way for the Lord's coming. John was his name; John to whom was given the grace to go ahead of the King of kings, to point out to the world the Word made flesh, to baptize him with that baptism in which the Spirit would manifest his divine Sonship, to give witness through his teaching and martyrdom to the eternal light.

John Scotus Eriugena, *Homilies on the Prologue of John*, 13: SC 151, 275–7

Third Sunday of Advent Year C: Luke 3.10–18 [7–18]

A READING FROM A HOMILY ON LUKE BY ORIGEN

The baptism that Jesus gives us is a baptism in the Holy Spirit and in fire. Baptism is one and the same no matter who receives it, but its effect depends on the recipient's disposition. He who is portrayed as baptizing in the Holy Spirit and in fire *holds a winnowing fan in his hand, which he will use to clear his threshing floor. The wheat he will gather into his barn, but the chaff he will burn with fire that can never be quenched.*

I should like to discover our Lord's reason for holding a winnowing fan and to inquire into the nature of the wind that scatters the light chaff here and there, leaving the heavier grain lying in a heap – for you must have a wind if you want to separate wheat and chaff.

I suggest that the faithful are like a heap of unsifted grain, and that the wind represents the temptations which assail them and show up the wheat and the chaff among them. When your soul is overcome by some temptation, it is not the temptation that turns you into chaff. No, you were chaff already, that is to say fickle and faithless; the temptation simply discloses the stuff you are made of. On the other hand, when you endure temptations bravely it is not the temptation that makes you faithful and patient; temptation merely brings to light the hidden virtues of patience and fortitude that have been present in you all along. *Do you think I had any other purpose in speaking to you,* said the Lord to Job, *than to reveal your virtue?* In another text he declares: *I humbled you and made you feel the pangs of hunger in order to find out what was in your heart.*

In the same way, a storm will not allow a house to stand firm if it is built upon sand. If you wish to build a house, you must build it upon rock.

Then any storms that arrive will not demolish your handiwork, whereas the house built upon sand will totter, proving thereby that it is not well founded.

So while all is yet quiet, before the storm gathers, before the squalls begin to bluster or the waves to swell, let us concentrate all our efforts on the foundations of our building and construct our house with the many strong, interlocking bricks of God's commandments. Then when cruel persecution is unleashed like some fearful tornado against Christians, we shall be able to show that our house is built upon Christ Jesus our rock.

Far be it from us to deny Christ when that time comes. But if anyone should do so, let that person realize that it was not at the moment of his public denial that his apostasy took place. The seeds and roots had been hidden within him for a long time; persecution only brought into the open and made public what was already there. Let us pray to the Lord then that we may be firm and solid buildings that no storm can overthrow, founded on the rock of our Lord Jesus Christ, to whom be glory and power for ever and ever. Amen.

Origen, *Homilies on Luke*, 26.3–5: SC 87, 340–2

Fourth Sunday of Advent Year A: Matthew 1.18–24

A READING FROM A HOMILY BY THE VENERABLE BEDE

Matthew the evangelist gives us an account of the way in which the eternal Son of God, begotten before the world began, appeared in time as the Son of Man. His description is brief but absolutely true. By tracing the ancestry of our Lord and Saviour Jesus Christ through the male line he brings it down from Abraham to Joseph, the husband of Mary. It is indeed fitting in every respect that when God decided to become incarnate for the sake of the whole human race none but a virgin should be his mother, and that, since a virgin was privileged to bring him into the world, she should bear no other son but God.

Behold, a virgin will conceive and bear a son, and he will be called Emmanuel, a name which means God-with-us. The name God-with-us, given to our Saviour by the prophet, signifies that two natures are united in his one person. Before time began he was God, born of the Father, but in the fullness of time he became Emmanuel, God-with-us, in the womb of his mother, because when the Word was made flesh and lived among us he deigned to unite our frail human nature to his own person. Without ceasing to be what he had always been, he began in a wonderful fashion to be what we are, assuming our nature in such a way that he did not lose his own.

And so Mary gave birth to her firstborn son, the child of her own flesh and blood. She brought forth the God who had been born of God before creation began, and who, in his created humanity, rightfully surpassed the whole of creation. And Scripture says *she named him Jesus.*

Jesus, then, is the name of the Virgin's son. According to the angel's explanation, it means one who is to save his people from their sins. In doing so he will also deliver them from any defilement of mind and body they have incurred on account of their sins.

But the title 'Christ' implies a priestly or royal dignity. In the Old Testament it was given to both priests and kings on account of the anointing with chrism or holy oil which they received. They prefigured the true king and high priest who, on coming into this world, was anointed with the oil of gladness above all his peers. From this anointing or chrismation he received the name of Christ, and those who share in the anointing which he himself bestows, that is the grace of the Spirit, are called Christians.

May Jesus Christ fulfil his saving task by saving us from our sins; may he discharge his priestly office by reconciling us to God the Father; and may he exercise his royal power by admitting us to his Father's kingdom, for he is our Lord and God who lives and reigns with the Father and the Holy Spirit for ever and ever. Amen.

Ven. Bede, *Homily 5 on the Vigil of the Nativity*: CCSL 122, 32–6

Fourth Sunday of Advent Year B: Luke 1.26–38

A READING FROM A HOMILY BY THE VENERABLE BEDE

Today's reading of the gospel calls to mind the beginning of our redemption, for the passage tells us how God sent an angel from heaven to a virgin. He was to proclaim the new birth, the incarnation of God's Son, who would take away our age-old guilt; through him it would be possible to be made new and numbered among the children of God. And so, if we are to deserve the gifts of the promised salvation, we must listen attentively to the account of its beginning.

The angel Gabriel was sent from God to a city of Galilee named Nazareth, to a virgin betrothed to a man whose name was Joseph of the house of David; and the virgin's name was Mary. What is said of the house of David applies not only to Joseph but also to Mary. It was a precept of the law that each man should marry a wife from his own tribe and kindred. St Paul also bears testimony to this when he writes to Timothy: *Remember Jesus Christ, risen from the dead, descended from David, as preached in my Gospel.* Our Lord is truly descended from David, since his spotless mother took her ancestry from David's line.

The angel came to her and said, 'Do not be afraid, Mary, for you have found favour with God. And behold, you will conceive in your womb and bear a son, and you shall call his name Jesus. He will be great, and will be called the son of the Most High; and the Lord God will give to him the throne of his father David.' The angel refers to the kingdom of the Israelite nation as the throne of David because in his time, by the Lord's command and assistance, David governed it with a spirit of faithful service. The Lord God gave to our Redeemer the throne of his father David, when he decreed that he should take flesh from the lineage of David. As David had once ruled the people with temporal authority, so Christ would now lead them to the eternal kingdom by his spiritual grace. Of this kingdom the Apostle said: *He has delivered us from the dominion of darkness and transferred us to the kingdom of his beloved Son.*

He will reign over the house of Jacob forever. The house of Jacob here refers to the universal Church which, through its faith in and witness to Christ, shares the heritage of the patriarchs. This may apply either to those who are physical descendants of the patriarchal families, or to those who come from gentile nations and are reborn in Christ by the waters of baptism. In this house Christ shall reign forever, and of his kingdom there will be no end. During this present life, Christ rules in the Church. By faith and love he dwells in the hearts of his elect, and guides them by his unceasing care toward their heavenly reward. In the life to come, when their period of exile on earth is ended, he will exercise his kingship by leading the faithful to their heavenly country. There, for ever inspired by the vision of his presence, their one delight will be to praise and glorify him.

Ven. Bede, Homily 2 on Advent: CCSL 122, 14–17

Fourth Sunday of Advent Year C: Luke 1.39–45 [39–55]

A READING FROM A SERMON BY BLESSED GUERRIC OF IGNY

Our King and Saviour is coming; let us run to meet him! *Good news from a far country*, in the words of Solomon, *is like cold water to a thirsty soul*; and to announce the coming of our Saviour and the reconciliation of the world, together with the good things of the life to come, is to bring good news indeed. *How beautiful are the feet of those who bring good tidings and publish peace!* Such messengers truly bear a refreshing draught to the soul that thirsts for God; with their news of the Saviour's coming, they joyfully draw and offer us water from the springs of salvation. In the words and spirit of Elizabeth, the soul responds to the message, whether it be of Isaiah four of his fellow-prophets: *Why is this granted to me, that my Lord should come to me? For behold, when the voice of your greeting came to my ears*, my spirit leapt for joy within me in eager longing to run ahead to meet my God and Saviour.

Let us too arise with joy and run in spirit to meet our Saviour. Hailing him from afar, let us worship him, saying, Come, Lord, *save me and I shall be saved!* Come and *show us your face, and we shall all be saved. We have been waiting for you; be our help in time of trouble.* This was how the prophets and saints of old men went to meet the Messiah, filled with immense desire to see with their eyes, if possible, what they already saw in spirit.

We must look forwards to the day, so soon to come, on which we celebrate the anniversary of Christ's birth. Scripture itself insists on the joy which must fill us – a joy which will lift our spirit out of itself in longing for his coming, impatient of delay as it strains forward to see even now what the future holds in store.

I believe that the many texts of Scripture which urge us to go out to meet him speak of Christ's first coming as well as his second. Surely, however, we are to understand that as our bodies will rise up rejoicing at his second coming, so our hearts must run forwards in joy to greet his first.

Between these two comings of his, the Lord frequently visits us individually in accordance with our merits and desires, forming us to the likeness of his first coming in the flesh, and preparing us for his return at the end of time. He comes to us now, to make sure that we do not lose the fruits of his first coming nor incur his wrath at his second. His purpose now is to convert our pride into the humility which he showed when he first came, so that he may refashion our lowly bodies into the likeness of that glorious body which he will manifest when he comes again.

Grace accompanied his first coming; glory will surround his last. This intermediate coming is a combination of both, enabling us to experience in the consolations of his grace a sort of foretaste of his glory. Blessed are those whose burning love has gained for them such a privilege!

And so, my brothers, though we have not yet experienced this wonderful consolation, we are encouraged by firm faith and a pure conscience to wait patiently for the Lord to come. In joy and confidence let us say with St Paul: *I know the one in whom I have put my trust, and I am confident of his power to guard what has been put into my charge until the day when our great God and Saviour Jesus Christ comes in glory.* May he be praised for ever and ever. Amen.

Bd Guerric of Igny, *Advent Sermons*, 2.1–4: SC 166, 104–16

CHRISTMAS

LET us strive to comprehend the mystery. The reason God is in the flesh is to kill the death that lurks there. As diseases are cured by medicines and assimilated by the body, and as darkness in a house is dispelled by the coming of light, so death, which held sway over human nature, is done away with by the coming of God. How great is God's goodness, how deep his love for us! Let us join the shepherds in giving glory to God, let us dance with the angels and sing: *Today a Saviour has been born to us; he is Christ the Lord*. This feast belongs to the whole of creation. Let our voices too ring out in songs of jubilation.

St Basil the Great

WHILE all things were in quiet silence and night was in the midst of her swift course, your almighty Word, O Lord, leapt down from heaven out of your royal throne.

Antiphon, *Dum medium silentium* (Wisdom 18.14–15)

WE venerate this holy day adorned with three miracles: today the star led the Magi to the manger; today water was turned into wine at the wedding; today Christ desired to be baptized in the Jordan by John, that he might save us, Alleluia.

Magnificat antiphon for Epiphany, *Tribus miraculis*

ETERNAL God, who made this most holy night to shine with the brightness of your one true light: bring us, who have known the revelation of that light on earth, to see the radiance of your heavenly glory; through Jesus Christ your Son our Lord, who is alive and reigns with you, in the unity of the Holy Spirit, one God, now and for ever. Amen.

Collect for Christmas night, *Common Worship*

'Now we give you thanks because, by the power of the Holy Spirit, [Jesus Christ] took our nature upon him and was born of the Virgin Mary his mother, that being himself without sin, he might make us clean from all sin.'[3] The Christmas season has two parts, after Christmas and after Epiphany, but it is really only one multi-faceted mystery that is celebrated: God became human and was revealed to Jews and Gentiles. It is distinct from the other parts of the Christian year in that it is based on a succession of feasts rather than a series of Sundays. It begins on the feast of the Nativity, Christmas, and can end with the Sunday of the Baptism of the Lord, as in the Roman calendar, or the feast of the Presentation of the Lord (2 February), as in the calendar of the Church of England. The Presentation is the last feast that depends on the date of Christmas, forty days before, and thereafter the liturgical year looks forward to Easter (with the significant exception of the Feast of the Annunciation on 25 March, nine months before Christmas, which commemorates the conception of Jesus in the womb of the Virgin Mary). The Sunday Gospels of the *Revised Common Lectionary* and the *Roman Lectionary*, however, start the series of semi-continuous readings from the Gospels on the Sunday after the Baptism of the Lord and so this section will only concern the Sundays up to this day.

The two great feasts of Christmas (25 December) and Epiphany (6 January) seem to have originated in the early fourth century. Christmas is first mentioned in Rome about the year AD 335 and Epiphany in Gaul before the year AD 360 although it probably came from the Christian East. Christ is the Sun of Justice (Malachi 4.2) and the Light of the World (John 8.12) and some have argued that it is no coincidence that 25 December was the pagan feast of the Unconquered Sun and 6 January was a midwinter feast, but others say that the days were chosen by reason of complicated calendrical reasons associated with their connection to Easter. Christmas commemorates the incarnation, the Son of God becoming human in the womb of the Virgin Mary and being born at Bethlehem. It was only by being both truly God and truly human that Jesus was able to be the Saviour of the human race, and so the mystery of Christmas is a necessary pre-condition for the paschal mystery celebrated at Easter.

Around the year AD 600 St Gregory the Great began a Christmas sermon by saying that 'the Lord in his generosity allows us to celebrate Mass three times on this day', and this Roman custom spread beyond the Alps to other parts of Europe. The first was the Mass of the Day, first celebrated in Rome at St Peter's but then at the Basilica of St Mary Major,

---

3 Christmas short preface, *Common Worship*.

at which was read the Prologue of John's Gospel – the great Gospel of Christmas; the second was the Mass at Night ('midnight Mass') with its Gospel of the Nativity which was celebrated at the replica of the manger in the Church of St Mary Major in imitation of the nocturnal liturgy at the Basilica of the Nativity in Bethlehem; the third was the Mass of the Dawn, originally celebrated in the Basilica of St Anastasia on her feast day (25 December) but later turned into another Christmas celebration with the Gospel of the shepherds. In their different ways these Gospels all present the birth of Christ as the dawning of God's promised salvation. These Masses are still in the *Roman Missal* and the *Revised Common Lectionary* has preserved their Gospels but it does not specify the times at which they should be used, although Anglican prayer books such as *Common Worship* often give liturgical formularies for celebrations at Christmas Night and Christmas Day.

The Sundays after Christmas continue the Christmas theme and the first Sunday after Christmas is named after the Holy Family – Jesus, Mary and Joseph – in the Roman calendar. This feast, with its roots in popular devotion to the Holy Family, was established in 1893 on the third Sunday after Epiphany, it was moved to 19 January in 1914 and then to the first Sunday after Epiphany in 1921 when it was made obligatory throughout the Roman Rite. In 1969 it moved to its present day because of its close connection with the mystery of Christmas. Its Gospels give the opportunity to read passages from the infancy narratives that are otherwise omitted from the Christmas season, the flight into Egypt, the Presentation and the finding of the boy Jesus in the Temple. Again we find that the liturgy is primarily a celebration of the mystery not history, as these passages of the Gospel are read before the visit of the Magi at Epiphany which historically happened first. If 1 January occurs on this Sunday, the feast of the Holy Family is moved to the previous Friday and replaced by the Mass of Mary, Mother of God.

Great Christian feasts such as Easter often have an 'octave' (from the Latin *octava*, eighth), a period of eight days during which the feast continues to be celebrated, and the eighth and final day (*octava dies*) is sometimes marked by special solemnity. The octave day of Christmas, 1 January, was originally a feast of Mary at Rome but soon became a commemoration of the circumcision of Jesus which the Gospel tells us occurred eight days after his birth (Luke 2.21). In 1969 the Roman Catholic Church renamed this feast 'Mary, Mother of God'. The Gospel of the feast also notes that this is when the Lord was called 'Jesus', according to the message of the angel, and so in the Church of England it is now called 'The Naming and Circumcision of Jesus'. Some Churches, such as the Anglican Church of

Canada, celebrate this day simply as the 'Feast of the Naming of Jesus'. The Gospel, however, is always the same, as is the Gospel from the Prologue to John for the second Sunday of Christmas, which can be displaced by the Epiphany when that is assigned to the Sunday between 2 and 8 January in the Roman calendar.

The Epiphany is celebrated on 6 January but in some regions it may be celebrated on the Sunday after 1 January. As we have noted in the introduction to Advent, Epiphany is from the Greek *epiphaneia* and means 'manifestation', 'appearance' or 'coming', and it could be used of the manifestation of a God (which is also called a 'theophany', from the Greek *theophaneia*) or the triumphant entry of a king into a city. In the Western Christian calendar the feast celebrates the visit of the Magi or wise men to offer their gifts to the infant Christ, which was the first manifestation of Christ to the Gentiles. It also celebrates the baptism of Jesus by John (the main content of the feast in the Christian East) and the miracle at Cana (John 2.1–11) which is described as the first of Jesus' signs which 'manifested his glory'.

The baptism of Jesus is now commemorated in Western calendars on the Sunday after Epiphany. This feast has its origin in a celebration of the Baptism of Christ on the octave of the Epiphany in the time of Charlemagne and it entered the Roman calendar in 1960, being assigned to this Sunday in the 1969 Roman calendar (it is celebrated on the following Monday when 6 January, the Epiphany, is a Sunday). The liturgical Gospels are the accounts of Jesus' baptism in Matthew, Mark and Luke and the feast has been adopted by the *Revised Common Lectionary*.

The Feast of the Presentation is celebrated on 2 February, forty days after Christmas. It is traditionally the end of the Christmas season but is discussed in the introduction to the next section of this book, 'Ordinary Time before Lent', as it occurs in the series of Gospels of Ordinary Time.

The Christmas season and its Gospels are thus a sustained meditation on the mystery of Christ's incarnation and first manifestation to Jews and Gentiles as recorded in the first chapters of the Gospels. The richness of the mystery is shown by the various feasts celebrated and the Gospel passages read. From Advent to Candlemas we are led through salvation history in preparation for the great saving drama of the Lord's death and resurrection which is celebrated in the Easter season but is present each week in the celebration of Sunday.

Christmas I, Midnight Mass: Luke 2.1–14 [1–20]

A READING FROM A HOMILY BY THEODOTUS OF ANCYRA

The Lord of all comes as a slave amidst poverty. The huntsman has no wish to startle his prey. Choosing for his birthplace an unknown village in a remote province, he is born of a poor maiden and accepts all that poverty implies, for he hopes by stealth to ensnare and save us.

If he had been born to high rank and amidst luxury, unbelievers would have said the world had been transformed by wealth. If he had chosen as his birthplace the great city of Rome, they would have thought the transformation had been brought about by civil power. Suppose he had been the son of an emperor. They would have said: 'How useful it is to be powerful!' Imagine him the son of a senator. It would have been: 'Look what can be accomplished by legislation!'

But in fact, what did he do? He chose surroundings that were poor and simple, so ordinary as to be almost unnoticed, so that people would know it was the Godhead alone that changed the world. This was his reason for choosing his mother from among the poor of a very poor country, and for becoming poor himself.

The manger teaches you how poor the Lord was: he was laid on it because he had no bed to lie on. This lack of the necessaries of life was a most appropriate prophetic foreshadowing. He was laid in a manger to show that he would be the food even of the inarticulate. The Word of God drew to himself both the rich and the poor, both the eloquent and the slow of speech as he lay in the manger in poverty.

Do you not see how his lack of worldly goods was a prophecy and how his poverty, accepted for our sake, showed his accessibility to all? No one was afraid to approach Christ, overawed by his immense wealth; no one was kept from coming to him by the grandeur of his royal estate. No, he who was offering himself for the salvation of the world came as an ordinary worker.

The Word of God in a human body was laid in a manger, so that both the eloquent and the slow of speech would have courage to share in the food of salvation. Perhaps this is what the prophet foretold when he said, speaking of the mystery of the manger: *The ox knows its owner and the ass its master's manger, but Israel does not know me; my people have not understood.* He whose godhead made him rich became poor for our sake, so as to put salvation within the reach of everyone. This was the teaching of St Paul when he said: *He was rich, but for our sake he became poor, to make us rich through his poverty.*

Who was rich, what was his wealth, and how did he become poor for our sake? Tell me, who was this possessor of great wealth who became a sharer in my poverty? Could he have been a mere man? If so he would never have been rich, for his parents were poor just as he was. Then who was this person possessed of great riches and what were the riches of him who became poor for our sake? Scripture says it is God who enriches his creatures. It must then have been God who became poor, who made his own the poverty of one who can be seen. His divinity made God rich, but he became poor for our sake.

Theodotus of Ancyra, *Homily 1 on the Nativity of the Lord*:
PG 77, 1360–1

Christmas II, Dawn Mass: Luke 2.15–20 [1–20, or 8–20]

A READING FROM A SERMON BY ST AELRED

Today, in the city of David, the Saviour of the world is born for us: he is Christ the Lord. That city is Bethlehem. We must run there as the shepherds did when they heard these tidings, and so put into action the words we traditionally sing in this season: *They sang of God's glory, they hastened to Bethlehem.*

And this shall be a sign for you: you will find the child wrapped in swaddling bands and lying in a manger. Now this is what I say: you must love. You fear the lord of angels, yes, but love the tiny babe; you fear the Lord of majesty, yes, but love the infant wrapped in swaddling clothes; you fear him who reigns in heaven, yes, but love him who lies in the manger.

What sort of sign were the shepherds given? *You will find the child wrapped in swaddling clothes and lying in a manger.* It was by this that they were to recognize their Saviour and Lord. But is there anything great about being wrapped in swaddling clothes and lying in a stable – are not other children also wrapped in swaddling clothes? What kind of sign, then, can this be?

Indeed it is a great one, if only we understand it rightly. Such understanding will be ours if this message of love is not restricted to our hearing, but if our hearts too are illuminated by the light which accompanied the appearance of the angels. The angel who first proclaimed the good tidings appeared surrounded by light to teach us that only those whose minds are spiritually enlightened can truly understand the message.

Much can be said of this sign; but as time is passing I shall say little, and briefly. Bethlehem, the *house of bread*, is holy Church. The manger at Bethlehem is the altar of the church; it is there that Christ's creatures are fed. This is the table of which it is written, *You have prepared a banquet for me*. In this manger is Jesus, wrapped in the swaddling clothes which are the outward form of the sacraments. Here in this manger, under the forms of bread and wine, is the true body and blood of Christ. We believe that Christ himself is here, but he is wrapped in swaddling clothes; in other words, he is invisibly contained in these sacraments. We have no greater or clearer proof of Christ's birth than our daily reception of his body and blood at the holy altar, and the sight of him who was once born for us of a Virgin daily offered in sacrifice for us.

And so let us hasten to the manger of the Lord. But before drawing near we must prepare ourselves as well as we can with the help of his grace; and then, in company with the angels, with pure heart, good conscience, and unfeigned faith, we may sing to the Lord in all that we do throughout the whole of our life: *Glory to God in the highest, and on earth peace to people of good will*; through our Lord Jesus Christ, to whom be honour and glory for ever and ever. Amen.

St Aelred, *Sermon 2 on the Birth of the Lord*: PL 195, 226–7, 1471–4

Christmas III, Day Mass: John 1.1–18 [1–14]

A READING FROM A HOMILY BY ST BASIL THE GREAT

God is on earth, God is among us, not now as lawgiver – there is no fire, trumpet blast, smoke-wreathed mountain, dense cloud, or storm to terrify whoever hears him – but as one gently and kindly conversing in a human body with his fellow men and women. God is in the flesh. Now he is not acting intermittently as he did through the prophets. He is bringing back to himself the whole human race, which he has taken possession of and united to himself. By his flesh he has made the human race his own kin.

But how can glory come to all through only one? How can the God-head be in the flesh? In the same way as fire can be in iron: not by moving from place to place but by the one imparting to the other its own properties. Fire does not speed toward iron, but without itself undergoing any change it causes the iron to share in its own natural attributes. The fire is not diminished and yet it completely fills whatever shares in its nature. So is it also with God the Word. He did not relinquish his own nature and yet *he dwelt among us*. He did not undergo any change and yet *the Word became flesh*. Earth received him from heaven, yet heaven was not deserted by him who holds the universe in being.

Let us strive to comprehend the mystery. The reason God is in the flesh is to kill the death that lurks there. As diseases are cured by medicines and assimilated by the body, and as darkness in a house is dispelled by the coming of light, so death, which held sway over human nature, is done away with by the coming of God. And as ice formed on water covers its surface as long as night and darkness last but melts under the warmth of the sun, so death reigned until the coming of Christ; but when the grace of God our Saviour appeared and the Sun of Justice rose, death was swallowed up in victory, unable to bear the presence of true life. How great is God's goodness, how deep his love for us!

Let us join the shepherds in giving glory to God, let us dance with the angels and sing: *Today a saviour has been born to us. He is Christ the Lord. The Lord is God and he has appeared to us*, not as God, which would have been terrifying for our weakness, but as a slave so as to free those who live in slavery. Who could be so lacking in sensibility and so ungrateful as not to join all here present in our gladness, exultation, and radiant joy? This feast belongs to the whole of creation. Let everyone contribute and be grateful. Let our voices too ring out in songs of jubilation.

St Basil the Great, *Homily 2 on the Holy Birth of the Lord*:
PG 31, 1459–62, 1471–4

Holy Family/First Sunday of Christmas Year A: Matthew 2.13–15, 19–23 [13–23]

A READING FROM A HOMILY BY ST JOHN CHRYSOSTOM

Today, as a firstborn son, Christ went down into Egypt to end the mourning its ancient bereavement had brought upon that land. Instead of plagues he brought joy, instead of night and darkness he gave the light of salvation.

Of old the river's water had been polluted by the untimely deaths of murdered infants. Therefore he who long ago had stained the waters red went down into Egypt and purified those waters by the power of the Holy

Spirit, making them the source of salvation. When the Egyptians were afflicted they raged against God and denied him. Therefore he went down into Egypt, filled devout souls with the knowledge of God and made the river more productive of martyrs than it was of ears of grain.

What more shall I say of this mystery? I see a carpenter and a manger, an infant and swaddling clothes, a virgin giving birth without the necessaries of life; nothing but poverty and complete destitution. Have you ever seen wealth in such great penury? How could he who was rich have become, for our sake, so poor that he had neither bed nor bedding but was laid in a manger? O immeasurable wealth concealed in poverty! He lies in a manger, yet he rocks the whole world. He is bound with swaddling bands, yet he breaks the bonds of sin. Before he could speak he taught the wise men and converted them. What else can I say? Here is the newborn babe, wrapped in swaddling clothes and lying in a manger. With him are Mary, virgin and mother, and Joseph who was called his father.

Joseph was only betrothed to Mary when the Holy Spirit overshadowed her; so he was at a loss as to what he should call the child. While he was in this perplexity a message from heaven came to him by the voice of an angel: *Do not be afraid, Joseph. It is by the Holy Spirit that she has conceived this child.* In her virginity the Holy Spirit overshadowed her.

Why was Christ born of a virgin and her virginity preserved inviolate? Because of old the devil had deceived the virgin Eve, Gabriel brought the Good News to the Virgin Mary. Having fallen into the trap, Eve spoke the word that led to death. Having received the Good News, Mary gave birth to the Incarnate Word who has brought us eternal life.

St John Chrysostom, *Homily on the Day of Christ's Birth*: PG 56, 392

Holy Family/First Sunday of Christmas Year B: Luke 2.22–40 or 2.22, 39–40

A READING FROM A HOMILY BY ST CYRIL OF ALEXANDRIA

We see Emanuel as a newborn infant lying in a manger. In his human condition he is wrapped in swaddling clothes, but in his divine nature he is hymned by angels. Angels brought the shepherds the good news of his birth, for God the Father had given those who dwell in heaven the special privilege of being his first heralds.

Today we also see him submitting to the law of Moses; or rather, we see

God the lawgiver subject as man to his own decrees. The reason for this we learn from the wisdom of Paul. He says: *When we were under age we were slaves of the elemental spirits of the universe, but when the fullness of time had come God sent his Son, born of a woman, born under the law, to redeem those who were under the law.*

Christ ransomed from the law's curse those who were subject to the law but had never kept it. How did he ransom them? By fulfilling the law. Or to put it in another way, to blot out the reproach of Adam's transgression, he offered himself on our behalf to God the Father, showing him in all things ready obedience and submission. Scripture says: *As through one man's disobedience many were made sinners, so through one man's obedience many will be made righteous.* And so, Christ submitted to the law together with us, and he did so by becoming man in accordance with the divine dispensation.

It was fitting that Christ should do everything that justice required. He had in all truth assumed the condition of a slave; and so, reckoned among those under the yoke by reason of his humanity, he once paid the half-shekel to those who demanded it, although as the Son he was by nature free and not liable to this tax. When you see him keeping the law, then, do not misunderstand it, or reduce one who is free to the rank of household slaves, but reflect rather on the depths of God's plan.

When the eighth day arrived on which it was customary for the flesh to be circumcised as prescribed by the law, he received the name, Jesus, which means 'salvation of the people'; for it was the wish of God the Father that his own Son, born of a woman, should be so named. It was then that he first became the salvation of the people and not of one people only but of many, indeed of all peoples and of the whole world.

Christ thus became the light of revelation to the Gentiles, but he is also the glory of Israel. Even though some members of that race were insolent and unbelieving, a remnant has been saved and glorified by Christ. The holy disciples were the first fruits of Israel, and the brightness of their glory illuminates the whole world. Christ is the glory of Israel in another way too, for in his human nature he came from that people, even though he is God, sovereign, ruler of all and blessed forever.

The wise Evangelist helps us, then, by teaching us all the Son of God made flesh endured for our sake and in our name, and that he did not disdain to take upon himself our poverty, so that we might glorify him as Redeemer, as Lord, as Saviour, and as God; for to him, and with him to God the Father and the Holy Spirit, belong glory and power for endless ages. Amen.

St Cyril of Alexandria, *Homily* 12: PG 77, 1042, 1046, 1047, 1050

Holy Family/First Sunday of Christmas Year C: Luke 2.41–52

A READING FROM A HOMILY ON LUKE BY ORIGEN

When Jesus was twelve years old, he stayed behind in Jerusalem. Not knowing this, his parents sought him anxiously, but did not find him. Though they searched the whole caravan, looking for him among their kinsfolk and acquaintances, he was nowhere to be found.

It was his own parents who were looking for him – the father who had brought him up and cared for him when they fled into Egypt – and even they did not find him at once. This shows that Jesus is not found among relatives and acquaintances, not among those bound to him by physical ties. We do not find him in a crowd. Let us learn where it was that Joseph and Mary discovered him, then in their company we too shall be able to find him.

They found him, Scripture says, in the temple. Not just anywhere, but in the temple; and not just anywhere in the temple, but among the doctors, listening to them and asking them questions. And so we too must look for Jesus in the temple of God; we must look for him in the Church, among the doctors who belong to the Church and are faithful to its teaching. If we seek him there, we shall find him. Moreover, anyone who claims to be a doctor without possessing Christ is a doctor in name only; Jesus, the Word and Wisdom of God, will not be found with him.

They found him, then, *sitting among the doctors*, or rather not merely sitting, but learning from them and listening to them. At this very moment Jesus is present among us too, questioning us and listening to us speaking. It is further written, *And they were all amazed*. What caused their astonishment? Not his questions – though these were certainly extraordinary – but his answers. He questioned the doctors, and since they could not always give an answer, he himself replied to his own questions. These replies were not mere disputation, but real teaching, exemplified for us in holy Scripture where the divine law declares: *Moses spoke, and God answered him*. In this way the Lord instructed Moses about those matters of which he was ignorant. So it was that sometimes Jesus asked questions, sometimes he answered them; and, as we have already said, wonderful though his questions were, his replies were even more wonderful.

In order, therefore, that we too may be his hearers and that he may put to us questions which he himself will then answer, let us pray to him earnestly, seeking him with great effort and anguish, and then our search will be rewarded. Not for nothing was it written, *Your father and I have been looking for you anxiously.* The search for Jesus must be neither careless nor indifferent, nor must it be only a transitory affair. Those who seek in this manner will never find him. We must truly be able to say: *We have been looking for you anxiously*; if we can say this then he will reply to our weary and anxious soul in the words: *Did you not know that I must be in my Father's house?*

Origen, *Homilies on Luke*, 18.2–5: GCS 9, 112–13

Mary, Mother of God/The Naming and Circumcision of Jesus/The Holy Name Year A: Luke 2.16–21

A READING FROM A SERMON BY BLESSED GUERRIC OF IGNY

One and unique was Mary's child, the only Son of his Father in heaven and the only Son of his mother on earth. Mary alone was virgin-mother, and it is her glory to have borne the Father's only Son. But now she embraces that only Son of hers in all his members. She is not ashamed to be called the mother of all those in whom she recognizes that Christ her Son has been or is on the point of being formed.

Our ancient mother Eve was more of a stepmother than a true mother, passing on to her children the sentence of death before bringing them into the light of day. Her name indeed means 'mother of all the living', but she proved more truly to be the slayer of the living or the mother of the dying, since for her to give birth was to transmit death.

Eve being unable to respond faithfully to the meaning of her name, its mysterious import was fully expressed by Mary. Like the Church of which she is the model, Mary is the mother of all who are born again to new life. She is the mother of him who is the Life by which all things live; when she bore him, she gave new birth in a sense to all who were to live by his life.

Recognizing that by virtue of this mystery she is the mother of all Christians, Christ's blessed mother also shows herself a mother to them by her care and loving kindness. She never grows hard toward her children, as though they were not her own. The womb that once gave birth is not dried up; it continues to bring forth the fruit of her tender compassion. Christ, the blessed fruit of that womb, left his mother still fraught with inexhaustible love, a love that once came forth from her but remains always within her, inundating her with his gifts.

It can be seen that the children themselves recognize her as their mother. A natural instinct, inspired by faith, prompts them to have recourse to her in all dangers and difficulties, invoking her and taking refuge in her arms like little ones running to their mother. To this day we dwell in the shelter of the mother of the Most High, remaining under her protection as it were beneath the shadow of her wings. And in the days to come we shall share in her glory; we shall know the warmth of her loving embrace. Then there will be one joyful voice proclaiming the praise of our mother: Holy Mother of God, *in you we all find our home*!

Bd Guerric of Igny, *Sermon 1 on the Assumption of Mary*, 2–4:
PL 185, 187–9

Mary, Mother of God/The Naming and Circumcision of Jesus/The Holy Name Year B: Luke 2.16–21

A READING FROM A HOMILY BY ST BASIL OF SELEUCIA

Born of the Virgin Mother of God, the Creator and Lord of all shared our human nature, for he had a real body and soul even though he had no part in our misdeeds. *He committed no sin*, says Scripture, *and no falsehood ever came from his mouth*. O holy womb in which God was received, in which the record of our sins was effaced, in which God became man while remaining God! He was carried in the womb, condescending to be born in the same way as we are. Yet when he was received into the arms of his mother he did not leave the bosom of his Father. God is not divided as he carries out his will, but saves the world without suffering any division in himself. When Gabriel came into the presence of the Virgin Mother of God he left heaven behind, but when the Word of God who fills all creation took flesh within her, he was not separated from the adoring hosts of heaven.

Is there any need to enumerate all the prophecies foretelling Christ's birth of the Mother of God? What tongue could worthily hymn her through whom we have received such magnificent blessings? With what flowers of praise could we weave a fitting crown for her from whom sprang the flower of Jesse, who has crowned our race with glory and honour? What gifts could we bring that would be worthy of her of whom the whole world is unworthy? If Paul could say of the other saints that

33

the world was not worthy of them, what can we say of the Mother of God, who outshines all the martyrs even as the sun outshines the stars? O Virgin, well may the angels rejoice in you! Because of you they who long ages ago had banished our race are now sent to our service, and to his joy Gabriel is entrusted with the news of a divine child's conception. *Rejoice, most favoured one,* let your face glow with gladness. You are to give birth to the joy of all the world, who will put an end to the age-old curse, destroying the power of death and giving to all the hope of resurrection.

Emmanuel came into the world he had made long before. God from all eternity, he came as a newborn infant. He who had prepared eternal dwellings lay in a manger, for there was no room for him at the inn. He who was made known by a star came to birth in a cave. He who was offered as a ransom for sin received gifts from the wise men. He who as God enfolds the whole world in his embrace was taken into the arms of Simeon. The shepherds gazed upon this baby; the angelic host, knowing he was God, sang of his glory in heaven and of peace to his people on earth. And all these things together with other marvels concerning him the holy mother of the Lord of all creation, the mother of the very truth of God, *pondered in her heart,* and her heart was filled with great gladness. She was radiant with joy and amazed when she thought of the majesty of her Son who was also God. As her gaze rested upon that divine child I think she must have been overwhelmed by awe and longing. She was alone conversing with the Alone.

St Basil of Seleucia, *Sermons*, 39.4, 5: PG 85, 438, 442, 446

Mary, Mother of God/The Naming and Circumcision of Jesus/The Holy Name Year C: Luke 2.16–21

A READING FROM A HOMILY BY ST CYRIL OF ALEXANDRIA

Deep, unfathomable, and really to be marvelled at is the mystery of our religion. Even the holy angels long to comprehend it. Referring somewhere to sayings of the prophets concerning Christ our Saviour, the Saviour's disciple says that *the angels long for insight into the things which the bringers of the Good News, by the power of the Holy Spirit sent from heaven, have now revealed to you.* And those angels who penetrated the tremendous mystery of our faith when Christ was born in the flesh give thanks for us as they sang, *Glory to God in the highest, and peace to his people on earth.*

True God by his very nature was the Word of God the Father, consubstantial with the Father and co-eternal, and resplendent also in his own sublime majesty. Yet although he was one in nature with his Father and his equal *he did not regard equality with God as something to be clung to, but gave up everything to take* from holy Mary *the nature of a slave. He was born as a human being, and existing then in human condition he humbled himself even to the extent of dying, dying on a cross.* He who held all things in his plenitude freely descended to our condition. Being under no compulsion but of his own free will, he who by his own nature was free lowered himself for our sake to assume the nature of a slave. He who was exalted above every creature became one of ourselves; he who gives life to all, for *he is the living bread that gives life to the world*, became one of those subject to death. He who, being God, was the lawgiver and himself above the law became subject to the law like us. He existed before time was and was in fact the maker of time, and yet he became one of those who must be born, who must have a beginning.

How then did he become like us? By taking a body from the holy Virgin; not a body without a soul, but one possessed of a rational soul, so that he came forth from a woman as a real man, though without sin. He was a man in all reality, he did not merely appear to be one, and yet there was no belittling of his divinity or casting out of his godhead, which had always been his, is his now, and shall be his for ever. For this reason, therefore, we declare the holy Virgin to be the Mother of God.

St Cyril of Alexandria, *Homilies on the Incarnation of the Word of God*,
15.1–3: PG 77, 1090–1

Second Sunday of Christmas Year A: John 1.1–18 or 1–5, 9–14

A READING FROM A SERMON BY ST LEO THE GREAT

The infancy which the Son of God in his majesty did not disdain to assume developed with the passage of time into the maturity of manhood. After the triumph of the passion and the resurrection all the lowly acts he performed on our behalf are in the past. Nevertheless today's feast of Christmas renews for us the sacred beginning of the life of Jesus, son of the Virgin Mary, and we find that in celebrating our Saviour's birth we also celebrate our own.

The birth of Christ is the origin of the Christian people, and the birthday of the head is also the birthday of the body. It is true that each of us is called in turn and that the children of the Church are separated from one another by being born at different times. Nevertheless, as the whole community of the faithful which comes into being in the baptismal font is crucified with Christ in his passion, raised up with him in his resurrection, and by his ascension placed at the right hand of the Father, so too it is born with him in his nativity. All over the world believers regenerated in Christ break with their former way of life that was marked by original sin, and by a second birth are transformed into new people. Henceforth they are reckoned to be of the stock, not of their earthly father, but of Christ, who became the Son of Man, so that we could become children of God. Had he not so lowered himself as to come down to us, none of us could ever have gone to him by any merits of our own.

Therefore the greatness of the gift which he has bestowed on us demands an appreciation proportioned to its excellence; for blessed Paul the apostle truly teaches: *We have received not the spirit of this world but the Spirit that comes from God to help us understand the gifts God has given us.* The only way that we can worthily honour him is by presenting to him what he himself has given us.

But what can we find in the treasury of the Lord's bounty more in keeping with the glory of this feast than that peace which was first announced by the angelic choir on the day of his birth? For peace makes us children of God; it nourishes love and is the mother of unity; it is the repose of the blessed and our home in eternity. The work of peace and its special blessing is to unite to God those whom it separates from the world.

Therefore, let those *who have been born not of blood, nor of the will of the flesh, nor of the will of human beings, but of God,* offer to the Father their harmony as sons and daughters united in peace; and let all those whom he has adopted as his members meet in the firstborn of the new creation who came not to do his own will but the will of the one who sent him. The Father has not given the grace of being adopted as his heirs to people at variance with one another, possessing no common ground, but to those who are one in thought and love. Between the hearts and minds of those refashioned according to a single image there should be harmony.

The birthday of the Lord is the birthday of peace. As the Apostles says: *He is our peace, who has made us both one*; for whether we are Jews or Gentiles, *through him we have access in one Spirit to the Father.*

St Leo the Great, *Sermon 6 on the Nativity of the Lord*, 2–3, 5:
PL 54, 213–16

Second Sunday of Christmas Year B: John 1.1–18 or 1.1–5, 9–14

A READING FROM A SERMON BY BLESSED GUERRIC OF IGNY

You have assembled here to listen to the word of God, but God has provided something better. Today it is given us not only to hear the word of God, but even to see it, if only we will *go over to Bethlehem and see this word which the Lord has brought to pass and shown to us.*

God knew that human perceptions could not reach the things invisible. Human beings were incapable of learning heavenly teaching, finding it difficult to believe anything not brought visibly before their senses. The fact of the matter is that although faith comes by hearing, it comes much more readily and quickly by sight. We learnt this from the example of the apostle to whom it was said: *You believe because you have seen me; as long as you only had the evidence of your ears, you remained in unbelief.*

But God desires to accommodate himself to our slowness in every way, and therefore his Word, which formerly he had made audible, he has today made visible and even tangible. For this reason people of flesh and blood like ourselves have been able to talk of *that which was from the beginning, which we have seen with our eyes, which we have looked upon and touched with our hands.* They could speak of the Word of Life.

From the beginning the Word was of that eternity which had no beginning; we have heard him promised from the beginning of time; they have seen and touched with our hands the one who is now shown to us at the end of time. Sometimes I have noticed that God's words arouse no interest when they are merely heard with the ears, but if anyone actually saw the Word which is God, how could he fail to rejoice? I will pass judgement on myself in the first place. The Word which is God offers himself to me today to be seen in my own nature; if this does not fill me with joy, then I am an unbeliever. If it does not instruct me, I am a castaway.

If anyone here finds it tedious to listen to this second-rate sermon, far be it from me to weary him with my poor words. Let him go over to Bethlehem, and there let him contemplate that Word on which the angels desire to gaze, the Word of God which the Lord has shown to us. Let him picture in his heart what the living and active Word of God was like as he lay there in the manger.

This is a faithful saying and worthy to be received: your almighty Word, O Lord, which made its way down in deep silence from the Father's royal throne into the cattle stall, speaks to us the better for its silence. Let anyone who has ears to hear listen to what this holy and loving silence of the eternal Word is saying to us, for if I have heard aright, peace is one of the words he speaks to his holy people, who out of reverence for him and following his example have taken upon themselves the observance of monastic silence.

Bd Guerric of Igny, *Sermon 5 on the Nativity of the Lord*, 1–2:
SC 166, 223–6

Second Sunday of Christmas Year C: John 1.1–18 or 1–5, 9–14

A READING FROM A SERMON BY JULIAN OF VÉZELAY

While everything was hushed and still, and night was halfway through its course, your almighty Word, O Lord, leaped down from your royal throne in the heavens. In this text of Scripture, written long before, the most sacred moment of all time is made known to us, the moment when God's almighty Word would leave his Father's tender embrace and come down into his mother's womb to bring us his message of salvation: *For God, who in many in various ways in the past spoke to our fathers through the prophets, in these last days has spoken to us through this Son*, declaring: *This is my beloved Son in whom I am well pleased; listen to him.* And so from his royal throne the Word of God came to us, humbling himself in order to raise us up, becoming poor to make us rich, and human to make us divine.

But the people he was to redeem needed to have great trust and hope that the Word would come to them with effective power. Hence the description of God's word as almighty: *Your almighty Word* the Bible calls him. So lost, so wholly abandoned to unhappiness was the human race, that it could only trust in a Word that was almighty, otherwise it would experience no more than a weak and tremulous hope of being set free from sin and its effects. To give poor lost humanity an absolute assurance of being saved, the Word that came to save it was therefore called almighty.

And see how truly almighty was that Word! *Neither heaven nor anything under the heavens as yet had any existence; he spoke, and they came into being*, made out of nothing. The almighty power of the Word created substance and shape simultaneously. At his command, 'Let there be a world', the world came into being, and when he decreed, 'Let there be human beings', human beings were created.

But the Word of God did not remake his creatures as easily as he made them. He made them by simply giving a command; he remade them by dying. He made them by commanding; he remade them by suffering. 'You have burdened me', he told them, 'with your sinning. To direct and govern the whole fabric of the world is no effort for me, for *I have power to reach from one end of the earth to the other and to order all things as I please.* It is only human beings, with their obstinate disregard for the law I laid down for them, who have caused me distress by their sins. That is why I came down from my royal throne, why I did not shrink from enclosing myself in the Virgin's womb nor from entering into a personal union with poor lost humanity. A newborn babe in swaddling bands, I lay in a manger, since the Creator of the world could find no room in the inn.'

And so there came a deep silence. Everything was still. The voices of prophets and apostles were hushed, since the prophets had already delivered their message, while the time for the apostles' preaching had yet to come. Between these two proclamations a period of silence intervened, and in the midst of this silence the Father's almighty Word leaped down from his royal throne. There is a beautiful fitness here: in the intervening silence the Mediator between God and the human race also intervened, coming as a human being to human beings, as a mortal to mortals, to save the dead from death.

I pray that the Word of the Lord may come again today to those who are silent, and that we may hear what the Lord God says to us in our hearts. Let us silence the desires and importunings of the flesh and the vainglorious fantasies of our imagination, so that we can freely hear what the Spirit is saying. Let our ears be attuned to the voice that is heard above the vault of heaven, for the Spirit of life is always speaking to our souls; as Scripture says: *A voice is heard above the firmament which hangs over our heads.* But as long as we fix our attention on other things, we do not hear what the Spirit is saying to us.

Julian of Vézelay, *Sermon 1 on the Nativity*: SC 192, 45, 52, 60

Epiphany Year A: Matthew 2.1–12

A READING FROM A HOMILY BY ST BASIL THE GREAT

The star came to rest above the place where the child was. At the sight of it the wise men were filled with great joy, and that great joy should fill our hearts as well. It is the same as the joy the shepherds received from the glad tidings brought by the angels. Let us join the wise men in worship and the shepherds in giving glory to God. Let us dance with the angels and sing: *To us is born this day a saviour who is Christ the Lord. The Lord is God and he has appeared to us*, not as God which would have terrified us in our weakness, but as a slave in order to free those living in slavery. Could anyone be so lacking in sensibility and so ungrateful as not to join us in our gladness, exultation, and radiant joy? This feast belongs to the whole universe. It gives heavenly gifts to the earth, it sends archangels to Zechariah and to Mary, it assembles a choir of angels to sing, *Glory to God in the highest, and peace to his people on earth.*

Stars cross the sky, wise men journey from pagan lands, earth receives its saviour in a cave. Let there be no one without a gift to offer, no one without gratitude as we celebrate the salvation of the world, the birthday of the human race. Now it is no longer, *Dust you are and to dust you shall return*, but 'You are joined to heaven and into heaven you shall be taken up.' It is no longer, *In sorrow you shall bring forth children*, but, 'Blessed is she who has borne Emmanuel and blessed the breast that nursed him.' *For a child is born to us, a son is given to us, and dominion is laid upon his shoulder.*

Come, join the company of those who merrily welcome the Lord from heaven. Think of shepherds receiving wisdom, of priests prophesying, of women who are glad of heart, as Mary was when told by the angel to rejoice and as Elizabeth was when John leapt in her womb. Anna announced the good news; Simeon took the child in his arms. They worshipped the mighty God in a tiny baby, not despising what they beheld but praising his divine majesty. Like light through clear glass the power of the Godhead shone through that human body for those whose inner eye was pure. Among such may we also be numbered, so that beholding his radiance with unveiled face we too may be transformed from glory to glory by the grace and loving kindness of our Lord Jesus Christ, to whom be honour and power for endless ages. Amen.

St Basil the Great, *Homily 2 on the Holy Birth of the Lord*:
PG 31, 1472–6

Epiphany Year B: Matthew 2.1–12

A READING FROM A SERMON BY ST ODILO OF CLUNY

This is the day on which Christ was clearly revealed to the world, the day on which he consecrated the sacrament of baptism by receiving it in person, and also the day, according to the belief of the faithful, on which he changed water into wine at the wedding feast. On this day too water became wine in a spiritual sense; the letter of the law ceased to apply, and the grace of the Gospel shone out through Christ.

Christ was baptized, and the world was renewed. At his baptism the world put off the old man and put on the new. The earth cast off the first man who is earthly by nature and put on the second man who comes from heaven. When Christ was baptized the mystery of holy baptism was consecrated by the presence of the whole Trinity. The Father's voice thundered, *This is my beloved Son in whom I am well pleased.* The Holy Spirit appeared in the form of a dove. But it was the divine will that only the Son should be baptized by blessed John. Although the whole Trinity was at work in the incarnation of the Word and the mystery of his baptism, the Son alone was baptized by John, just as he alone was born of the Virgin. With the exception of sin, he experienced all the sufferings of the humanity he had assumed, yet in his divinity he remained untouched by suffering.

Today is festive enough in its own right, but it stands out all the more clearly because of its proximity to Christmas. When God is worshipped in the Child, the honour of the virgin birth is revered. When gifts are brought to the God-man, the dignity of the divine motherhood is exalted. When Mary is found with her child, Christ's true manhood is proclaimed, together with the inviolate chastity of the Mother of God. All this is contained in the Evangelist's statement: *And entering the house they found the child with Mary his mother, and bowing down they worshipped him. Then, opening their treasures, they offered him gifts, gold, frankincense, and myrrh.*

The gifts brought by the wise men reveal hidden mysteries concerning Christ. To offer gold is to proclaim his kingship, to offer incense is to adore his godhead, and to offer myrrh is to acknowledge his mortality. We too must have faith in Christ's assumption of our mortal nature. Then we shall realize that our twofold death has been abrogated by the death he died once for all. You will find a description in Isaiah of how Christ appeared as a mortal man and freed us from our debt to death. It is written: *He was led like a lamb to the slaughter.*

The necessity of faith in the kingship of Christ can be demonstrated on divine authority, since he says of himself in one of the psalms: *I have been appointed king by him,* that is, by God the Father. And speaking as Wisdom personified he claims to be the King of kings, saying, *It is through me that kings reign and princes pronounce judgement.*

As to Christ's divinity, the whole world created by him testifies that he is the Lord. He himself says in the gospel: *All power has been given to me in heaven and earth*, and the blessed Evangelist declares: *All things were made through him, and without him nothing came into being*. If we know, then, that everything was created to him and subsists in him, it follows that all creation must have been aware of his coming.

St Odilo of Cluny, *Sermon 2 on the Epiphany of the Lord*:
PL 142, 997–8

Epiphany Year C: Matthew 2.1–12

A READING FROM A HOMILY BY ST BRUNO OF SEGNI

Dearly beloved, the last verse of the gospel reading, which is still ringing in your ears, is intended for the instruction of believers. It tells how, when they had entered the house in which the blessed Virgin Mother was staying with her child, they opened their treasures, and offered the Lord three gifts – gold, frankincense, and myrrh – thereby acknowledging him as true Lord, true man, and true king.

Holy Church also offers the same gifts to her Saviour every day without ceasing. She offers him frankincense by acknowledging and believing him to be the true Lord and Creator of all. She offers him myrrh when she affirms that he assumed the substance of our flesh, in which he willed to suffer and to die for our salvation. And she offers him gold by believing without doubt that he reigns eternally with the Father and the Holy Spirit.

Alternatively, the offering of these gifts may be taken in a mystical sense. Heavenly wisdom is symbolized by gold, according to the verse of Solomon which says: *A priceless treasure lies in the mouth of the sage*; and elsewhere Scripture says: *The mouth of the just will utter wisdom*. By frankincense pure prayer is to be understood, as the psalmist says: *Let my prayer rise like incense in your sight, O Lord*. For when our prayer is pure, it yields a purer fragrance to the Lord than the smoke of burning incense, and just as such smoke rises upward, so does our prayer ascend to the Lord. Myrrh can be taken as the mortification of our flesh.

Thus, we offer the Lord gold when we shine in his sight with the light of heavenly wisdom. We offer him frankincense when we send up pure prayer before him, and myrrh when, mortifying our flesh with its vices and passions by self-control, the carry the cross behind Jesus.

St Bruno of Segni, *Sermon 1 on the Epiphany of the Lord*:
PL 165, 863–4

The Baptism of the Lord: First Sunday in Ordinary Time/Epiphany 1 Year A: Matthew 3.13–17

A READING FROM A HOMILY ATTRIBUTED TO ST GREGORY THE WONDERWORKER

I am the voice, the voice crying in the wilderness. Prepare the way for the Lord. So I cannot be silent, Lord, in your presence. *I need to be baptized by you, and do you come to me?* At my birth I took away my mother's barrenness, and while still an infant I healed my father's dumbness, for you gave me in childhood the gift of working miracles. But when you were born of the Virgin Mary, in the way you willed and in a manner known to you alone, you did not take away her virginity, but while preserving it intact you gave her in addition the name of 'mother'. Her virginity did not hinder your birth, nor did your birth destroy her virginity. On the contrary, two opposites, motherhood and virginity, were easily united by you, because the laws of nature have their origin in you. I am a mere man, sharing in the grace of God, but you are both God and man because of your love for humankind.

I need to be baptized by you, and do you come to me? You existed from the beginning, you were with God and you were God. You are the radiance of the Father's glory, the perfect image of the perfect Father. *You are the true light enlightening every person who comes into the world.* You were in the world, yet you have come to where you were already. You have become flesh, but you have not been changed into flesh. You have lived among us, appearing to your servants in the likeness of a servant. You by your holy name have bridged heaven and earth, and do you come to me? You, so great, to such as I? King to herald, master to servant?

You were not ashamed to be born within the lowly limits of our human nature, but I cannot pass its bounds. I know the distance between the earth and the Creator, between the clay and the potter. I know how far I, a lamp lit by your grace, am outshone by you, the Sun of Righteousness. You are concealed by the pure cloud of your body, but I still recognize your sovereignty. I acknowledge my servile condition; I proclaim your greatness. I admit your absolute authority, and my own lowly estate. I am unworthy to undo the strap of your sandal; how then could I dare to touch your immaculate head? How could I stretch out my hand over you, who stretched out the heavens like a tent, and set the earth upon the waters? How could I lay my hands, the hands of a servant, on your divine head? How could I enlighten the light? Surely it is not for me to pray over you, for you are the one who receives the prayers even of those who have no knowledge of you.

St Gregory the Wonderworker, *Homily 4 on the Holy Theophany*:
PG 10, 1181, 1183

The Baptism of the Lord: First Sunday in Ordinary Time/Epiphany 1 Year B: Mark 1.7–11 [4–11]

A READING FROM A HOMILY BY ST GREGORY OF ANTIOCH

This is my beloved Son in whom I am well pleased. This is he who, without leaving my side, dwelt in the womb of Mary. It is he who was neither separated from me, nor confined in her; he who, indivisible in heaven, was not defiled in the Virgin's womb.

My Son and the Son of Mary are not two sons, but one. He who lay in a cave is not one and he who was worshipped by the wise men another. He who was baptized is not one and he who was not baptized another. No, this is my Son. One and the same is he who is perceived by the mind and he who is perceived by the eyes; he who is invisible and he whom you have seen; he who is eternal and he who is subject to time; he who is one with me in my divinity, and he who is one with you in your humanity in all things except sin.

He is the mediator between myself and his servants, for in his own person he reconciles with me all who have sinned. He is my Son and the lamb, priest and victim, offerer and offering. He himself is both the sacrifice and the one who receives the sacrifice.

Such was the Father's testimony to his only Son after his baptism in the Jordan. And when in the sight of his disciples Christ was transfigured on the mountain, and his face shone with a radiance surpassing the radiance of the sun, again those words were repeated, *This is my beloved Son in whom I am well pleased. Listen to him.*

If he says, *I am in the Father and the Father is in me,* listen to him. If he says, *Whoever has seen me has seen the Father also,* listen to him as to one who speaks the truth. If he says, *The Father who sent me is greater than I,* know that these words refer to his condescension in becoming man. If he says: *This is my body which is broken for you for the forgiveness of sins,* look at the body he shows you, look at what he took from you, what became his own and was broken for you. If he says: *This is my blood*, believe it to be the blood of him who speaks to you, and of no one else.

We have been instructed in these things by God the Father; we have been taught them by God's only Son; they have been stated explicitly in the holy Scriptures; they have been proclaimed by the holy fathers. Let us keep what we have received. Why should we uselessly quarrel with one another? God has not called us to conflict but to peace. Let us persevere in that calling. Let us be filled with awe before the holy table at which we share in the heavenly mysteries. Let us not share a common table and at the same time be at enmity with one another; in communion with each other here and at odds outside, for then the Lord may say of us: *I have begotten children and reared them, feeding them with my own flesh, but they have rebelled against me.*

May he who is the saviour of the world and the author of peace grant to his Church tranquillity. May he himself watch over this holy flock, protect its pastor, and gather the sheep that stray into his fold, so that there may be one flock and one sheepfold. To him be glory and power for ever and ever. Amen.

St Gregory of Antioch, *Homily 2 on the Baptism of Christ*, 5, 6, 9, 10:
PG 88, 1876–7, 1880–4

The Baptism of the Lord: First Sunday in Ordinary Time/Epiphany 1 Year C: Luke 3.15–16, 21–22

A READING FROM A HOMILY ATTRIBUTED TO ST HIPPOLYTUS

As soon as he had been baptized, Jesus came out of the water. The heavens were opened to him and the Spirit of God in the form of a dove came down and rested on him. Then a voice from heaven said: 'This is my beloved Son in whom I am well pleased.'

If the Lord had yielded to John's persuasion and had not been baptized, do you realize what great blessings and how many we should have been deprived of? Heaven was closed until then; our homeland on high was inaccessible. Once we had descended into the depths we were incapable of rising again to such lofty heights. The Lord was not only baptized himself; he also renewed our fallen nature and restored to us our status as God's children. At once *the heavens were opened to him*. The world we see was reconciled with the world that lies beyond our vision; the angels were filled with joy; earthly disorders were remedied; mysteries were revealed; enemies were made friends.

The heavens were opened to him, you have heard the Evangelist say. This happened for three wonderful reasons. The heavenly bridal chamber had to open its shining gates to Christ at his baptism because he was the bridegroom. The gates of heaven had also to be lifted up to allow the Holy Spirit to descend in the form of a dove and the Father's voice to resound far and wide. *The heavens were opened to him and a voice said, This is my beloved Son in whom I am well pleased.*

This is my beloved Son who appeared on earth without leaving his Father's side. He both appeared and did not appear, for he was not what he seemed. As far as appearance goes the one who confers baptism is superior to the one who receives it. This is why the Father sent the Holy Spirit down on him from heaven. As in Noah's ark a dove revealed God's love for the human race, so now it was in the form of a dove, as though with an olive branch in its beak, that the Spirit descended and rested on him to whom the Father would bear witness. He did so to make sure that the Father's voice would be recognized and the ancient prophecy believed. Which prophecy? The one that says, *The Lord's voice resounded over the waters. The God of glory thunders, the Lord thunders across many waters.* And what does he say? *This is my beloved Son in whom I am well pleased.*

Pay close attention now, I beg you, for I want to return to the fountain of life and contemplate its healing waters at their source. The Father of immortality sent his immortal Son and Word into the world; he came to us to cleanse us with water and the Spirit. To give us a new birth that would make our bodies and souls immortal, he breathed into us the Spirit of life and armed us with incorruptibility.

Therefore in a herald's voice I cry: 'Peoples of every nation, come and receive the immortality given in baptism. To you who have spent all your days in the darkness of ignorance I bring the Good News of life. Leave your slavery for freedom, the tyrant's yoke for a kingdom, corruptibility for eternal life. Do you wish to know how to do this? By water and the Holy Spirit. This is to say, by the water through which we are born again and given life, and by the Spirit who is the Comforter sent for your sake to make you a child of God.'

St Hippolytus (attr.), *Sermon on the Holy Theophany*, 6–9:
PG 10, 858–9

ORDINARY TIME BEFORE LENT

I ENTREAT you therefore: Let us put our whole trust in God's promise; let our thoughts be completely taken up with longing for spiritual graces; let us consider everything else of secondary importance compared with the joys to come. To these may we all attain by the grace and loving kindness of our Lord Jesus Christ, to whom with the Father and the Holy Spirit be glory, power and honour now and for ever, and for endless ages. Amen.

St John Chrysostom

O LORD, who hast taught us that all our doings without charity are nothing worth: Send thy Holy Ghost, and pour into our hearts that most excellent gift of charity, the very bond of peace and of all virtues, without which whosoever liveth is counted dead before thee. Grant this for thine only Son Jesus Christ's sake. Amen.

Collect for Quinquagesima, *Book of Common Prayer*

ADORN your bridal chamber, O Sion, and receive Christ the King; embrace Mary, who is the gate of heaven, for she herself is carrying the King of glory who is the new light; she remains a Virgin although she bears in her hands the Son begotten before the daystar; Simeon takes him in his arms, proclaiming him to the peoples as Lord of life and death and the Saviour of the world.

Antiphon for Candlemas, *Adorna thalamum*

'Now we give you thanks because, in the incarnation of the Word, a new light has dawned upon the world, that all the nations may be brought out of darkness to see the radiance of your glory.'[4] Between the season of Christmas and Epiphany and the season of Lent which begins on Ash Wednesday there is a period of time in the liturgical year which different Churches have arranged in different ways at different times.

In the traditional liturgical books of the West this season consists of Sundays after Epiphany followed by a period called Septuagesima which was the beginning of the Easter cycle. Septuagesima means 'seventieth', just as Lent was called Quadragesima or 'fortieth' after the forty days of Lent. This season seems to have developed in the sixth century out of a desire to extend the Lenten fast backwards towards Christmas. First came Quinquagesima, 'fiftieth', which was the Sunday before Ash Wednesday, then Sexagesima, 'sixtieth', on the Sunday before that, and then finally, at the end of the century at Rome, Septuagesima on the Sunday before Sexagesima. Quinquagesima is the fiftieth day before Easter but the other names are not mathematically exact in the same way, although medieval writers added Easter week to the total and said that these ten weeks or seventy days symbolized the seventy-year captivity of the People of Israel in Babylon (Jeremiah 25.9–12; 29.10). The Byzantine Church has a similar pre-Lent period.

With the adoption of the Roman liturgy all over Western Europe from the eighth century, this arrangement of Sundays after Epiphany followed by Septuagesima came into general use and thence it came into the *Book of Common Prayer* of the Church of England in the sixteenth century. Septuagesima was similar to Lent in the Roman liturgy, alleluia was not sung or said in the liturgy, purple vestments were worn, and the *Gloria* and *Te Deum* were not sung on Sundays. In some ways it was a season of beginnings, as the traditional Bible readings at Matins began with Genesis and took the story of salvation history up to Moses before Lent. The reform of the Roman liturgy in the second half of the twentieth century, however, abolished the distinctive features of this season replacing it with the first part of Ordinary Time with its green vestments (green had previously been worn from the second Sunday after Epiphany until Septuagesima), which lasts from after the feast of the Baptism of the Lord until Shrove Tuesday. It thus includes most of the old Sundays after Epiphany and the Septuagesima season and gives greater relief to the important seasons of Christmas and Lent which are separated by a 'green' period of Ordinary Time which resumes after Pentecost.

---

4 Short preface from the Epiphany until the eve of the Presentation, *Common Worship*.

The Sunday Gospels during Ordinary Time before and after Lent and Eastertide form one series based on the three-year cycle of readings from the three synoptic Gospels. This has been followed by the *Revised Common Lectionary* although different Churches follow different customs in naming these Sundays, with the Roman Catholic Church simply having 'Sundays in Ordinary Time' (with three to eight before Lent depending on how early Easter falls) and the Church of England having Sundays of Epiphany followed, after Candlemas, by Sundays before Lent. The readings in this book are thus simply those of the Ordinary Time cycle but there are some variants where the *Revised Common Lectionary* or the *Common Worship Lectionary* change the readings that are in the *Roman Lectionary*. On the last Sunday before Lent the *Revised Common Lectionary* allows the Lutheran custom of reading the Gospel of the Transfiguration, which is read in the *Roman Lectionary* on the Second Sunday of Lent. When read before Lent it both concludes the Epiphany or 'manifestation' theme of the Sundays before Lent and acts as a turning point at the time when the liturgical year begins to emphasize Jesus' journey towards the cross, just as the story of the Transfiguration does in the Gospels themselves.

The Feast of the Presentation of Christ in the Temple, or Candlemas, has been included in *The Fathers on the Sunday Gospels* because it divides the Sundays of Epiphany from the Sundays before Lent in the calendar of the Church of England and may be celebrated on the Sunday falling between 28 January and 3 February instead of its traditional date of 2 February. Forty days after Christmas it celebrates the presentation of Jesus to God the Father in the Jerusalem Temple by his parents in accordance with the Law of Moses (Luke 2.22–40). Known in the East as the feast of 'The Meeting of the Lord with Simeon', from the eighth to the twentieth century the feast was generally known in the West as the 'Purification of the Blessed Virgin Mary' (Luke 2.22), although the texts of the Missal continued to emphasis the Presentation. French liturgies of the eighteenth century used the title 'Presentation of the Lord' which was adopted by the Roman calendar in 1969 and by many Anglican Churches. The feast has been celebrated in the East since the fourth century and in the West since the seventh century. A procession with candles is found in both East and West from an early date and the blessing of candles is first recorded in the tenth century in the Germanic lands. The beautiful antiphon *Adorna thalamum* is traditionally sung in the procession and is an early Latin translation of a Greek chant.

Second Sunday in Ordinary Time/Epiphany 2
Year A: John 1.29–34

A READING FROM THE COMMENTARY ON JOHN BY ST CYRIL OF ALEXANDRIA

When he saw Jesus coming toward him John said: 'Behold the Lamb of God, who takes away the sin of the world.' No longer does he say: 'Prepare.' That would be out of place now that at last he who was prepared for is seen, is before our very eyes. The nature of the case now calls for a different type of homily. An explanation is needed of who is present, and why he has come down to us from heaven. So John says: *Behold the Lamb of God*, of whom the prophet Isaiah told us in the words: *He was led like a sheep to the slaughter, and like a lamb before his shearer he opened not his mouth.* In past ages he was typified by the law of Moses, but because the law was merely a figure and a foreshadowing its salvation was only partial; its mercy did not reach out to embrace the whole world. But now the true lamb, the victim without blemish obscurely prefigured in former times, is led to the slaughter for all to banish sin from the world, to overthrow the world's destroyer, to abolish death by dying for the entire human race, and to release us from the curse: *Dust you are and to dust you shall return.* He will become the second Adam who is not of earth but of heaven and be for us the source of every blessing. He will deliver us from the corruptibility foreign to our nature; he will secure eternal life for us, reconcile us with God, teach us to revere God and to live upright lives, and be on our way to the kingdom of heaven.

One Lamb died for all to restore the whole flock on earth to God the Father; one died for all to make all subject to God; one died for all to gain all so that all *might live no longer for themselves, but for him who died and was raised to life for them.*

Because our many sins had made us subject to death and corruption, the Father gave his Son as our redemption, one for all, since all were in him and he was greater than all. One died for all so that all of us might live in him. Death swallowed the Lamb who was sacrificed for all, and then disgorging him disgorged all of us in him and with him; for we were all in Christ who died and rose again for us.

Once sin had been destroyed how could death, which was caused by sin, fail to be wholly annihilated? With the root dead how could the branch survive? What power will death have over us now that sin has been blotted out? And so, rejoicing in the sacrifice of the Lamb let us cry out: O *death, where is your victory? O grave, where is your sting? All wickedness shall hold its tongue,* as the Psalmist sings somewhere. Henceforth it will be unable to denounce sinners for their weakness, for God is the one who acquits us. *Christ redeemed us from the curse of the law by becoming a curse for our sake,* so we might escape the curse brought down on us by sin.

St Cyril of Alexandria, *Commentary on John,* 2: PG 73:191–4

Second Sunday in Ordinary Time/Epiphany 2 Year B (RL): John 1.35–42

A READING FROM A HOMILY BY ST BASIL OF SELEUCIA

Spurred on by the testimony of John the Baptist, the glorious apostle Andrew left his teacher and ran to the one pointed out by him. John's words were his signal, and, moving more swiftly than John could speak, he approached the master with obvious longing, his companion, John the Evangelist, running beside him. Both had left the lamp to come to the Sun.

Andrew was the first to become an apostle. It was he who opened the gates of Christ's teaching. He was the first to gather the fruits cultivated by the prophets, and he surpassed the hopes of all by being the first to embrace the one awaited by all. He was the first to show that the precepts of the law were in force only for a limited time. He was the first to restrain the tongue of Moses, for he would not allow it to speak after Christ had come. Yet he was not rebuked for this, because he did not dishonour the teacher of the Jews, but honoured more the Sender than the one sent. In fact Andrew was seen to be the first to honour Moses, because he was the first to recognize the one he foretold when he said: *The Lord God will raise up for you from amongst your kindred a prophet like myself. Listen to him.* Andrew set the law aside in obedience to the law. He listened to Moses who said: *Listen to him.* He listened to John who cried out: *Behold the Lamb of God,* and of his own accord went to the one pointed out to him.

Having recognized the Prophet foretold by the prophets, Andrew led his brother to the one he had found. Taking Peter with him, Andrew brought his brother to the Lord, thus making him his fellow-disciple. This was Andrew's first achievement: he increased the number of the apostles by bringing Peter to Christ, so that Christ might find in him the disciples' leader. When later on Peter won approval, it was thanks to the seed sown by Andrew. But the commendation given to the one redounded to the other, for the virtues of each belonged to both, and each was proud of the other's merits. Indeed, when Peter promptly answered the Master's question, how much joy he gave to all the disciples by breaking their embarrassed silence! Peter alone acted as the mouthpiece of those to whom the question was addressed. As though all spoke through him, he replied clearly on their behalf, *You are the Christ, the Son of the living God.* In one sentence he acknowledged both the Saviour and his saving plan.

Notice how these words echo Andrew's. By prompting Peter the Father endorsed from above the words Andrew used when he led Peter to Christ. Andrew had said, *We have found the Messiah.* The Father said, prompting Peter: *You are the Christ, the Son of the living God,* almost forcing these words on Peter. 'Peter,' he said, 'when you are questioned, use Andrew's words in reply. Show yourself very prompt in answering your Master. Andrew did not lie to you when he said: *We have found the Messiah.* Turn the Hebrew words into Greek and cry out: *You are the Christ, the Son of the living God!*

St Basil of Selucia, *Exhortatory Sermon*, 3–4: PG 28:1104–1106

Second Sunday of Epiphany Year B (RCL): John 1.43–51

A READING FROM THE *TRACTATES ON JOHN* BY ST AUGUSTINE

What sort of a man was Nathanael? The Lord himself bears testimony, *Behold an Israelite indeed, in whom is no guile.* Great testimony! Not of Andrew, nor of Peter, nor of Philip was that said which was said of Nathanael. Should this man then be the first among the apostles? Not only is Nathanael not found as first among the apostles, but he is neither the middle nor the last among the twelve. The reason seems to be Nathanael was learned and skilled in the law and the Lord chose unlearned persons, that by them he might confound the world. Our Lord Jesus Christ, wishing to break the necks of the proud, did not seek the orator by means of the fisherman, but by the fisherman he gained the emperor. Great was Cyprian as an orator, but before him was Peter the fisherman, by means of whom not only the orator, but also the emperor, should believe. No noble was chosen in the first place, no learned man, because *God chose the weak things of the world that he might confound the strong.* This man, then, was great and without guile, and for this reason only was not chosen, lest the Lord should seem to any to have chosen the learned.

Jesus said to him, *Before Philip called you, when you were under the fig-tree, I saw you.* Nathanael answered, *Rabbi, you are the Son of God; you are the King of Israel.* His words were not dissimilar to those of Peter when the Lord said to him, *Blessed are you, Simon Barjona, for flesh and blood has not revealed it unto you, but my Father which is in heaven.* What does this fig-tree signify? Listen, my brethren. We find the fig-tree cursed because it had leaves only, and not fruit. In the beginning of the human race, when Adam and Eve had sinned, they made themselves girdles of fig leaves. Fig leaves then signify sins. Nathanael then was under the fig-tree, as it were under the shadow of death. He whom an apostle had already called, Christ perceived to already belong to his Church. O you Church, O you Israel, in whom is no guile! If you are the people of Israel, in whom is no guile, you have even now known Christ by his apostles, as Nathanael knew Christ by Philip. But his compassion beheld you before you knew him, when you were lying under sin. For did we first seek Christ, and not he seek us?

The Lord then says to Nathaniel, *You shall see a greater thing than these, you shall see heaven open, and angels ascending and descending upon the Son of man.* Jacob saw a ladder in a dream; and on a ladder he saw angels ascending and descending, and he anointed the stone which he had placed at his head. Christ is the Anointed. For Jacob did not place the stone, the anointed stone, that he might come and adore it, otherwise that would have been idolatry. What was done was a pointing out of Christ. *Behold, I lay in Zion a stone, elect, precious, and he that believes in him shall not be confounded.*

Augustine, *Tractates on John*, 7.16, 17, 20, 21

Second Sunday in Ordinary Time/Epiphany 2
Year C: John 2.1–12

A READING FROM A SERMON BY ST MAXIMUS OF TURIN

The Son of God went to the wedding so that marriage, which had been instituted by his own authority, might be sanctified by his blessed presence. He went to a wedding of the old order when he was about to take a new bride for himself through the conversion of the Gentiles, a bride who would for ever remain a virgin. He went to the wedding not to drink wine, but to give it, for when there was none left for the wedding guests, the most blessed Mary said to him: *They have no wine.* Jesus answered as though he were displeased. *Woman,* he said, *is that my concern or yours?* It can hardly be doubted that these were words of displeasure. However, this I think was only because his mother mentioned to him so casually the lack of earthly wine, when he had come to offer the peoples of the whole world the new chalice of eternal salvation. By his reply, *My hour has not yet come,* he was foretelling the most glorious hour of his passion, and the wine of our redemption which would obtain life for all. Mary was asking for a temporal favour, but Christ was preparing joys that would be eternal. Nevertheless, the Lord in his goodness did not refuse this small grace while great graces were awaited.

Holy Mary, therefore, since she was in very truth the Mother of the Lord, and in her spirit knew in advance what would happen and foresaw the Lord's will, took care to advise the servants to do whatever he told them. Of course this holy Mother knew that the rebuke of her Son and Lord was not an insult born of anger, but that it contained a mysterious compassion. Then, to save his Mother from embarrassment because of his reproach, the Lord revealed his sovereign power. Addressing the expectant servants he said: *Fill the jars with water.* The servants promptly obeyed, and suddenly in a marvellous way the water began to acquire potency, take on colour, emit fragrance, and gain flavour – all at once it changed its nature completely!

Now this transformation of the water from its own substance into another testified to the powerful presence of the Creator. Only he who had made it out of nothing could change water into something whose use was quite different. Scripture says that *this sign at Cana in Galilee was the first that Jesus performed. He manifested his glory, and his disciples believed in him.* It was not what they saw happening that the disciples believed, but what could not be seen by bodily eyes. They did not believe that Jesus Christ was the son of the Virgin – that was something they knew. Rather they believed that he was the only Son of the Most High, as this miracle proved. Let us too believe not only that he shared our nature, but also that he was consubstantial with the Father; for as a man he was present at the wedding, and as God he changed the water into wine. If such is our faith, the Lord will give us also to drink of the sobering wine of his grace.

St Maximus of Turin, *Homily* 23: PL 57, 274–276

Third Sunday in Ordinary Time/Epiphany 3
Year A: Matthew 4.12–23 or 4.12–17

A READING FROM *THE HOMILIES ON THE GOSPELS*
BY ST GREGORY THE GREAT

You have heard how, at a single command, Peter and Andrew left their nets and followed our Redeemer. They had not yet seen him work one miracle, or heard any mention of an eternal reward, and yet one word from the Lord was enough to make them forget all their possessions.

How many miracles we see, how many punishments we suffer, how many ominous threats fill us with fear, and yet we refuse to follow the one who calls us! He who urges us to amend our lives is now enthroned in heaven. He has already bent the necks of the nations beneath the yoke of faith; he has already cast down the glory of this world. Growing reports of disaster and ruin warn us that his day of strict reckoning is at hand. And yet in our arrogance we refuse freely to abandon things we daily lose whether we will or no. What are we going to say on the day of judgement, we who are not turned from love of this world by commands or corrected by punishments?

But then perhaps someone is saying to himself: 'How much did these two fishermen give up at the Lord's bidding? They had practically nothing!' That may be so, but in this matter what counts is motive rather than wealth. Those who keep nothing back for themselves give up much; those who abandon all they have, even if it is very little, give up a great deal. We, on the other hand, are possessive about the things we have and covetously try to obtain those we do not have. Peter and Andrew gave up a great deal because they gave up even the desire to possess anything.

Therefore let none of us who see other people giving up great possessions say to ourselves, 'I should like to imitate people like these who have such contempt for the world, but I have nothing to give up.' You give up much if you give up the desire to possess. The Lord looks at your heart, not your fortune; he considers the love that prompts your offering, not its amount. If we're going to weigh material goods, our holy traders gave their nets and boats to purchase the eternal life of the angels. The real value of that is beyond price, but for you its price is just what you possess. For Zacchaeus it was worth half his fortune, since he kept the other half to restore fourfold whatever he had unjustly extorted. For Peter and Andrew it was worth the value of their nets and boat; for the widow it cost two small coins; another may buy it with a cup of cold water. As I said, the kingdom of God costs whatever you have.

St Gregory the Great, *Forty Gospel Homilies*, 1.5: PL 76, 1093–4

Third Sunday in Ordinary Time/Epiphany 3
Year B: Mark 1.14–20

A READING FROM A SERMON BY ST CAESARIUS OF ARLES

In today's gospel, beloved, we heard the exhortation to repent, for the kingdom of heaven is at hand. Now the kingdom of heaven is Christ, who, as we know, is the judge of good and evil and scrutinizes the motives for all our actions. We should therefore do well to forestall God's judgement by freely acknowledging our sins and correcting our wrong-headed attitudes; for by failing to seek out the needful remedies and apply them, we place ourselves in danger. And our knowledge that we shall have to account for the motives behind our shortcomings makes the need for such a change of heart even greater.

We must recognize the greatness of God's love for us; so generous is it that he is willing to be appeased by the amends we make for our evil deeds, provided only that we freely admit them before he has himself condemned them. And though his judgements are always just, he gives us a warning before he passes them, so as not to be compelled to apply the full rigour of this justice. It is not for nothing that our God draws floods of tears from us; he does so to incite us to recover by penance and a change of heart what we had previously let slip through carelessness. God is well aware that human judgement is often at fault, that we are prone to fleshly sins and deceitful speech. He therefore shows us the way of repentance, with which we can compensate for damage done and atone for our faults. And so to be sure of obtaining forgiveness, we ought to be always bewailing our guilt. Yet no matter how many wounds our human nature has sustained, we're never justified in giving ourselves over to despair, for the Lord is magnanimous enough to pour out his compassion abundantly on all who need it.

But perhaps one of you will say: 'What have I to fear? I have never done anything wrong.' On this point hear what the apostle Johns says: *If we claim to be sinless, we deceive ourselves and are blind to the truth.* So let no one lead you astray; the most pernicious kind of sin is the failure to realize one's own sinfulness. Once let wrongdoers admit their guilt and repent of it, and this change of heart will bring about their reconciliation with the Lord; but no sinner is more in need of the tears of others than the one who thinks he has nothing to weep for. So I implore you, beloved, to follow the advice given you by holy Scripture and *humble yourselves beneath the all powerful hand of God.*

As none of us can be wholly free from sin, so let none of us fail to make amends; here too we do ourselves great harm if we presume our own innocence. It may be that some are less guilty than others, but no one is entirely free from fault; there may be degrees of guilt, but no one can escape it altogether. Let those then whose offences are more grievous be more earnest in seeking pardon; and let those who have so far escaped contamination by the more heinous crimes pray that they may never be defiled by them, through the grace of our Lord Jesus Christ, who with the Father and the Holy Spirit lives and reigns for ever and ever. Amen.

St Caesarius of Arles, *Sermon* 144, 1–4: CCSL 104, 593–5

Third Sunday of Epiphany Year B (CWL): John 2.1–11

SEE THE READING FOR SUNDAY 2C BY ST MAXIMUS OF TURIN, PAGE 55

Third Sunday in Ordinary Time/Epiphany 3 Year C: Luke 1.1–4; 4.14–21

A READING FROM A HOMILY ON LUKE BY ORIGEN

When you read about Jesus teaching in the synagogues of Galilee and everyone there praising him, take care not to regard those people as uniquely privileged, and yourselves as deprived of his teaching. If Scripture is true, it was not only to the Jewish congregations of his own generation that our Lord spoke. He still speaks to us assembled here today – and not only to us, but to other congregations also. Throughout the world Jesus looks for instruments through which he can continue his teaching. Pray that I may be one of them, and that he may find me ready and fit to sing his praises.

Then Jesus came to Nazareth, where he had been brought up, and went into the synagogue on the Sabbath day as was his custom. When he stood up to read they handed him the scroll of the prophet Isaiah. Unrolling the scroll he found the place where it is written, 'The Spirit of the Lord has been given to me, for he has anointed me.'

It was no coincidence, but in accordance with the plan of divine providence, that Jesus unrolled the scroll and found in it this chapter prophesying about himself. Since it is written, *Not a single sparrow will*

58

fall to the ground without your Father's permission, and the apostles were told that every hair on their heads have been counted, we can be sure that it was not by chance that the scroll of the prophet Isaiah was produced rather than some other and this precise passage found which speaks of the mystery of Christ, *The Spirit of the Lord has been given to me, for he has anointed me.*

When Jesus had read this prophecy, *he rolled up the scroll, handed it back to the assistant and sat down. Every eye in the synagogue was fixed upon him.*

Here too in this synagogue, that is in this present assembly, you can at this very moment fix your eyes upon your Saviour if you wish. Whenever you direct your inward gaze toward wisdom and truth and the contemplation of God's only Son, then your eyes are fixed upon Jesus. Blessed was that congregation of which the gospel says, *All eyes in the synagogue were fixed upon him!* How I long for our own assembly to deserve the same testimony; for all of you, catechumens as well as the faithful, women, men, and children, to have your eyes, not those of the body but of the soul, turned toward Jesus! When you look at Jesus your own faces will become radiant with his reflected glory, and you will be able to say, *The light of your face has shed its brightness upon us, O Lord!* To you be glory and power for ever and ever! Amen.

Origen, *Homilies on Luke*, 32, 2–6: SC 87, 386–92

Fourth Sunday in Ordinary Time/Epiphany 4 Year A: Matthew 5.1–12

A READING FROM A HOMILY BY ST CHROMATIUS OF AQUILEIA

While our Lord and Saviour was going the rounds of the various cities and regions preaching and healing every disease and infirmity among the people, *he saw the crowds coming to him and went up on the mountain*, as today's reading tells us. There is a fittingness in this: the Most High God goes up to a high place in order to preach a lofty message to those who desire to reach the heights of virtue.

It is appropriate that the new law should be promulgated on a mountain, because it was on a mountain that the law had been given to Moses. The old law comprised ten commandments that were intended to guide its adherents on the path of instruction and discipline in this present life; the new law consists of eight beatitudes, because it lead its followers to eternal life and the heavenly fatherland.

Blessed are the meek, for they shall possess the land. The meek must be calm of soul and sincere of heart; the Lord clearly shows that their merit is by no means negligible, for he says they shall possess the land. The 'land' here is the land of which it is written: *I believe I shall see the Lord's goodness in the land of the living.* The heritage proper to that land is immortality of body and the glory of eternal resurrection. Now meekness is a stranger to pride, boasting and ambition. Quite rightly, then, does the Lord exhort his disciples in another passage: *Learn of me, for I am meek and humble of heart, and you will find rest for your souls.*

Blessed are those who mourn, for they shall be comforted. The reference here is not to those who mourn for the loss of their dear ones, but to those who weep for their own sins and wash them away with their tears, or to those who grieve before the wickedness of this world or lament the sins of others.

Blessed are the peacemakers; they shall be called the children of God. If you can see how great the merit of peacemakers is, when they are no longer called servants but children of God. This reward is fully justified, since the lover of peace loves Christ, the author of peace, to whom Paul the Apostle even gives 'peace' as a name: *He is our peace,* he says. Someone who does not love peace goes in pursuit of discord, for he loves its author, the devil. In the beginning the devil caused discord between God and the human race by leading the first man to violate God's precept. The reason why the Son of God came down from heaven was to condemn the devil, the author of discord, and to make peace between God and the human race by reconciling its members to God and making God propitious to them.

We must therefore become peacemakers so that we may deserve to be called children of God. Without peace, we lose the name not only of children but even of servants, since the apostle says to us: *Love peace, for without it none of us can be pleasing to God.*

St Chromatius of Aquileia, *Sermon* 39: SC 164, 216–20

Fourth Sunday of Epiphany Year A (CWL): John 2.1–11

SEE THE READING FOR SUNDAY 2C FROM ST
MAXIMUS OF TURIN, PAGE 55

Fourth Sunday in Ordinary Time/Epiphany 4 Year B: Mark 1.21–28

A READING FROM A HOMILY ON THE LETTER TO
THE HEBREWS BY ST JOHN CHRYSOSTOM

Think of Jesus Christ, the apostle and high priest of our religion. He was faithful to God who appointed him, just as Moses was faithful in all God's house. What does his being faithful to God who appointed him mean? It means that he governed with care all that belonged to him, not lightly allowing his property to be pillaged, *just as Moses was faithful in all God's house.* If then you recognize who your high priest is, and how great he is, you will need no other consolation or encouragement.

The text calls Jesus Christ an apostle because he was sent, and also *high priest of our religion*, or in other words, of our faith. It does well to compare Christ with Moses, for like Moses Christ was entrusted with the government of a people, although his was a greater authority, exercised on a higher plane. Moses governed as a servant; Christ governed as a Son. Moses took charge of another's domain; Christ took charge of his own.

Moses had *to testify to the things that would be spoken later.* What do I mean? That God accepts human testimony? Yes, indeed he does. He calls upon heaven and earth and the hills to be his witnesses when he says through the prophet: *Listen, heaven, and hearken, earth, for the Lord has spoken*; and: *Listen, ravines, you foundations of the earth for the Lord is accusing his people.* Much more therefore does he call on human beings to testify to him. They are bound to witness to him when others behave shamelessly.

Christ, however, was faithful as a Son. Moses took charge of another's domain; Christ takes charge of his own.

St John Chrysostom, *Homily 5 on Hebrews*: Bareille, 20, 158

Fourth Sunday in Ordinary Time/Epiphany 4
Year C: Luke 4.21–30

A READING FROM THE COMMENTARY ON ISAIAH BY ST CYRIL OF ALEXANDRIA

Desiring to win over the whole world and bring its inhabitants to God the Father, raising all things to a higher condition and, in a sense, renewing the face of the earth, the Lord of the universe took the form of a servant and brought the Good News to the poor. This, he said, was why he had been sent.

Now by the poor we may understand those who were then deprived of all spiritual blessings and who lived in the world without hope and without God, as Scripture says. They are those among the Gentiles who, enriched by faith in Christ, have gained the divine, the heavenly treasure, which is the saving proclamation of the gospel. Through this they have become sharers in the kingdom of heaven and companions of the saints. They have inherited blessings impossible to express or comprehend, for *eye has not seen*, says Scripture, *nor ear heard, nor human heart conceived what God has prepared for those who love him.*

To the broken-hearted Christ promises healing and release, and to the blind he gives sight. For those who worship created things, and say to a piece of wood, *You are my father*, and to a stone, *You gave me birth*, thus failing to recognize him who is really and truly God, are they not blind? Are not their hearts devoid of the spiritual and divine light? To these the Father sends the light of true knowledge of God. Having been called by faith, they know God, or rather, they are known by him. They were children of night and of darkness, but they have become children of light. The Day has shone upon them, the Sun of Righteousness has risen, the Morning Star has appeared in all its brilliance.

All that has been said, however, could also be applied to the Israelites, for they too were poor, broken-hearted, captives in a certain sense, and in darkness. But Christ came, and it was to the Israelites first that he made known the purpose of this coming; he came to proclaim the acceptable year of the Lord, and the day of retribution. That was the acceptable year, when Christ was crucified for us, when we became acceptable to God the Father. Through Christ we bear fruit, as he himself told us when he said: *I tell you truly that unless a grain of wheat falls into the ground and dies, it remains as it is, a single grain; but if it dies, it bears a rich harvest*; and again: *When I am lifted up from the earth, I will draw the whole world to myself.* Moreover, on the third day he came to life again, after trampling death's power underfoot. He then addressed these words to his disciples: *All power has been given to me in heaven and on earth. Go and make disciples of all nations, baptizing them in the name of Father, and of the Son, and of the Holy Spirit.*

St Cyril of Alexandria, *On Isaiah*, 5.5: PG 70, 1352–3

Fourth Sunday of Epiphany Year C (CWL), Luke 2.22–40

SEE THE READINGS FOR THE PRESENTATION OF
CHRIST YEARS A–C, BELOW

The Presentation of Christ in the Temple Year A: Luke 2.22–40

(Candlemas, the Feast of the Presentation of Christ in the Temple, is celebrated on 2 February; in the Church of England it may be celebrated on the Sunday between 28 January and 3 February)

A READING FROM A SERMON BY ST CYRIL OF
ALEXANDRIA

Christ was carried into the temple, being still a little child at the breast: and the blessed Symeon who was endowed with the grace of prophecy took him in his arms and, filled with the highest joy, blessed God and said: *Lord, now lettest thou thy servant depart in peace.* For the mystery of Christ had been prepared even before the very foundation of the world, but it was manifested in the last ages of time and became a light for those who in darkness and error had fallen under the devil's hand.

Christ therefore became the Gentiles' light for revelation, but also for the glory of Israel. For even granting that some of them proved insolent and disobedient, yet is there a remnant saved and admitted into glory through Christ. And the first fruits of these were the divine disciples, the brightness of whose renown lightens the whole world. In another sense Christ is the glory of Israel, for he came of them according to the flesh, although he is *God over all, and blessed for ever, Amen.*

What does the prophet Symeon say of Christ? *Behold this child is set for the fall and rising again of many in Israel, and for a sign that shall be spoken against.* For the Emmanuel is set by God the Father as the foundations of Sion, *being a chosen stone, the cornerstone*. Those then who trusted in him were not ashamed: but those who were unbelieving and ignorant, and unable to perceive the mystery regarding him, fell and were broken in pieces. For God the Father again has said, *Behold I lay in Sion a stone of stumbling and a rock of offence, and he that believes in it shall not be ashamed; but on whomsoever it shall fall, it will winnow him*.

And by the sign that is spoken against, he means the precious Cross, for as the most wise Paul writes, *to the Jews it is a stumbling-block and it is foolishness to the heathen*; and again, *To those who are perishing it is foolishness: but to us who are being saved, it is the power of God unto salvation*. The sign therefore is spoken against if to those that perish it seems to be folly; while to those who acknowledge its power it is salvation and life.

And Symeon furthermore said to the holy Virgin, *And a sword shall pierce your own soul also*, meaning by the sword the pain which she suffered for Christ, when she saw whom she brought forth crucified when she had no idea that he would be more mighty than death and rise again from the grave. Nor may you wonder that the Virgin did not know this, when we shall find even the holy Apostles themselves had little faith. For truly the blessed Thomas, had he not thrust his hands into Christ's side after the resurrection and felt also the prints of the nails, would not have believed the other disciples who had told him that Christ was risen and had shown himself to them.

Cyril of Alexandria, Sermon 4 on Luke, 28–9

The Presentation of Christ in the Temple Year B: Luke 2.22–40

A READING FROM A SERMON BY ST AUGUSTINE

Concerning that time it was written, *And of Sion it shall be reported that he was born in her, and the Most High shall establish her*. O how blessed is the omnipotence of him who was born! Yea, how blessed is the glory of him who came down from heaven to earth! While he was yet in his Mother's womb, he was saluted by St John the Baptist. And when he was presented in the temple, he was recognized by the old man Simeon, a worthy man who was full of years, tested and crowned. This ancient one, as soon as he knew him, worshipped and said, *Lord, now lettest thou thy servant depart in peace, for mine eyes have seen thy salvation*.

He had lingered long in the world to see the birth of him who made the world. The old man knew the child, and in that child became a child himself, for in the love with which he regarded the Father of all, he felt his own years to be as but yesterday. The ancient Simeon bore in his arms the new-born Christ, and all the while Christ ruled and upheld the old man. Simeon had been told by the Lord that he should not taste of death before he had seen the birth of the Christ of the Lord. Now that Christ was born, all the old man's wishes on earth were fulfilled. He that came into a decrepit world now also came to an old man.

Simeon did not wish to remain long in the world, but with great desire he had desired to see Christ in the world, for he had sung with the Prophet, *O Lord, show thy mercy upon us, and grant us thy salvation.* And now at last, that you might know how, to his joy, his prayer was granted, he said, *Now lettest thou thy servant depart in peace, for mine eyes have seen thy salvation.* The Prophets have sung that the Maker of heaven and earth would converse on earth with men. An Angel has declared that the Creator of flesh and spirit would come in the flesh. The unborn John, while still in the womb, has saluted the unborn Saviour who was still in the womb. The old man Simeon has seen God as little child.

St Augustine, *Sermon 13 de Tempore*, from the old Roman Breviary

The Presentation of Christ in the Temple Year C: Luke 2.22–40

A READING FROM A SERMON BY ST AMBROSE

Behold, there was a man in Jerusalem whose name was Simeon, and this man was just and devout, waiting for the consolation of Israel. The birth of the Lord is attested not only by angels, prophets and shepherds but also by elders and just men. Every age and both sexes, as well as the wonders of the events themselves, are present here to strengthen our faith. A virgin conceives, a barren woman bears, a dumb man speaks, Elisabeth prophesies, the wise man worships, the unborn child leaps, the widow praises, and the just man waits.

Rightly is he called just, who looked not for favour for himself but for consolation for his people. He desired to be set free from the bondage of this frail body, but he waited to see the Promised One; for he knew that blessed are the eyes that see him. Then took he him up in his arms, and blessed God, and said, *Lord, now lettest thou thy servant depart in peace, according to thy word*. Behold a just man, confined in the weary prison of his body, desiring to depart and to begin to be with Christ! *For it is far better to depart and to be with Christ.*

Whoever desires to depart and be with Christ, let him come into the temple. Yes, let him come to Jerusalem and wait for the Christ of the Lord. Let him take hold of the Word of God, let him embrace the Word of God with good works, as it were, with arms of faith. Then let him depart in peace, for he who has seen Life shall not see death. Behold how the Lord's birth overflows with abounding grace for all, and how prophecy was not denied except to the unbelieving. Behold, Simeon prophesied that the Lord Jesus Christ has come for the fall and rising again of many. Yea, he shall separate the just from the unjust by their rewards, and according as our work shall be, so shall the true and righteous Judge command us to be punished or rewarded in the life to come.

St Ambrose, *Sermons on Luke*

Fifth Sunday in Ordinary Time/Epiphany 5
Year A: Matthew 5.13–16 [13–20]

A READING FROM A BAPTISMAL HOMILY BY ST JOHN CHRYSOSTOM

We who have once for all clothed ourselves in Christ, and been made worthy to have him dwelling within us, may show everyone, if we choose, simply by the strict discipline of our life and without saying a word, the power of him who dwells in us. Therefore Christ said, *Let your light so shine before all, that people may see your good works and praise your Father in heaven.* This is a light that reaches not only the bodily senses, but illuminates also the beholder's mind and soul. It disperses the darkness of evil, and invites those who encounter it to let their own light shine forth, and to follow the example of virtue.

Let your light shine before all, Christ said; and he used the words *before all* advisedly. He meant, 'Let your light be so bright that it illuminates not only yourself, but shines also before those needing its help.' As the light our senses perceive puts darkness to flight, and enables those travelling along a road perceptible to the senses to follow a straight course, so also the spiritual light which shines from blameless conduct illuminates those who cannot see clearly how to live a virtuous life, because their spiritual eyesight has been blurred by the darkness of error. It purifies their inward vision, leads them to live upright lives, and makes them walk henceforward in the path of virtue.

That people may see your good works and praise your Father in heaven. Christ means: let your virtue, the perfection of your life, and the performance of good works inspire those who see you to praise the common Master of us all. And so I beg each of you to strive to live so perfectly that the Lord may be praised by all who see you. By the perfection of your lives attract to yourselves the grace of the Spirit, so that the Church of God may exult and be full of joy at your progress, so that the Lord of all creation may be glorified, and so that we may all be found worthy of the kingdom of heaven by the grace, mercy, and goodness of God's only-begotten Son our Lord Jesus Christ, to whom with the Father and the Holy Spirit be glory, might, and honour now and for ever and for endless ages. Amen.

St John Chrysostom, *Baptismal Catecheses*, 4.18–21, 26, 33:
SC 50, 192–3, 196, 199

Fifth Sunday in Ordinary Time/Epiphany 5 Year B: Mark 1.29–39

A READING FROM A SERMON BY ST PETER CHRYSOLOGUS

Those who have listened attentively to today's gospel will have learnt why the Lord of heaven, by whom all creation was renewed, entered the houses of his servants on earth. Nor should it surprise us that he so courteously adapted himself to every situation, since his motive in coming among us was to bring mercy and help to all.

You can easily see what drew Christ to Peter's house on this particular occasion; it was no desire to sit down and rest himself, but compassion for a woman stricken down by sickness. He was prompted not by the need to eat but by the opportunity to heal, his immediate preoccupation being the performance of a work which only his divine power could carry out, rather than the enjoyment of human company at table. In Peter's house that day it was not wine that flowed, but tears. Consequently Christ did not enter to obtain sustenance for himself, but to restore vitality to another. God wants human beings, not human goods. He desires to bestow what is heavenly, not to acquire anything earthly. Christ came to seek not our possessions but us.

As soon as Jesus crossed the threshold he saw Peter's mother-in-law lying ill in bed with a fever. On entering the house he immediately saw what he had come for. He was not interested in the comfort the house itself could offer, nor the crowds awaiting his arrival, nor the formal welcome prepared for him, nor the assembled household. Still less did he look for any outward signs of preparation for his reception. All he had eyes for was the spectacle of a sick woman, lying there consumed with a raging fever. At a glance he saw her desperate plight, and at once stretched out his hands to perform their divine work of healing; nor would he sit down to satisfy his human needs before he had made it possible for the stricken woman to rise up and serve her God. *So he took her by the hand, and the fever left her.* Here you see how fever loosens its grip on a person whose hand is held by Christ's; no sickness can stand its ground in the face of the very source of health. Where the Lord of life has entered, there is no room for death.

St Peter Chrysologus, *Sermon* 18: PL 52, 246–9

Fifth Sunday in Ordinary Time/Epiphany 5 Year C: Luke 5.1–11

A READING FROM A SERMON BY ST AUGUSTINE

While he was on the mountain with Christ the Lord in company with the two other disciples James and John, the blessed apostle Peter heard a voice from heaven saying, *This is my beloved Son, in whom I am well pleased. Listen to him.* The apostle remembered this and made it known in his letter. *We heard a voice coming from heaven,* he said, *when we were with him on the holy mountain*; and he added: *so we have confirmation of what was prophesied.* A voice came from heaven, and prophecy was confirmed.

How great was Christ's courtesy! This Peter who spoke these words was once a fisherman, and in our day a public speaker deserves high praise if he is able to converse with a fisherman! Addressing the first Christians the apostle Paul says: *Brothers and sisters, remember what you were when you were called. Not many of you were wise according to human standards; not many of you were influential or of noble birth. But God chose what the world regards as weak in order to disconcert the strong; God chose what the world regards as foolish in order to abash the wise; God chose what the world regards as common and contemptible, of no account whatever, in order to overthrow the existing order.*

If Christ had first chosen a man skilled in public speaking, such a man might well have said: 'I have been chosen on account of my eloquence.' If he had chosen a senator, the senator might have said: 'I have been chosen because of my rank.' If his first choice had been an emperor, the emperor surely might have said: 'I have been chosen for the sake of the power I have at my disposal.' Let these worthies keep quiet and defer to others; let them hold their peace for a while. Saying they should be passed over or despised; I am simply asking all those who can find any grounds for pride in what they are to give way to others just a little.

Christ says, 'Give me this fisherman, this man without education or experience, this man to whom no senator would deign to speak, not even if he were buying fish. Yes, give me him; once I have taken possession of him, it will be obvious that it is I who am at work in him. Although I mean to include senators, orators, and emperors among my recruits, even when I have won over the senator I shall still be surer of the fisherman. The senator can always take pride in what he is; so can the orator and the emperor, but the fishermen can glory in nothing except Christ alone. Any of these other men may come and take lessons from me in the importance of humility for salvation, but let the fisherman come first. He is the best person to win over an emperor.'

Remember this fisherman, then, this holy, just, good, Christ-filled fisherman. In his nets cast throughout the world he has the task of catching this nation as well as all the others. So remember that claim of his: *We have confirmation of what was prophesied.*

St Augustine, *Sermon* 43.5–6: PL 38, 256–7

Sixth Sunday in Ordinary Time/Epiphany 6
Year A: Matthew 5.17–37 [21–37]
A READING FROM A HOMILY ON THE TREACHERY OF JUDAS BY ST JOHN CHRYSOSTOM

Christ gave his life for you, and do you hold a grudge against your fellow servant? How then can you approach the table of peace? Your Master did not refuse to undergo every kind of suffering for you, and will you not even forgo your anger? Why is this, when love is the root, the wellspring and the mother of every blessing?

He has offered me an outrageous insult, you say. He has wronged me times without number, he has endangered my life. Well, what is that? He has not yet crucified you as the Jewish elders crucified the Lord. If you refuse to forgive your neighbour's offence your heavenly Father will not forgive your sins either. What does your conscience say when you repeat the words: *Our Father who art in heaven, hallowed be thy name*, and the rest? Christ went so far as to offer his blood for the salvation of those who shed it. What could you do that would equal that? If you refuse to forgive your enemy you harm not him but yourself. You have indeed harmed him frequently in this present life, but you have earned for yourself eternal punishment on the Day of Judgement. There is no one God detests and repudiates more than the person who bears a grudge, whose heart is filled with anger, whose soul is seething with rage.

Listen to the Lord's words: *If you are bringing your gift to the altar, and there remember that your brother or sister has something against you, leave your gift there before the altar and first go and be reconciled with your brother or sister. Then come and offer your gift.* What do you mean? Am I really to leave my gift, my offering there? Yes, he says, because this sacrifice is offered in order that you may live in peace with your brother or sister. So if the attainment of peace with your neighbour is the object of the sacrifice and you fail to make peace, even if you share in the sacrifice your lack of peace will make this sharing fruitless. Before all else therefore make peace, for the sake of which the sacrifice is offered. Then you will really benefit from it.

The reason the Son of God came into the world was to reconcile the human race with the Father. As Paul says: *Now he has reconciled all things to himself, destroying enmity in himself by the cross.* Consequently, as well as coming himself to make peace he also calls us blessed if we do the same, and shares his title with us. *Blessed are the peacemakers*, he says, *for they shall be called children of God.*

So as far as a human being can, you must do what Christ the Son of God did, and become a promoter of peace both for yourself and for your neighbour. Christ calls the peacemaker a child of God. The only good deed he mentions as essential at the time of sacrifice is reconciliation with one's brother or sister. This shows that of all the virtues the most important is love.

St John Chrysostom, *Homily* 2: Bareille, 3, 655–6

Sixth Sunday in Ordinary Time/Epiphany 6
Year B: Mark 1.40–45

A READING FROM THE COMMENTARY ON MATTHEW BY ST PASCHASIUS RADBERTUS

However great our sinfulness, each one of us can be healed by God every day. We have only to worship him with humility and love, and wherever we are to say with faith, *Lord, if you want to you can make me clean. It is by believing from the heart that we are justified*, so we must make our petitions with the utmost confidence, and without the slightest doubt of God's power. If we pray with a faith springing from love, God's will need be in no doubt. He will be ready and able to save us by an all-powerful command. He immediately answered the leper's request, saying: *I do want to*. Indeed, no sooner had the leper begun to pray with faith than the Saviour's hand began to cure him from his leprosy.

This leper is an excellent teacher of the right way to make petitions. He did not doubt the Lord's willingness through disbelief in his compassion, but neither did he take it for granted, for he knew the depths of his own sinfulness. Yet because he acknowledged that the Lord was able to cleanse him if he wished, we praise this declaration of firm faith just as we praise the Lord's mighty power. For obtaining a favour from God rightly depends as much on having a real living faith as on the exercise of the Creator's power and mercy. If faith is weak it must be strengthened, for only then will it succeed in obtaining health of body or soul. The Apostle's words, *purifying their hearts by faith*, referred, surely, to strong faith like this. And so, if the hearts of believers are purified by faith, we must give thought to this virtue of faith, for, as the Apostle says, *Anyone who doubts is like a wave in the sea*.

A faith shown to be living by its love, steadfast by its perseverance, patient by its endurance of delay, humble by its confession, strong by its confidence, reverent by its way of presenting petitions, and discerning with regard to the content – such a faith may be certain that in every place it will hear the Lord saying: *I do want to*.

Pondering this wonderful reply, let us put the words together in their proper sequence. The leper began: *Lord, if you want to*, and the Lord spoke his powerful word of command, *Be clean*. All that the sinner's true confession maintained with faith, love and power immediately conferred. And in case the gravity of his sins should make anyone despair, another Evangelist says this man who was cured had been completely covered with leprosy. For *all have sinned and forfeited the glory of God*. Since, as we rightly believe, God's power is operative everywhere, we ought to believe the same of his will. For *his will is that all should be saved and come to the knowledge of the truth.*

St Paschasius Radbertus, *On Matthew*, 5.8: PL 120, 341–2

Sixth Sunday in Ordinary Time/Epiphany 6 Year C: Luke 6.17, 20–26 [17–26]

A READING FROM A HOMILY ON THE SECOND LETTER TO THE CORINTHIANS BY ST JOHN CHRYSOSTOM

Only Christians have a true sense of values; their joys and sorrows are not the same as other people's. The sight of the wounded boxer wearing a victor's crown would make someone ignorant of the games think only of the boxer's wounds and how painful they must be. Such a person would know nothing of the happiness the crown gives. And it is the same when people see the things we suffer without knowing why we do so. It naturally seems to them to be suffering pure and simple. They see us struggling and facing danger, but beyond their vision are the rewards, the crowns of victory – all we hope to gain through the contest!

When Paul said, *We possess nothing, and yet we have everything,* what did he mean by 'everything'? Wealth of both the earthly and the spiritual order. Did he not possess every earthly gift when whole cities received him as an angel, when people were ready to pluck out their eyes for him, or bare their necks to the sword? But if you would think of spiritual blessings, you will see that it was in these above all that he was rich. The King of the universe and Lord of angels loved him so much that he shared his secrets with him. Did he not surpass all others in wealth then? Did he not possess all things? Had it been otherwise, demons would not have been subject to him, nor sickness and suffering put to flight by his presence.

We too, then, when we suffer anything for Christ's sake, should do so not only with courage, but even with joy. If we have to go hungry, let us be glad as if we were at a banquet. If we are insulted, let us be elated as though we had been showered with praises. If we lose all we possess, let us consider ourselves the gainers. If we provide for the poor, let us regard ourselves as the recipients. Anyone who does not give in this way will find it difficult to give at all. So when you wish to distribute alms, do not think only of what you are giving away; think rather of what you are gaining, for your gain will exceed your loss.

And that not only in the matter of almsgiving, but also with every virtue you practise: do not think of the painful effort involved, but of the sweetness of the reward; and above all remember that your struggles are for the sake of our Lord Jesus. Then you will easily rise above them, and live out your whole lifetime in happiness; for nothing brings more happiness than a good conscience.

St John Chrysostom, *Homily* 12.4: Bareille, 17, 480–1

Seventh Sunday in Ordinary Time/Epiphany 7 Year A: Matthew 5.38–48

A READING FROM THE TREATISE *ON JEALOUSY AND ENVY* BY ST CYPRIAN

To assume the name of Christ without following the way of Christ – what else is that but to make a sham of the divinely given name and to abandon the path of salvation? When Christ himself teaches that the person who keeps his commandments will have life and that wisdom belongs to the one who not only listens to his words but acts on them, that the distinction of being called the greatest teacher in the kingdom of heaven is awarded to the one who not only teaches but acts in accordance with his teaching, then he means that if anything good and useful has been preached it will benefit the preacher only insofar as he lives by what he preaches.

Now is there anything the Lord more frequently urged on his disciples, any salutary counsel or heavenly precept he wanted them to cherish and observe more assiduously than his commandment that we should love one another with the same love as he himself showed for his disciples? Yet how can anyone preserve the peace and love of the Lord if jealousy has rendered him incapable of being either peaceable or loving toward his neighbour?

This is why, after his eulogy of peace and charity and his uncompromising assertion that neither faith nor alms nor even the suffering of the confessor or martyr would be of any value unless he had observed the claims of love in their entirety and without exception, the apostle Paul went on to say: *Love is generous, love is kind, love is not jealous.* The point he wished to make was that only the person who is generous, kind, and free from jealousy and envy can continue to be loving. Elsewhere, when he is teaching that once one has been filled with the Holy Spirit and has through a heavenly birth become a child of God, one must pursue only spiritual and divine in ends, the Apostle declares: *I was unable to address you, brothers and sisters, as spiritual people; I had to talk to you as to worldly men and women who were still infants in the Christian life. When there is jealousy, contention, and strife among you, is it not clear that you are unspiritual people living by worldly standards?*

We cannot bear the heavenly image within us unless we show a likeness to Christ in the life upon which we have now entered. This means changing from what we used to be and becoming something altogether new, so that our divine birth may be seen in us, so that we may imitate the Father by our holy way of life, and so that our lives may give honour and praise to God and he may be glorified in us. This is what he himself has taught and urged us to do, promising that those who glorify him will be rewarded. *I will glorify those who glorify me*, he says, and those who despise me shall be despised. To instruct us and prepare us for this glorification and produce in us a likeness to God the Father, our Lord, the Son of God, says in his gospel: *You have heard it said, 'Love your neighbour and hate your enemy.' But I tell you to love your enemies and pray for those who persecute you, so that you may be like your Father in heaven.*

St Cyprian, *On Jealousy and Envy*, 12–13: CSEL 3/1, 427–30

Seventh Sunday in Ordinary Time/Epiphany 7 Year B: Mark 2.1–12

A READING FROM A HOMILY ON MATTHEW BY ST JOHN CHRYSOSTOM

The scribes asserted that only God could forgive sins, yet Jesus not only forgave sins, but showed that he had also another power that belongs to God alone: the power to disclose the secrets of the heart. They, of course, did not reveal what they were thinking. Scripture says that *some of the scribes said within themselves: 'This man is talking blasphemy.' And Jesus, aware of their thoughts, said: 'Why do you think evil in your hearts?'* Now only God knows the secrets of the heart. As the prophet says: *You alone know the heart*, and: *God searches the mind and the heart*. And so, to prove his divinity and his equality with the Father, Jesus brought their secret thoughts into the open, which they had not dared to do for fear of the crowds.

In doing this, he showed his great compassion. *Why do you think evil in your hearts?* he said. After all, if anyone had reason for complaint it was the invalid. As though cheated he might well have asked: 'Have you come to heal something else then? To put right a different malady? How can I be sure that my sins are forgiven?' In fact, however, he said nothing of the sort, but surrendered himself to the Healer's power.

The scribes, on the other hand, feeling left out and envious, plotted against the good of others. Jesus therefore rebuked them, but with forbearance. He said: 'If you do not believe the first proof, and regard it as an empty boast, then see, I offer you another by revealing your secret thoughts; and to this I will add a third.' What is the third to be? The healing of the paralytic.

Jesus did not give a clear manifestation of his power when he first spoke to the paralytic. He did not say: 'I forgive you your sins', but: *Your sins are forgiven.* When the scribes forced him, however, he showed his power more clearly, *that you may know*, he said, *that the Son of Man has power on earth to forgive sins.*

Before doing this Jesus asked the scribes: *Which is easier to say, 'Your sins are forgiven', or to say, 'Pick up your mat and go home?'* This was the same as asking: 'Which seems easier to you, to heal the body, or to forgive the soul its sins? Obviously, it is easier to heal the body. Indeed, as far as the soul is above the body, so far does the forgiveness of sins surpass physical healing. However, since the one is invisible, but the other visible, I grant you as well this lesser, visible miracle as proof of the one which is greater but invisible.' Thus he showed by his deeds the truth of what John had said of him: that he takes away the sins of the world.

St John Chrysostom, *Homilies on Matthew*, 29.1: Bareille, 12, 87–9

Seventh Sunday in Ordinary Time/Epiphany 7 Year C: Luke 6.27–38

A READING FROM THE COMMENTARY ON THE PSALMS BY ST AUGUSTINE

All the ways of the Lord are mercy and faithfulness, for those who keep his covenant and will. We have here a tremendous statement on the subject of faithfulness and mercy. Mercy is mentioned because it is not our deserts but his own goodness that God regards. He forgives us all our sins and promises us eternal life. But it also speaks of faithfulness, because God never fails to honour his promises. Acknowledging this to be so, let us practise these virtues ourselves in our present circumstances. Just as God has shown us his mercy and faithfulness – his mercy by forgiving our sins and his faithfulness by keeping his promises – so we too should practise mercy and faithfulness in our own lives. Let us show mercy to the sick and needy, even our enemies, and practise faithfulness by refraining from sin. Never let us add sin to sin, because whoever presumes too much on God's mercy has secretly consented to the suggestion that he can cause God to be unjust. Such a person imagines that even if he persists in sin and refuses to give up his wrongdoing, God will still come and give him a place among his obedient servants.

Would this be justice, for God to assign an obstinate sinner like you the same place as those who have turned their backs on sin? Would you be so unjust as to expect God to be unjust too? Why then are you trying to bend God to your will? Bend yourself, rather, to his. Yet how many people do, in fact, bend their wills to God's? Only those few of whom it is said, *The one who perseveres to the end will be saved.*

It is with good reason that Scripture asks: *Who will seek God's mercy and faithfulness for his own sake?* What precisely does *for his own sake* mean? Surely it would have been enough to say *Who will seek* without adding *for his own sake.*

The answer is that many people seek to discover God's mercy and faithfulness from the sacred books, and yet, when their learning is done, they live for their own sakes and not for God's. They are intent on their own interests, not those of Jesus Christ. They preach mercy and faithfulness without practising them. Their preaching proves that they know their subject, for they would not preach without knowledge. But it is a different matter in the case of someone who loves God and Christ. When such a person preaches God's mercy and faithfulness, he seeks to make them known for God's sake, not his own. This means that he is not out to gain temporal benefits from his preaching; his desire is to help Christ's members, that is, those who believe in him, by faithfully sharing with them the knowledge he himself possesses, so *that the living may no longer live for themselves, but for him died for all.*

St Augustine, *On the Psalms* 60, 9: CCSL 39, 771

Eighth Sunday in Ordinary Time/Epiphany 8/ Proper 3 Year A: Matthew 6.24–34

A READING FROM A BAPTISMAL HOMILY BY ST JOHN CHRYSOSTOM

If spiritual things hold first place in our lives, material needs will cause us no concern, for God in his goodness will give them to us in abundance. On the other hand, if we devote ourselves entirely to earthly pursuits and neglect our spiritual life, if we are always concerned with what this life has to offer without any care for our souls, then we shall forfeit not only spiritual graces but worldly profit as well.

I urge you, therefore: let us not overturn the established order. We know that our Master is good, so let us commit everything to him and not be taken up with the cares of this life. He who in his loving kindness created us out of nothing will be even more ready now to lavish his care upon us. As Scripture says: *Your heavenly Father knows that you need all these things even before you ask him.*

God wishes us, then, to be free from every anxiety regarding temporal affairs, and to have all possible leisure for the things of the Spirit. He says: 'Your part is to seek spiritual blessings, and I myself will provide amply for your material needs. *Look at the birds in the sky. They neither sow nor reap nor gather crops into barns, and yet your Father feeds them.*' In other words, 'If I take such care of irrational birds as to supply them with all they need without ploughing or sowing, I will take much greater care of you who are endowed with reason, if only you make up your minds to put spiritual things before temporal ones. If I made these creatures for your sake, as well as the whole of creation, and if I take such care of them, of what great care will I not deem you worthy – you for whom I created all of this?'

I entreat you therefore: let us put our whole trust in God's promise; let our thoughts be completely taken up with longing for spiritual graces; let us consider everything else of secondary importance compared with the joys to come. To these may we all attain by the grace and loving kindness of our Lord Jesus Christ, to whom with the Father and the Holy Spirit be glory, power and honour now and for ever, and for endless ages. Amen.

St John Chrysostom, *Baptismal Catecheses*, 8.19–21, 23–5:
SC 50, 257–60

Eighth Sunday in Ordinary Time/Epiphany 8/ Proper 3 Year B: Mark 2.18–22 [13–22]

A READING FROM THE COMMENTARY ON MATTHEW BY ST PASCHASIUS RADBERTUS

A most strange, indeed, unheard of, marriage took place when, in the womb of the Virgin, *the Word became flesh and* so *dwelt among us.* Just as when Christ rose again all the elect rose again in him, so also this marriage was solemnized in Christ. The Church was joined to her Bridegroom by a marriage covenant when the Man-God received in their entirety the gifts of the Holy Spirit, and the fullness of the divine nature became embodied in him. The bride has already received as a marriage present a pledge from among these gifts, the gifts of the same Holy Spirit who dwelt fully in Christ, through whom he became man and like a bridegroom came forth from the womb of the Virgin, since her womb was his bridal chamber. When the Church is reborn of water in this same Spirit, she becomes one body in Christ, so that they are two in a single body. This is *a great mystery concerning Christ and the Church.*

This wedding lasts from the first moment of Christ's incarnation until his return, so that all its rites may be completed. Then those who are ready, having duly fulfilled the requirements of so exalted a marriage, it will go into the eternal wedding banquet with Christ, filled with awe. Meanwhile, Christ's promised bride is brought to her husband, and in faith and mercy they pledge themselves to one another every day until he comes again. This is what Paul said, *I have betrothed you to Christ to present you as a pure virgin to this one husband,* so that when Christ comes he may embrace the Church, made up as it is of both Jews and Gentiles, as his bride, his consort, his spouse.

All the saints of the Old Testament, all who have lived since the beginning of the world and have believed in Christ's future coming to save the human race – all these shall share in this marriage feast which by faith they glimpsed from afar. As Scripture says, *He sent his servants to summon the invited guests to the marriage feast.* Those summoned had already received their invitation, since God had inspired them all, from the righteous Abel onward, to look forward to the coming of Christ.

St Paschasius Radbertus, *On Matthew,* 10.22: PL 120, 741–2

Eighth Sunday of Epiphany Year B (CWL): John 1.1–14

SEE THE READINGS FOR ADVENT 3B BY JOHN SCOTUS ERIUGENA, CHRISTMAS III BY ST BASIL THE GREAT, OR CHRISTMAS 2 A–C, PAGES 13, 27 AND 35–9.

Eighth Sunday in Ordinary Time/Epiphany 8/ Proper 3 Year C: Luke 6.39–45 [39–49]

A READING FROM THE COMMENTARY ON LUKE BY ST CYRIL OF ALEXANDRIA

The blessed disciples were to be the spiritual guides and teachers of the whole world. It had therefore to be clearly seen by all that they held fast to the true faith. It was essential for them to be familiar with the gospel way of life, skilled in every good work, and to give teaching that was precise, salutary, and scrupulously faithful to the truth they themselves had long pondered, enlightened by the divine radiance. Otherwise they would be blind leaders of the blind. Those imprisoned in the darkness of ignorance can never lead others in the same sorry state to knowledge of the truth. Should they try, both would fall headlong into the ditch of the passions.

To destroy the ostentatious passion of boastfulness and stop people from trying to win greater honour than their teachers, Christ declared: *The disciple is not above his teacher.* Even if some should advance so far as to equal the teachers in holiness, they ought to remain within the limits set by them, and follow their example. Paul also taught this when he said, *Be imitators of me, as I am of Christ.* So then, if the Master does not judge, why are you judging? He came not to judge the world, but to take pity on it.

What he is saying, then, is this, 'If I do not pass judgement, neither must you, my disciple. You may be even more guilty of the faults of which you accuse another. Will you not be ashamed when you come to realize this?' The Lord uses another illustration for the same teaching when he says: *Why do you look for the speck in your brother's eye?*

With compelling arguments he persuades us that we should not want to judge others, but should rather examine our own hearts, and strive to expel the passions seated in them, asking this grace from God. He it is

79

who heals the contrite of heart and frees us from our spiritual disorders. If your own sins are greater and worse than other people's, why do you censure them, and neglect what concerns yourself?

This precept, then, is essential for all who wish to live a holy life, and particularly for those who have undertaken the instruction of others. If they are virtuous and self restrained, giving an example of the gospel way of life by their own actions, they will rebuke those who do not choose to live as they do in a friendly way, so as not to break their own habit of gentleness.

St Cyril of Alexandria, *On Luke*, 6: PG 72, 602–3

Eighth Sunday of Epiphany Year C (CWL): Luke 8.22–25

SEE THE READING FOR ORDINARY TIME 12B FROM ST AUGUSTINE, PAGE 190.

Ninth Sunday in Ordinary Time/Epiphany 9/ Proper 4 Year A: Matthew 7.21–27

A READING FROM A HOMILY BY ST PHILOXENUS OF MABBUG

This saying of our Master obliges us to be diligent not only in hearing God's word, but also in obeying it. We do well to listen to the law, because it moves us to good works; it is a good thing to read and meditate on Scripture, because our inmost thoughts are thus purified from all evil; to be assiduous in reading, listening to and meditating on the law of God without doing what it says is a wickedness that the Spirit of God has already condemned, forbidding those guilty of it even to pick up the holy book in their unclean hands. *God said to the sinner: 'Do not touch the book of my commandments, because you have taken my covenant on your lips, but have hated correction and cast my words behind you.'*

Assiduous readers who do no good works are accused by their very reading, and merit a more severe condemnation because each day they scorn and despise what they have heard that day. They are like dead people, corpses without souls. The dead will not hear thousands of trumpets and horns sounding in their ears; in the same way souls dead in sin, minds that have forgotten God, do not hear the sound and cry of divine words; the spiritual trumpet leaves them unmoved. They sleep the sleep of death and find it pleasant.

God's disciples need to have firmly anchored in their souls the remembrance of their Master, Jesus Christ, and to think of him day and night. They must learn where to begin, and how and where to construct the rooms in their buildings, and how to bring those buildings to completion. Otherwise all the passers-by will mock them, as our Lord said about the man who set out to build a tower and could not finish it.

The foundation is already laid, as St Paul said: it is Jesus Christ our God. *If anyone builds on this foundation with gold or silver or precious stones, or with wood or straw or stubble, his work will be brought to light, because fire will reveal it and test the quality of each one's work.*

Good habits and righteousness in all its beauty are what Paul compared to gold, silver, and precious stones. Faith is like gold; temperance, fasting, abstinence, and the other good works are like silver; while the precious stones are peace, hope, pure and holy thoughts, and spiritual understanding that contemplates God and the grandeur of his being, and keeps silence, trembling before the inexplicable, incommunicable mysteries of the Godhead.

St Philoxenus of Mabbug, *Homily* 1: SC 44, 27–31

Ninth Sunday of Epiphany Year A (RCL alternative): Matthew 17.1–9

SEE THE READINGS FOR LENT 2A BY ST EPHREM THE SYRIAN, PAGE 98.

Ninth Sunday in Ordinary Time/Epiphany 9/ Proper 4 Year B: Mark 2.23 – 3.6 or 2.23–28

A READING FROM A HOMILY BY AN UNKNOWN GREEK AUTHOR

Listen, my child, and I will tell you the reason why this tradition of observing the Lord's Day and refraining from work has been handed down to us. When our Lord gave the Sacrament to his disciples, he took bread and blessed it. Then he broke it and handed it to them saying, *Take, eat; this is my body, which is broken for you for the forgiveness of sins. In the same way he also gave the cup to them saying: 'Drink of this, all of you. This is my blood, the blood of the new covenant, which is poured out for you and for many for the forgiveness of sins. Do this', he said, 'in memory of me.'*

Now this is the day we dedicate to the Lord's memory, so it is called the Lord's Day. Before the Lord's passion it was not called the Lord's Day, but the first day. On this day the Lord began the creation of the world, and on this day he gave the first fruits of the resurrection to the world. This is the day on which, as we have said, he bade us celebrate the holy mysteries. This great day has therefore become for us the beginning of all graces. It was the beginning of the world's creation, the beginning of the resurrection, and it is the beginning of the week. Because of its three beginnings, this day signifies the primordial power of the holy Trinity.

Now every week has seven days. Six of these God has given to us for work, and one for prayer, rest, and making preparations for our sins, so that on the Lord's Day we may atone to God for any sins we have committed on the other six days.

Therefore, arrive early in the church of God; draw near to the Lord and confess your sins to him, repenting in prayer and with a contrite heart. Attend the holy and divine liturgy; finish your prayer and do not leave before the dismissal. Contemplate your Master as he is broken and distributed, yet not consumed. If you have a clear conscience, go forwards and partake of the body and blood of the Lord. But if your conscience condemns you for being guilty of wicked and immoral deeds, refrain from receiving communion until your conscience has been purified by repentance. Remain for the prayer, however, and do not leave the church until you are dismissed. Remember Judas, the traitor. Not remaining in prayer with all the others was the beginning of his downfall and destruction.

This day, as we have often said was given to you for prayer and rest. *This is the day which the Lord has made; let us rejoice and be glad in it,* and give glory to him who rose on this day, together with the Father and the Holy Spirit, now, always, and for endless ages. Amen.

Unknown Greek author, *Sermon* 6.1–2, 6: PG 86/1, 416, 421

Ninth Sunday of Epiphany Year B (RCL alternative): Mark 9.2–9

SEE THE READINGS FOR LENT 2B BY ST AMBROSE,
PAGE 100.

Ninth Sunday in Ordinary Time/Epiphany 9/ Proper 4 Year C: Luke 7.1–10

A READING FROM A SERMON BY ST AUGUSTINE

In the gospel we heard our own faith extolled as it was manifested by humility. The Lord Jesus agreed to go to the centurion's house to cure his servant, but he replied: *I am not worthy to have you under my roof; only say the word and my servant will be healed.* In protesting his unworthiness the centurion showed himself worthy to have Christ enter not his house but his heart. Yet he could not have said this with such faith and humility unless he already bore within his heart the one he was too overawed to have within his house. In any case, there would have been no great happiness at the entry of the Lord Jesus within his walls if he were not present in his heart. The Master who taught humility by both word and example dined in the house of a certain proud Pharisee called Simon; but though he was in his house, the Son of Man found nowhere in the Pharisee's heart where he could lay his head. The centurion's house he did not in fact enter, but he took possession of his heart. The centurion said, *I am not worthy to have you under my roof.* The Lord praised the faith shown by his humility, replying, *I tell you, not even in Israel have I've found faith like this.* He meant Israel in a physical sense, for the centurion was already an Israelite in spirit.

The Lord had come to the people of Israel, that is to the Jews, to seek out the lost sheep first among that people in whom and from whom he had taken flesh; but not even there, he says, did he find such faith. We can only judge a person's faith from a human viewpoint; but he who sees the heart and whom no one ever deceives testified to the state of this man's heart: I'm hearing the centurion's humble words he pronounced his assurance of healing.

But what emboldened the centurion to act as he did? *I am under authority myself*, he said, *and have soldiers under me; and I say to one man, Go, and he goes; to another, Come here, and he comes; to my servant, Do this, and he does it.* I exercise authority over my subordinates, and am myself subject to those with authority over me. If I then, a man subject to authority, have authority to give orders, what must be the extent of your authority which all authorities obey?

Now the man who said this was a Gentile as well as a centurion. He was a professional soldier and, as a centurion, acted according to his rank; subject to authority and exercising authority, obeying as a subordinate and giving orders to those subordinate to him. As for the Lord, though living among the Jewish people, he was already beginning to make it known that his Church would extend throughout the whole world into which he was about to send his apostles. Although the Gentiles would not see him they would believe in him, whereas the Jewish leaders who saw him would put him to death.

The Lord did not enter the centurion's house in person, but, though absent in body, he was present by his divine power, bringing healing of body and soul. And it was the same with the Gentiles. Only among the Jews was he bodily present. Among no other people was he born of a virgin, among no others did he suffer, travel on foot, endure our human lot, or perform divine wonders. No, he did none of these things among other peoples, and yet the prophecy about him was fulfilled: *People unknown to me served me.* How was that possible if they did not know him? *As soon as they heard of me they obeyed me.* Indeed, the whole world has heard and has obeyed.

St Augustine, *Sermon* 62.1, 3–4: PL 38, 414–16

Ninth Sunday of Epiphany Year C (RCL alternative): Luke 9.28–36 [28–43]

SEE THE READING FOR LENT 2C BY ST CYRIL OF ALEXANDRIA, PAGE 103.

LENT

REMEMBER that thou art dust and to dust thou shalt return.

Words at the administration of the ashes, Ash Wednesday
(Genesis 3.19)

WHEN someone asks you why you fast, you should not answer: because of the Passover, or because of the Cross. Neither of these is the reason for our fasting. We fast because of our sins, since we are preparing to approach the sacred mysteries. The Christian Passover is a time for neither fasting nor mourning, but for great joy, since the Cross destroyed sin and made expiation for the whole world. It reconciled ancient enmities and opened the gates of heaven. It made friends of those who had been filled with hatred, restoring them to the citizenship of heaven. Through the Cross our human nature has been set at the right hand of the throne of God, and we have been granted countless good things besides. Therefore we must not give way to mourning or sadness; we must rejoice greatly instead over all these blessings.

St John Chrysostom

ALMIGHTY and everlasting God, who hatest nothing that thou hast made, and dost forgive the sins of all them that are penitent: Create and make in us new and contrite hearts, that we worthily lamenting our sins, and acknowledging our wretchedness, may obtain of thee, the God of all mercy, perfect remission and forgiveness; through Jesus Christ our Lord. Amen.

Collect for Ash Wednesday, *Book of Common Prayer*

HEAR us, O Lord, and have mercy upon us, for we have sinned against
you.
Crying, we raise our eyes to you, Sovereign King, Redeemer of all.
Listen, O Christ, to the pleas of the sinners who cry to you.
You are at the right hand of God the Father, you are the Keystone,
the Way of Salvation and the Gate of Heaven, cleanse the stains of our
sins.

Tenth-century Latin chant, *Attende, Domine*

'Now we give you thanks because you have given us the spirit of discipline, that we may triumph over evil and grow in grace, as we prepare to celebrate the paschal mystery with mind and heart renewed.'[5] Lent is a season of prayer, penance and almsgiving in preparation for the Passover of Christ at Easter. The English word 'Lent' means the season of spring and is probably derived from an Old English word meaning 'long' because of the lengthening of days in this season. In the Middle Ages it was adopted for this season of the Christian year which other Western European languages usually call by a name derived from the Latin *quadragesima*, 'the fortieth' (fortieth day before Easter), as in the French *carême*, the Italian *quaresima*, and the Spanish *cuaresma* (the German is *Fastenzeit*, period of fasting).

Easter always included a period of fasting in preparation for the celebration of the Lord's resurrection on Easter night. At first this was a total fast of a couple of days with a less strict fast for the preceding days of the week. In the fourth century a forty-day fast came to be adopted throughout the whole Church. It originally began on the first Sunday of Lent, which gave forty days before the Triduum (the 'three days' from the evening of Maundy Thursday until Easter Day) – which included the original Easter fast on the two days before Easter. In the sixth century at Rome the fast came to begin on the Wednesday before the first Sunday of the six weeks so that, as Christians do not fast on Sundays, the whole season consisted of forty fasting days and lasted until the Easter Vigil. The rite of imposition of ashes on people's heads on Ash Wednesday began in the Germanic lands and spread to Italy in the tenth century. As well as a period of preparation for Easter, Lent in the early Church was also a period of preparation for those catechumens who were to be baptized and enter the Church at the Easter Vigil and those penitents who had committed public sins and were to be received back into the community of the Church on Thursday of Holy Week.

The first Sunday of Lent has the Gospel of the temptation of Christ and the second his transfiguration in the *Roman Lectionary*, but the *Revised Common Lectionary* has the option (mandatory in the Church of England) of transferring the transfiguration Gospels to the Sunday before Lent and replacing them with the gospel stories of Nicodemus (Year A), a prophecy of the passion (Year B) and Jesus' lament over Jerusalem (Year C). The Gospel of John dominates the remaining Sundays of Lent. The Year A Gospels from John – the woman at the well, the man born blind and the raising of Lazarus – were perhaps the ancient Gospels of these Sundays when they were used for the 'scrutinies' of those preparing for

---

5 Lent short preface, *Common Worship*.

baptism. These three Gospel passages were later transferred to weekdays but returned to the Sundays with the restoration of the catechumenate in the Roman Catholic Church in the later twentieth century. In years B and C other readings are given, emphasizing the exaltation of Christ on the cross in year B and repentance and the mercy of God in Year C, but the *Roman Lectionary* allows the Year A readings also to be used in the other years.

In the ancient Roman liturgy the last two weeks of Lent are traditionally called Passiontide, the liturgical formularies focus more strongly on the approaching passion of the Lord and images are veiled in churches. Passiontide is part of the calendar of the Church of England and there are remnants of this in the ordinary form of the Roman liturgy, although Palm Sunday has been renamed Passion Sunday. The final week of Lent is called Holy Week and begins with Palm Sunday with its liturgical procession commemorating Christ's entry into Jerusalem. The main liturgical Gospel for Palm Sunday is the passion but *The Fathers on the Sunday Gospels* provides commentaries on the Gospels for the 'Liturgy of Palms' or 'Commemoration of the Lord's Entry into Jerusalem' which is celebrated at the start of the Palm Sunday liturgy. This is a Sunday lectionary and so commentaries are not given for the Gospels provided in *Revised Common Lectionary* for the Monday, Tuesday and Thursday in Holy Week (traditionally the Tuesday and Wednesday had the reading of the passion in Mark and Luke but these are now read on Palm Sunday). Although the Holy Eucharist is not celebrated on Good Friday or Holy Saturday, commentaries are provided for the Gospels read at the monastic office of Vigils which reflects the origin of this lectionary in a Benedictine Abbey and also provides texts for meditation which may be useful as inspiration for preachers in this holy season. On Good Friday the *Roman Lectionary* and the *Revised Common Lectionary* prescribe St John's Passion and the *Revised Common Lectionary* gives the story of Joseph of Arimathea in Matthew 27 and John 19 for Holy Saturday before the Easter Vigil.

The Easter or Paschal Triduum is a term that became popular from the 1930s and has been incorporated in the Roman liturgical books, but already in the fourth century St Ambrose was speaking of the 'sacred triduum' in which Christ 'suffered, rested and rose' (Letter 23.13) and St Augustine also wrote of 'the most holy triduum of the crucified, buried and risen Lord' (Letter 54.14). It is an unpacking of the mystery celebrated at Easter and runs from the evening Eucharist of the Lord's Supper on Maundy Thursday to Evensong on Easter Day (before 1955 in the Roman Catholic Church the Thursday Mass was in the morning and the Easter Vigil was held in the morning of Holy Saturday so the Triduum did not include Easter Day, but this has now changed). The Triduum seems to have had its roots in the liturgy of the Church of Jerusalem where the faithful wanted to celebrate the events of the Gospel in the appropriate order at the places where they occurred. This is what is described by the pilgrim Egeria who visited the Holy Land in the 380s. As the Triduum includes Easter Day it forms a transition from Lent to Eastertide and discussion of it will continue in the introduction to that season.

Ash Wednesday Years A–C, Reading I:
Matthew 6.1–6, 16–21

A READING FROM A SERMON BY ST JOHN CHRYSOSTOM

Why do we fast for forty days? Formerly many believers approached the sacraments without any particular preparation, especially at the time when Christ first gave them to us. But when the fathers realized the harm that could result from such neglect, they took counsel together and decreed that a period of forty days of fasting be set aside, during which the people would meet to pray and listen to the word of God. During this Lenten season each of the faithful would undergo a thorough purification by means of prayer, almsgiving, fasting, watching, repentant tears, confession, and every other remedial measure. Then when they had done all in their power to cleanse their consciences, they could approach the sacraments.

It is certain that the fathers did well to use such lenience in their desire to establish us in the habit of fasting. As we know, we could proclaim a fast throughout the whole year, and no one would pay any attention. But now, with a set time for fasting of only forty days, even the most sluggish need no exhortation to rouse themselves to undergo it; they accept it as a regular observance and recurring encouragement.

So, when someone asks you why you fast, you should not answer: because of the Passover, or because of the Cross. Neither of these is the reason for our fasting. We fast because of our sins, since we are preparing to approach the sacred mysteries. Moreover, the Christian Passover is a time for neither fasting nor mourning, but for great joy, since the Cross destroyed sin and made expiation for the whole world. It reconciled ancient enmities and opened the gates of heaven. It made friends of those who had been filled with hatred, restoring them to the citizenship of heaven. Through the Cross our human nature has been set at the right hand of the throne of God, and we have been granted countless good things besides. Therefore we must not give way to mourning or sadness; we must rejoice greatly instead over all these blessings.

Listen to the exultant words of Saint Paul: *God forbid that I should boast of anything but the Cross of our Lord Jesus Christ.* And elsewhere he writes: *God shows his own love for us because when we were still sinners Christ died for our sake.*

Saint John's message is the same. *God loved the world so much*, he declares, and then, passing over every other manifestation of God's love, he comes at once to the crucifixion. *God loved the world so much that he gave his only Son*, that is, he gave him up to be crucified, *so that those who believed in him might not perish but might have eternal life*. If, then, the Cross has its foundation in love and is our glory, we must not say we mourn because of the Cross. Far from it. What we have to mourn over is our own sinfulness, and that is why we fast.

St John Chrysostom, *Oration 3 Against the Jews*: PG 48, 867–8

Ash Wednesday Years A–C, Reading II: Matthew 6.1–6, 16–21

A READING FROM A SERMON BY ST PETER CHRYSOLOGUS

Perseverance in faith, devotion, and virtue is assured by three things: prayer, fasting, and mercy. Prayer knocks at the door, fasting gains entrance, mercy receives. These three things, prayer, fasting, and mercy are all one and they give life to each other.

Fasting is the soul of prayer, mercy is the lifeblood of fasting. Let no one try to separate them, for this is impossible. If we have only one of them, if we have not all three together, we have nothing. Whoever prays, then, must also fast; whoever fasts must also show mercy. If we want our own petitions heard we must hear the petitions of others. God's ear will be open to us if we do not turn a deaf ear to other people.

When we fast we should understand what it means to be really hungry. If we want God to take account of our hunger we must feel for the hunger of others. If we hope for mercy we must show mercy. If we look for kindness we must show kindness. If we want to receive we must give. Only a shameless person would ask for himself what he refused to give to others. In showing mercy this should be the rule: show it in the same way, with the same generosity, with the same promptness as you would wish it to be shown to you.

Let prayer, mercy, and fasting, then, be one single appeal to God on our behalf, one speech in our defence, one threefold plea in our favour. What we have lost by despising others let us regain by fasting. By fasting let us offer our souls in sacrifice, for we can make no better offering to God, as is proved by the prophet's words: *A sacrifice pleasing to God is a contrite spirit. A contrite and humbled heart, O God, you will not spurn.*

Offer your soul to God, make him an oblation of your fasting so that your soul may be a pure offering, a holy sacrifice, a living victim, remaining your own and at the same time made over to God. Whoever fails to give this gift to God will not be excused for you are never without the means of giving if the gift to be given is yourself.

To make these offerings acceptable mercy must be added. Fasting bears no fruit unless it is watered by mercy. When mercy dries up fasting is arid. Mercy is to fasting as rain is to the earth. However much you may cultivate your heart, clear the soil of your nature, root out your vices and sow virtues, if you do not release the springs of mercy your fasting will bear no fruit. When you fast, a thin sowing of mercy will mean a thin harvest. When you fast, what you pour out in mercy overflows into your barn. So do not lose by saving, but gather in by scattering. Give to the poor and you give to yourself. You will not be allowed to keep what you have refused to give to others.

St Peter Chrysologus, *Sermon* 43: PL 52, 320, 322

Ash Wednesday Years A–C, Reading III: Matthew 6.1–6, 16–21

A READING FROM A SERMON BY ST AUGUSTINE

As we begin our annual Lenten observance with its solemn call to conversion, it is incumbent upon me to make the customary solemn exhortation to all of you. Indeed, it is more than ever my pastoral duty to nourish your minds with the word of God when you are about to mortify your bodies by fasting, for once you have been inwardly refreshed by the food of the spirit you will be able to undertake physical hardships more courageously and endure them with greater stamina.

We are soon to celebrate the Passion of our crucified Lord. It is therefore in keeping with our commitment to him that we should crucify ourselves by restraining the desires of the flesh. As the Apostle says: *You cannot belong to Christ Jesus unless you crucify all your self-indulgent passions and desires.* Such is the Cross upon which we Christians must continually hang, since our whole lives are beset by trials and temptations. Not for us, as long as we live, to be rid of those nails we read of in the psalm: *Pierce my flesh with the nails of your fear.* Flesh means the desires of our lower nature; nails, the demands of God's justice and holiness. With these the fear of the Lord pierces our flesh and fastens us to the Cross as an acceptable sacrifice to him. In a similar passage the apostle Paul appeals to us by the mercy of God to offer our bodies as a living sacrifice, holy and acceptable to God.

To hang on such a Cross brings no shame to the servants of God; it is something in which they glory, as Saint Paul does when he says: *Far be it from me to glory in anything except in the Cross of our Lord Jesus Christ, through whom the world has been crucified to me, and I to the world.*

This crucifixion, I repeat, is something that must continue throughout our life, not for forty days only. It is true that Moses, Elijah, and our Lord himself fasted for forty days; but in Moses, Elijah, and Christ we are meant to see the Law, the Prophets, and the Gospel, and to learn from them not to cling to this present world or imitate its ways, but to nail our unregenerate selves to the Cross. Christians must always live in this way, without any wish to come down from their Cross, otherwise they will sink beneath the world's mire. But if we have to do so all our lives, we must make an even greater effort during these days of Lent. It is not a simple matter of living through forty days; Lent is the epitome of our whole life.

St Augustine, *Sermon* 205.1: PL 38, 1039–40

Ash Wednesday, CWL alternative Gospel: John 8.1–11

SEE THE READING FOR LENT 5C (RL) BY
ST AMBROSE, PAGE 115.

First Sunday of Lent Year A: Matthew 4.1–11

A READING FROM THE ORATIONS OF ST GREGORY
NAZIANZEN

We must not expect baptism to release us from the temptations of our persecutor. The body that concealed him made even the Word of God a target for the enemy; his assumption of a visible form made even the invisible light an object of attack. Nevertheless, since we have at hand the means of overcoming our enemy, we must have no fear of the struggle. Flaunt in his face the water and the Spirit. In them will be extinguished all the flaming darts of the evil one.

Suppose the tempter makes us feel the pinch of poverty, as he did even to Christ, and taking advantage of our hunger talks of turning stones into bread: we must not be taken in by him, but let him learn what he has still not grasped. Refute him with the word of life, with the word that is the bread sent down from heaven and that gives life to the world.

He may try to ensnare us through our vanity, as he tried to ensnare Christ when he set him on the pinnacle of the temple and said, 'Prove your divinity: throw yourself down.' Let us beware of succumbing to pride, for the tempter will by no means stop at one success. He is never satisfied and is always pursuing us. Often he beguiles us with something good and useful, but its end is always evil. That is simply his method of waging war.

We also know how well-versed the devil is in Scripture. When Christ answered the temptation to turn stones into bread with a rebuke from Scripture beginning: *It is written*, the devil countered with the same words, tempting Christ to throw himself down from the pinnacle of the temple. *For it is written*, he quoted, *he will give his angels charge of you, and on their hands they will bear you up.* O past master of all evil, why suppress the verse that follows? You did not finish the quotation, but I know full well what it means: that we shall tread on you as on an adder or a cobra; protected by the Trinity, we shall trample on you as on serpents or scorpions.

If the tempter tries to overthrow us through our greed, showing us at one glance all the kingdoms of the world – as if they belonged to him – and demanding that we fall down and worship him, we should despise him, will we know him to be a penniless impostor. Strong in our baptism, each of us can say: 'I too am made in the image of God, but unlike you, I have not yet become an outcast from heaven through my pride. I have put on Christ; by my baptism I have become one with him. It is you that should fall prostrate before me.' By these words he can only surrender and retire in shame; as he retreated before Christ, the light of the world, so will he depart from those illumined by that light. Such are the gifts conferred by baptism on those who understand its power; such the rich banquet it lays before those who hunger for the things of the Spirit.

St Gregory Nazianzen, *Oration* 40.10: PG 36, 370–1

First Sunday of Lent Year B: Mark 1.12–15 [9–15]

A READING FROM A HOMILY BY JOHN JUSTUS LANDSBERG

Everything the Lord Jesus decided to do, everything he chose to endure, was ordained by him for our instruction, our correction, and our advantage; and since he knew that the teaching and consolation we should derive from it all was far from negligible, he was loath to let slip any opportunity that might profit us. And so when he was led out into the wilderness there is no doubt that his guide was the Holy Spirit whose intention was to take him to a place where he would be exposed to temptation, a place where the devil would have the audacity to accost him and put him to the test. The circumstances were so greatly in the devil's favour that he was prompted to capitalize on them: here was Jesus alone, at prayer, physically worn out by fasting and abstinence. A chance indeed to find out whether this man really was the Christ, whether or not he was the Son of God.

From this episode therefore our first lesson is that human life on earth is a life of warfare, and the first thing Christians must expect is to be tempted by the devil. As Scripture tells us, we have to be prepared for temptation, for it is written: *When you enter God's service, prepare your soul for an ordeal.* For this reason, the Lord desires the newly baptized and recent converts to find comfort in his own example. Reading in the gospel that Christ too was tempted by the devil immediately after he was baptized, they will not grow fainthearted and fearful if they experience keener temptations from the devil after their conversion or baptism than before – even if persecution should be their lot.

The second lesson Christ desires to impress upon us by his own example is that we should not lightly expose ourselves to temptation, for we read that it was the Holy Spirit who led Jesus into the wilderness. Mindful of our frailty rather, we must be on the watch, praying not to be put to the test, and keeping ourselves clear of every occasion of temptation.

John Justus Landsberg, *Sermons: Opera omnia* 1 [1888], 120

First Sunday of Lent Year C: Luke 4.1–13

A READING FROM THE COMMENTARY ON THE SONG OF SONGS BY ORIGEN

We live in constant danger of being ensnared by sin, caught in the nets concealed in our path by Nimrod, that mighty hunter in opposition to the Lord, who is in fact none other than the devil, the adversary of God himself. This is why we call these nets, or temptations, the snares of the devil.

When the enemy had spread his nets everywhere and almost the whole world was enmeshed in them, it was necessary for someone stronger, whom they could not hold, to come and destroy them, so as to clear the way for those who came after him. And so, before entering into union and fellowship with the Church, the Saviour too was tempted by the devil. By overcoming temptation and escaping its snares he was able to make a path through those snares for the Church and to call her to himself through them, thus teaching and showing her most clearly that the way to Christ is not along the primrose path of ease but through many tribulations and trials.

No one but Christ could have broken through those snares, for *all have sinned*, says Scripture. *In the whole world there is not a single upright person who does good and never sins*, says another text, and a third declares: *No one is free from stain, not even the child a day old*. The only one who never sinned is Jesus, our Lord and Saviour, but *for our sake* the Father *made him one with human sinfulness*, so that *in the likeness of sinful flesh and of sin he might condemn sin*.

He came, then, to the devil's nets – he, the only one who could not be caught in them. By breaking them and trampling them underfoot he gave his Church courage, so that she now dares to trample on the snares and pass over the nets, saying with all gladness: *Our soul has escaped like a bird from the snare of the fowlers. The snare has been broken and we have escaped.*

Who broke the net but he who was the only one it could not hold? He died, it is true, but willingly and not, as we do, to pay the debt of sin. He alone was *free among the dead*, and being freed from death's power, he could conquer the one who wielded it and to deliver all held in its thrall. At one and the same time he raised from death both himself and death's captives, enthroning them with himself in heaven. *When he ascended on high he led a host of captives*, not only bringing forth their souls but also raising their bodies as the gospel bears witness in the text: *Many bodies of the saints were raised and appeared to many; and they went in to Jerusalem, the city of the living God.*

Origen, *On the Song of Songs*, 3.13: GCS 8, 221, 19 – 223, 5

Second Sunday of Lent Year A: Matthew 17.1–9

A READING FROM A HOMILY BY ST EPHREM THE SYRIAN

After six days Jesus took Simon Peter with James and his brother John and led them up a high mountain, where he was transfigured before them. His face shone like the sun and his clothing became white as light.

Jesus took the three apostles up into the mountain for three reasons: first, to show them the glory of his divinity: then to declare himself Israel's redeemer as he had already foretold by the prophets; and thirdly to prevent the apostles being scandalized at seeing him soon afterward enduring the human suffering which he had freely accepted for our sake. The apostles knew that Jesus was a man; they did not know that he was God. To their knowledge he was the son of Mary, a man who shared their daily life in this world. On the mountain he revealed to them that he was the Son of God, that he was in fact God himself. Peter, James, and John were familiar with the sight of their Master eating and drinking, working and taking rest, growing tired and falling asleep, experiencing fear and breaking out in sweat. All these things were natural to his humanity, not to his divinity. He therefore took them up onto the mountain so that they could hear his Father's voice calling him Son, and he could show them that he was truly the Son of God and was himself divine.

He took them up onto the mountain in order to show them this kingship before they witnessed his passion, to let them see his mighty power before they watched his death, to reveal his glory to them before they beheld his humiliation. Then when the Jews took him captive and condemned him to the cross, the apostles would understand that it was not for any lack of power on his part that Jesus allowed himself to be crucified by his enemies, but because he had freely chosen to suffer in that way for the world's salvation.

He took them up onto the mountain before his resurrection and showed them the glory of his divinity, so that when he rose from the dead in that same divine glory they would realize that this was not something given him as a reward for his labour, as if he were without it previously. That glory had been his from all eternity with the Father, as is clear from what he said on approaching his freely chosen passion: *Father, glorify me now with the glory I had with you before the world came into being.* So then, it was the glory of the Godhead hitherto concealed by his human condition which Jesus revealed to the apostles on the mountain. They saw his face shining like the sun, and his clothing white with the brilliance of light.

St Ephrem the Syrian, *Sermon 16 on the Transfiguration of the Lord,*
1, 3, 4

Second Sunday of Lent Year A (RCL alternative): John 3.1–17

A READING FROM THE COMMENTARY ON JOHN BY ST CYRIL OF ALEXANDRIA

Nicodemus is ready to believe, but he is overcome by fear and does not despise the opinion of men. He refuses to be bold and is divided in two. O Nicodemus, faith is not what you think. The will of the Father is that humans participate in the Holy Spirit, that the citizens of earth are reborn into new life and are called citizens of heaven. When Christ calls the new birth of the Spirit a birth *from above*, he clearly shows that the Spirit is of the essence of God the Father, as indeed he says of himself, *I am from above.*

Since Nicodemus did not understand what being born from above meant, Christ instructed him with plainer teaching, giving him the know-ledge of the Mystery. Our Lord Jesus Christ called the new birth through the Spirit *from above*, showing that the Spirit is of the essence above all essences through whom we become *partakers of the Divine Nature.* Through him and in him we are re-formed to the Archetype of Beauty, re-born into newness of life, and re-moulded to the divine sonship. But Nicodemus did not understand this and so the Saviour answered gently and, removing the veil that seemed to be thrown over his words, he said openly, *Except a man be born again of water and of the Spirit, he cannot enter into the Kingdom of God.* For since man is not simple in his nature but is composed of body and soul, he requires a two-fold healing for his new birth: by the Spirit the human spirit is sanctified; by the sanctified water, the body.

No one has ascended up to heaven but he who came down from heaven, the Son of Man. He says that the Son of Man came down because after the

Incarnation he refused to be divided into two persons. As he is the Word of God, he is also man born of a woman, but he is one Christ of both, undivided in his sonship and God-befitting glory. Now he says that *the Son of Man has come down from heaven*; but at the time of his passion, he is afraid and he is recorded as suffering the sufferings which pertain to his human nature alone.

Having explained these things to Nicodemus, his teaching then turns to those things done in figures and types by Moses of old. He says he must *be lifted up, as the serpent was by Moses*, showing that the study of history is necessary, all but saying to this man of little understanding, *Search the Scriptures, for they testify of me*. For serpents sprung upon Israel in the wilderness, and they cried for salvation from above. God, since he was good and full of compassion, commanded Moses to set up a brazen serpent, and commanded them to look at the serpent as a foreshadowing of salvation by faith. So much for the history, but it does represent the whole Mystery of the Incarnation. For the serpent signifies the sin that was destroying the whole human race and no one could escape it except by the help which is from heaven. The Word of God was then made *in the likeness of sinful flesh* that he might *condemn sin in the flesh* and that those who gaze on him with faith and search into the divine doctrines might be saved. The serpent being lifted up signifies that Christ himself was *lifted up from the earth* by his passion on the cross. *For God so loved the world, that he gave his only-begotten Son, that whoever believes in him should not perish, but have everlasting life.*

St Cyril of Alexandria, Commentary on John, 2.3

Second Sunday of Lent Year B: Mark 9.2–10

A READING FROM A COMMENTARY ON THE PSALMS BY ST AMBROSE

It was the will of the Lord Jesus that Moses alone (although he was accompanied, it is true, by Joshua) should climb the mountain to receive the law. In the gospel too, out of his many disciples he limited the revelation of his risen glory to three: Peter, James, and John. Wishing to put no stumbling block in the way of his weaker followers, whose vacillating minds might prevent them from taking in the full meaning of the paschal mystery, he chose to keep his redemptive plan a secret, and repeatedly warned Peter, James, and John not to talk freely about what they had seen.

Peter, in fact, did not know what to say. He thought of setting up three shelters for the Lord and his attendants. Then he found himself unable to bear the brilliance of the glory radiating from his transfigured Lord. Together with those sons of thunder, James and John, he fell to the ground. A cloud enveloped the three of them, and they were unable to rise until Jesus came and touched them, bidding them stand up and dismiss their fears.

They entered the cloud in order to receive knowledge of hidden, secret matters, and there they heard the voice of God saying: *This is my beloved Son in whom I am well pleased. Listen to him.*

What does *This is my beloved Son* mean? The implication is as follows. Make no mistake, Simon. Do not imagine God's Son can be put into the same category as the servants who attend him. This man is my Son, neither Moses nor Elijah can be given that title, even though the one opened up the sea and the other closed the heavens. Both of them exercised dominion over the elements, but it was by the power of the Lord's word that they did so. They were only servants; it was the Lord who made the waters into a solid wall, the Lord who caused the drought that closed the heavens, and the Lord who, in his own time, opened them to release the rain.

For evidence of the resurrection to be accepted, the combined witness of those servants is required; but when the glory of their risen Lord is revealed, the servants' aureole is lost in shadow. Sunrise obscures the stars; the light of the heavenly bodies grows pale before the brilliance of the sun shining on this material world. How then could human stars attract notice in the presence of the eternal Sun of Justice and that divine radiance? Where are those luminaries now that used to shine so brightly in your sight on account of a miracle worked in the past? The whole created universe is darkness in comparison with eternal light. Let others hasten to make themselves pleasing to God by serving him, but this man alone is the true and eternal light in which the Father takes pleasure.

It is as if the Father said: 'I find my delight in acknowledging everything this man has done as my own work, and in having all my own work attributed to my Son. Listen to what he says: *The Father and I are one.* He never said, "Moses and I are one", nor did he ever say there was any partnership in divine glory between Elijah and himself. Why make three shelters? My Son has no shelter on earth; his dwelling place is in heaven.'

St Ambrose, *On Psalm* 45, 2: CSEL 64, pars 6, 330–1

Second Sunday of Lent Year B (RCL alternative): Mark 8.31–38

A READING FROM THE COMMENTARY ON LUKE BY ST CYRIL OF ALEXANDRIA

When Peter had professed his faith, Jesus commanded them to tell no one, *for the Son of Man is about to suffer many things, and be rejected, and killed, and on the third day rise again*. But wasn't it the duty of disciples to proclaim him everywhere? Sacred Scripture, however, says, *There is a time for everything*. There were things yet unfulfilled which must also be included in their preaching of him: the cross, passion, death in the flesh and the resurrection from the dead, that great and truly glorious sign which gives witness that the Emanuel is truly God, the Son of the Father. He utterly abolished death, spoiled hell, overthrew the tyranny of the enemy, took away the sin of the world, opened the gates above to the dwellers upon earth, and united earth to heaven – these things proved him to be in truth God. He commanded them, therefore, to guard the mystery by a seasonable silence until the whole plan of the dispensation should arrive at a suitable conclusion.

For then, when he had risen from the dead, he commanded that the mystery should be revealed to all the inhabitants of the earth, setting before every man justification by faith and the cleansing efficacy of holy baptism. For he said, *All power is given unto me in heaven and in earth. Go, make disciples of all nations, baptizing them in the Name of the Father, and of the Son, and of the Holy Spirit, and teaching them to observe all those things I have commanded you. And behold, I am with you always, even to the end of the world*. For Christ is with us and in us by the Holy Spirit, and dwells in the souls of us all. We must wonder at the love of Christ the Saviour of us all towards the world; for he not only consented to suffer and bear so great ignominy, humbling himself even to the cross and death for our sakes, but he also rouses his chosen followers to the same excellent desire.'

Next, however, Christ also brings fear to birth in them, for he says that he shall descend from heaven, not in his former lowliness and humiliation, but in the glory of his Father. He shall descend in godlike and transcendent glory, with the holy angels keeping guard around him. It would be miserable and ruinous to be condemned of cowardice and indolence when the Judge has descended from above with the angelic ranks at his side; but great and most blessed, and a foretaste of final blessedness, is it to be able to rejoice in labours already accomplished and await the recompense of past toils. Christ himself shall praise such as this, saying to them, *Come, blessed of my Father, inherit the kingdom prepared for you from the foundation of the world.*

Cyril of Alexandria, *Commentary on Luke*, 49–50

Second Sunday of Lent Year C: Luke 9.28b–36

A READING FROM A HOMILY BY ST CYRIL OF ALEXANDRIA

With three chosen disciples Jesus went up the mountain. Then he was transfigured by a wonderful light that made even his clothes seem to shine. Moses and Elijah stood by him and spoke with him of how he was going to complete his task on earth by dying in Jerusalem. In other words, they spoke of the mystery of his incarnation, and of his saving passion upon the cross. For the law of Moses and the teaching of the holy prophets clearly foreshadowed the mystery of Christ. The law portrayed it by types and symbols inscribed on tablets. The prophets in many ways foretold that in his own time he would appear, clothed in human nature, and that for the salvation of all our race he would not refuse to suffer death upon the cross.

The presence of Moses and Elijah, and their speaking together, was meant to show unmistakably that the law and the prophets were the attendants of our Lord Jesus Christ. He was their master, whom they had themselves pointed out in advance in prophetic words that proved their perfect harmony with one another. The message of the prophets was in no way at variance with the precepts of the law.

Moses and Elijah did not simply appear in silence; the spoke of how Jesus was to complete his task by dying in Jerusalem, they spoke of his passion and cross, and of the resurrection that would follow. Thinking no doubt that the time for the kingdom of God had already come, Peter would gladly have remained on the mountain. He suggested putting up three tents, hardly knowing what he was saying. But it was not yet time for the end of the world; nor was it in this present time that the hopes of the saints would be fulfilled – those hopes founded on Paul's promise that Christ *would transform our lowly bodies into the likeness of his glorious body.*

Only the initial stage of the divine plan had as yet been accomplished. Until its completion was it likely that Christ, who came on earth for love of the world, would give up his wish to die for it? For his submitting to death was the world's salvation, and his resurrection was death's destruction.

As well as the vision of Christ's glory, wonderful beyond all description, something else occurred which was to serve as a vital confirmation, not only of the disciples' faith, but of ours as well. From a cloud on high came the voice of God the Father saying: *This is my beloved Son in whom I am well pleased. Listen to him.*

St Cyril of Alexandria, *Homily 9 on the Transfiguration of the Lord.*
PG 77, 1011–14

Second Sunday of Lent Year C (RCL alternative): Luke 13.31–35

A READING FROM THE COMMENTARY ON LUKE BY ST CYRIL OF ALEXANDRIA

Why did the wicked Pharisees draw near to Christ and say, *Depart hence for Herod wishes to kill you.* The Pharisees imagined that the power of Herod would terrify him, and humble him by fear, although he is Lord of powers and begets in us spiritual bravery by his words, *Fear not those who kill the body but cannot kill the soul.* Christ answered them gently, and with his meaning veiled, *Go and tell this fox.* Listen carefully to the force of the expression. The words used seem to be directed to the person of Herod, but they really refer to the craftiness of the Pharisees. For while he would naturally have said, 'Tell *that* fox', he does not do so, but he skilfully used a middle sort of expression and pointed to the Pharisee, who was close beside him, and said, '*this* fox'. He compares the man to a fox, for it is always a very crafty animal, even a malicious one, just like the Pharisees.

Christ showed he took no account of human violence by saying, *I must go on my way today and tomorrow and the day after.* By saying, *I must,* he does not imply that an inevitable necessity was laid upon him, but rather that by the power of his own free will, he would go wherever he chose, and traverse Judaea without anyone opposing him, until of his own accord he received his consummation upon the precious cross.

Those who killed the Lord did not win a victory over one who fled from suffering, they did not prevail over one who refused to be caught in the meshes of their craftiness. Of his own will he consented to suffer, because he knew that by the death of his flesh he would abolish death and return again to life. For he rose from the dead and raised up with him the whole nature of man, having fashioned it anew unto the life incorruptible.

He says, *you shall not see me again until you say, blessed is he that comes in the name of the Lord.* The Lord withdrew from Jerusalem and left as unworthy of his presence those who had said, *Depart and go hence.* After he had traversed Judaea, saved many, and performed miracles which no words can adequately describe, he returned again to Jerusalem upon a foal and an ass, while vast multitudes and young children, holding up branches of palm-trees, went before him, praising him, and saying, *Hosanna to the Son of David, blessed is he who comes in the name of the Lord.* At the time of his passion he went up to Jerusalem, and entered amid praises, and at that very time endured his saving passion on our behalf, that by suffering he might save and renew unto incorruption all the inhabitants of the earth.

St Cyril of Alexandria, Commentary on Luke, 100

Third Sunday of Lent Year A: John 4.5–42 or 4.5–15, 19b–26, 39a, 40–42

A READING FROM THE *TRACTATES ON JOHN* BY ST AUGUSTINE

A woman came. She is a symbol of the Church not yet justified, but about to be justified, for this is the drift of their conversation. She comes in ignorance, she finds him, and he talks with her.

Let us consider what this Samaritan woman was, and why she had come to draw water. The Samaritans did not belong to the Jewish nation; they were foreigners. It is part of the allegory that this woman, who stands for the Church, came from a foreign nation, for the Church was to come from the Gentiles, who were aliens to the Jews.

Let us therefore hear ourselves speaking in her; let us recognize ourselves in her, and in her person give thanks to God for ourselves. She was an image, not the reality, which she both foreshadowed and then became the reality by believing in Christ, who made her a symbol for us.

She *came* then *to draw water.* She had come simply to draw water, like any other woman. *Jesus said to her, 'Let me have a drink.' (His disciples had gone into the city to buy food.) The Samaritan woman said to him: 'You are a Jew; why do you ask me for a drink, when I am a Samaritan? The Jews had no dealings with the Samaritans.'* They were foreigners. In fact, the Jews would not even use their utensils. And since the woman was carrying a vessel to draw water, she was amazed that against all custom a Jew should ask her for a drink. Yet in asking her for a drink, he was really thirsting for that woman's faith.

Now hear who it is who is asking for a drink. *Jesus answered her: 'If you knew the gift of God, and who it is who says to you, Let me have a drink, you might have asked him, and he would have given you living water.'*

He asks for a drink and he promises a drink. He is in need and wants to receive; he is rich and wants to satisfy the needs of others. *If only you knew the gift of God*, he says. The gift of God is the Holy Spirit. Still speaking to the woman in veiled language, and entering her heart only gradually. Perhaps he is already teaching her, for what could be kinder or more gentle than his exhortation: *If you knew the gift of God, and who it is who says to you, Let me have a drink, you might have asked him, and he would have given you living water.*

From what water does Jesus intend to give her a drink, if not from that of which it is said, *With you is the fountain of life*? For how can they thirst who *will be inebriated by the bounty of your house*? He was promising the kind of nourishment and abundance that comes from the Holy Spirit. She did not yet understand, and because she did not understand, what did she reply? *The woman said to him: 'Sir, give me that water, so that I may never be thirsty, nor have to come here to draw water.'* This work was forced on her by her poverty, but her frailty made her shrink from it. If only she had understood the words: *Come to me, all you who labour and are overburdened, and I will give you rest!* Jesus was saying this to her so that her labour would be at an end.

St Augustine, *Tractates on John*, 15.10–12, 16–17: CCSL 36, 154–6

Third Sunday of Lent Year B: John 2.13–25

A READING FROM THE COMMENTARY ON THE PSALMS BY ST AUGUSTINE

We should not listen to the psalmist's voice as though he were an individual singer; we need to take it as the voice of all who belong to the body of Christ. Since all are members of his body, Christ speaks as a single person. He himself is both one and manifold, for his members are many among themselves but one in him who is unique. This is the mystery of

God's temple. The Apostle says of it that *the temple of God is holy, and that temple is yourselves* – all of you, that is, who believe in Christ and whose faith expresses itself in love. Believing in Christ means loving him. The demons believed without loving, and so, in spite of their belief, they demanded: *What have you to do with us, Son of God?* But ours must be a faith that leads to love. Not for us the cry: *What have you to do with us?* Rather let us say: 'We belong to you; you have redeemed us.' All who have this kind of faith are like the living stones that are built up into the temple of God, or like the incorruptible wood used to construct the ark no flood could submerge.

Human beings themselves are the temple where God's gifts are asked for and received. The gift of eternal life is only granted to those who pray in the temple of God; but those who pray in the temple of God are those who pray in harmony with the Church, in the unity of the body of Christ which consists of the multitude of believers throughout the whole world. Because they are praying in the temple, that is in harmony with the Church, they gain a hearing, for they are praying in spirit and truth. But to pray in the temple of Jerusalem gave no such assurance, for that temple was the scene of a symbolic action in which the Lord drove out those who were bent on their own ends, frequenting the place for the purpose of buying and selling.

However, if that temple was a figure of the true one which is the body of Christ, it is apparent that even in the body of Christ people can be found who have only their own interests at heart, not those of Jesus Christ. And since their own sins, like so many cords, form the scourge with which people are chastised, the Lord made a scourge of cords with which to drive such traders out of the temple.

The voice of the psalmist, then, belongs to the temple which is the body of Christ, and it is here, not in that temple made by hands, that God's gifts are sought and received in spirit and truth. The old temple was only the place of foreshadowing; consequently it has now been demolished. Does this mean that our house of prayer has been destroyed? Certainly not. How could that fallen temple be called *a house of prayer for all nations*? You know what our Lord Jesus Christ said: *It is written, my house shall be called a house of prayer for all people, and you have turned it into a robbers' den.* Now we cannot suppose that the people who tried to turn the house of God into a robbers' den intended to destroy the temple. It is the same with those who live evil lives within the Catholic Church; they do their best to make the house of God into a robbers' den, but they do not on that account destroy it. The time will come when they will be driven out with the scourge of their own sins.

But as for the temple of God which is the body of Christ and the assembly of the faithful, it chants this psalm of ascent with the voice of a single man. We have already heard him in psalm after psalm; let us listen to him again now. If we wish, his voice is ours; we can listen to its music and sing it in our hearts. But if we refuse, we shall be like the traders in the temple of old, pursuing our own selfish interests. We may indeed enter the church, but it will not be in order to seek what is pleasing to God.

St Augustine, *On the Psalms* 130: CCSL 40, 1899–1900

Third Sunday of Lent Year C: Luke 13.1–9

A READING FROM A HOMILY BY ST SYMEON THE NEW THEOLOGIAN

Every unrepented and unconfessed sin and every lapse into despair is a mortal wound inflicted by our own deliberate choice and will. If we refuse to abandon ourselves to the pit of indifference and despair, no evil spirit will have the slightest power over us. Even after we are wounded, we can still learn from this experience and become more courageous for the future if we repent with our whole heart. To save ourselves from every wound is not within our power, but whether we are to be mortal or immortal depends entirely upon ourselves. As long as we do not despair we shall not die, death will have no power over us. We shall always be strong when by repentance we fly for refuge to our almighty and loving God.

This is why I exhort myself, and all of you together with myself, to show by the good we do all our zeal and courage in patient endurance. Then, after journeying with eager hearts along the way of Christ's commandments, we shall be led by the Spirit into the eternal dwellings and be judged worthy to stand before and to worship the one indivisible Trinity in the same Christ our God, to whom be glory and power for endless ages. Amen.

St Symeon the New Theologian, *Catecheses*, 3.347–70:
SC 96, 308–10

Fourth Sunday of Lent Year A: John 9.1–41 or 9.1, 6–9, 13–17, 34–38

A READING FROM THE LETTERS OF ST AMBROSE

You have heard that story in the gospel where we are told that the Lord Jesus, as he was passing by, caught sight of a man who had been blind from birth. Since the Lord did not overlook him, neither ought we to overlook the story of a man whom the Lord considered worthy of his attention. In particular we should notice the fact that he had been blind from birth. This is an important point.

There is, indeed, a kind of blindness, usually brought on by serious illness, which obscures one's vision, but which can be cured, given time; and there is another sort of blindness, caused by cataract, that can be remedied by a surgeon; he can remove the cause and so the blindness is dispelled. Draw your own conclusion: this man, who was actually born blind, was not cured by surgical skill, but by the power of God.

When nature is defective the Creator, who is the author of nature, has the power to restore it. This is why Jesus also said, *As long as I am in the world, I am the light of the world*, meaning, all who are blind are able to see, so long as I am the light they are looking for. Come, then, and receive the light, so that you may be able to see.

What is he trying to tell us, he who brought human beings back to life, who restored them to life by a word of command, who said to a corpse, *Come out!* and Lazarus came out of the tomb; who said to a paralytic, *Arise and pick up your stretcher*, and the sick man rose and picked up the very bed in which he used to be carried as a helpless cripple? Again, I ask you, what is he trying to convey to us by spitting on the ground, mixing his spittle with clay and putting it on the eyes of a blind man, saying: *Go and wash yourself in the pool of Siloam (a name that means 'sent')*? What is the meaning of the Lord's action in this? Surely one of great significance, since the person whom Jesus touches receives more than just his sight.

In one instance we see both the power of his divinity and the strength of his holiness. As the divine light, he touched this man and enlightened him; as priest, by an action symbolizing baptism he wrought in him his work of redemption. The only reason for his mixing clay with the spittle and smearing it on the eyes of the blind man was to remind you that he who restored the man to health by anointing his eyes with clay is the very one who fashioned the first man out of clay, and that this clay that is of our flesh can receive the light of eternal life through the sacrament of baptism.

You, too, should come to Siloam, that is, to him who was sent by the Father (as he says in the gospel, *My teaching is not my own, it comes from him who sent me*). Let Christ wash you and you will then see. Come and be baptized, it is time; come quickly, and you too will be able to say, *I was blind, and now I can see*, and as the blind man said when his eyes began to receive the light, *The night is almost over and the day is at hand.*

St Ambrose, *Letter* 80.1–5: PL 16, 1326–7

Fourth Sunday of Lent Year B: John 3.14–21

A READING FROM THE TREATISE *ON PROVIDENCE* BY ST JOHN CHRYSOSTOM

Although we praise our common Lord for all kinds of reasons, we praise and glorify him above all for the cross. It fills us with awe to see him dying like one accursed. It is this death for people like ourselves that Paul constantly regards as a sign of Christ's love for us. He passes over everything else that Christ did for our advantage and consolation and dwells incessantly on the cross. *The proof of God's love of us*, he says, *is that Christ died for us while we were still sinners.* Then in the following sentence he gives us the highest ground for hope: *When we were alienated from God we were reconciled to him through the death of his Son; surely now that we are reconciled we can count on being saved by his life.* It is this above all that made Paul so proud, so happy, so full of joy and exultation, when he wrote to the Galatians: *God forbid that I should boast of anything but the cross of our Lord Jesus Christ!* What wonder, indeed, if Paul rejoices and glories in the cross, when the Lord himself spoke of his passion as his glory. *Father*, he prayed, *the hour has come: glorify your Son.*

The disciple who recorded these things also told us that the Holy Spirit had not yet come among them because Jesus was not yet glorified. In these words he spoke of the cross as the Lord's glory. When the same disciple wanted to describe the love of God, did he do so by referring to signs, wonders, or miracles of any sort? By no means: he pointed to the cross, saying: *God so loved the world that he gave his only Son, so that all who believe in him may not perish but have eternal life.* And Paul writes: *He did not spare his own Son but gave him up for us all; can we not trust him to give us all we need together with his Son?*

Even when he is urging his readers to be humble, Paul bases his exhortation on the example of the cross, begging them to have the same understanding as Christ Jesus, who, though he had the same nature as God, did not wish to cling to his equality with God, but, emptying himself and taking the nature of a servant, assumed human form. And being revealed in his humanity he humbled himself, following the way of obedience, not only to death, but to death on a cross.

Again, on the subject of love, Paul insists that we should love one another as Christ loved us, giving himself up for us as a fragrant offering and sacrifice to God.

Now when Christ explained how greatly he desired what was to come, and how he welcomed the hour of his passion, the reaction of Peter, the first of the apostles, founder of the Church and leader of the disciples, was to cry out in his ignorance: *God forbid, Lord! This shall never happen to you.* But Christ answered: *Get behind me, Satan. You are an obstacle in my way.* This exclamation of indignant reproof expressed the Lord's great eagerness to undergo what lay ahead. How radiantly the cross shone for Christ during his earthly life! No wonder he called it his glory, and Paul made it his boast.

St John Chrysostom, *On Providence*, 17.1–8: SC 79, 225–9

Fourth Sunday of Lent Year C: Luke 15.1–3, 11–32
A READING FROM THE HOMILIES OF ST JOHN CHRYSOSTOM

All that God looks for from us is the slightest opening and he forgives a multitude of sins. Let me tell you a parable that will confirm this.

There were two brothers: they divided their father's goods between them and one stayed at home, while the other went away to a foreign country, wasted all he had been given, and then could not bear the shame of his poverty. Now the reason I have told you this parable is so that you will understand that even sins committed after baptism can be forgiven if we face up to them. I do not say this to encourage indolence but to save you from despair, which harms us worse than indolence.

The son who went away represents those who fall after baptism. This is clear from the fact that he is called a son, since no one is called a son unless he is baptized. Also, he lived in his father's house and took a share of all his father's goods. Before baptism no one receives the Father's goods or enters upon the inheritance. We can therefore take all this as signifying the state of believers. Furthermore, the wastrel was the brother of the good man, and no one is a brother unless he has been born again through the Spirit.

What does he say after falling into the depths of evil? *I will return to my father.* The reason the father let him go and did not prevent his departure for a foreign land was so that he might learn well by experience what good things are enjoyed by the one who stays at home. For foreign words would not convince us God often leaves us to learn from the things that happen to us.

When the profligate returned after going to a foreign country and finding out by experience what a great sin it is to leave the father's house, the father did not remember past injuries but welcomed him with open arms. Why? Because he was a father and not a judge. And there were dances and festivities and banquets and the whole house was full of joy and gladness.

Are you asking: 'Is this what he gets for his wickedness?' Not for his wickedness, but for his return home; not for sin, but for repentance; not for evil, but for being converted. What is more, when the elder son was angry at this the father gently won him over, saying: *You were always with me, but he was lost and has been found; he was dead and has come back to life.* 'When someone who was lost has to be saved,' says the father, 'it is not the time for passing judgement or for making minute enquiries, but only for mercy and forgiveness.'

St John Chrysostom, *On Repentance*, 1.3–4: PG 49, 282–3

Fifth Sunday of Lent Year A: John 11.1–45 or 11.3–7, 17, 20–27, 33b–45

A READING FROM A SERMON BY ST PETER CHRYSOLOGUS

On his return from the underworld, Lazarus comes forth from the tomb like death confronting its conqueror, an image of the resurrection to come. Before we can fathom the depths of meaning behind this miracle, we must consider the way in which our Lord raised Lazarus to life. This action appears to us as the greatest of all his signs; we see in it the supreme example of divine power, the most marvellous of all his wonderful works.

Our Lord had raised up the daughter of Jairus, the ruler of the synagogue; but although he restored life to the dead girl, he left the law of death still in force. He also raised the widow's only son. He halted the bier, forestalled the young man's burial, arrested the onset of physical decay; but the life he restored had not completely fallen into the power of death. The case of Lazarus was unique. His death and resurrection to life had nothing in common with the other two. Death had already exerted its full power over him, so that in him the sign of the resurrection shone out in all its fullness. I think it is possible to say that if Lazarus had remained only three days in the tomb it would have deprived our Lord's resurrection of its full significance, since Christ proved himself Lord by returning to life after three days, whereas Lazarus, as his servant, had to lie in the grave for four days before he was recalled. However, let us see if we can verify the suggestion by reading the gospel text further.

His sisters sent a message to Jesus saying, 'Lord, the friend whom you love is sick.' By these words they appeal to his affection, they lay claim to his friendship, they call on his love, urging their familiar relationship with him to persuade him to relieve their distress. But for Christ it was more important to conquer death than to cure disease. He showed his love for his friend not by healing him but by calling him back from the grave. Instead of a remedy for his illness, he offered him the glory of rising from the dead.

We are next told that *when Jesus heard that Lazarus was sick, he remained where he was for two days.* You see how he gives full scope to death. He grants free reign to the grave; he allows corruption to set in. He prohibits neither putrefaction nor stench from taking their normal course; he allows the realm of darkness to seize his friend, drag him down to the underworld, and take possession of him. He acts like this so that human hope may perish entirely and human despair reach its lowest depths. The deed he is about to accomplish may then clearly be seen to be the work of God, not of man.

He waited for Lazarus to die, staying in the same place until he could tell his disciples that he was dead; then he announced his intention of going to him. *Lazarus is dead*, he said, *and I am glad.* Was this a sign of his love for his friend? Not so. Christ was glad because their sorrow over the death of Lazarus was soon to be changed into joy at his restoration to life. *I am glad for your sake*, he said. Why for their sake? Because the death and raising of Lazarus were a perfect prefiguration of the death and resurrection of the Lord himself. What the Lord was soon to achieve in himself had already been achieved in his servant. This explains why he said to them: *I am glad for your sake not to have been there, because now you will believe.* It was necessary that Lazarus should die, so that the faith of the disciples might also rise with him from the dead.

St Peter Chrysologus, *Sermon* 63: PL 52, 375–7

Fifth Sunday of Lent Year B: John 12.20–33

A READING FROM THE COMMENTARY ON NUMBERS
BY ST CYRIL OF ALEXANDRIA

As the first fruits of our renewed humanity, Christ escaped the curse of the law precisely by becoming accursed for our sake. He overcame the forces of corruption by himself becoming once more *free among the dead.* He trampled death under foot and came to life again, and then he ascended to the Father as an offering, the firstfruits, as it were, of the human race. *He ascended,* as Scripture says, *not to a sanctuary made by human hands, a mere copy of the real one, but into heaven itself, to appear in God's presence on our behalf.* He is the life-giving bread that came down from heaven, and by offering himself to God the Father as a fragrant sacrifice for our sake, he also delivers us from our sins and frees us from the faults that we commit through ignorance. We can understand this best if we think of him as symbolized by the calf that used to be slain as a holocaust and by the goat that was sacrificed for our sins committed through ignorance. For our sake, to blot out the sins of the world, he laid down his life.

Recognized then in bread as life and the giver of life, in the calf as a holocaust offered by himself to God the Father as an appeasing fragrance, in the goat as one who became sin for our sake and was slain for our transgressions, Christ is also symbolized in another way by a sheaf of grain, as a brief explanation will show.

The human race may be compared to spikes of wheat in a field, rising, as it were, from the earth, awaiting their full growth and development, and then in time being cut down by the reaper, which is death. The comparison is apt, since Christ himself spoke of our race in this way when he said to his holy disciples: *Do you not say, 'Four months and it will be harvest time?' Look at the fields I tell you, they are already white and ready for harvesting. The reaper is already receiving his wages and bringing in a crop for eternal life.*

Now Christ became like one of us; he sprang from the holy Virgin like a spike of wheat from the ground. Indeed, he spoke of himself as a grain of wheat when he said, *I tell you truly, if a grain of wheat falls into the ground and dies, it remains as it was, a single grain; but if it dies its yield is very great.* And so, like a sheaf of grain, the firstfruits, as it were, of the earth, he offered himself to the Father for our sake.

For we do not think of a spike of wheat, any more than we do of ourselves, in isolation. We think of it rather as part of a sheaf, which is a single bundle made up of many spikes. The spikes have to be gathered into a bundle before they can be used, and this is the key to the mystery they represent, the mystery of Christ who, though one, appears in the image of a sheaf to be made up of many, as in fact he is. Spiritually, he contained in himself all believers. *As we have been raised up with him*, writes St Paul, *so we have also been enthroned with him in heaven.* He is a human being like ourselves, and this has made us one body with him, the body being the bond that unites us. We can say, therefore, that in him we are all one, and indeed he himself says to God, his heavenly Father: *It is my desire that as I and you are one, so they also may be one in us.*

St Cyril of Alexandria, *Commentary on Numbers*, 2: PG 69, 617–24

Fifth Sunday of Lent Year C (RL): John 8.1–11
A READING FROM THE LETTERS OF ST AMBROSE

The scribes and Pharisees brought in a woman who had been caught committing adultery. This they did to harm our Lord, since if he were to forgive her he would appear to be abrogating the law. On the other hand, if he were to condemn her he would alter the very purpose of his coming, which was to judge no one, but to take away the sins of the whole world.

They made her stand there before him and said: *Master, we caught this woman in the very act of committing adultery, and in the law of Moses it is written that every adulteress is to be stoned. Give us your opinion.*

While they were saying this, Jesus bent down and began to write on the ground with his finger. When they waited to hear his answer he looked up and said: *If there is any among you who has not sinned, let him be the first to throw a stone at her.* What could be more authentically divine than this verdict? Let him who is sinless punish her for her sin? Is it tolerable that a man should punish another person's sins and himself be allowed to sin with impunity? To condemn someone else for the very sins he has himself committed can only be to pronounce his own condemnation.

Jesus said these words and then continued to write on the ground. If you wish to know what he wrote, surely it was: *Why do you point out the splinter in your brother's eye and never notice the beam in your own?* He wrote on the ground with the finger that had traced the characters of the law. The names of sinners are written in the dust; those of saints are inscribed in heaven. We learn this from Christ's words to his disciples: *Rejoice that your names are written in heaven.*

When they heard what he said they went out one by one, beginning with the eldest, and, sitting down, they began to examine their consciences.

Jesus was left alone with the woman, who remained standing there. The Evangelist does well to remark that they went out, since they had no desire to be with Christ. The letter of the law remains outside; the mystery is found within. In their interpretation of holy Scripture they were looking only for the leaves on the tree, not for the fruit; they were living under the shadow of the law, unable to see the Sun of Justice.

At last they had all gone out, and Jesus found himself alone with the woman. He whose mission is to forgive sins is left alone; as he himself said: *The time will come – in fact it has come already – when you will be scattered, each one going his own way, and leaving me by myself.* Indeed, *it was neither messenger nor angel, but the Lord himself who saved his people.* He stays there by himself; the power to forgive sins belongs to Christ and cannot be shared with any man. It is the work of Christ who alone has taken away the sins of the world. The woman, moreover, deserved to be pardoned, because when the Jews went out she was the only one to stay behind with Jesus.

Jesus looked up and said: *Where are those who were accusing you? Has no one thrown a stone at you? No one, sir, she replied. Neither do I condemn you, said Jesus. Go, and sin no more.* See what a mystery this is, and see the goodness of Christ! While the woman is being accused, Christ bends down; when her accusers go out he looks up. If you want to know the meaning of the words, *Go, and sin no more,* let me tell you. Christ has set you free. Let grace now set right in you what punishment has been unable to correct.

St Ambrose, *Letter* 26, 11–20: PL 16, 1044–46

Fifth Sunday of Lent Year C (RCL): John 12.1–8

A READING FROM THE *TRACTATES ON JOHN* BY ST AUGUSTINE

Mary anointed the feet of Jesus; such was the deed, let us look into the mystery it signified. Anoint the feet of Jesus: follow the Lord's footsteps by a good life. Wipe them with your hair (the abundance of your possessions), give to the poor, and you have wiped the feet of the Lord. Perhaps on this earth the Lord's feet are still in need. For of whom but his members is he to say in the end, *Inasmuch as you did it to one of the least of mine, you did it unto me?* But what follows? We can certainly understand *the poor are always with you*; when were the poor wanting in the Church? But what does he mean by *you will not always have me?*

Don't be alarmed, it was addressed to Judas. Why, then, did he speak in the plural not the singular? Because Judas is not here a single unit. One wicked man represents the whole body of the wicked; in the same way as Peter represents the whole body of the good in Church. If in Peter's case there were no sacramental symbol of the Church, the Lord would not have said to him, *I will give unto you the keys of the kingdom of heaven.* If this was said to Peter alone, it means nothing to the Church; but when the Church excommunicates, the excommunicated person is bound in heaven. Peter, in receiving the keys, represented the holy Church; in Judas was represented the bad in the Church, and it was to these it was said, *you will not always have me.* If you are good and belong to the body represented by Peter, you have Christ both now and hereafter. Now by faith, by sign, by the sacrament of baptism, by the bread and wine of the altar; and you will always have him, for when you have departed, you will come to him who said to the robber, *Today shall you be with me in paradise.* But if you live wickedly, you may seem to have Christ now, because you enter the Church, sign yourself with the sign of Christ, are baptized with his baptism, mingle with the members of Christ, and approach his altar: now you have Christ, but by living wickedly you will not have him always.

It may be also understood in this way: that he was speaking of his bodily presence. For in respect of his majesty, providence and grace, his own words are fulfilled, *Behold, I am with you always, even to the end of the world.* But in respect of the flesh he assumed as the Word, as the son of the Virgin, of that in which he was seized by the Jews, nailed to the tree, taken down from the cross, enveloped in a shroud, laid in the sepulchre, and manifested in his resurrection, *you will not have him always.* And why? Because in respect of his bodily presence he spent forty days with his disciples, and then, having taken them along for the purpose of beholding and not of following him, he ascended into heaven and is no longer here. He is there, sitting at the right hand of the Father; and he is here also, having never withdrawn the presence of his glory. In other words, in respect of his divine presence we always have Christ; in respect of his presence in the flesh it was rightly said to the disciples, *you will not always have me.* In this respect the Church enjoyed his presence only for a few days: now it possesses him by faith, without seeing him with the eyes. Whatever he meant when he said this, it can no longer, I suppose, after this twofold solution, remain as a subject of doubt.

St Augustine, *Tractates on John,* 50.6, 12, 13

Palm Sunday (Passion Sunday) Year A: Matthew 21.1–11

A READING FROM A HOMILY BY ST GREGORY PALAMAS

Because of all he had done, the simple people believed in the Lord not only with a silent faith, but with a faith that proclaimed his divinity both by word and by deed. After raising Lazarus, who had been dead four days, the Lord found the young donkey his disciples had brought for him, as the Evangelist Matthew relates. Seated on it he entered Jerusalem, in fulfilment of the prophecy of Zechariah: *Fear not, daughter of Zion; behold your king comes to you, the just one, the saviour. He is gentle, and rides on a beast of burden, on the colt of a donkey.*

By these words the Prophet shows that Christ was the king he was foretelling, the only true king of Zion. He is saying: 'Your king will not frighten those who look upon him; he is not an overbearing kind of person, or an evildoer. He does not come with a bodyguard, an armed escort, at the head of hosts of cavalry and foot soldiers. Nor does he live by extortion, demanding taxes and the payment of tribute and ignoble services, hurtful to those who perform them. No, he is recognized by his lowliness, poverty, and frugality, for he enters the city riding on a donkey, and with no crowd of attendants. Therefore, this king alone is just, and in justice he saves. He is also meek, meekness is his own special characteristic. In fact, the Lord's own words regarding himself were: *Learn from me, for I am meek and lowly in heart.*'

He who raised Lazarus from the dead enters Jerusalem today as king, seated on a donkey. Almost at once all the people, children and grown-ups, young and old alike, spread their garments on the road; and taking palm branches, symbols of victory, they went to meet him as the giver of life and conqueror of death. They worshipped him, and formed an escort. Within the temple precincts as well as without they sang with one voice, *Hosanna to the Son of David! Hosanna In the highest!* This *hosanna* is a hymn of praise addressed to God. It means, 'Lord, save us.' The other words, *in the highest*, show that God is praised not only on earth by human beings, but also on high by the angels of heaven.

St Gregory Palamas, *Homily* 15: PG 151, 184–5

Palm Sunday (Passion Sunday) Year B: Mark 11.1–10 [or John 12.12–16]

A READING FROM A SERMON BY BLESSED GUERRIC OF IGNY

When Jesus entered Jerusalem like a triumphant conqueror, many were astonished at the majesty of his bearing; but when a short while afterward he entered upon his passion, his appearance was ignoble, an object of derision. If today's procession and passion are considered together, in the one Jesus appears as sublime and glorious, in the other as lowly and suffering. The procession makes us think of the honour reserved for a king, whereas the passion shows us the punishment due to a thief.

In the one Jesus is surrounded by glory and honour, in the other *he has neither dignity nor beauty*. In the one he is the joy of men and women and the glory of the people, in the other *the butt of men and a laughingstock of the people*. In the one he receives that acclamation: *Hosanna to the Son of David! Blessed is he who comes as the king of Israel*; in the other there were shouts that he is guilty of death and he is reviled for having set himself up as king of Israel.

In the procession the people meet Jesus with palm branches, in the passion men slap him in the face and strike his head with a rod. In the one they extol him with praises, in the other they heap insults upon him. In the one the people compete to lay their clothes in his path, in the other he is stripped of his own clothes. In the one he is welcomed to Jerusalem as a just king and saviour, in the other he is thrown out of the city as a criminal, condemned as an impostor. In the one he is mounted on an ass and accorded every mark of honour; in the other he hangs on the wood of the cross, torn by whips, pierced with wounds, and abandoned by his own. If, then, we want to follow our leader without stumbling through prosperity and through adversity, let us keep our eyes upon him, honoured in the procession, undergoing ignominy and suffering in the passion, yet unshakeably steadfast in all such changes of fortune.

Lord Jesus, you are the joy and salvation of the whole world; whether we see you seated on an ass or hanging on the cross, let each one of us bless and praise you, so that when we see you reigning on high we may praise you for ever and ever, for to you belong praise and honour throughout all ages. Amen.

Bd Guerric of Igny, *Sermon 3 on Palm Sunday*, 2, 3:
SC 202, 190–3, 198–201

Palm Sunday (Passion Sunday) Year C: Luke 19.28–40

A READING FROM THE COMMENTARY ON ISAIAH BY ST CYRIL OF ALEXANDRIA

Behold, a righteous king will reign, and princes will rule with justice. The only-begotten Word of God, together with God the Father, has always been king of the universe, and to him all creatures, visible and invisible, are subject. People on earth, having been caught in the snares of sin, were persuaded by the devil to reject his sovereignty and to despise his royal power, but the judge and dispenser of all justice brought them back under his own dominion.

All his ways are straight, says Scripture, and by the ways of Christ we mean the divine precepts laid down in the gospel. By observing them we make progress in every virtue, do honour to ourselves by the moral beauty of our lives, and attain the heavenly reward to which we have been called. These are straight, not winding ways; they are direct and easily followed. As it is written, *The way of the upright is straight; the road of the just is made smooth.* Its many decrees make the law a rugged way and its difficulty intolerable, but the way of gospel commands is smooth, without any roughness or steep ascents.

The ways of Christ are straight, then, and as for the holy city, which is the Church, he himself was its builder and he makes it his own dwelling. In other words, he makes the saints his dwelling; sharing as we do in the Holy Spirit, we have Christ within us and have become temples of the living God. Christ is both a founder of the Church and its foundation, and upon this foundation we, like precious stones, are built into a holy temple to become, through the Spirit, a dwelling place for God.

Since it has in Christ such a firm foundation, the Church can never be shaken. Scripture says, *I am laying the foundation stone of Zion, the cornerstone, chosen and precious. No one who believes in him will ever be put to shame.* When he founded the Church, Christ delivered his people from bondage. He saved us from the power of Satan and of sin, freed us and subjected us to his own rule, but not by paying a ransom or by bribes. As one of his disciples wrote, We have been freed from the futile ways handed down to us by our ancestors, not by anything perishable like silver and gold, but by the precious blood *of Christ, like that of a lamb without mark or blemish.* He gave his own blood for us, so that we no longer belong to ourselves, but to him who bought us and saved us. Those therefore who turn aside from the noble rule of the true faith are justly accused by all the saints of denying the Lord who redeemed them.

St Cyril of Alexandria, *Commentary on Isaiah*, 4.2: PG 70, 967–70

Good Friday Year A: Matthew 27.1–2, 11–56
A READING FROM THE COMMENTARY ON JOHN BY ST CYRIL OF ALEXANDRIA

They took Jesus in charge and carrying his own cross he went out of the city to what was called the Place of the Skull, or in Hebrew, Golgotha. There they crucified him.

They led away the author of life to die – to die for our sake. In a way beyond our understanding, the power of God brought from Christ's passion an end far different from that intended by his enemies. His sufferings served as a snare for death and rendered it powerless. The Lord's death proved to be our restoration to immortality and newness of life.

Condemned to death though innocent, he went forth bearing on his shoulders the cross upon which he was to suffer. He did this for our sake, taking on himself the punishment which the Law justly imposed upon sinners. *He was accursed for our sake according to the saying all Scripture: 'A curse is on everyone who is hanged on a tree.'* We who have all committed many sins were under the ancient curse for our refusal to obey the law of God. To set us free he who was without sin took that curse upon himself. Since he is God who is above all, his sufferings sufficed for all, his death in the flesh was the redemption of all.

And so Christ carried the cross, a cross that was rightfully not his but ours, who were under the condemnation of the Law. As he was numbered among the dead not on his own account but on ours, to destroy the power of death and to become for us the source of eternal life, so he accepted the cross we deserved. He passed the Law's sentence on himself *to seal the lips of lawlessness forever*, as the psalm says, by being condemned sinless as he was for the sins of all.

Christ's example of courage in God's service will be of great profit to us, for only by putting the love of God before our earthly life and being prepared when occasion demands to fight zealously for the truth can we attain the supreme blessing of perfect union with God. Indeed, our Lord Jesus Christ has warned us that anyone who does not take up his cross and follow him is not worthy of him. And I think taking up the cross means simply renouncing the world for God's sake and, if this is required of us, putting the hope of future blessings before the life we now live in the body. Our Lord Jesus Christ was not ashamed to carry the cross we deserved, and he did so because he loved us.

Those united to Christ are also crucified with him by dying to their former way of life and entering upon a new way of life based on the teaching of the gospel. Paul spoke for all when he said, *I have been crucified with Christ and the life I live now is not my life, but the life that Christ lives in me.*

St Cyril of Alexandria, *Commentary on John*, 12.19: PG 74, 650–4

Good Friday Year B: Mark 15.1–41

A READING FROM THE *TRACTATES ON JOHN* BY ST AUGUSTINE

Jesus' hour had not yet come – not the hour he would be forced to die, but the hour when he would choose to be put to death. He knew the appointed hour for him to die; he had pondered all the prophecies concerning himself and was waiting until everything had taken place that the prophets state would occur before his passion began. When all was accomplished the passion would then follow, in the due ordering of events and not at the compulsion of fate.

Listen to these prophecies, and see if they are true. Among the other things that were foretold of Christ it is written, *They mingled gall with my food, and in my thirst they gave me vinegar to drink.* How this came about we know from the gospel. First they gave Jesus gall; he took it, tasted it and rejected it. Then, to fulfil the Scriptures as he hung on the cross, he said, *I am thirsty.* They took a sponge soaked in vinegar, tied it to a reed, and lifted it up to him where he hung. When he had taken it he said: *It is finished.* What did he mean by that? It is as though he said, 'All the prophecies foretelling what would happen before my passion have been fulfilled. What then is left for me to do?' So, after saying, *It is finished*, he bowed his head and yielded up his spirit.

Did the thieves crucified beside him choose when to die? They were imprisoned in the flesh with no power over its limitations. But it was when he himself chose to do so that the Lord took flesh in a virgin's womb. He chose the moment of this coming among us and the duration of his life on earth. He also chose the hour when he would depart this earthly life. It was in his power to do all this; he was under no compulsion. So when waiting for the hour of his choice, not the hour decreed by fate, he had said: *I have power to lay down my life, and I have power to take it up again. No one can take it from me; I lay it down by my own accord, and I will take it up again.* He showed that same power when the Jewish authorities came in search of him. *Who are you looking for?* he asked them. *Jesus of Nazareth*, they answered, and he in turn replied: *I am he. By these words they recoiled and fell to the ground.*

Someone is sure to ask: 'If he had such power, why did he not demonstrate it when his enemies were taunting him and saying: *if he is the Son of God, let him come down from the cross?*' He was showing us how to endure; that was why he deferred the exercise of his power. If he were to come down because he was stung by their words, they would think he had succumbed to their mockery. He chose not to come down. He chose to stay where he was, refusing to die until the moment of his choice.

If Jesus had the power to rise from the tomb, could he have found it so very difficult to come down from the cross? We, then, for whom all these things were done, should understand that the power of our Lord Jesus Christ, which was then hidden, will be revealed at the Last Judgement. *Our God will come openly*, we are told. *He will no longer keep silence.* What does this mean? It means that previously when he was being judged he had been silent, in order to fulfil the prophecy: *He was led away like a sheep to be sacrificed; and like a lamb, dumb before the shearer, he did not open his mouth.*

Thus, unless he had been willing he would not have suffered, his blood would not have been shed; and if that blood had not been shed, the world would not have been redeemed. So let us pour out our thanks to him, before the power of his divinity and for the compassion of his suffering humanity.

St Augustine, *Tractates on John*, 37.9–10: CCSL 36, 336–8

Good Friday Year C: Luke 23.1–49

A READING FROM THE COMMENTARY ON JOHN BY ST CYRIL OF ALEXANDRIA

When Jesus had taken the vinegar he said: 'It is finished', and bowing his head, he gave up his spirit. The time had come for him to preach to the spirits in the underworld and by visiting them to establish his lordship over the dead as well as over the living. To despoil the underworld and make possible our return to life he endured in his flesh the lot of every human being. Although in his divine nature he was life itself he died, becoming as Scripture says: *the firstfruits of all who have fallen asleep and the firstborn from the dead.*

The Evangelist said *He bowed his head*, because this is what the dying do when the spirit or soul, which controls the body, departs. As for the expression, *He gave up his spirit*, that was only a way of saying that he died, but it seems very likely that there was a special reason why the holy Evangelist did not say simply that he died, but rather, that he gave up his spirit. He meant that he gave it into the hands of God the Father, because this was what Jesus himself had said: *Father, into your hands I commend my spirit.*

Our own hope is founded upon these words, for thanks to the goodness and mercy of God we surely have every reason to be confident that, when they leave their earthly bodies, the souls of the saints are surrendered into the hands of a most loving Father. They do not haunt their tombs awaiting for libations as some unbelievers imagine; nor are they, like the souls of sinners, thrust down into hell to suffer eternal punishment. Instead, they pass swiftly into the hands of the Father of all, along the way opened up for us by Christ our Saviour. He surrendered his soul into the hands of his Father to give us a firm faith and a sure hope that in him and through him we too shall pass when we die into the hands of God and to a life that infinitely transcends our life in the flesh. This is why St Paul tells us that it is better *to depart and to be with Christ.*

St Cyril of Alexandria, *Commentary on John*, 12: PG 74, 667–70

Holy Saturday Year A: Matthew 27.57–66

A READING FROM THE COMMENTARY ON JOHN BY ST CYRIL OF ALEXANDRIA

They took the body of Jesus and wrapped it in linen cloths with the spices, according to the Jewish burial custom. At the place where he had been crucified there was a garden, and in this garden a new tomb in which no one had yet been buried.

Christ was numbered among the dead. For our sake he was put to death in the body, even though of himself and through his Father we believe him to be, and indeed he is, life itself. In order to do all that was required by

God, all that was involved in his having become man, he freely submitted the temple of his body not only to death, but to everything that accompanies it, to the laying out of his body and its burial in a tomb.

The Evangelist says that his tomb was in a garden and that it was new. This teaches us in a symbolic way that it is through Christ's death that we gain entry into paradise: he entered as the forerunner on our behalf. The newness of the tomb suggests the new and untrodden path from death to life and the renewal by which Christ frees us from corruption. By Christ's death, our death has been transformed into something quite new, more like a kind of sleep. We are *alive to God now*, as Scripture says, and destined to live for ever. This is why St Paul frequently refers to those who have died in Christ as 'those who have fallen asleep'.

In the past the power of death had always prevailed against our nature. *From the time of Adam to the time of Moses, death ruled over all, even over those who did not sin, as Adam did, by disobeying God's command. We bore the image of the earthly man*, Adam, and underwent the death inflicted by the divine curse, but when the second Adam who is divine and from heaven appeared among us, he fought for the lives of us all, purchased them by his own death in the flesh and then, having destroyed the power of corruption, he rose again. In this way he transformed us into his own image, so that the death we now undergo is of a new kind: it does not lead to eternal destruction, but is rather a sleep, full of good hope. In fact, it resembles the death of Christ, who opened up for us this new pathway to life.

St Cyril of Alexandria, *Commentary on John*, 12.19: PG 74, 679–82

Holy Saturday Year B: Mark 15.42–47

A READING FROM THE COMMENTARY ON THE LETTER TO THE ROMANS BY ORIGEN

Christ has presented each Christian with the death of sin itself, a gift of faith, as it were, deriving from his own death. Sin can have no more freedom of action in people who believe themselves to be dead, crucified, and buried with Christ, than in those who have suffered bodily death. They are therefore said to be dead to sin. This is why the Apostle says, *If we have died with him, we believe we shall also live with him*. It is important to note the difference of expression: St Paul does not say 'we have lived' as he says 'we have died', but 'we shall live'. This is his way of showing that death is at work in the present world, but not in the life to come, *when Christ is revealed. He is our life, hidden away in God.* For the time being, therefore, as Paul himself teaches, *death is at work in us.*

But it seems to me that this death that is at work in us has certain decisive moments. As with Christ there was the moment when Scripture says that *he cried out with a loud voice and gave up his spirit;* then there was the time when he was laid in the grave and its entrance was sealed up; and there was the morning when the women looked for him in the tomb and did not find him because he had already risen, though his actual resurrection was visible to none; so also in each of us who believe in Christ, there must be this threefold pattern of death.

First of all, Christ's death must be manifested in us by a verbal acknowledgement of our faith in him, since *the faith that leads to righteousness is in the heart, and the confession that leads to salvation is on the lips.* In the second place, we must show it by putting to death those passions which belong to earth, as we carry Christ's death about with us wherever we go; this is what is meant by *death is at work in us.* Thirdly, we have to proclaim Christ's death by showing that we ourselves have already risen from the dead and are walking in newness of life. To sum up briefly and clearly: the first day of death is when we renounce the world; the second, when we renounce the sins of the flesh; the third, the day of resurrection, when we are fully perfected in the light of wisdom. In each believer, however, these different stages and his degree of progress can be discerned and known only by God, to whom alone are revealed the secrets of our hearts.

Christ chose to empty himself and take the form of a slave. He submitted to a despot's rule, and became obedient even to death. By that death he destroyed the lord of death, that is the devil, and set free all those whom death held captive. He tied up the Strong One, conquering him on the cross, and broke into his house in the underworld, the stronghold of death. He then plundered his goods; in other words, he carried off the souls whom the devil held in bondage. This is the meaning of Christ's own parable in the gospel, *How can anyone break into a strong man's house and plunder his goods unless he begins by tying the strong man up?* First of all, then, he bound him on the cross and so entered his house, that is the underworld. *From there he ascended on high, leading a host of captives,* namely those who rose with him from the dead and entered the holy city, the heavenly Jerusalem. Because of this, St Paul rightly declares that *death no longer has any power to touch him.*

Origen, *Commentary on Romans,* 5.10: PG 14, 1048–52

Holy Saturday Year C: Luke 23.50–56

A READING FROM A HOMILY ATTRIBUTED TO ST AUGUSTINE

Today, my dearest friends, there is every reason for heaven to rejoice and earth to be glad. It is a day on which more light shines forth from the tomb than rays from the sun. When our Lord and Saviour was born as man he brought light into the world; so also today, being dead in the body, he has illumined the underworld with the powerful presence of his divinity as well as of his human soul. Today at the Lord's visitation there is leaping and dancing in the nether regions over the fulfilment of the prophecy, *The people that sat in darkness* (that is to say, the whole human race enveloped in the gloom of Sheol) *have seen a great light*. He who created Adam has this day sought him out in the underworld, and by his own power has set him free.

Wonderful beyond words is the loving kindness of our God! Death had indeed invaded Paradise, but life has now conquered the abyss, and by assuming our mortality the Son of God has trodden underfoot the law that all must die. Thus he has made good the prophet's assertion: *O death, I will be your death!* Those whom you have caused to die through sin I will gather up from that place of eternal ruin, and by dying myself I will deliver them from everlasting death.

Look now at the author of our undoing! With what snares he is entangled and fettered! As he deceived us, so he is himself deceived; in the very act of killing he is destroyed.

When the Lord's body was laid in the tomb, he himself descended into the lowest and most hidden abode of the infernal regions. There, where he was presumed to be held captive, he bound death fast, and so broke the chains of all who had died. And from that place whence none had ever returned before, not even one, he carried off an immense booty with which he penetrated the heavens.

See what tremendous things God's surpassing love has accomplished for our healing and restoration! For our sake *he was led like a sheep to the slaughter*, having taken upon himself the evils of this present life in order to bestow upon us the good things of eternity.

St Augustine, *Sermons*, Mai 146: PLS 2, 1242–3

EASTERTIDE

CHRIST is risen from the dead, trampling down death by death, and on those in the tombs bestowing life!

Byzantine Paschal Troparion

THE sacred work of our salvation was of such value in the sight of the creator of the universe that he counted it worth the shedding of his own blood. After his passion weakness was turned into strength, mortality into eternal life, and disgrace into glory. At Easter the Lord's resurrection was the cause of our joy, now it is his ascension into heaven. Having made careful provision for the preaching of the Gospel and the mysteries of the new covenant, our Lord Jesus Christ was taken up to heaven before the eyes of his disciples. His bodily presence among them came to an end, and so what was visible in our Redeemer has passed into the sacraments.

St Leo the Great (abridged)

FOR this is the Passover feast, when Christ, the true Lamb of God, is slain whose blood consecrates the homes of all the faithful. This is the night when Jesus Christ vanquished hell, broke the chains of death and rose triumphant from the grave. Most blessed of all nights! Evil and hatred are put to flight and sin is washed away, lost innocence regained, and mourning turned to joy. For Christ the morning star has risen in glory; Christ is risen from the dead and his flame of love still burns within us! Christ sheds his peaceful light on all the world!

From the Exsultet, sung at the Easter Vigil, Common Worship

'Chiefly we are bound to praise you because you raised Jesus Christ glori- ously from the dead. For he is the true paschal lamb who was offered for us and has taken away the sins of the world. By his death he has destroyed death, and by his rising to life again he has restored to us everlasting life.'[6] Easter is not just one feast among many in the liturgical year, it is the Great Feast, the Feast of Feasts, as it is the day on which Christ rose from the dead, the central event of our faith: 'if Christ has not been raised, then our preaching is in vain and your faith is in vain' (1 Corinthians 15.14).

Easter is the central point of the liturgical year and maintains the link, found in the Gospels, between the death and resurrection of Christ and the Jewish feast of Passover, as St Paul wrote, 'Christ our Passover has been sacrificed, let us therefore celebrate the feast' (1 Corinthians 5.7). The mystery of the cross and resurrection of Christ is rightly called the 'paschal mystery', from the Greek (*pascha*) and Hebrew (*pesach*) names for Passover. It is the mystery of Christ's Passover through death to life, something in which believers share through baptism: 'when you were bur- ied with him in baptism, you were also raised with him through faith in the power of God, who raised him from the dead' (Colossians 2.12). It is the same paschal mystery of Christ which we celebrate in the Eucharist where, 'we recall his blessed passion and death, his glorious resurrec- tion and ascension, and we look for the coming of his kingdom' (*Scottish Liturgy 1982*).

The Gospels on the Sundays of Eastertide offer us a sustained medi- tation on the resurrection of Christ. With their emphasis on Jesus, his relationship with the Father and, at Pentecost, the sending of the Holy Spirit, the whole of Eastertide may also be seen as a meditation on the revelation of the mystery of the Holy Trinity – which is also celebrated on the Sunday after Pentecost, Trinity Sunday.

Sunday, the first day of the week and the Lord's day, was the first feast of the resurrection but at the start of the second century we find Christians celebrating the resurrection annually, either on the date of the Jewish Passover or on the following Sunday. The date was later fixed by the Council of Nicaea in 325 as the Sunday following the first full moon after the spring equinox. The original shape of Easter seems to have been a fast, which developed into Lent, and a nocturnal vigil which ended with the celebration of the Eucharist. From at least the beginning of the third century the feast was extended into a period of fifty days including seven more Sundays, a 'week of weeks' (St Hilary of Poitiers), and from the following century the fiftieth day, Pentecost, became a focus of special celebration. The fifty-day period came to conform to the chronology of

---

6 Easter short preface, *Common Worship*.

the Book of Acts with the ascension of Christ celebrated forty days after Easter (Acts 1.3), on a Thursday, and the descent of the Holy Spirit at Pentecost after fifty days (Acts 2.1). This is found, for example, in the sermons of SS John Chrysostom and Augustine. Thus, just as the paschal mystery was unpacked into the Sacred Triduum and Holy Week, so different aspects of the same mystery were celebrated at different times during the fifty days of Easter.

From the end of the second century Easter became the prime site for celebrating baptism, later joined by Pentecost, and the liturgy reflects this. In the fourth century Easter gained an octave (a period of eight days ending on the following Sunday) during which the newly baptized received more teaching on the mystery they had entered through the sacraments. Some say that Whitsun or Whit Sunday, the English name for Pentecost, is derived from the white garments worn by the newly baptized on this day. Pentecost later received its own octave but this was lost during the twentieth-century liturgical reforms in order to emphasize the importance of the celebration of the Paschal Mystery during the fifty days. The nine days between Ascension and Pentecost, however, are often celebrated as a period of prayer in preparation for the coming of the Holy Spirit. The names of the Sundays have also been changed, for example the second Sunday **after** Easter is now the third Sunday **of** Easter, to emphasize the unity of the season. The *Roman Lectionary* allows the Ascension to be celebrated on the seventh Sunday of Easter despite the fact that this breaks the chronology of the Acts of the Apostles.

Easter Day has two Masses, the Eucharist that is the culmination of the Paschal Vigil and the Eucharist of the Day, but the *Revised Common Lectionary* provides only four Gospels for these and so only three patristic readings are provided in *The Fathers on the Sunday Gospels*. The Gospel for the second Sunday of Easter is the same in all three years of the lectionary, the incredulity of St Thomas in John 20 which mentions this very day 'a week later' after the resurrection (John 20.26). Despite this, three commentaries have been provided for this Sunday. During Eastertide most Gospel readings are taken from the Gospel of John. The Gospels for the third Sunday also recount the appearances of the risen Christ and have in common a meal shared by the disciples and the risen Christ. The fourth Sunday has readings about Jesus as the Good Shepherd from John 10 with its references to the paschal mystery, 'I lay down my life in order to take it up again' (John 10.17), and the fifth, sixth, and seventh Sundays have excerpts from the discourse and prayer of Jesus at the last supper. The most important reading for the feast of the Ascension is the account of the ascension of Christ in Acts and the Gospels are taken from the end of the three synoptic Gospels which emphasize the enthronement of Jesus at God's right hand, two of which mention the ascension. Pentecost has readings from John on the sending of the Holy Spirit. The original revised *Roman Lectionary* of 1969 had John 20.19–23, when Jesus breathed the Holy Spirit on his disciples on the evening after his resurrection, for all three years (this is also the first part of the Gospel for the second Sunday of Easter) but the 1981 edition adds passages promising the Spirit from John 15 and 14 in Years B and C. The *Revised Common Lectionary* takes the three Gospels for the day but provides the promise of the Spirit in John 7.37–39 as an alternative in Year A. Patristic commentaries are provided for all of these.

The liturgical colour for Eastertide is white (sometimes gold or the best vestments that the church possesses) and for Pentecost it is red to symbolize the tongues of fire which descended on the apostles as they were filled with the Holy Spirit. The joy of the resurrection means that this is the pre-eminent season of that great shout of praise, the alleluia, as St Augustine writes:

Because there are these two periods of time – the present, beset with the trials and troubles of this life, and the other yet to come, a life of everlasting serenity and joy – we are given two liturgical seasons, one before Easter and the other after. What we commemorate before Easter is what we experience in this life; what we celebrate after Easter points to something we do not yet possess. This is why we keep the first season with fasting and prayer; but now the fast is over and we devote the present season to praise. Such is the meaning of the Alleluia we sing. Now therefore, friends, we urge you to praise God. That is what we are all telling each other when we say Alleluia. You say to your neighbour, 'Praise the Lord!' and he says the same to you. We are all urging one another to praise the Lord, and all doing what each of us urges the other to do. But see that your praise comes from your whole being; in other words, see that you praise God not with your lips and voices alone, but with your minds, your lives and all your actions.

On Psalm 148.1–2, abridged

Easter Day Years A–C, Reading I:
John 20.1–9 [1–20]; Matthew 28.1–10;
[Mark 16.1–8]; [Luke 24.1–12]

A READING FROM A HOMILY BY ST JOHN CHRYSOSTOM

How shall I recount for you these hidden realities or proclaim what surpasses every word and concept? How shall I lay open before you the mystery of the Lord's resurrection, the saving sign of his cross and of his three days' death? Each and every event that happened to our Saviour is an outward sign of the mystery of our redemption.

Just as Christ was born from his mother's inviolate virginal womb, so too he rose again from the closed tomb. As he, the only-begotten Son of God, was made the firstborn of his mother, so, by his resurrection, he became the firstborn from the dead. His birth did not break the seal of his mother's virginal integrity; nor did his rising from the dead break the seals on the sepulchre. And so, just as I cannot fully express his birth in words, neither can I wholly encompass his going forth from the tomb.

Come, see the place where he lay. Come, see the place where the outward signs of your own resurrection are portrayed, where death lies entombed. Come, see the place where the unsown seed of mortality has brought forth a rich harvest of immortality.

Go and tell my disciples, *Go and tell my brethren to go into Galilee, and there they will see me.* Tell my disciples the mysteries which you yourselves have beheld. Thus did our Lord speak to the women. And still today, to those who believe, he is present, although unseen, in the baptismal font. As friends and brethren he embraces the newly baptized; with rejoicing and gladness he fills their hearts and souls. The Lord himself washes away their stains with streams of grace and anoints those who have been reborn with the precious ointment of the Spirit. The Lord becomes not only the one who feeds them, but also their very food; to his own servants he offers the daily largesse of spiritual bread. To all the faithful he says, 'Take and eat the bread from heaven; receive from out of my side the spring of water, ever flowing and never dried up. Let those who are hungry have their fill; let those who are thirsty drink the wine that brings true fulfilment and salvation.'

O Christ our God, you alone are the good Lord and lover of all; to you, with the Father of all purity and the life-giving Spirit belong the power and the glory, now and always and for endless ages. Amen.

St John Chrysostom, *Easter Homily*, 10–11, 12: PG 88, 1859–66

Easter Day Years A–C, Reading II: John 20.1–9 [1–20]; Matthew 28.1–10; [Mark 16.1–8]; [Luke 24.1–12]

A READING FROM AN EASTER SERMON BY BLESSED GUERRIC OF IGNY

Blessed and holy are those who share in the first resurrection. Christ is the firstfruits of those who have fallen asleep and the firstborn from the dead. His Resurrection, which is the prototype of all others, has guaranteed the rising of our souls in the first resurrection and of our bodies in the second, for he offers his own risen body to our souls as Sacrament and to our bodies as exemplar. Even for our souls Christ's single Resurrection has prepared a twofold grace, through the living out of the paschal mystery in our daily lives we rise from the death of sin, and by our joyful celebration of the paschal feast today we rouse ourselves from the torpor of sleep.

I slept and I arose, Christ says. *Awake*, then, my sleeping soul, *and rise from the dead, and Christ will give you light!* As the new sun rises from below, the grace of the Resurrection already casts its radiance over the whole world, a radiance reflected in the eyes of those who have watched for him since daybreak, a dawn that ushers in the day of eternity. This is the day that knows no evening, the day whose sun will never set again. Only once has that sun gone down, and now once and for all it has ascended above the heavens, leading death captive in its train.

This is the day that the Lord has made; let us rejoice and be glad. And you also, if you watch daily at the threshold of wisdom, fixing your eyes on the doorway and, like the Magdalen, keeping vigil at the entrance to his tomb, you also will find what she found. You will know that what was written of Wisdom was written of Christ, *She hastens to make herself known to those who desire her. Anyone who rises early to seek her will have no trouble; he will find her sitting at his gates.*

While it was still dark Mary had come to watch at the tomb, and she found Jesus whom she sought standing there in the flesh. But you must know him now according to the spirit, not according to the flesh, and you can be sure of finding his spiritual presence if you seek him with a desire like hers, and if he observes your persevering prayer. Say then to the Lord Jesus, with Mary's love and longing: *My soul yearns for you in the night, my spirit within me earnestly seeks for you.* Make the Psalmist's prayer your own as you say, *O God, my God, I watch for you at morning light;*

my soul thirsts for you. Then see if you do not also find yourselves singing with them both: *In the morning fill us with your love; we shall exult and rejoice all our days*.

Bd. Guerric of Igny, *Sermon 3 on the Resurrection*, 1–2:
PL 185, 148–9

Easter Day Years A–C, Reading III: John 20.1–9 [1–20]; Matthew 28.1–10; [Mark 16.1–8]; [Luke 24.1–12]

A READING FROM A PASCHAL HOMILY ATTRIBUTED TO ST HIPPOLYTUS

Now the holy rays of the light of Christ shine forth, the pure stars of the pure Spirit rise, the heavenly treasures of glory and divinity lie open. In this splendour the long dark night has been swallowed up and the dreary shadows of death have vanished. For us who believe in him a glorious day has dawned, a long unending day, the mystical Passover symbolically celebrated by the Law and effectually accomplished by Christ, a wonderful Passover, a miracle of divine virtue, a work of divine power. This is the true festival and the everlasting memorial, the day upon which freedom from suffering comes from suffering, immortality from death, life from the tomb, healing from a wound, Resurrection from the fall, and Ascension into heaven from the descent into hell.

To show that he had power over death Christ had exercised his royal authority to loose death's bonds even during his lifetime, as for example when he gave the command, *Lazarus, come out* and *Arise, my child*. For the same reason he surrendered himself completely to death, so that in him that gluttonous beast with his insatiable appetite would die completely. Since *death's power comes from sin*, it searched everywhere in his sinless body for its accustomed food, for sensuality, pride, disobedience or, in a word, for that ancient sin which was its original sustenance. In him, however, it found nothing to feed on and so, being entirely closed in upon itself and destroyed for lack of nourishment, death became its own death.

Many of the just, proclaiming the Good News and prophesying, were awaiting him who was to become by his Resurrection *the firstborn from the dead*. And so, to save all members of the human race, whether they lived before the Law, under the Law, or after his own coming, Christ dwelt three days beneath the earth. After his Resurrection it was the women who were the first to see him, for as a woman brought the first sin into the world, so a woman first announced the news of life to the world. Thus they heard the holy words, *Women, rejoice*; for sadness was to be swallowed up by the joy of the Resurrection.

When Christ had clothed himself completely in the humanity created in God's image and transformed into *the heavenly man* the *old man* he had put on, the image united to himself ascended with him into heaven. At the sign of the great mystery of human nature now ascending with God the angelic powers cried out with joy, commanding the hosts of heaven: *Lift up your gates, you princes, be lifted up, you everlasting doors, and the king of glory shall enter.* They, seeing the unheard of wonder of human nature united to God, exclaimed in their turn: *Who is this King of glory?* and received the reply: *The Lord of hosts, he is the King of glory, the strong, the mighty, the powerful in battle.*

St Hippolytus (attr.), *Paschal Homily*: SC 27, 116–18, 184–90

Second Sunday of Easter Year A: John 20.19–31

A READING FROM THE COMMENTARY ON JOHN BY ST CYRIL OF ALEXANDRIA

By his miraculous entry through closed doors Christ proved to his disciples that by nature he was God and also that he was none other than their former companion. That by showing them his side and the marks of the nails, he convinced them beyond a doubt that he had raised the temple of his body, the very body that had hung upon the cross. He had destroyed death's power over the flesh, for as God he was life itself.

Because of the importance he attached to making his disciples believe in the resurrection of the body, and in order to prevent them from thinking that the body he now possessed was different from that in which he had suffered death upon the cross, he willed to appear to them as he had been before, even though the time had now come for his body to be clothed in a supernatural glory such as no words could possibly describe.

They have only to recall Christ's transfiguration on the mountain in the presence of his holy disciples, to realize that mortal eyes could not have endured the glory of his sacred body had he chosen to reveal it before ascending to the Father. St Matthew describes how Jesus went up the mountain with Peter, James, and John, and how he was transfigured before them. His face shone like lightning and his clothes became white as snow. But they were unable to endure the sight and fell prostrate on the ground.

And so, before allowing the glory that belonged to it by every right to transfigure the temple of his body, our Lord Jesus Christ in his wisdom appeared to his disciples in the form that they had known. He wished them to believe that he had risen from the dead in the very body that he had received from the blessed Virgin, and in which he had suffered crucifixion and death, as the Scriptures had foretold. Death's power was over the body alone, and it was from the body that it was banished. If it was not Christ's dead body that rose again, how was death conquered, how was the power of corruption destroyed? It could not have been destroyed by the death of a created spirit, of a soul, of an angel, or even of the Word of God himself. Since death held sway only over what was corruptible by nature, it was in this corruptible nature that the power of the resurrection had to show itself in order to end death's tyranny.

When Christ greeted his holy disciples with the words, *Peace be with you*, by peace he meant himself, for Christ's presence always brings tranquillity of soul. This is the grace St Paul desired for believers when he wrote: *The peace of Christ, which passes all understanding, will guard your hearts and minds*. The peace of Christ, which passes all understanding, is in fact the Spirit of Christ, who fills all those who share in him with every blessing.

St Cyril of Alexandria, *Commentary on John*, 12: PG 74, 704–5

Second Sunday of Easter Year B: John 20.19–31
A READING FROM *THE HOMILIES ON THE GOSPELS* BY ST GREGORY THE GREAT

The first question to arise in our minds when we read this passage of the gospel is: how could the Lord's body have been a real one after his resurrection, when it could pass through locked doors? We must realize, however, that there would be nothing wonderful in a work of divine power if we could explain it rationally; nor would it exercise our faith if we could prove it possible by human reasoning.

What we must do, then, when confronted by those works of our Redeemer which are incomprehensible in themselves, is to consider them in relation to his other works. In this way we shall find that miraculous occurrences gain credibility in the light of even greater marvels. For example, the body of the Lord which came into the presence of the disciples through locked doors was the same body which, at his birth, passed through the Virgin's inviolate womb, and was seen by human eyes. Need it surprise us, then, if he who rose from the dead to live for ever came forth from the unopened womb of a virgin? However, since those who beheld his visible body hesitated to believe that it was real: he showed them his hands and his side, inviting them to handle that body which had come through the locked doors into their presence.

The reason why our risen Redeemer showed his disciples, in such a wonderful way, that his body was at one and the same time incorruptible and yet capable of being touched, was that he wanted to inspire them with hope in their own resurrection and to strengthen their belief in his. He proved to them, therefore, that while his body was now imperishable, they could still touch it with their hands, to convince them beyond any doubt that after his resurrection his body was the same as their own, different only by reason of its being glorified.

Peace be with you, he said. *As the Father sent me, so I am sending you.* In other words, as I who am God was sent by the Father who is God, so I, who am also a man, send you who are men. The Father sent his Son, having decreed that he should become incarnate for the redemption of the whole human race. It was his will that he should come into the world to suffer. Nevertheless, he loved the Son whom he sent to suffer. In the same way, when the Lord chose his apostles, he did not send them into the world to enjoy its pleasures; on the contrary, he sent them to face suffering, as he himself had done. Just as the Father sent the Son whom he loved into the world to suffer, so the Lord sent the disciples whom he loved into the world to suffer. That is why he said: *As the Father sent me, so I am sending you*, meaning, I am sending you out into the midst of traps laid for you by persecutors; even so, I love you as my Father loved me, when he decreed that I should come into the world to suffer.

St Gregory the Great, *Forty Gospel Homilies*, 26.1–2: PL 76, 1197–8

Second Sunday of Easter Year C: John 20.19–31

A READING FROM A SERMON BY ST AUGUSTINE

My dear people, you, like myself, are well aware that our Lord and Saviour Jesus Christ is the one physician capable of bringing us eternal healing and salvation. We know, too, that it was in order to accomplish this that he took upon himself the weakness of our human nature, otherwise that weakness would have remained with us forever. He equipped himself with a human body liable to death, so that in and through that body he might conquer death itself. And though, as the Apostle tells us, it was his human weakness that made it possible for him to be crucified, it was his divine power that enabled him to return to life.

The same Apostle says: *He will never die again, neither will death have any further hold upon him.* All this you already know and believe, and also the consequences flowing from it; we can be sure that the miracles he wrought while he lived among us were meant to encourage us to accept gifts from him that should never pass away nor have an end. Thus he gave back sight to blind eyes that would shortly be closed again in death; he raised Lazarus from the dead only for him to die again. His bodily cures, indeed, were never meant to last forever, even though at the end of time he is to give the body itself life everlasting. But because 'seeing is believing', he used those visible wonders to build up people's faith in even greater marvels that could not be seen.

Let no one then be found to say that Christ Jesus our Lord no longer works such miracles among us, the Church was better off in its early days. On the contrary, in one recorded statement, the same Lord sets those who have never seen and yet believe before those who believe only because they see. Indeed, so great was the disciples' weakness at that time, that when they saw the Lord they found it necessary to touch him before they could believe he had really risen from the dead. They were unable to believe the testimony of their own eyes, until they had handled his body and explored his recent wounds with their fingers. Only after this was done could that most hesitant of all his disciples exclaim: *My Lord and my God!* Thus it was by his wounds that Christ, who had so often healed the manifold wounds of others, came to be recognized himself.

Now we may ask: could not the Lord have risen with a body from which all marks of wounds had been erased? No doubt he could have; but he knew his disciples bore within their hearts a wound so deep that the only way to cure it was to retain the scars of his own wounds in his body. And when that confession: *My Lord and my God!* was uttered, what was his answer to it? *You believe*, he said, *because you have seen me; blessed are those who have not seen and yet believe.*

And who, my brothers and sisters, are those if not ourselves and those who were to follow after us? When, later on, the Lord had departed from human sight and faith had had time to strike roots into people's hearts, those who believed in him made their act of faith without seeing him in whom they made it. The faith of such believers is highly meritorious, for it springs from a devoted heart rather than from an exploring hand.

St Augustine, *Sermon* 88.1–2: Edit. Maurist., 5, 469–70

Third Sunday of Easter Year A: Luke 24.13–35

A READING FROM A SERMON BY ST AUGUSTINE

We are accustomed at this season of the year to read all four gospel accounts of Christ's resurrection. We have to read them all, because no single one among them gives us a full account of the event, each one providing something that the others leave out. Indeed, it almost seems as if each had purposely kept itself incomplete so that it would be necessary to retain all four to make up a finished picture.

Mark alludes no more than briefly to an incident that Luke develops in far greater detail – the episode, namely, of those two men who, though not numbered among the twelve, were genuine disciples for all that. The Lord appeared to these two on the road and accompanied them on their journey. Mark simply chronicles the Lord's appearance to two disciples on their way into the country; but Luke reports his conversation with them, describing how he went all the way with them and how they recognized him in the breaking of the bread.

What comment, if any, must we now make upon this story? We may say at once that it greatly helps to confirm our faith in Christ's resurrection. True, we had already come to believe in it before listening to the gospel story just now; otherwise it is hardly likely we should be here in church today. And yet we like to hear this passage read to us again, if only to refresh our memories. Are we not also given new heart when we see ourselves so much better off than those to whom the Lord appeared, as they were walking down the road that day? We believe what they as yet did not believe; they had lost hope, and we have no doubts about the things that caused their uncertainty.

That Christ's death upon the cross had shattered all their hopes is clear from the tenor of the conversation into which he broke when he said to them: *What are you talking about that so clearly fills you with sadness?* To which they answered: *Are you the only stranger in Jerusalem who has not heard of the things that have been happening in the city?* So he said, *What things?* Although he knew everything already, he asked this question about himself, because he wished to enter into their hearts and minds. They told him: *The things they did to Jesus of Nazareth, a man who had proved himself a prophet outstanding in word and deed. But the chief priests had him crucified, and that was three days ago. We had been hoping* ... Oh, you had been hoping? And now you are not hoping any more? Is that all you have gained from his teaching up to now? Why, even the robber on the cross could acquit himself better than that! While you had forgotten both your teacher and his lesson, that poor ignorant thief was able to recognize him as he hung beside him. We had been hoping ... And what had you been hoping for? *That he would be the one to redeem Israel.* You lost this hope when Jesus was crucified, but the robber knew his Redeemer when he was crucified with him, and said to him, *Lord, remember me when you come into your kingdom.* Yes, it was indeed he who was to redeem Israel. The cross became the rostrum from which the master taught the robber; the gibbet upon which he hung became his magisterial chair. Now, in giving himself back to you, he has restored to you your hope.

Do not forget, my friends, that it was in the breaking of the bread that the Lord Jesus wished to be recognized by those who till then had been kept from seeing who he was. Believers will know what I mean. They know Christ in the breaking of the bread, not any kind of bread, but the bread which has been blessed by Christ and has now become his body.

St Augustine, *Sermon* 234.1–2: Edit. Maurist., 5, 987–8

Third Sunday of Easter Year B: Luke 24.35–48

A READING FROM A HOMILY BY ST JOHN CHRYSOSTOM

Christ rose from the dead and showed himself to his disciples. But even among these there was one who refused to believe it. This was Thomas, called the twin. He wanted to put his finger into the marks of the nails and even to probe Christ's wounded side. Here was a disciple who had spent three years with the Lord, sharing his daily life and breaking bread with him. He had seen great signs and wonders, and heard the Lord speaking, but when he saw him risen from the dead he would not believe until he had seen the marks of the nails and the wound caused by the lance. Was it likely then that the rest of the world would believe if it saw Christ raised from the dead? Indeed not; and elsewhere we shall find that miracles were more persuasive than the appearance of the risen Lord in person.

For example, after the crowds heard Peter say to the cripple: *In the name of Jesus Christ, stand up and walk*, the number of believers rose from three to five thousand. Yet that disciple who had seen the Lord risen from the dead refused to believe it. How much easier this miracle made it to believe in the resurrection! His own disciple would not believe it when he saw his risen master, but even the Lord's enemies became believers when they saw the healing of the cripple. Because this was more striking and more obvious than the Lord's appearance to his disciples, so much the greater was its power to persuade those who witnessed it to believe in the resurrection of Jesus.

I have singled out Thomas, but we know from the gospel that the rest of the disciples were equally disbelieving when they first saw the risen Lord. Nevertheless, my friends, do not pass judgement on them: if Christ did not condemn them, neither should we. It was a strange and marvellous thing that the disciples should see the firstborn himself risen from the dead. But great wonders of such a kind naturally cause terror at first sight, until they have had time to become established in the minds of believers. So it was, now, with the disciples. When Christ rose from the dead and said to them: *Peace be with you*, the gospel tells us: *they were terrified with amazement and thought they were seeing a ghost. Then Jesus said to them: 'Why are you so frightened?' After this he showed them his hands and feet, and while they still could not believe for joy and wonder, he asked them: 'Have you anything to eat?'* This was the way in which he wanted to bring home to them the reality of his resurrection. They had seen his side and his wounds and were not convinced. Then surely the sight of him sharing their meal should persuade them of the truth.

St John Chrysostom, *Homily 4 on the beginning of Acts*, 6:
PG 51, 106–7

Third Sunday of Easter Year C: John 21.1–19 or 21.1–14

A READING FROM A SERMON BY ST AUGUSTINE

When you hear the Lord saying to Peter: *Do you love me?* see in this an image of yourself. For here Peter stands for the whole Church of which he is the symbol. When the Lord questioned Peter he was really questioning us, questioning the Church itself. To understand how Peter stood for the whole Church, you have only to recall that gospel passage which says: *You are Peter, and on this rock I will build my Church, and the gates of hell will be powerless against it. To you I will give the keys of the kingdom of heaven.* Only one man is to receive the keys. But the Lord was careful to explain the function of those heavenly keys. He said: *Whatever you bind on earth shall be bound in heaven, and whatever you loose on earth shall be loosed in heaven.* And indeed if this promise had been made exclusively to Peter, he alone would have been empowered to implement it, and after he was dead and gone, no one would have had the power to bind and loose. But I would go so far as to claim that we also have the power of those keys today. What do I mean by this? That we bind and loose? We do indeed; but so do you: you also bind and loose. Anyone who is bound is excluded from your community, and when someone is thus excommunicated is it not you that bind him? Likewise, when such a person is reconciled, it is you that loose him, because you pray to God on his behalf.

We all love Christ and are his members. When he had entrusted his beloved sheep to their respective shepherds, he reduces the total number of shepherds to one in the person of the one chief Pastor, all the many pastors being incorporated into his body. Now Peter was undoubtedly a pastor in the fullest sense. But Paul too was a pastor: this is certain. John, James, Andrew, and the other apostles were pastors, together with all holy bishops. How can this be in keeping with the words of the gospel: *There will be one flock and one shepherd*? If that saying is to be realized and there is indeed to be a single flock and a single shepherd, then all the many pastors must somehow be incorporated into the body of the one shepherd of them all. And you also will be there as members of that body.

It was the members of that body whom Saul – the persecutor, later to be Paul the preacher – was trampling underfoot, breathing out threats, delaying to believe himself, and that campaign of his was brought to an end by one short sentence spoken by the Lord: *Saul, Saul, why are you persecuting me?* We may well ask what harm Saul could do to one who had already taken his seat in heaven, how his language could hurt him, what difference his rantings here on earth could make to Christ in heaven. Whatever Saul could hope to do was powerless to affect him. And yet the incarnate truth could say: *You are persecuting me.* Thus in saying, *You are persecuting me*, he made it clear that we are members of his body.

So let our love for Christ, whom we love in you and whom you love in us, guide us through all the temptations, labours, struggles, weariness, and trials of this present time to that place where there will be no more sighs or groans, labour, or vexation, where there will be neither birth nor death, where the frowns of the mighty are no longer to be feared, but each of us is forever rapt in contemplation of the face of almighty God.

St Augustine, *Sermons, Guelferbytanus* 16.2–3: PLS 2, 580–1

Fourth Sunday of Easter Year A: John 10.1–10

A READING FROM *THE TEACHER* BY ST CLEMENT OF ALEXANDRIA

In our sickness we need a saviour, in our wanderings a guide, in our blindness someone to show us the light, in our thirst the fountain of living water which quenches forever the thirst of those who drink from it. We dead people need life, we sheep need a shepherd, we children need a teacher, the whole world needs Jesus!

If we would understand the profound wisdom of the most holy shepherd and teacher, the ruler of the universe and the Word of the Father, when using an allegory he calls himself the shepherd of the sheep, we can do so for he is also the teacher of little ones.

Speaking at some length through Ezekiel to the Jewish elders, he gives them a salutary example of true solicitude. *I will bind up the injured*, he says; *I will heal the sick; I will bring back the strays and pasture them on my holy mountain.* These are the promises of the Good Shepherd.

Pasture us like sheep, Lord. Fill us with your own food, the food of righteousness. As our guide we pray you to lead us to your holy mountain, the Church on high, touching the heavens.

I will be their shepherd, he says, *and I will be close to them*, like their own clothing. He desires to save my flesh by clothing it in the robe of immortality and he has anointed my body. *They shall call on me*, he says, *and I will answer, 'Here I am.'* Lord, you have heard me more quickly than I ever hoped! *And if they pass over they shall not fall says the Lord,* meaning that we who are passing over into immortality shall not fall into corruption, for he will preserve us. He has said he would and to do so is his own wish. Such is our Teacher, both good and just. He said he had not come to be served but to serve, and so the gospel shows him tired out, he who laboured for our sake and promised *to give his life as a ransom for many*, a thing which, as he said, only the Good Shepherd will do.

How bountiful the giver who for our sake gives his most precious possession, his own life! He is a real benefactor and friend, who desired to be our brother when he might have been our Lord, and who in his goodness even went so far as to die for us!

St Clement of Alexandria, *Paedagogus*, 9.83.3 – 85.a: SC 70, 258–61

Fourth Sunday of Easter Year B: John 10.11–18

A READING FROM A SERMON BY ST PETER CHRYSOLOGUS

By saying to us today: *I am the Good Shepherd, who lays down his life for his sheep*, Christ has indicated that his return to the earth will be the welcome return of a shepherd to his flock. It is because he is about to lay down his life that the master seeks for companions to assist him in his care of the entire world. In this search he makes use of the psalmist's words: *Let all the earth cry out with joy to God*. That is why, when the time draws near for him to ascend to heaven, he entrusts his sheep to Peter to feed in his stead, saying: *Peter, do you love me? Then feed my sheep*. And so as not to overdrive the tender little ones with relentless force on his return, but rather to carry them forward with loving care, he repeats his question once more and says: *Peter, do you love me? Feed my lambs*. In this way he entrusts his sheep to Peter together with their young, for as Chief Shepherd he knows how prolific his future flock will be. *Peter*, he says for the third time, *do you love me? Be a shepherd to my flock*.

Paul, the shepherd Peter's colleague, in his solicitude for the well-being of these lambs, offers them milk to drink in preference to solid food. The holy king David is also thinking of the Divine Shepherd's care for the weaklings of his flock when he sings: *The Lord is my shepherd, there is nothing I shall want; in places of green pasture he has set me down, and he has led me to refreshing waters*.

The next verse of our psalm announces the coming joy of gospel peace to those who are at last emerging from captivity after the miseries of endless wars and this whole wretched life of bloodshed. The human race had formerly been the slave of sin, the prisoner of death, the vassal of iniquity. When indeed did men and women not repine under sin's dominion, when did they not groan beneath the yoke of death or despair of escaping from the toils of wickedness? So long as they remained in bondage to such cruel masters, their misery was extreme. But seeing how we have at last been freed from these tyrants and restored to the service of our Creator, to friendship with our Father, and to willing allegiance to the one good Lord, the prophet rightly exclaims: *Serve the Lord with gladness, enter into his presence with joy*; for those whom guilt had cast out and an accusing conscience driven forth have now been brought once more into the Lord's presence by grace and the renewal of their innocence.

We are his people and the sheep of his pasture. In many passages we are told of the joy with which the Shepherd will come from heaven to recall his wandering sheep to life-giving pastures – sheep who have grown weak and sick through feeding on noxious weeds. *Enter his gates*, says the psalmist, *giving thanks.* Praise is the only way to enter the gates of faith. *Let us enter his courts to the accompaniment of song, declaring his greatness, praising and blessing his holy name.* It is through that name that we are saved, it is at the sound of that name that all in heaven and on earth and beneath the earth shall bend the knee, and every creature confess his love for the Lord his God.

The Lord is gracious; his mercy endures for ever. Truly his mercy entitles him to be called gracious, since it is because of his compassion alone that he has cancelled the bitter sentence passed upon the whole world. *Behold the Lamb of God, who takes away the sins of the world.*

St Peter Chrysologus, *Sermon* 6: PL 52, 202–4

Fourth Sunday of Easter Year C: John 10.27–30 [22–30]

A READING FROM THE COMMENTARY ON JOHN BY ST CYRIL OF ALEXANDRIA

The mark of Christ's sheep is their willingness to hear and obey, just as the sign of those who are not his is their disobedience. We take the word 'hear' to imply obedience to what has been said. People who hear God are known by him. No one is entirely unknown by God, but to be known in this way is to become his kin. Thus, when Christ says, *I know mine,* he means, 'I will receive them, and give them permanent mystical kinship with myself.'

It might be said that inasmuch as he has become man, he has made all human beings his kin, since all are members of the same race; we are all united to Christ in a mystical relationship because of his incarnation. Yet those who do not preserve the likeness of his holiness are alienated from him. *My sheep follow me*, says Christ. By a certain God-given grace, believers follow in the footsteps of Christ. No longer subject to the shadows of the law, they obey the commands of Christ, and guided by his words rise in grace to his own dignity, for they are called children of God. When Christ ascends into heaven, they also follow him.

Christ promises his followers as a recompense and reward eternal life, exemption from death and corruption, and from the torments the judge inflicts upon transgressors. By giving life Christ shows that by nature he *is* life. He does not receive it from another, but supplies it from his own resources. And by eternal life we understand not only length of days which all, both good and bad, shall possess after the resurrection, but also the passing of those days in peace and joy.

We may also see in the word 'life' a reference to the Eucharist, by means of which Christ implants in believers his own life through their sharing in his flesh, according to the text, *He who eats my flesh and drinks my blood has eternal life.*

St Cyril of Alexandria, *Commentary on John*, 7: PG 74, 20

Fifth Sunday of Easter Year A: John 14.1–12

A READING FROM THE TREATISE *ON DEATH AS A BLESSING* BY ST AMBROSE

Let us march forward intrepidly to meet our Redeemer, Jesus, pursuing our onward course without swerving until we come to the assembly of the saints and are welcomed by the company of the just. It is to join our Christian forebears that we are journeying, to those who taught us our faith – that faith which comes to our aid and safeguards our heritage for us even when we have no good works to show. In the place where making for the Lord will be everyone's light; the true light which enlightens every human person will shine upon all. In the house where we are going the Lord Jesus has prepared many resting places for his servants, so that where he is we also may be. This was his express desire. Listen to his own words: *In my Father's house there are many resting places.* And: *I will come again and take you to myself, so that where I am you also may be.*

You may say, perhaps, that he was speaking only to his disciples, and it was to them alone that he promised there would be many resting places. So you suppose he was preparing only for the eleven? And what of that statement of his about people coming from all sides to take their seats in the kingdom of God? Have we any grounds for doubting that God's will is effective? With Christ, surely, to will a thing is to accomplish it. In short, the Lord has not only shown us the way we are to travel, he has also pointed out our destination. *Where I am going you know*, he says, *and the way there is known to you.* This destination is our Father's house, and our way to it is Christ, as his own words assure us: *I am the way, the truth, and the life. No one can come to the Father except through me.*

Let us set out, then, upon this way, holding fast to the truth and following in the footsteps of life. Christ is the way that leads us, the truth that strengthens us, and the life that restores us to life in him.

To make sure that we really understand his will, our Lord prays a few minutes later: *Father, it is my desire that those whom you have given me be with me where I am, so that they may see my glory.* How graciously our Lord asks his Father here to grant what he himself had promised earlier! The promise came first and then the request, not the other way round. Conscious of his authority and knowing the gift was at his own disposal, he made the promise; then as if to exemplify his filial submission, he asked his Father to grant it. Through the one instance we are made aware of his power; through the other, his loving deference to his Father.

Yes, Lord Jesus, we do follow you. But we can only come at your bidding. No one can make the ascent without you, for you are our way, our truth, our life, our strength, our faith, our reward. We belong to you; be the way that carries us onward, the truth that inspires us with courage, and the life that fills us with renewed vigour.

St Ambrose, *On Death as a Blessing*, 12.52–55: CSEL 32, 747–50

Fifth Sunday of Easter Year B: John 15.1–8

A READING FROM THE *TRACTATES ON JOHN* BY ST AUGUSTINE

The passage from the gospel in which the Lord calls himself the vine and his disciples the branches affirms in its own way that, as mediator between God and the human race, the man Christ Jesus is head of the Church and we are his members. It is beyond dispute that a vine and its branches are of one and the same stock. Since Christ, therefore, possessed a divine nature not shared by ourselves, he became man precisely in order that in his own person there might be a vine of human stock whose branches we could become.

Dwell in me, said Jesus, *and I will dwell in you*. His disciples, however, do not dwell in Christ in the same way as Christ dwells in them. In either case, the benefit is theirs, not his. If branches are attached to a vine, it is not to confer any advantage on the vine; it is rather that the branches themselves may draw their sustenance from the vine. The vine is attached to the branches to provide them with their vital nourishment, not to receive anything from them. In the same way Christ's presence in his disciples and their presence in him both profit the disciples rather than Christ. If a branch is cut off, another can grow from the life-giving root; but once severed from the root no branch can remain alive.

The incarnate Truth goes on to say: *I am the vine, you are the branches. Whoever dwells in me and I in him yields fruit in plenty, because without me you can do nothing.* These are words to be weighed and pondered continually. Someone hearing Jesus say, *he yields fruit in plenty*, might perhaps think that the branch can bear at least a certain amount of fruit on its own. Our Lord's words, however, were not: *You can do little without me*, but: *You can do nothing*. Little fruit or plenty, that can be neither without him, because without him nothing can be done. Even if a branch does produce a little fruit, the vinedresser prunes it away so that it may produce more. But if the branch does not remain attached to the vine and draw its life from the root, it can bear no fruit at all.

Now, although Christ could not be the vine if he were not human, he could not offer such a grace to his branches if he were not at the same time divine. Since without this grace it is impossible to have life and consequently death is the result of one's free choice, he said: *Whoever does not dwell in me will be thrown away like a branch and will wither, to be gathered in and cast on the fire to burn*. And so the shame incurred by those branches that refuse to dwell in the vine is in direct proportion to the glory they will have if they do remain in him. Indeed, what the Lord also says through the prophet Ezekiel is true of them: when such branches are cut off they are useless to the vinedressers, nor are they worth the carpenters' labour. The proper place for a branch is the vine or the fire. Branches that do not adhere to the vine will end up in the fire. So if they are to avoid burning, let them remain in the vine.

If you dwell in me, said Jesus, *and my words dwell in you, you will ask for whatever you desire and it will be yours.* Can a person dwelling in Christ desire anything out of harmony with Christ? The very fact that people dwell in their Saviour must mean that they have no desire that is opposed to their salvation. And yet we do indeed desire one thing insofar as we are in Christ, and another insofar as we are still in this world. Because of our sojourn here below, a thought sometimes steals into our ignorant minds to ask for something which cannot be good for us. But this may not be, if we are dwelling in Christ. He does what we ask only if it is for our good. To dwell in him, therefore, is to have his words dwelling in us; whatever we desire we shall then ask for, and it will be given us.

St Augustine, *Tractates on John*, 80.1; 81.1, 3, 4: CCSL 36, 527, 530–1

Fifth Sunday of Easter Year C: John 13.31–33a, 34–35 [31–35]

A READING FROM THE COMMENTARY ON JOHN BY ST CYRIL OF ALEXANDRIA

I give you a new commandment, said Jesus: *love one another*. But how, we might ask, could he call this commandment new? Through Moses, he had said to the people of old: *You shall love the Lord your God with all your heart and with all your mind, and your neighbour as yourself.* Notice what follows. He was not content simply to say, *I give you a new commandment: love one another.* He showed the novelty of his command and how far the love he enjoined surpassed the old conception of mutual love by going on immediately to add: *Love one another as I have loved you.*

To understand the full force of these words, we have to consider how Christ loved us. Then it will be easy to see what is new and different in the commandment we are now given. Paul tells us that *although his nature was divine, he did not claim his equality with God, but stripped himself of all privilege to assume the condition of a slave. He became as we are, and appearing in human form humbled himself by being obedient even to the extent of dying, dying on a cross.* And elsewhere Paul writes: *Though he was rich, he became poor.*

Do you not see what is new in Christ's love for us? The law commanded people to love their brothers and sisters as they love themselves, but our Lord Jesus Christ loved us more than himself. He who was one in nature with God the Father and his equal would not have descended to our lowly estate, nor endured in his flesh such a bitter death for us, nor submitted to the blows given him by his enemies, to the shame, the derision, and all the other sufferings that could not possibly be enumerated; nor, being rich, would he have become poor, had he not loved us far more than himself. It was indeed something new for love to go as far as that!

Christ commands us to love as he did, putting neither reputation, nor wealth, nor anything whatever before love of our brothers and sisters. If need be we must even be prepared to face death for our neighbour's salvation as did our Saviour's blessed disciples and those who followed in their footsteps. To them the salvation of others mattered more than their own lives and they were ready to do anything or to suffer anything to save souls that were perishing. *I die daily*, said Paul. *Who suffers weakness without my suffering too? Who is made to stumble without my heart blazing with indignation?*

The Saviour urged us to practise this love that transcends the law as the foundation of true devotion to God. He knew that only in this way might we become pleasing in God's eyes, and that it was by seeking the beauty of the love implanted in us by himself that we should attain to the highest blessings.

St Cyril of Alexandria, *Commentary on John*, 9: PG 74, 161–4

Sixth Sunday of Easter Year A: John 14.15–21

A READING FROM THE HOMILIES ON JOHN BY ST JOHN CHRYSOSTOM

If you love me, said Christ, *keep my commandments.* I have commanded you to love one another and to treat one another as I have treated you. To love me is to obey these commands, to submit to me your beloved. *And I will ask the Father, and he will give you another Counsellor.* This promise shows once again Christ's consideration. Because his disciples did not yet know who he was, it was likely that they would greatly miss his companionship, his teaching, his actual physical presence, and be completely disconsolate when he had gone. Therefore he said: *I will ask the Father, and he will give you another Counsellor*, meaning another like himself.

They received the Spirit after Christ had purified them by his sacrifice. The Spirit did not come down on them while Christ was still with them, because this sacrifice had not yet been offered. But when sin had been blotted out and the disciples, send out to face danger, were preparing themselves for the battle, they needed the Holy Spirit's coming to encourage them. If you ask why the Spirit did not come immediately after the resurrection, this was in order to increase their gratitude for receiving him by increasing their desire. They were troubled by nothing as long as Christ was with them, but when his departure had left them desolate and very much afraid, they would be most eager to receive the Spirit.

He will remain with you, Christ said, meaning his presence with you will not be ended by death. But since there was a danger that hearing of a Counsellor might lead them to expect another incarnation and to think they would be able to see the Holy Spirit, he corrected this idea by saying: *The world cannot receive him because it does not see him.* For he will not be with you in the same way as I am, but will dwell in your very souls, *He will be in you.*

Christ called him the Spirit of truth because the Spirit would help them to understand the types of the old law. By *He will be with you*, he meant, *He will be with you as I am with you*, but he also hinted at the difference between them, namely, that the Spirit would not suffer as he had done, nor would he ever depart.

The world cannot receive him because it does not see him. Does this imply that the Spirit is the simple? By no means; Christ is speaking here of knowledge, for he adds: *or know him.* Sight being the sense by which we perceive things most distinctly, he habitually used this sense to signify knowledge. By *the world*, he means here the wicked, thus giving his disciples the consolation of receiving a special gift. He said that the Spirit was another like himself, that he would not leave them, that he would come to them just as he himself had come, and that he would remain in them. Yet even this did not drive away their sadness, for they still wanted Christ himself and his companionship. So to satisfy them he said, *I will not leave you orphans; I will come back to you.* Do not be afraid, but when I promised to send you another Counsellor I did not mean that I was going to abandon you forever, nor by saying that he would remain with you did I mean that I would not see you again. Of course I also will come to you; *I will not leave you orphans.*

St John Chrysostom, *Homilies on John*, 75.1: PG 59, 403–5

Sixth Sunday of Easter Year B: John 15.9–17

A READING FROM *A TREATISE UPON THE PASSION* BY ST THOMAS MORE

Let us deeply consider the love of our Saviour Christ who so loved his own unto the end that for their sakes he willingly suffered that painful end, and therein declared the highest degree of love that can be. For, as he himself says: *A greater love no one has than to give his life for his friends*. This is indeed the greatest love that ever anyone had. But yet had our Saviour a greater, for he gave his for both friend and foe.

But what a difference is there now, between this faithful love of his and other kinds of false and fickle love found in this wretched world. The flatterer pretends to love you because he dines well with you. But now if adversity so diminish your possessions that he find your table not laid, then – farewell, adieu – your brother flatterer is gone and gets himself to some other table. And he might even sometime turn into your enemy and cruelly speak evil of you.

Who can in adversity be sure of many of his friends when our Saviour himself was, at his capture, left alone and forsaken by his? When you go forth who will go with you? If you were a king would not all your realm send you on your way alone and then forget you? Will not your own family let you depart a naked, feeble soul, you know not whither?

Let us all in time, then, learn to love as we should, God above all things, and all other things for him. And whatsoever love be not referred to that end, namely, to the good pleasure of God, is a very vain and unfruitful love. And whatsoever love we bear to any creature whereby we love God the less, that love is a loathsome love and hinders us from heaven. Love no child of yours so tenderly but that you could be content to sacrifice it to God, as Abraham was ready with Isaac, if God so commanded you. And since God will not do so, offer your child in another way to God's service. For whatever we love that makes us break God's commandment, we love better than God, and that is a love deadly and damnable. Now, since our Lord has so loved us, for our salvation, let us diligently call for his grace that in return for his great love we be not found ungrateful.

St Thomas More, *A Treatise upon the Passion*, 1

Sixth Sunday of Easter Year C: John 14.23–29

A READING FROM A PENTECOST SERMON BY ST LEO THE GREAT

In the gospel reading we hear the Lord Jesus telling his disciples: *If you loved me you would be glad, because I go to the Father*, and: *the Father is greater than I*. But we have also heard those other sayings of his: *I and the Father are one*, and: *He who sees me sees the Father*, and so we are able to accept the first passage without concluding that it implies any difference in Godhead, or that it refers to that essential being which we know to be co-eternal and co-natural with the Father. What the apostles are given to understand is that it is human nature that is promoted in the incarnation of the Word. In spite of their dismay at the announcement of our Lord's departure, they are spurred on by their own increased dignity to look forward to the joys that never end. *If you loved me*, our Lord says, you would be glad, because I am going to the Father. In other words, if you could comprehend the glory that is bestowed on you by the fact that I, who was begotten of God the Father, was also born of a human mother; that I, the Lord of eternity, chose to become mortal with mortals; that I, the Invisible, have shown myself in visible form; that I, who have the *nature of the everlasting God*, have assumed the *nature of a slave*: if you had knowledge of these things, I say, *you would indeed be glad that I am going to the Father*. The truth is that this ascension of mine is a free gift to you; it is your lowly existence that is raised up in me to the Father's right hand. But I who share the Father's nature dwell with him inseparably; when I came to you I did not leave him, and now that I am returning to him I do not abandon you.

Rejoice, then, *because I go to the Father, for the Father is greater than I*; I have united you to myself, and have become the Son of Man to enable you to become the children of God. Although I am one and the same person in both natures, in my co-naturality with you I am less than the Father, but in that nature which is inseparable from the Father's, I am greater even than myself. And so let what is less than the Father go to the Father; where the Word has his eternal dwelling, there let the flesh dwell also; and let the Catholic Church be united in believing that he who in his humanity is undeniably less than the Father is equal to the Father in his divinity.

St Leo the Great, *Sermon* 77.5: CCSL 138A, 490–3

The Ascension Year A: Matthew 28.16–20 [Luke 24.44–53]

A READING FROM A SERMON ON THE ASCENSION BY ST LEO THE GREAT

The sacred work of our salvation was of such value in the sight of the creator of the universe that he counted it worth the shedding of his own blood. From the day of his birth until his passion and death this work was carried out in conditions of self-abasement; and although he showed many signs of his divinity even when he bore the form of a slave, yet, strictly speaking, the events of that time were concerned with proving the reality of the humanity he had assumed. But he was innocent of any sin, and so when death launched its attack upon him he burst its bonds and robbed it of its power. After his passion weakness was turned into strength, mortality into eternal life, and disgrace into glory. Of all this our Lord Jesus Christ gave ample proof in the sight of many, until at last he entered heaven in triumph, bearing with him the trophy of his victory over death.

And so while at Easter it was the Lord's resurrection which was the cause of our joy, our present rejoicing is on account of his ascension into heaven. With all due solemnity we are commemorating that day on which our poor human nature was carried up in Christ above all the hosts of heaven, above all the ranks of angels, beyond the highest heavenly powers to the very throne of God the Father. It is upon this ordered structure of divine acts that we have been firmly established, so that the grace of God may show itself still more marvellous when, in spite of the withdrawal from our sight of everything that is rightly felt to command our reverence, faith does not fail, hope is not shaken, charity does not grow cold.

For such is the power of great minds, such the light of truly believing souls, that they put unhesitating faith in what is not seen with the bodily eye; they fix their desires on what is beyond sight. Such fidelity could never be born in our hearts, nor could anyone be justified by faith, if our salvation lay only in what was visible. This is why Christ said to that man who seemed doubtful about his resurrection unless he could see and touch the marks of his passion in his very flesh: *You believe because you see me; blessed are those who have not seen and yet believe.*

It was in order that we might be capable of such blessedness that on the fortieth day after his resurrection, after he had made careful provision for everything concerning the preaching of the Gospel and the mysteries of the new covenant, our Lord Jesus Christ was taken up to heaven before the eyes of his disciples, and so his bodily presence among them came to an end. From that time onward he was to remain at the Father's right hand until the completion of the period ordained by God for the Church's children to increase and multiply, after which, in the same body with which he ascended, he will come again to judge the living and the dead.

And so what was visible in our Redeemer has passed into the sacraments. Our faith is nobler and stronger because sight has been replaced by a doctrine whose authority is accepted by believing hearts, enlightened from on high.

St Leo the Great, *Sermon* 74.1–2: CCSL 138A, 455–7

The Ascension Year B: Mark 16.15–20 [Luke 24.44–53]

A READING FROM THE HOMILIES ON THE FIRST LETTER OF JOHN BY ST AUGUSTINE

We believe in Jesus whom we have not seen. Those who have seen and touched him with their own hands, who have heard the word from his mouth, are the ones who have borne witness to him. It was to teach these things to the world that they were sent by him. They did not presume to go out on their own initiative. And where did he send them? You've heard the answer to that in the gospel reading: *Go, proclaim the Good News to every creature under heaven.* The disciples were sent to the ends of the earth, with signs and wonders accompanying them in confirmation of their testimony, because they spoke of what they had actually seen.

We believe in him though we have not seen him, and we await his return. Whoever waits for him in faith will rejoice when he comes, but those without faith will be put to shame at the appearance of what they cannot at present see. Then let us abide in his word, so that his coming may not put us to shame. In the gospel he himself says to those who have believed in him: *If you persevere in my word, you will truly be my disciples.* And to their unspoken question, 'What will this profit us?' he adds: *You will know the truth, and the truth will set you free.*

At present we possess our salvation in hope, not in fact; we do not yet possess what we have been promised, but we hope to do so in the future. The one who promised it is faithful; he will not deceive you, so long as you wait for his promised gift without growing weary. The truth cannot possibly deceive. Make sure then that you yourself are not a liar, professing one thing and doing another; keep faith with him, and he will keep his word to you. If you do not keep faith, it will be you who deceive yourself, not he who made the promise.

If you know that he is righteous, you can be sure that everyone who acts rightly is born of him. Our righteousness in this life comes through faith. None but the angels are perfectly righteous, and they have only a shadow of righteousness in comparison with God. Nevertheless, if there is any perfect righteousness to be found in the souls and spirits created by God, it is in the holy angels who are good and just, who have not fallen away from God nor been thrust out of heaven by their pride. They abide for ever in the contemplation of God's word and find their happiness in nothing apart from him who made them. In them is found the perfection of righteousness, but in us righteousness has its beginning through faith, as the Spirit leads us.

St Augustine, *Homilies on 1 John*, 4.2–3: SC 75, 220–4

The Ascension Year C: Luke 24.46–53 [44–53]

A READING FROM THE COMMENTARY ON JOHN BY ST CYRIL OF ALEXANDRIA

If there had not been many dwelling places in the house of God the Father, our Lord would have told us that he was going on ahead to prepare the dwelling places of the saints. He knew, however, that many such dwelling places already prepared were awaiting the arrival of those who love God. Therefore he did not give this as the reason for his departure, but rather his desire to open the way for our ascent to those heavenly places and to prepare a safe passage for us by making smooth the road that had previously been impassable. For heaven was then completely inaccessible to us – human foot had never trodden that pure and holy country of the angels. It was Christ who first prepared the way for our ascent there. By offering himself to God the Father as the firstfruits of all who are dead and buried, he gave us a way of entry into heaven and was himself the first human being the inhabitants of heaven ever saw. The angels in heaven, knowing nothing of the sacred and profound mystery of the incarnation, were astonished at his coming and almost thrown into confusion by an event so strange and unheard of. *Who is this coming from Edom?* they asked; that is, from the earth. But the Spirit did not leave the heavenly throng ignorant of the wonderful wisdom of God the Father. Commanding them to open the gates of heaven in honour of the King and Master of the universe, he cried out: *Lift up your gates, you princes, and be lifted up you everlasting doors, that the king of glory may come in.*

And so our Lord Jesus Christ has opened up for us *a new and living way*, as Paul says, *not by entering a sanctuary made with hands, but by entering heaven itself to appear before God on our behalf.* For Christ has not ascended in order to make his own appearance before God the Father. He was, is, and ever will be in the Father and in the sight of him from whom he receives his being, for he is his Father's unfailing joy. But now the Word, who has never before been clothed in human nature, has ascended as a man to show himself in a strange and unfamiliar fashion. And he has done this on our account and in our name, so that being like us, though with his power as the Son, and hearing the command, *Sit at my right hand*, as a member of our race, he might transmit to all of us the glory of being children of God. For since he became man it is as one of us that he sits at the right hand of God the Father, even though he is above all creation and one in substance with his Father, having truly come forth from him as God from God and Light from Light.

As man then he appeared before the Father on our behalf, to enable us from whom original sin had excluded from his presence once more to see the Father's face. As the Son he took his seat to enable us as sons and daughters through him to be called children of God. So Paul, who claims to speak for Christ, teaching that the whole human race has a share in the events of Christ's life, says that *God has raised us up with him and enthroned us with him in heaven.* To Christ as the Son by nature belongs the prerogative of sitting at the Father's side; this honour can rightly and truly be ascribed to him alone. Yet because his having become man means that he sits there as one who is in all respects like ourselves, as well as being, we believe, God from God, in some mysterious way he passes this honour on to us.

St Cyril of Alexandria, *Commentary on John*, 9: PG 74, 182–3

Seventh Sunday of Easter Year A: John 17.1–11

A READING FROM A HOMILY BY ST JOHN CHRYSOSTOM

Father, the hour has come: glorify your Son. Christ called the cross glory. How then could he have sought to avoid it at one time when he longed for it at another? That the cross is glory we can learn from the Evangelist, who says: *The Holy Spirit had not yet been given because Jesus had not yet been glorified*, by which he meant that grace had not yet been given because Christ had not yet gone forth to be crucified and so to end the hostility existing between God and the human race. For the cross reconciled us with God, made earth heaven, caused human beings to mingle with angels, destroyed the citadel of death, broke the strength of the devil, freed the world from error, and founded churches.

The cross was the will of the Father, the glory of the Son, the joy of the Holy Spirit. It was the boast of Paul, who said: *Let me boast of nothing except the cross of our Lord Jesus Christ*. The cross is brighter than the sun, its rays are more brilliant. When the sun is darkened the cross shines forth, for the darkening of the sun does not mean it no longer exists, but that it is outshone by the splendour of the cross. The cross destroyed the bond that was against us and opened the prison-house of death. The cross is the proof of God's love, for *God loved the world so much that he gave his only Son to save those who believe in him from perishing*. The cross unlocked the gates of paradise, admitted the thief, and led to the kingdom of heaven the human race which, unworthy even of the earth, was on the point of being destroyed.

Since such great blessings have come and come still from the cross, could Christ have been unwilling to be crucified? If he was unwilling, who compelled him? Why did he even send prophets before him to foretell his crucifixion if he did not intend and was unwilling to be crucified? Why did he call the cross a cup? For this shows his desire. As someone who is thirsty welcomes a drink so Christ welcomes the cross. This is why he said, *With all my heart I have longed to eat this passover with you*, for he knew that the next day he would be crucified.

How could he have prayed to escape the cross? He called it glory; he rebuked the disciple who tried to stand in his way; he taught that he was the Good Shepherd because he was going to die for his sheep; he longed for the cross with all his heart, and he came to it of his own free will.

St John Chrysostom, *Homily on 'Father, if it is possible ...'*:
PG 51, 34–5

Seventh Sunday of Easter Year B: John 17.11b–19 [6–19]

A READING FROM THE COMMENTARY ON JOHN BY ST CYRIL OF ALEXANDRIA

Holy Father, keep those whom you have given me in your name, that they may be one as we are one. Christ desired his disciples to be preserved in unity of mind and will, blended as it were with one another in soul and spirit by the law of peace and mutual love. He wished them to be united by love's unbreakable bond, and so to advance to such perfect oneness that their freely chosen unity might mirror the natural unity that exists, as we know, between the Father and the Son.

This means that their unity was never to be broken, that it was to be permanent. Never must they be drawn from their singleness of purpose by love of pleasure, or by anything belonging to this world. Rather, they were to preserve intact the power of love in unity of worship and holiness, as in fact they did.

We read in the Acts of the Apostles that the whole company of believers was united in heart and soul in a unity that came from the Spirit. Paul also says the same thing. *There is one body and one spirit. We who are many form one body in Christ, for we all partake of the one loaf,* and we have all been anointed by the one Spirit, which is the Spirit of Christ. And so, since the disciples were to form one body and to share in one and the same Spirit, Christ wished them to be preserved in unimpaired spiritual unity, unbroken concord.

It may be thought that in this respect the unity of the disciples resembles that of the Father and the Son, who are united not only in substance, but also in will (for in the holy nature of God there is in everything one will and one intention). To think thus is permissible and not mistaken, for although we are not consubstantial with one another as are the Father and the Word that proceeds from him and is in him, in their deepest desires true Christians are seen to be united.

St Cyril of Alexandria, *Commentary on John*, 11.9: PG 74, 516–17

Seventh Sunday of Easter Year C: John 17.20–26

A READING FROM THE COMMENTARY ON JOHN BY ST CYRIL OF ALEXANDRIA

Our Lord Jesus Christ did not pray only for the twelve disciples. He prayed for all in every age whom their exhortation would persuade to become holy by believing and to be purified by sharing in the Holy Spirit. *May they all be one*, he prayed. *As you Father are in me and I am in you, may they also be one in us.*

The only Son shines out from the very substance of the Father and possesses the Father completely in his own nature. He became man, according to the Scriptures, blending himself, so to speak, with our nature by an inexplicable union with an earthly body. In himself he somehow united totally disparate natures to make us sharers in the divine nature.

The communion and abiding presence of the Spirit has passed even to ourselves. This was experienced first through Christ and in Christ when he was seen to have become like us, that is, a human being anointed and sanctified. By nature however he was God, for he proceeded from the Father. It was with his own Spirit that he sanctified the temple of his body and also, in a way befitting it, the world of his creation. Through the mystery of Christ, then, sharing in the Holy Spirit and union with God has become possible also for us, for we are all sanctified in him.

By his own wisdom and the Father's counsel he devised a way of bringing us all together and blending us into a unity with God and one another, even though the differences between us give us each in both body and soul a separate identity. For in Holy Communion he blesses with one body, which is his own, those who believe in him, and makes them one body with himself and one another. Who would separate those who are united to Christ through that one sacred body, or destroy their true union with one another? If *we all share one loaf* we all become one body, for Christ cannot be divided.

So it is that the Church is the body of Christ and we are its members. For since we are all united to Christ through his sacred body, having received that one indivisible body into our own, our members are not our own but his.

St Cyril of Alexandria, *Commentary on John*, 11.11: PG 74, 553–60

Pentecost Sunday Year A: John 20.19–23

A READING FROM A PENTECOST HOMILY BY ST JOHN CHRYSOSTOM

Great beyond all description, beloved, are the gifts which in his love God gave us on this day. Let us then rejoice together and be glad as we give our Lord praise: this is a great feast for us. Like the changing seasons which succeed one another throughout the year, the feast days of the Church follow an orderly progression, each one leading on to the next. Not long ago we celebrated the passion and resurrection of our Lord Jesus Christ and then his ascension into heaven. Today we have reached the supreme and final grace, the most important feast, the actual fulfilment of the Lord's promise.

If I go away, he said, *I will send you another Comforter; I will not leave you orphans*. Do you not see his care for us and his boundless love? He first ascended to heaven once more to sit on his royal throne at the right hand of the Father. Now, on this day, he gives us the Holy Spirit and through him he sends us innumerable heavenly graces. Indeed, which of the graces necessary for our salvation is not given us through the Holy Spirit? Through the Holy Spirit we are freed from slavery and called to liberty; we are raised to the status of sons and daughters; we are in a sense recreated and we lay down the heavy and foul burden of our sins. Through the Holy Spirit we are given priests and teachers; from the same source come revelations and the gift of healing; and all the other adornments of the Church have their origin in him. *It is one and the same Spirit who does all this*, says Paul. *He divides his gifts among us as he wills.*

As he wills, he says, not as he is bidden; he divides them, he is not himself divided; he acts on his own authority, not in subjection to the authority of another. Paul attributes to the Spirit exactly the same power as to the Father. Just as he says of the Father, *It is one and the same Spirit who does all this. He divides his gifts among us as he wills.* Do you not see how complete the power of the Spirit is? Clearly, those who have the same nature must have the same authority; those who have the same dignity must have the same power and dominion.

Through the Holy Spirit we have obtained the remission of our sins and we have washed away all defilement. By his gift, we who have had recourse to grace have been changed from human beings into angels. I do not mean that our nature has been changed, but something much more wonderful: while remaining human we live the way the angels do. So great is the power of the Holy Spirit.

St John Chrysostom, *Homilies on Pentecost*, 2.1: PG 50, 463–5

Pentecost Sunday Year A: John 7.37–39 [RCL alternative]

A READING FROM THE *TRACTATES ON JOHN* BY ST AUGUSTINE

What does it mean when Jesus says, *For the Spirit was not yet given, because Jesus was not yet glorified*? Not that the Spirit of God, which was with God, was not yet in being; but rather that it was not yet in those who had believed on Jesus. For the Lord Jesus arranged it that they would not be given the Spirit until after his resurrection. Why then did the Lord Jesus Christ decide not to give the Holy Spirit until he should be glorified? How was the Spirit not yet in holy people, when we read in the early passages of the Gospel that Simeon recognized Christ by the Holy Spirit; that Anna the widow, a prophetess, also recognized him; that John, who baptized him, recognized him; that Zechariah, being filled with the Holy Spirit, said many things; that Mary herself received the Holy Spirit to conceive the Lord? There is much evidence of the activity of the Holy Spirit before the Lord was glorified by the resurrection of his flesh. It was the same Spirit whom the prophets had, who proclaimed beforehand the coming of Christ.

There was, however, to be a special way of giving the Spirit which had not appeared before. Nowhere do we read before Pentecost that people who had been gathered together spoke in the tongues of all nations by receiving the Holy Spirit. After his resurrection, when he first appeared to his disciples, Jesus said to them: *Receive the Holy Spirit.* It was of this giving then that it was said, *The Spirit was not given, because Jesus was not yet glorified.* After his resurrection, which the evangelist calls his glorifying, the Lord first gave the Holy Spirit to his disciples. Then having stayed with them forty days, as the Acts of the Apostles shows, he ascended into heaven in their sight, and, at the end of ten days, on the day of Pentecost, he sent the Holy Spirit from above and they spoke in the tongues of all nations.

Why then, if one is baptized in Christ and believes in him, does he not now speak in the tongues of all nations? Has he not received the Holy Spirit? No, it is because the Church herself now speaks in the tongues of all nations. Beforehand, the Church was in one nation and it spoke in the tongues of all. This signified what was to come to pass; that by growing among the nations, it would speak in the tongues of all. Whoever is not in this Church, does not now receive the Holy Spirit; therefore we too receive the Holy Spirit if we love the Church, if we are joined together by love, if we rejoice in the Catholic name and faith.

St Augustine, *Tractates on John*, 32.6–8

Pentecost Sunday Year B: John 15.26–27; 16.12–15 [4–15]

A READING FROM A SERMON BY ST AELRED OF RIEVAULX

Today's holy solemnity puts new heart into us, for not only do we revere its dignity, we also experience it as delightful. On this feast it is love which we specially honour, and among human beings there is no word pleasanter to the ear, no thought more tenderly dwelt on, than love. The love we celebrate is nothing other than the goodness, kindness, and charity of the Lord. His goodness is identical with his Spirit, with God himself.

In his work of disposing all things *the Spirit of the Lord has filled the whole world* from the beginning, *reaching from end to end of the earth in strength, and delicately disposing everything*; but as sanctifier *the Spirit of the Lord has filled the whole world* since Pentecost, for on this day the gracious Spirit himself was sent by the Father and the Son on a new mission, in a new mode, by a new manifestation of his mighty power, for the sanctification of every creature. Before this day *the Spirit had not been given, for Jesus was not yet glorified*, but today he came forth from his heavenly throne to give himself in all his abundant riches to the human race, so that the divine outpouring might pervade the whole wide world and be manifested in a variety of spiritual endowments.

It is surely right that this overflowing delight should come down to us from heaven, since it was heaven that a few days earlier received from our fertile earth a fruit of wonderful sweetness. When has our land ever yielded a fruit more pleasant, sweeter, holier, or more delectable? Indeed, *faithfulness has sprung up from the earth*. A few days ago we sent Christ on ahead to the heavenly kingdom, so that in all fairness we might have in return whatever heaven held that should be sweet to our desire. The full sweetness of earth is Christ's humanity, the full sweetness of heaven Christ's Spirit. Thus a more profitable bargain was struck: Christ's human nature ascended from us to heaven, and on us today Christ's Spirit has come down.

Now indeed *the Spirit of the Lord has filled the whole earth*, and all creation recognizes his voice. Everywhere the Spirit is at work, everywhere he speaks. To be sure, the Holy Spirit was given to the disciples before our Lord's ascension when he said, *Receive the Holy Spirit: if you forgive anyone's sins they are forgiven, if you withhold forgiveness, unforgiven they shall be*; but before the day of Pentecost the Spirit's voice was still in a sense unheard. His power had not yet leaped forth, nor had the disciples truly come to know him, for they were not yet confirmed by his might; they were still in the grip of fear, cowering behind closed doors.

From this day onward, however, *the voice of the Lord has resounded over the waters; the God of majesty has thundered and the Lord makes his voice echo over the flood.* From now on *the voice of the Lord speaks with strength, the voice of the Lord in majesty, the voice of the Lord fells the cedars, the voice of the Lord strikes flaming fire, the voice of the Lord shakes the desert, stirring the wilderness of Kadesh, the voice of the Lord strips the forest bare, and all will cry out, 'Glory!'*

St Aelred of Rievaulx, Sermons: Talbot 1, 112–14

Pentecost Sunday Year C: John 14.15–16, 23b–26 [8–17, 25–27]

A READING FROM A PENTECOST SERMON BY ST LEO THE GREAT

Every Catholic knows that today's solemnity ranks as one of the principal feasts of the Church. The reference due to it is beyond all question, because this day is consecrated by the most sublime and wonderful gift of the Holy Spirit. Ten days after the Lord ascended high above the heavens to sit at the right hand of God the Father, and fifty days after his resurrection, on the very same day of the week this joyful season began, the day of Pentecost has dawned upon us. In itself the feast of Pentecost contains great mysteries relating to the old dispensation as well as to the new, signs which clearly show that the race was heralded by the law and the law fulfilled by grace. Fifty days after the sacrifice of the lamb marking the deliverance of the Hebrews from the Egyptians, the law was given on Mount Sinai; and fifty days from the raising up of Christ after his passion and immolation as the true lamb of God, the Holy Spirit came down upon the apostles and assembled believers. Thus the thoughtful Christian may easily perceive that the origin of the Old Testament laid the foundations of the Gospel, and that the Spirit who was the author of the second covenant was the same Spirit who had established the first.

As the apostles' story testifies, *when the days of Pentecost were fulfilled and all the disciples were together in one place, suddenly there came from heaven a sound like that of a strong driving wind which filled the whole house where they were sitting. And there appeared to them tongues like flames of fire which came to rest on each one of them. And they were all filled with the Holy Spirit and began to speak in other tongues as the Spirit gave them the power of utterance.* O how swift is the word of wisdom, and where God is master how quickly the lesson is learnt! One needs no interpretation in order to understand, no practice in order to gain facility, no time in order to study. *The Spirit* of truth *breathes where he will,* and each nation's own language has become common property in the mouth of the Church.

And so, ever since that day, the clarion call of the Gospel has rung out; since the day of Pentecost a rain of charismatic gifts, a river of blessings, has watered every desert and dry land, for *the Spirit of God has swept over the waters to renew the face of the earth,* and a blaze of new light has shone out to dispel our former darkness. In the light of those flaming tongues the word of the Lord has shone out clearly, and a fiery eloquence has been enkindled which is charged with the energy to enlighten, the ability to create understanding, and the power to burn away and destroy sin.

St Leo the Great, *Sermons,* 75.1–3: CCSL 138A, 465–9

ORDINARY TIME AFTER PENTECOST
SUNDAYS AFTER TRINITY

AS soon as we have celebrated the coming of the Holy Spirit at Pentecost we greet with song the feast of the Holy Trinity on the following Sunday, a well-chosen place in the calendar for immediately after the descent of the Holy Spirit preaching and conversion began and faith through baptism and confession in the name of the Father and of the Son and of the Holy Spirit.

Rupert of Deutz

ALMIGHTY God, you have broken the tyranny of sin and have sent the Spirit of your Son into our hearts whereby we call you Father; give us grace to dedicate our freedom to your service, that we and all creation may be brought to the glorious liberty of the children of God; through Jesus Christ your Son our Lord, who is alive and reigns with you, in the unity of the Holy Spirit, one God, now and for ever. Amen.

Collect for the Third Sunday after Trinity, *Common Worship*

FOR as the heavens are higher than the earth, so are my ways higher than your ways and my thoughts than your thoughts. As the rain and the snow come down from above, and return not again but water the earth, bringing forth life and giving growth, seed for sowing and bread to eat, so is my Word that goes forth from my mouth, it will not return to me fruitless, but it will accomplish that which I purpose, and succeed in the task I give it.

A Song of the Word of the Lord (Isaiah 55), *Common Worship*

'For Jesus Christ is your living Word; through him you have created all things from the beginning, and formed us in your own image. Through him you have freed us from the slavery of sin, giving him to be born of a woman and to die upon the cross; you raised him from the dead and exalted him to your right hand on high. Through him you have sent upon us your holy and life-giving Spirit, and made us a people for your own possession.'[7] Sunday, also called the Lord's Day, is the first Christian feast-day, the first day of the week on which our Lord rose from the dead and on which the first disciples gathered for prayer and the Eucharist (Matthew 28.1; John 20.19; Acts 20.7; *Didache* 14). The pristine shape of Sunday as the commemoration of the Lord's resurrection takes central stage in the Sundays in Ordinary Time.

The *Revised Common Lectionary* follows the revised *Roman Lectionary* in having a series of Gospel readings from the three synoptic Gospels on the Sundays before Lent and after Pentecost, which the 1970 Roman Missal has called 'Sundays in Ordinary Time'. These follow the sequence of each Gospel, although the reading of the shorter Gospel of Mark in Year B has a major insert on Sundays of Ordinary Time 17–21 from the Gospel of John, the sermon on the bread of life in John 6, which replaces the Marcan story of the miraculous feeding and fits well with Mark's concern with Jesus' revelation of himself on the surrounding Sundays. The short Gospel readings of the Sundays of Ordinary Time do not give enough space to read all the Gospel text between the early passages of the Christmas cycle and the passion and resurrection stories of Eastertide. Those who created the *Roman Lectionary* sought to include as much of the story of Jesus' public ministry as possible and to emphasize the special qualities of each Evangelist while ensuring that the same basic story was told in each of the three years. About three-quarters of the stories of Jesus' public life are thus included and Years A and C contain much material that is special to Matthew and Luke while all three years repeat important episodes that are found in all three Gospels such as the calling of the disciples and the confession of Peter. The old Roman Missal had called these Sundays at the end of the Church's year, 'Sundays after Pentecost'. Other Churches have other names for these Sundays while following the same cycle of readings. For the 'Sundays after Pentecost' the Church of England followed the ancient Calendar of Salisbury (the 'Sarum Use'), widely followed in the British Isles in the Middle Ages, and called them 'Sundays after Trinity'. In most Churches today the liturgical colour for this season in green.

---

7 Common preface from Eucharistic Prayer A, *Common Worship*.

Three major feast days that occur in this period are included in this book. The Feast of the Most Holy Trinity (Trinity Sunday) is the first Sunday after Pentecost; Corpus Christi ('The Solemnity of the Most Holy Body and Blood of Christ' or 'The Day of Thanksgiving for the Institution of Holy Communion') is the Thursday after Trinity and may be celebrated on the following Sunday; the Roman Catholic Church keeps the Solemnity of the Sacred Heart of Jesus on the Friday after the Second Sunday after Pentecost and calls these three feasts, the 'Solemnities of the Lord in Ordinary Time'.

Trinity Sunday has its roots in a commemoration of the mystery of the Trinity on the Sunday after Pentecost in the seventh-century book of prayers for the Eucharist called the 'Gelasian Sacramentary'. About the year 800 the great English scholar Alcuin composed a Mass for the Holy Trinity and the celebration of the feast on various days became popular in the Middle Ages. It was eventually fixed on this day and ordered to be celebrated everywhere in the Christian West by Pope John XXII in 1334. The feast of this great biblical mystery of our faith has been preserved in Anglican and Lutheran calendars.

Corpus Christi was celebrated for the first time at Liège in 1247 at the suggestion of a nun, St Juliana of Mont-Cornillon. In 1264 the feast was extended to the whole Latin Church by Pope Urban IV and a Mass was composed for the feast, probably by St Thomas Aquinas. It became popular in the following century. The feast takes up themes from the commemoration of the institution of the Eucharist on Maundy Thursday and is also in the calendar of the Church of England and other Anglican Churches. It is celebrated on the Thursday after Trinity, although some Roman Catholic Churches keep it on the following Sunday.

The feast of the Sacred Heart has its remote roots in medieval devotion to the wound in Jesus' side when he was on the cross but was first celebrated by St John Eudes in France in the seventeenth century. It became popular because of the visions of a nun, St Margaret Mary Alacoque, but was only extended to the whole Roman Catholic Church by Pope Pius IX in 1856. The feast celebrates the great love of Jesus for humanity and is celebrated on the Friday after the second Sunday after Pentecost.

In among the Sundays of Ordinary Time, the *Common Worship Lectionary* adds readings for the commemoration of the dedication of a church-building which may be used on the first Sunday in October or the last Sunday after Trinity if the anniversary of the actual rite of dedication is not commemorated. The dedication of a church, in which the community of the Church meets, is a feast of the Church which is the Body of Christ and the Temple of the Holy Spirit: 'Do you not know that you are

God's temple and that God's Spirit dwells in you?' (1 Corinthians 3.16). The Gospels for this feast are of the cleansing of the Temple and the feast of the dedication of the Temple, showing that the relationship of Jesus to the Jerusalem Temple was central to his ministry. Liturgical rites for the dedication of a church reveal the relationship that still exists between the sacred space of a Christian church and the Temple of the Old Covenant.

This liturgical season of 'Sundays in Ordinary Time', 'Sundays after Trinity' or 'Sundays after Pentecost' represents the Age of the Church or the Age of the Spirit when the people of God gather Sunday by Sunday to hear the story of Jesus, to celebrate his paschal mystery in the sacraments, and to await his glorious return. At the end of this season, which is the end of the liturgical year, on the last Sundays before Advent our attention begins to turn more strongly to the Last Things and the consummation of all in Christ.

Trinity Sunday Year A: John 3.16–18
[RCL Trinity B]

A READING FROM A HOMILY BY ST JOHN CHRYSOSTOM

God loved the world so much that he gave his only Son so that those who believed in him might not perish, but might have eternal life. As you see, the reason for the Son's coming was to enable people heading for ruin to be saved by believing in him. Could anyone have imagined the great generosity, wonderful beyond description, which God has shown to us? By the grace of baptism he has freed us from all our sins! But why continue? The mind cannot count, words cannot enumerate all the rest of God's gifts. However much I said would leave much more unsaid. Who could ever have thought of the way of repentance which God in his indescribable love for us has provided for our race, or of the wonderful commandments that we may, if we wish, gain his grace after baptism?

Do you not see, beloved, how boundless God's blessings are? I have counted a great many, but there are many more which I have not yet been able to mention. How can a human tongue tell all God has done for us? Yet although the blessings he has lavished on us are many and great, to those walking in the way of virtue he has promised others much greater and more inexpressible when they have left this world for the next. To show us their sublimity in a few words the blessed Paul said: *No eye has seen, nor ear heard, no human heart conceived what God has prepared for those who love him.*

Do you not see the excellence of these gifts, and how God's blessings surpass all human understanding? No human heart has even imagined them, says St Paul. If then we desire to reckon them up and give thanks for them as best we can, that in itself will win for us an increase of grace and help us to grow in virtue. It will make us ready to rise above present circumstances and place all our hope in the giver of such great gifts, longing for him more and more every day.

St John Chrysostom, *Homilies on Genesis*, 27.1–2: PG 53, 241

Trinity Sunday Year B: Matthew 28.16–20 [RCL Trinity A]

A READING FROM *THE LIFE IN CHRIST* BY ST NICHOLAS CABASILAS

Although it was by a common benevolence that the Trinity saved our race, each one of the blessed Persons played his own part. The Father was reconciled, the Son reconciled, and the Holy Spirit was the gift bestowed upon those who were now God's friends. The Father set us free, the Son was our ransom, and the Spirit our liberty, for Paul says, *Where the Spirit of the Lord is, there is liberty.* The Father recreated us through the Son, but *it is the Spirit who gives life.*

Even in the first creation there was a shadowy indication of the Trinity, for the Father created, the Son was the Creator's hand, and the Paraclete was the life-giver's breath. But why speak of this? For in fact it is only in the new creation that the distinctions within the Godhead are revealed to us.

God bestowed many blessings on his creation in every age, but you will not find any of them being ascribed to the Father alone, or to the Son, or to the Spirit. On the contrary, all have their source in the Trinity, which performs every act by a single power, providence, and creativity. But in the dispensation by which the Trinity restored our race, something new occurred. It was still the Trinity that jointly willed my salvation, and providentially arranged the means for its accomplishment, but the Trinity no longer acted as one. The active role belonged not to the Father, or to the Spirit, but to the Word alone. It was the only-begotten Son alone who assumed flesh and blood, who was scourged, who suffered and died, and who rose again.

Through these acts of his our nature received new life; through these acts baptism was instituted – a new birth and a new creation. Only in this new creation are the distinctions within the Godhead revealed. Therefore, when those who have obtained this holy re-creation call on God over the sacred bath, it is fitting that they should distinguish between the persons by invoking them as Father, Son, and Holy Spirit.

St Nicholas Cabasilas, *The Life in Christ*, 2: PG 150, 532–3

Trinity Sunday Year C: John 16.12–15

A READING FROM THE TREATISE *ON THE TRINITY* BY ST HILARY OF POITIERS

According to the Apostle, Lord, your Holy Spirit fully understands and penetrates your inmost depths; he also intercedes on my behalf, saying to you things for which I cannot find the words. Nothing can penetrate your being but what is divine already; nor can the depths of your immense majesty be measured by any power which itself is alien or extrinsic to you. So, whatever enters into you is yours already, nor can anything which has the power to search your very depths ever have been other than your own.

Your Holy Spirit proceeds through your Son from you; though I may fail to grasp the full meaning of that statement, I give it nonetheless the firm assent of my mind and heart.

I may indeed show dullness and stupidity in my understanding of these spiritual matters; it is as your only Son has said: *Do not be surprised if I have said to you: 'You must be born again.' Just as the wind blows where it pleases and you hear the sound of it without knowing where it is coming from or going to, so will it be with everyone who is born again of water and the Holy Spirit.* By my regeneration I have received the faith, but I am still ignorant; and yet I have a firm hold on something which I do not understand. I am born again, capable of rebirth but without conscious perception of it. The Spirit abides by no rules; he speaks when he pleases, what he pleases, and where he pleases. We are conscious of his presence when he comes, but the reasons for his approach or his departure remain hidden from us.

John tells us that all things came into being through the Son who is God the Word abiding with you, Father, from the beginning. Paul in his turn enumerates the things created in the Son, both visible and invisible, in heaven and on earth. And while he is specific about all that was created in and through Christ, of the Holy Spirit he considers it enough simply to say that he is your Spirit.

Therefore I concur with those chosen men in thinking that just as it is not expedient for me to venture beyond my mental limitation and predicate anything of your only begotten Son save that, as those witnesses have assured us, he was born of you, so it is not fitting for me to go beyond the power of human thought and the teaching of those same witnesses by declaring anything regarding the Holy Spirit other than that he is your Spirit. Rather than waste time in a fruitless war of words, I would prefer to spend it in the firm profession of an unhesitating faith.

I beg you therefore, Father, to preserve in me that pure and reverent faith and to grant that to my last breath I may testify to my conviction. May I always hold fast to what I publicly professed in the creed when I was baptized in the name of the Father and of the Son and of the Holy Spirit. May I worship you, the Father of us all, and your Son together with you and may I be counted worthy to receive your Holy Spirit who through your only Son proceeds from you. For me there is sufficient evidence for this faith in the words: *Father, all that I have is yours, and all that is yours is mine*, spoken by Jesus Christ my Lord who remains, in and from and with you, the God who is blessed for endless ages. Amen.

St Hilary of Poitiers, *On the Trinity*, 12.55–6: PL 10, 468–72

Corpus Christi Year A: John 6.51–59 [RCL A–C]
(The Feast of Corpus Christi, the Day of Thanksgiving for the Institution of Holy Communion, is the Thursday after Trinity Sunday, although Roman Catholics sometimes celebrate it on the following Sunday)

A READING FROM A SERMON BY ST AUGUSTINE

You see on God's altar bread and a cup. That is what the evidence of your eyes tells you, but your faith requires you to believe that the bread is the body of Christ, the cup the blood of Christ. In these few words we can say perhaps all that faith demands.

Faith, however, seeks understanding; so you may now say to me, 'You have told us what we have to believe, but explain it so that we can understand it, because it is quite possible for someone to think along these lines: we know from whom our Lord Jesus Christ took his flesh – it was from the Virgin Mary. As a baby, he was suckled, he was fed, he developed, he came to young man's estate. He was slain on the cross, he was taken down from it, he was buried, he rose again on the third day. On the day of his own choosing, he ascended to heaven, taking his body with him; and it is from heaven that he will come to judge the living and the dead. But now that he is there, seated at the right hand of the Father, how can bread be his body? And the cup, or rather what is in the cup, how can that be his blood?'

These things, my friends, are called sacraments, because our eyes see in them one thing, our understanding another. Our eyes see the material form; our understanding, its spiritual effect. If, then, you want to know what the body of Christ is, you must listen to what the Apostle tells the faithful: *Now you are the body of Christ, and individually you are members of it.*

If that is so, it is the sacrament of yourselves that is placed on the Lord's altar, and it is the sacrament of yourselves that you receive. You reply 'Amen' to what you are, and thereby agree that such you are. You hear the words 'The body of Christ' and you reply 'Amen'. Be, then, a member of Christ's body, so that your 'Amen' may accord with the truth.

Yes, but why all this in bread? Here let us not advance any ideas of our own, but listen to what the Apostle says over and over again when speaking of the sacrament: *Because there is one loaf, we, though we are many, form one body.* Let your mind assimilate that and be glad, for there you will find unity, truth, piety, and love. He says, *one loaf.* And who is this one loaf? *We, though we are many, form one body.* Now bear in mind that bread is not made of a single grain, but of many. Be, then, what you see, and receive what you are.

So much for what the Apostle says about the bread. As for the cup, what we have to believe is quite clear, although the Apostle does not mention it expressly. Just as the unity of the faithful, which holy Scripture describes in the words: *They were of one mind and heart in God,* should be like the kneading together of many grains into one visible loaf, so with the wine. Think how wine is made. Many grapes hang in a cluster, but their juice flows together into an indivisible liquid.

It was thus that Christ our Lord signified us, and his will that we should belong to him, when he hallowed the sacrament of our peace and unity on his altar. Anyone, however, who receives this sacrament of unity and does not keep the bond of peace, does not receive it to his profit, but as a testimony against himself.

St Augustine, *Sermon* 272: Edit. Maurist., 5, 1103–4

Corpus Christi Year B: Mark 14.12–16

A READING FROM A HOMILY ON MATTHEW BY ST JOHN CHRYSOSTOM

As they were eating, he took bread and broke it. Christ instituted this sacrament at the time of the Passover in order to teach us by every possible means both that he himself had been the lawgiver of the Old Testament, and also that the whole of the Old Testament had been a foreshadowing of these mysteries. He was replacing the type by the reality. The fact that it was evening signified that the fullness of time had come and that all was about to be accomplished. He gave thanks to teach us how we ought to celebrate these mysteries, to show that he was not going to his passion against his will, and to train us to accept with gratitude whatever we have to suffer and so to derive from it hope of future blessedness.

If the type was able to free a people from bondage, much more would the reality liberate the world, and Christ's death bring down blessings upon our race. We see then why he did not institute this sacrament before, but only when it was time to abolish the rites of the law. Christ put an end to the most important Jewish festival by offering his disciples another far more awe-inspiring meal. *Take, eat*, he said, *this is my body which is broken for many.*

These words might well have alarmed them; if they did not, it was because Christ had already told them many marvellous things about this sacrament. In fact, they had been so well prepared that there was no need for him to say any more. But he told them that the reason he was going to suffer was to take away our sins. He spoke of the blood of the new covenant, that is, of the promise, the new law. He had promised long before that the new covenant had been ratified by his blood. As the old covenant had been ratified by the blood of sheep and calves, so the new covenant was to be ratified by the blood of the Lord. Thus, by speaking of his covenant and by reminding them that the old covenant had also been inaugurated by the shedding of blood, he made known to them that he was soon to die. And he told them once again the reason for his death in the words, *This is my blood, which is poured out for all for the forgiveness of sins*, and, *Do this in memory of me.*

Notice how he leads them away from the Jewish customs by saying, 'Just as you used to do this in memory of the miracles performed in Egypt, so now you must do it in memory of me.' Blood was shed then for the salvation of the firstborn: it is to be shed now for the forgiveness of sins of the whole world. *This*, he said, *is my blood, which is shed for the forgiveness of sins*. He said this both to teach his disciples the sacramental nature of his death upon the cross, and also to comfort them. As Moses had said, *This shall be for you an everlasting memorial*, so now the Lord says, *Do this in memory of me until I come*. And so he also says, *I have longed to eat this Passover*, meaning, 'to hand over to you the new rites and to give you the Passover by which I am going to sanctify you.'

St John Chrysostom, *Homilies on Matthew*, 82.1: PG 58, 737–9

Corpus Christi Year C: Luke 9.11–17

A READING FROM THE HOMILIES ON THE FIRST LETTER TO THE CORINTHIANS BY ST JOHN CHRYSOSTOM

Christ gave us his flesh to eat in order to deepen our love for him. When we approach him, then, there should be burning within us a fire of love and longing. Otherwise the punishment awaiting us will be in proportion to the magnitude of the graces we have received and of which we have shown ourselves unworthy.

The wise men paid homage to Christ's body even when it was lying in a manger. Foreigners who did not worship the true God left their homes and their native land, set out on a long journey, and on reaching its end, worshipped in great fear and trembling. They only saw Christ in a manger, they saw nothing of what you now see, and yet they approached him with profound awe and reverence. You see him, not in a manger but on an altar, not carried by a woman but offered by a priest; and you see the Spirit bountifully poured out upon the offerings of bread and wine. Unlike the wise men, you do not merely see Christ's body: you know his power as well, and whole divine plan for our salvation. Having been carefully instructed, you are ignorant of none of the marvels he has performed. Let us then awaken in ourselves a feeling of awe and let us show a far greater reverence than did those foreigners, for we shall bring down fire upon our heads if we approach this sacrament casually, without thinking of what we do.

By saying this I do not mean that we should not approach it, but simply that we should not do so thoughtlessly. Just as coming to it in a casual way is perilous, so failing to share in this sacramental meal is hunger and death. This food strengthens us; it emboldens us to speak freely to our God; it is our hope, our salvation, our light, and our life. If we go to the next world fortified by this sacrifice, we shall enter its sacred portals with perfect confidence, as though protected all over by armour of gold.

But why do I speak of the next world? Because of this sacrament earth becomes heaven for you. Throw open the gates of heaven – or rather, not of heaven but of the heaven of heavens – look through and you will see the proof of what I say. What is heaven's most precious possession? I will show you it here on earth. I do not show you angels or archangels, heaven or the heaven of heavens, but I show you the very Lord of all these. Do you not see how you gaze, here on earth, upon what is most precious of all? You not only gaze on it, but touch it as well. You not only touch it, but even eat it, and take it away with you to your homes. It is essential therefore when you wish to receive this sacrament to cleanse your soul from sin and to prepare your mind.

St John Chrysostom, *Homilies on 1 Corinthians*, 24.4: PG 61, 204–5

Sacred Heart Year A (RL): Matthew 11.25–30
(The Solemnity of the Sacred Heart is the Friday after the second Sunday after Pentecost)

A READING FROM A SERMON BY ST BRUNO OF SEGNI

Be imitators of God as his dearest children, and walk in love, just as Christ loved us, and gave himself up for us as a sweet-smelling oblation and sacrifice. Dearly beloved, in everything but he did and said our Lord Jesus Christ left us a pattern of humility, and instruction in virtuous living, for he wished to teach us not only by words, but also by example. Hence it is written: *Jesus began to do and to teach.* As regards humility the Lord himself said: *Learn from me, for I am meek and humble of heart.*

Although he was the almighty Lord, he chose to be poor for our sakes; he refused honours, freely submitted to sufferings, and even went so far as to pray for his persecutors. And he did all this in order that we might not disdain to follow him insofar as our frailty allows. If we fail to do so we are not true Christians, for anyone who says he loves Christ must tread the path he trod.

Because the Lord freely submitted to suffering and the cross, he delivered us by his very death from the power of the devil. Moreover, he prayed for sinners as he hung on the cross to give us an example. After all, if so much was willingly endured by the very Lord of the universe at the hands of slaves, by the just One at the hands of sinners, it behoves us to bear with the greatest patience wrongs done us by our own kith and kin.

And when we are in the midst of affliction, we too must pray most earnestly. Afflictions are of two kinds. It is an affliction when we suffer some temporal injury, and it is an affliction – a much greater one – when we give way to any kind of wrongdoing. Our prayer, however, must be such that it will not be turned into sin. And we must also give alms, and do so in the perfect way. The perfection of almsgiving consists in two things, namely, giving and forgiving. As the Lord says in the gospel: *Give and it will be given you; forgive and you will be forgiven.* These are the virtues through which we are to come to the kingdom of heaven, to which may our Lord Jesus Christ lead us, who lives and reigns for ever and ever.

St Bruno of Segni, *Sermon 1 on Good Friday*: PL 165, 1007–8

Sacred Heart Year B (RL): John 19.31–37

A READING FROM A SERMON BY ST AUGUSTINE

I believe in God, the almighty Father. How little time it takes to say it; how much it means! God is both God and Father; God in that he is all-powerful, Father in that he is all-goodness. How blessed are we that have discovered that the Lord is our Father! Let us put our faith in him and be sure that we shall obtain all we need from his mercy, because he is almighty.

Let none of you say: 'He is powerless to forgive my sins.' How can the Almighty be powerless? You may say: 'I have sinned much', but I reply that he is almighty. And if you insist, 'I have committed such great sins that it is impossible for me to be freed from them and made clean', I still reply that he is almighty.

In another part of the creed we say: *I believe in the forgiveness of sins.* If the Church did not possess the power of forgiving sins, there would be no hope. If there were no forgiveness of sins in the Church, there would be no hope of a future life or of eternal freedom. Thanks be to God for bequeathing this gift to the Church!

Here you all are now, ready to come to the sacred font where you will be washed clean in baptism and made new by being born again in the saving waters. When you come up from the font, you will be without sin. All the things that burden you from your past will be blotted out. Your sins will be like the Egyptians who pursued the Israelites – they pursued them only as far as the Red Sea. Now what does 'as far as the Red Sea' mean? As far as the baptismal font, which has been consecrated by the cross and the blood of Christ. It is called the Red Sea because of its ruddy hue. And do you not see the stain of blood upon those who belong to Christ? Look with the eyes of faith. When you see the cross, visualize the blood also. When you see the body hanging on the cross, contemplate the blood streaming from it. Christ's side was pierced with a lance, and our ransom poured out. This is the reason why baptism, that is to say the water into which you are dipped, is signed by the cross of Christ; it is as if you were crossing over the Red Sea. Your sins are your enemies; they pursue you, but only as far as the sea.

When you enter the font you escape from them. They are wiped out, just as the Egyptians were engulfed by the waves while the Israelites escaped dry-shod. What does the Scripture say? *Not one of them remained.* Whether your sins are many or few, great or small, not the least one of them remains.

St Augustine, *Sermon* 213, 8: Edit. Maurist., 5, 942

Sacred Heart Year C (RL): Luke 15.3–7

A READING FROM A COMMENTARY ON PSALM 118 BY ST AMBROSE

The Lord Jesus himself declared that the shepherd in the gospel left the ninety-nine sheep and went after the one that had strayed. The lost sheep he spoke of was the hundredth. Now the number one hundred stands for perfection and fullness, and there should be a lesson in this for you. There are grounds for preferring the stray sheep to the others. The truth is that it is a greater thing to turn back from one's sins than scarcely to have committed any. When souls are steeped in sin, not only do they need perfect human virtue to shake off the tyranny of lust and mend their ways, but heavenly grace is also necessary. A man can make a resolution to amend in the future, but forgiveness of the past is a matter for divine power.

When the shepherd has at last found the sheep, he places it on his shoulders. I am sure you are aware of the symbolism contained in the way the weary sheep is revived; how it represents humanity, worn out and exhausted, incapable of restoration to health except by the mystery of the passion and blood of our Lord Jesus Christ, of whom it is written that the *symbol of dominion will be upon his shoulders.* On the cross he bore our infirmities, so that there he might cancel the sins of us all. The angels have good reason to rejoice, seeing the lost sheep straying no longer, seeing him, in fact, giving no further thought to wandering.

Like a lost sheep I have gone astray; give life to your servant, but I do not forget your commandment. I am your servant, Lord; come in search of me, for unless the shepherd seeks out the stray, it will die. Return is still possible for the one who is lost; he can still be recalled to the right path. Come, then, Lord Jesus, seek your servant, seek your exhausted sheep. Come as shepherd of the flock, seeking your sheep as Joseph sought his, the sheep that went astray while you were lingering in the mountains. Leave your ninety-nine sheep there and come in search of the one that is lost. Come, not with rod in hand, but in a spirit of love and gentleness.

Seek me, Lord; I need you. Seek me, find me, lift me up, carry me. You are expert at finding what you search for; and when you have found the stray you stoop down, lift him up, and place him on your own shoulders. To you he is a burden of love, not an object of revulsion; it is no irksome task to you to bring justification to the human race. Come then, Lord; I have gone astray, but *I have not forgotten your commandments.* I still hold on to the hope of healing. Come, Lord; none but you can bring back your erring sheep. Those whom you leave behind will not be grieved, because the sinner's return will be a joy to them too. Come, do your saving work on earth, and let there be joy in heaven.

Come in search of your sheep, not through the ministry of servants or hirelings, but in your own person. Take my human nature, which fell in Adam. Take my humanity, not from Sarah but from the spotless Virgin Mary, a virgin preserved through your grace from any stain of sin. Bear me on the cross where sinners find salvation, where alone there is rest for the weary, where alone there is life for the dying.

St Ambrose, *Sermons on Psalm 118*, 22.3, 27–30: CSEL 62, 489,
502–4

FOR THE READINGS FOR WEEKS SIX TO NINE OF ORDINARY TIME (RL) OR PROPERS THREE AND FOUR (RCL), SEE ORDINARY TIME BEFORE LENT

Tenth Sunday in Ordinary Time/Proper 5 Year A: Matthew 9.9–13 [& 18–36]

A READING FROM THE COMMENTARY ON THE PSALMS BY ST AUGUSTINE

Some people's strength is based on confidence in their own righteousness. It was this kind of strength that prevented the Jewish leaders from entering the eye of the needle. They took their righteousness for granted and seemed in their own eyes to be healthy. Therefore they refused the remedy and slew the physician. They were strong, not weak. They were not the ones he came to call who said: *The healthy have no need of a physician; it is the sick who need him. I did not come to call the righteous but sinners to repentance.* Those were strong people who taunted Christ's disciples because their master entered the homes of the sick and ate with them.

Why, they asked, *does your master eat with tax collectors and sinners?* O you strong ones who do not need the doctor! Yours is not the strength of health but of madness! God grant that we may never need that kind of strength. We should dread the possibility of anyone wanting to imitate it.

The teacher of humility, who shared our weakness and gave us a share in his own divinity, came to earth in order to teach us the way, even to be the Way himself. It was his humility, above all else, that he impressed upon us. He willingly submitted to baptism at the hands of one of his servants, so that we might learn to confess our own sins and become weak in order to be truly strong, repeating with the Apostle: *When I am weak, then I am strong.*

But as for the people who wished to be strong, that is, those who wanted to be righteous by their own power, they tripped over the stumbling block. In their eyes, the Lamb was a goat, and because, seeing him as a goat, they killed him, they did not deserve to be redeemed by the Lamb. In their strength they attacked Christ, priding themselves on their own righteousness. Listen to these strong ones talking. They had sent some people from Jerusalem to arrest Christ but they did not dare to do so. *Why did you not seize him?* they demanded. *No one ever spoke like this man*, they replied. To which the strong ones retorted: *You do not see any of the Pharisees believing in him, do you, or any of the Scribes? It is only the people who are ignorant of the law that believe in him.*

Thus they put themselves on a higher level than the weak crowd that ran to the doctor. Why did they exalt themselves? Because they were strong. What is worse, by their strength they drew the whole crowd to themselves and killed the physician who had power to heal them all. But the murdered physician, by his very death, compounded a medicine for the sick out of his own blood.

St Augustine, *On the Psalms* 58, 1.7: CCSL 39, 733–4

Tenth Sunday in Ordinary Time/Proper 5 Year B: Mark 3.20–35

A READING FROM AN UNKNOWN GREEK AUTHOR OF THE FIFTH CENTURY

The signs of the Lord's resurrection are obvious: deception has ceased, envy has been banished, strife is despised. Peace is held in honour, and war has been done away with. No longer do we bewail the Adam who was fashioned first; instead we glorify the Second Adam. No longer do we reproach Eve for transgressing God's command: instead we bless Mary for being the Mother of God. No longer do we avert our eyes from the wood of the tree: instead we carry the Lord's cross. We no longer fear the serpent: instead we revere the Holy Spirit. We no longer descend into the earth: instead we re-ascend into heaven. We are no longer exiles from paradise: instead we live in Abraham's bosom. We no longer hear, 'I have made your day like night': instead, inspired by the Holy Spirit, we sing: *This is the day which the Lord has made: let us keep it with gladness and rejoicing.* Why should we do so? Because the sun is no longer darkened: instead everything is bathed in light. Because the veil of the temple is no longer rent: instead the Church is recognized. Because we no longer hold palm branches: instead we carry the newly enlightened.

This is the day which the Lord has made: let us keep it with gladness and rejoicing. This is the day, this and no other, for there is only one queen, and not a throng of princesses. This is the day in the truest sense: the day of triumph, the day custom consecrates to the resurrection, the day on which we adorn ourselves with grace, the day on which we pertain to the spiritual Lamb. This is the day on which milk is given to those born again, and in which God's plan is realized. *Let us keep it with gladness and rejoicing*, not by running off to the taverns, but by hastening to the martyrs' shrines; not by esteeming drunkenness, but by loving temperance; not by dancing in the marketplace, but by singing psalms at home. This day is a day of resurrection, not of revelry. No one can ascend to heaven dancing; no one in a state of drunkenness can attend upon a king. See that none of us, therefore, dishonour this day.

This is the day on which Adam was set free, and Eve delivered from her affliction. It is the date on which cruel death shuddered, the strength of hard stones was shattered and destroyed, the bars of tombs were broken and set aside. It is the day on which the bodies of people long dead were restored to their former life, and the laws of the underworld, hitherto ever powerful and immutable, where repealed. It is the day on which the heavens were opened at the rising of Christ the Lord, and on which, for the good of the human race, the flourishing and fruitful tree of the resurrection sent forth branches all over the world, as if the world were a garden. It is the day on which the lilies of the newly enlightened sprang up, the streams that sustained sinners ran dry, the strength of the devil drained away, and demonic armies were scattered.

This, then, *is the day which the Lord has made: let us keep it with gladness and rejoicing* by the grace of Christ. By his resurrection he has illuminated the whole world, which was *in darkness and in the shadow of death*. May glory and adoration be given to him together with the Father and the Holy Spirit for endless ages. Amen.

Unknown Greek author of the fifth century, *Paschal Homilies*, 51.1–3:
SC 187, 318–22

Tenth Sunday in Ordinary Time/Proper 5 Year C: Luke 7.11–17

A READING FROM A SERMON BY ST AUGUSTINE

All believers are moved when they hear the accounts of the miracles wrought by Jesus, our Lord and Saviour, though they are affected by them in different ways. Some are astounded by his wonderful physical cures, but have not yet learnt to discern the greater miracles that lie beyond the world of sense. Others marvel that the miracles that they hear our Lord working on people's bodies are now being accomplished more wonderfully in their souls.

No Christian should doubt that even today the dead are being raised to life. Yet, while everyone has eyes capable of seeing the dead rise in the way the widow's son rose, as we have just heard in the gospel, the ability to see the spiritually dead arise is possessed only by those who have themselves experienced a spiritual resurrection.

It is a greater thing to raise what will live for ever than to raise what must die again. When the young man in the gospel was raised, his widowed mother rejoiced; when souls are daily raised from spiritual death, mother Church rejoices. The young man was dead in body, these latter are dead in spirit. Those who witnessed the lad's visible death mourned openly and visibly, but the invisible death of the dead in spirit was neither seen nor thought about.

The Lord Jesus sought out those he knew to be dead, and he alone could make them live again. Unless he had come to raise the dead the Apostle would not have said: *Rise up, sleeper, and rise from the dead, and Christ will enlighten you. Rise up, sleeper*, of course, makes you think of someone slumbering, but when the Apostle goes on to say, *rise from the dead*, you realize that he really means a dead person. The visibly dead are often said to be sleeping; and indeed for one who has power to wake them they are only sleeping. A person is dead as far as you are concerned if he does not waken no matter how much you slap or pinch or even wound him. But for Christ the young man he commanded to rise was only sleeping, because he immediately got up. Christ raises the dead from their graves more easily than another can rouse a sleeper from his bed.

Our Lord Jesus Christ wished us to understand that what he did for people's bodies he also did for their souls. He did not work miracles merely for miracles' sake; his object was that his deeds might arouse wonder in the beholders and reveal the truth to those capable of understanding.

A person who sees the letters in a beautifully written book without being able to read them will praise the skill of the copyist because he admires the graceful shape of the letters, but the purpose and meaning of these letters he does not grasp. What he sees with his eyes prompts him to praise, but his mind is not enriched with knowledge. Another, praising the artistry, will also grasp the meaning; one, that is, who is able not only to see what everyone else sees but also to read it, which is a skill that has to be learned. So too, those who observed Christ's miracles without grasping their purpose and the meaning they had for those able to understand, simply admired the deeds. Others went further: they admired the deeds and also grasped the meaning. As pupils in the school of Christ, we must be such as these.

St Augustine, *Sermon* 98, 1–3: PL 38, 591–2

Eleventh Sunday in Ordinary Time/Proper 6
Year A: Matthew 9.36 – 10.8 [9.36 – 10.23]
A READING FROM A HOMILY BY ST JOHN CHRYSOSTOM

All farm work is undertaken with a view to the harvest that will come at the end. How then could Jesus apply the word 'harvest' to work that was only beginning? Idolatry held sway all over the world. Everywhere there was fornication, adultery, licentiousness, everywhere greed, robbery, bloodshed. When the world was filled with so many evils, when the good seed had not yet been sown, when the land had not been cleared, and there were briars, thistles and weeds everywhere, when no ploughing had been done, no furrow cut, how could Jesus speak of a harvest and say it was plentiful? Why did he speak thus of the gospel?

Why indeed, if not that with things in such a state, he was about to send out his apostles all over the world. Most likely they were bewildered and anxious; they probably asked themselves: 'How can we even open our mouths, let alone stand up and preach in front of huge crowds of people? How can eleven of us put the whole world to rights? Can we speak to the wise when we are ignorant, to soldiers when we are unarmed, to rulers when we are subjects, to people of many different languages, people of foreign nations and alien speech, when we have only one language? Who will tolerate us if no one can understand what we say?'

It was to save them from the anxiety of such reasoning that the Lord called the gospel a harvest. It was almost as if he said: 'Everything is ready, all is prepared. I am sending you to harvest the ripe grain. You will be able to sow and reap on the same day. You must be like the farmer who rejoices when he goes out to gather in his crops. He looks happy and is glad of heart. His hard work and many difficulties forgotten, he hurries out eagerly to reap their reward, hastening to collect his annual returns. Nothing stands in the way, there is no obstacle anywhere, nor any uncertainty regarding the future. There will be no heavy rain, no hail or drought, no devastating legions of locusts. And since the farmer at harvest time fears no such disasters, the reapers set to work dancing and leaping for joy.

'You must be like them when you go out into the world – indeed your joy must be very much greater. You also are to gather in a harvest – a harvest easily reaped, a harvest already there waiting for you. You have only to speak, not to labour. Lend me your tongue, and you will see the ripe grain gathered into the royal granary.' And with this he sent them out, saying: *Remember that I am with you always, until the end of the world.*

St John Chrysostom, *Last Homilies*, 10.2–3: Bareille, 20, 562–4

Eleventh Sunday in Ordinary Time/Proper 6 Year B: Mark 4.26–34

A READING FROM A HOMILY ATTRIBUTED TO ST JOHN CHRYSOSTOM

What is greater than the kingdom of heaven, and what smaller than a mustard seed? How can the Lord compare the infinite kingdom of heaven with a tiny mustard seed? Well, if we consider what the kingdom of heaven is and what the mustard seed, we shall discover how right and apt the comparison.

The kingdom of heaven is obviously Christ, for he says of himself: *Behold, the kingdom of heaven is among you.* That there is nothing greater than Christ in his divine nature you may learn from the prophet's words: *This is our God: no other can be compared with him. He has the key to the whole way of knowledge, and he gave it to Jacob his servant and to Israel his beloved. Then he appeared upon earth and lived among us.*

On the other hand, what is less than Christ in the order of the incarnation, which made him lower than both angels and humans. Listen to David tell of his becoming lower than the angels: *What is man that you are mindful of him, or the son of man that you care for him? You have made him a little lower than the angels.* David refers here to Christ, as Paul explains to you when he says: *We see Jesus, who was made a little lower than the angels.*

But how can the same man be both the kingdom of heaven and a seed, and be described as both large and small? Because he had such great compassion for his own creatures Christ became all things to all in order to win all. He was God, as he still is and always will be in his own nature, and he became man for our salvation. *O the depths of the riches and wisdom and knowledge of God! How incomprehensible are his judgements and how unsearchable his ways!* O seed by which the world was made, through which darkness was dispersed and the Church brought into being! In this seed hanging on the cross was such tremendous power that by a mere word, though bound itself, it snatched the thief from his cross and transported him to the joy of paradise. This seed, its side pierced by a spear, poured out for the thirsty an immortal drink. This mustard seed, taken down from the cross and planted in a garden, branched out over the whole world. This mustard seed sown in a garden sent its roots down to Hades, gathered together the souls that were there, and after three days raised them with itself to heaven.

The kingdom of heaven, then, *is like a mustard seed which a man took and sowed in his garden.* Sow this mustard seed in the garden of your soul and the words of the prophet will apply to you as well: *You will be like a well-watered garden, like a spring whose waters never run dry.*

St John Chrysostom, Homily 7: PG 64, 21–6

Eleventh Sunday in Ordinary Time/Proper 6
Year C: Luke 7.36 – 8.3 or 7.36–50

A READING FROM A HOMILY BY AN ANONYMOUS SYRIAN WRITER

A sinful woman has proclaimed to us that God's love has gone forth in search of sinners. For when he called her, Christ was inviting our whole race to love; and in her person he was drawing all sinners to his forgiveness. He spoke to her alone, but he was drawing all creation to his grace. No one else persuaded him to help her come to forgiveness; only his love for the one he himself had formed persuaded him to do this, and his own grace besought him on behalf of the work of his hands.

Who would not be struck by the mercy of Christ, who accepted an invitation to a Pharisee's house in order to save a sinner! For the sake of the woman who hungered for forgiveness, he himself felt hunger for the table of Simon the Pharisee; and all the while, under the guise of a meal of bread, he had prepared for the sinner a meal of repentance!

The shepherd came down from heaven for the lost sheep, to catch in Simon's house the woman the cunning wolf had carried off. In the house of Simon the Pharisee he found the one he sought.

Seeing Jesus' feet, the sinner took them to be a symbol of his incarnation, and in grasping them believed herself to be grasping her God on the level of his corporal nature. By her words she besought him as her Creator – for clearly her words, though not written down, may be guessed at from her actions. She must surely have uttered words corresponding to her deeds when she bathed his feet with her tears, wiped them with her hair, and poured precious ointment over them. It was a prayer that she offered to the incarnate God: by bringing him her humility she showed her trust in him, and by the conversation they had with one another she proved him to be truly man.

Such then were the words addressed to Jesus by the sinner when she clasped his feet. He listened to them patiently, his silence proclaiming his steadfastness, his patience proclaiming his endurance. By his kindness in response to her boldness, he made it obvious that it was right for her to wrest pardon from him in the presence of all the guests. He did not speak at once and when he spoke he uttered only one word, but by that word he destroyed sins, abolished faults, chased away iniquity, granted pardon, uprooted evil, and made righteousness bud. All at once his forgiveness appeared within her soul and chased out of it the darkness of sin; she was cured, she recovered her wits, and gained both health and strength. For when Jesus gives graces he gives them lavishly, as he easily can, being the God of all things.

In order that you may have the same experience, reflect within yourself that your sin is great, but that it is blasphemy against God and damage to yourself to despair of his forgiveness because your sin seems to you to be too great. He has promised to forgive your sins, however many they are; would you tell him you cannot believe this and dispute with him, saying that your sin is too great; he cannot heal your sickness? Stop at this point, and cry out with the prophet, *Lord, I have sinned against you*. At once he will reply, 'As for me, I overlooked your fault: you shall not die.' Glory to him from all of us, for all the ages. Amen.

Anonymous Syrian writer, *Homily*: *Orient Syrien* 7 [1962], 180–1, 189, 193, 194

Twelfth Sunday in Ordinary Time/Proper 7 Year A: Matthew 10.26–33 [24–39]

A READING FROM THE COMMENTARY ON THE PSALMS BY ST AUGUSTINE

Thanks be to that grain of wheat who freely chose to die and so be multiplied! Thanks be to God's only Son, our Lord and Saviour Jesus Christ, for whom the enduring of our human death was not a thing to be scorned if it would make us worthy of his life! Mark how alone he was before his passing: his is the voice of the psalmist who said, *I am all alone until I depart from this place* – a solitary grain that nevertheless contained an immense fruitfulness, a capacity to be multiplied beyond measure.

How many other grains of wheat imitating the Lord's passion do we find to gladden our hearts when we celebrate the anniversaries of the martyrs! Many members has that one grain, all united by bonds of peace and charity under their one head, our Saviour himself, and, as you know from having heard it so often, all of them form one single body. Their many voices can often be heard praying in the psalms through the voice of a single speaker calling on God as if all were calling together, because all are one in him.

Let us listen to their cry. In it we can hear the words of the martyrs who found themselves hard pressed, beset by danger from violent storms of hatred in this world, a danger not so much to their bodies which, after all, they would have to part with some time, but rather to their faith. If they were to give way, if they should succumb either to the harsh tortures of their persecutors or to love of this present life, they would forfeit the reward promised them by the God who had taken away all ground for fear. Not only had he said: *Do not be afraid of those who kill the body but are unable to kill the soul*; he had also left them his own example. The precept he had enjoined on them he personally carried out, without attempting to evade the hands of those who scourged him, the blows of those who struck him, or the spittle of those who spat on him. Neither the crown of thorns pressed into his head nor the cross to which the soldiers nailed him encountered any resistance from him. None of these torments did he try to avoid. Though he himself was under no obligation to suffer them, he endured them for those who were to come, making his own person a remedy for the sick. And so the martyrs suffered, but they would certainly have failed the test without the presence of him who said: *Know that I am with you always, until the of time.*

St Augustine, *On the Psalms* 69; CCSL 39.930–1

Twelfth Sunday in Ordinary Time/Proper 7 Year B: Mark 4.35–41

A READING FROM A SERMON BY ST AUGUSTINE

With the Lord's help I want to speak to you about today's reading from the holy gospel, and to urge you in his name not to let your faith lie dormant in your hearts when you are buffeted by the winds and waves of this world. The Lord Christ's power is by no means dead, nor is it asleep. Do you think the Almighty was overcome by sleep in the boat against his will? If you do, then Christ is asleep in your hearts. If he were indeed keeping watch within you, then your faith too would be vigilant. The Apostle, remember, speaks of Christ dwelling in your hearts through faith.

This sleep of Christ has a symbolic meaning. The boat's crew are human souls sailing across the sea of this world in a wooden vessel. That vessel, of course, also represents the Church; but as each one of us is a temple of God, each one's heart is a sailing boat, nor can it be wrecked so long as we fill our minds only with what is good.

When you have to listen to abuse, that means you are being buffeted by the wind; when your anger is roused, you are being tossed by the waves. So when the winds blow and the waves mount high, the boat is in danger, your heart is imperilled, your heart is taking a battering. On hearing yourself insulted, you long to retaliate; but the joy of revenge brings with it another kind of misfortune – shipwreck. Why is this? Because Christ is asleep in you. What do I mean? I mean you have forgotten his presence. Rouse him, then; remember him, let him keep watch within you, pay heed to him. Now what was your desire? You wanted to get your own back. You have forgotten that when Christ was being crucified he said: *Father, forgive them, for they know not what they do.* Christ, the sleeper in your heart, had no desire for vengeance in his. Rouse him, then, call him to mind (to remember him is to recall his words; to remember him is to recall his commands). Then, when he is awake within you, you will ask yourself,

'Whatever kind of wretch am I to be thirsting for revenge? Who am I to threaten another? Suppose I were to die before I am avenged! Suppose I were to take leave of my body breathing out threats, inflamed with rage and thirsting for that vengeance which Christ himself never sought; would he not refuse to receive me? He who said, *Give and it shall be given you; forgive and you will be forgiven*, would indeed decline to acknowledge me. So I will curb my anger and restore peace to my heart.'

Now all is calm again. Christ has rebuked the sea. What I have said about anger must be your rule of conduct in every temptation. A temptation arises: it is the wind. It disturbs you: it is the surging of the sea. This is the moment to awaken Christ and let him remind you of those words: *Who can this be? Even the winds and the sea obey him.* Who is this whom the sea obeys? It is he to whom the sea belongs, for he made it; all things were made through him.

Try, then, to be more like the wind and the sea; obey the God who made you. The sea obeys Christ's command, and are you going to turn a deaf ear to it? The sea obeys him, the wind is still; will you persist with your blustering? Words, actions, schemes, what are all these but a constant huffing and puffing, a refusal to be still at Christ's command?

When your heart is in this troubled state, do not let the waves overwhelm you. If, since we are only human, the driving wind should stir up in us a tumult of emotions, let us not despair but awaken Christ, so that we may sail in quiet waters, and reach at last our heavenly homeland.

St Augustine, *Sermon* 63, 1–3: PL 38, 424–5

Twelfth Sunday in Ordinary Time Year C (RL): Luke 9.18–24

A READING FROM A HOMILY ON LUKE BY ST CYRIL OF ALEXANDRIA

One day when Jesus was praying alone with his disciples he asked them: 'Who do the crowd say that I am?' By praying alone accompanied only by his disciples the Lord and Saviour of the world was setting them an example of a life befitting saints. However, there was a danger that this might disturb them and give them mistaken ideas. When they saw praying like a human being one whom the day before they had seen working miracles like God, they might well say among themselves: 'This is very strange – who are we to think he is, God or a man?'

To put an end to any such mental turmoil and steady their unsettled faith, Jesus questioned them. He was not ignorant of what was being said of him by those outside the synagogue of the Jews or by the Israelites themselves, but he wanted to withdraw his disciples from the thinking of the multitude and establish right belief in them. *Who do the crowd say I am?* he asked.

Then Peter burst out before the rest and became the spokesman for the whole group, his words full of the love of God giving expression to a faith in Jesus which was correct and beyond reproach. *The Anointed of God,* he said. The disciple had weighed his words carefully and spoke of holy things with complete understanding. He did not say simply that Jesus was one anointed by God, but that he was *The Anointed.* For many were called anointed ones because God had anointed them in various ways, some as kings, some as prophets. Others like ourselves are called anointed ones because we have been saved by this Anointed One, the Saviour of all the world, and have received the anointing of the Holy Spirit. Yes, many have received an anointing, and are therefore called anointed ones, but there is only One who is the Anointed of God the Father.

When the disciple had made his profession of faith Jesus *gave them strict orders to tell this to no one. 'The Son of Man',* he said, *'must suffer greatly, and be rejected and killed, and raised up on the third day.'*

Yet why was it not rather their duty to preach him everywhere? Surely this was the task of those who had been consecrated by him as apostles. However, as Holy Scripture says, *Every work has its own time.* Preaching Jesus had to follow events which had not yet taken place, namely, the crucifixion, the passion, the physical death, and the resurrection from the dead – that great and truly glorious miracle by which Emmanuel was attested as true God and by nature the Son of God the Father.

Jesus therefore commanded that the mystery should be honoured by silence for the time being, until God's saving dispensation was brought to its proper conclusion. Then, when he had risen from the dead, he gave orders for it to be revealed to the whole world, and for all to be offered justification through faith and purification through holy baptism. *All authority in heaven and on earth has been given to me,* he said. *Go, therefore, and teach all nations. Baptize them in the name of the Father and of the Son and of the Holy Spirit, and instruct them to observe all the commandments I have given you. And remember that I am with you always, till the end of the world.*

St Cyril of Alexandria, Homily 49: ed. R. M. Tonneau, CSCO Script. Syri 70, 110–15

Sunday of Proper 7C (RCL): Luke 8.26–39

A READING FROM THE *LIFE OF HILARION* BY ST JEROME

Before I begin to write the life of the blessed Hilarion I invoke the aid of the Holy Spirit who dwelt in him, that the Spirit who bestowed upon him his virtues may grant me such power of speech to relate them that my words may be adequate to his deeds. For the virtue of those who have done great deeds is esteemed in proportion to the ability with which it has been praised.

Brute animals were daily brought to Hilarion in a state of madness, and among them a Bactrian camel of enormous size amid the shouts of thirty men or more who held him tight with stout ropes. He had already injured many. His eyes were bloodshot, his mouth filled with foam, his rolling tongue swollen, and above every other source of terror was his loud and hideous roar. The old man ordered him to be let go. At once those who brought him as well as the saint's attendants fled away without exception. The saint went by himself to meet the camel, and, addressing him in Syriac, said, 'You do not alarm me, devil, huge though your present body is. Whether in a fox or a camel you are just the same.' Meanwhile he stood with outstretched hand. The brute raging and looking as if he would devour Hilarion came up to him, but immediately fell down, laid its head on the ground, and to the amazement of all present showed suddenly no less tameness than it had previously exhibited ferocity.

The old man then told those who had fled how the devil, to persecute human beings, seizes even beasts of burden; that he is inflamed by such intense hatred for humans that he desires to destroy not only them but what belongs to them. As an illustration of this he added the fact that before he was permitted to try the saintly Job, he made an end of all his possessions. Nor ought it to disturb anyone that by the Lord's command two thousand swine were slain by the agency of demons, since those who witnessed the miracle could not have believed that so great a multitude of demons had gone out of the man unless an equally vast number of swine had rushed to ruin, thus demonstrating that it was a legion that impelled them.

St Jerome, *Life of Hilarion*, 1, 23–4

Thirteenth Sunday in Ordinary Time/Proper 8
Year A: Matthew 10.37–42

A READING FROM THE COMMENTARY ON MATTHEW
BY ST HILARY OF POITIERS

Christ commanded the apostles to leave everything in the world that they held most dear, adding: *Whoever does not take up his cross and follow me is not worthy of me.* For those who belong to Christ have crucified their lower nature with its sinful passions and desires. No one is worthy of him who refuses to take up his cross, that is to say, to share the Lord's passion, death, burial, and resurrection, and to follow him by living out the mystery of faith in the new received grace of the Spirit.

Whoever finds his life will lose it, and whoever loses his life for my sake will find it. This means that thanks to the power of the Word and the renunciation of past sins, temporal gains are death to the soul, and temporal losses salvation. Apostles must therefore take death into their new life and nail their sins to the Lord's cross. They must confront their persecutors with contempt for things present, holding fast to their freedom by a glorious confession of faith, and shunning any gain that would harm their souls. They should know that no power over their souls has been given to anyone, and that by suffering loss in this short life they will achieve immortality.

Whoever receives you receives me, and whoever receives me receives the one who sent me. Christ gives us all a love for his teaching and a disposition to treat our teachers with courtesy. Earlier he had shown the danger facing those who refused to receive the apostles by requiring these to shake the dust off their feet as a testimony against them; now he commends those who do receive the apostles, assuring them of a greater recompense than they might have expected for their hospitality, and he teaches that since he still acts as mediator, when we receive him God enters us through him because he comes from God. Thus whoever receives the apostles receives Christ, and whoever receives Christ receives God the Father, since what is received in the apostles is nothing else than what is received in Christ; nor is there anything in Christ but what is God. Through this disposition of graces to receive the apostles is to receive God, because Christ is in them and God is in Christ.

St Hilary of Poitiers, *Commentary on Matthew*, 10.25–27:
SC 254, 246–51

Thirteenth Sunday in Ordinary Time/Proper 8
Year B: Mark 5.21–43 or 5.21–24, 35–43

A READING FROM A SERMON BY ST PETER CHRYSOLOGUS

Every gospel reading, beloved, is most helpful both for our present life and for the attainment of the life to come. Today's reading, however, sums up the whole of our hope, banishing all grounds for despair.

Let us consider the synagogue official who took Christ to his daughter and in so doing gave the woman with a haemorrhage an opportunity to approach him. Here is the beginning of today's reading: An official came to Jesus and did homage, saying: *Lord, my little daughter has just died, but come and lay your hand on her and she will live.*

Christ could foresee the future and he knew this woman would approach him. Through her the Jewish official was to learn that there is no need to move God to another place, take him on a journey, or attract him by a physical presence. One must only believe that he is present in the whole of his being always and everywhere, and that he can do all things effortlessly by a single command; that far from depriving us of strength, he gives it; that he puts death to flight by a word of command rather than by physical touch, and gives life by his mere bidding, without need of any art.

My daughter has just died. Do come. What he means is that the warmth of life still remains, there are still indications that her soul has not departed, her spirit is still in this world, the head of the house still has a daughter, the underworld is still unaware of her death. Come quickly and hold back the departing soul!

In his ignorance the man assumed that Christ would not be able to raise his daughter unless he actually laid his hand on her. So when Christ reached the house and saw the mourners lamenting as though the girl were dead, he declared that she was not dead but sleeping, in order to move their understanding minds to faith and convince them that one can rise from death more easily than from sleep. *The girl is not dead*, he told them, *but asleep.* And indeed, for God death is nothing but sleep, since he can raise the dead to life more quickly than we can rouse a sleeper. He can restore life-giving warmth to limbs grown cold in death sooner than we can impart vigour to bodies sunk in slumber. Listen to the Apostle: *In an instant, in the twinkling of an eye, the dead will rise.* He used an image because it was impossible to express the speed of the resurrection in words. How could he explain its swiftness verbally when divine power outstrips the very notion of swiftness? How could time enter the picture when an eternal gift is given outside of time? Time implies duration, but eternity excludes time.

St Peter Chrysologus, *Sermon* 34: PL 52, 296–9

Thirteenth Sunday in Ordinary Time/Proper 8 Year C: Luke 9.51–62

A READING FROM THE COMMENTARY ON THE PSALMS BY ST HILARY OF POITIERS

Sure of protection on the day of battle, Christ prayed: *Lord, do not allow the wicked anything contrary to my desire.* He who said, *I have come not to do my own will, but the will of him who sent me*, hastened to fulfil the task he had undertaken out of obedience, though in such a way as to remind us that he possessed a will of his own. In fact, he willed whatever the Father willed. His saying: *I have come not to do my own will, but the will of him who sent me*, revealed who had sent him and whom he obeyed, but without detriment to his own power of willing.

Desiring to do everything the Father desired, Christ hastened to carry out his wishes with regard to his passion before the wicked could hinder him or prevent his doing so. He had a great longing to eat the passover with his disciples, and he celebrated the paschal meal in haste. He had an intense desire to drink the cup of his passion, for he said: *Shall I not drink the cup which my Father has given me?* When the search party came to arrest him and asked which man was Jesus, he stepped forward of his own accord. He asked for the sour wine which he knew he was destined to drink, and having drunk it and achieved his great purpose he said: *It is accomplished*, thus expressing his joy at obtaining his heart's desire.

In the psalms Christ had often prayed for his life to be delivered from the sword. He had shown in advance that not one of his bones was to be broken, and he had prophesied that his tunic was to be acquired by lot. He prayed that all these things willed by himself might come to pass so that prophecy might be fulfilled, that the wicked should have no control over them, that sinners should not hinder the celebration of that passover for which he so ardently longed, that fear should not stop them from presenting him with the cup of his passion – for those who came to arrest him all fell to the ground at the Lord's first reply to them. He prayed that the sour wine that was to be offered him might be ready, that the soldier's lance might not pierce his side before he had given up his spirit, and that no pretext for breaking his bones should be given by his slowness in dying. He prayed that no prophecy should be unfulfilled, but that everything not only prophesied but also willed by himself should be accomplished. He prayed about these things not because there was any danger of their not being accomplished, but so that everyone should perceive that the prophecies referred to himself.

St Hilary of Poitiers, *On Psalm 39*, 12: CSEL 22, 784–5

Fourteenth Sunday in Ordinary Time/Proper 9 Year A: Matthew 11. [16–19] 25–30

A READING FROM A HOMILY BY ST JOHN CHRYSOSTOM

Our Master is always the same, gentle and benevolent. In his constant concern for our salvation, he says explicitly in the gospel just read to us: *Come, learn from me.* The Master came to console his fallen servants. This is how Christ treats us. He shows pity when a sinner deserves punishment. When the race that angers him deserves to be annihilated, he addresses the guilty ones in the kindly words: *Come, learn from me, for I am gentle and humble in heart.*

God is humble, and we are proud! The judge is gentle; the criminal arrogant! The potter speaks in lowered voice; the clay discourses in the tones of a king! *Come, learn from me, for I am gentle and humble in heart.* Our Master carries a whip not to wound, but to heal us. Reflect upon his indescribable kindness. Who could fail to love a master who never strikes his servants? Who would not marvel at a judge who beseeches a condemned criminal? Surely the self-abasement of these words must astound you.

I am the Creator and I love my work. I am the sculptor and I care for what I have made. If I thought of my dignity, I should not rescue fallen humankind. If I failed to treat its incurable sickness with fitting remedies, it would never recover its strength. If I did not console it, it would die. This is why I apply the salve of kindness to it where it lies. Compassionately I bend down very low in order to raise it up. No one standing erect can lift a fallen man without putting a hand down to him.

Come, learn from me, for I am gentle and humble in heart. I do not make a show of words; I have left you the proof of my deeds. You can see that I am gentle and humble in heart from what I have become. Consider my nature, reflect upon my dignity, and marvel at the condescension I have shown you. Think of where I came from, and of where I am as I speak to you. Heaven is my throne, yet I talk to you standing on the earth! I am glorified on high, but because I am long-suffering I am not angry with you, *for I am gentle and humble in heart.*

St John Chrysostom, *Sermon on St Bassus*: Bareille, 4, 509–10

Fourteenth Sunday in Ordinary Time/Proper 9
Year B: Mark 6.1–6 [1–13]

A READING FROM A CONFERENCE BY ST SYMEON THE NEW THEOLOGIAN

Brothers and Fathers, many people never stop saying – I have heard them myself – 'If only we had lived in the days of the apostles, and been counted worthy to gaze upon Christ as they did, we should have become holy like them.' Such people do not realize that the Christ who spoke then and the Christ who speaks now throughout the whole world is one and the same. If he were not the same then and now, God in every respect, in his operations as in the sacraments, how would it be seen that the Father is always in the Son and the Son in the Father, according to the words Christ spoke through the Spirit: *My Father is still working and so am I?*

But no doubt someone will say that merely to hear his words now and to be taught about him and his kingdom is not the same thing as to have seen him then in the body. And I answer that indeed the position now is not the same as it was then, but our situation now, in the present day, is very much better. It leads us more easily to a deeper faith and conviction than seeing and hearing him in the flesh would have done.

Then he appeared to the uncomprehending Jews as a man of lowly station: now he is proclaimed to us as true God. Then in his body he associated with tax collectors and sinners and ate with them: now he is seated at the right hand of God the Father, and is never in any way separated from him. We are firmly persuaded that it is he who feeds the entire world, and we declare – at least if we are believers – that without him nothing came into being. Then even those of lowliest condition held him in contempt. They said: *Is this not the son of Mary, and of Joseph the carpenter?* Now kings and rulers worship him as Son of the true God, and himself true God, and he has glorified and continues to glorify those who worship him in spirit and in truth, although he often punishes them when they sin. He transforms them, more than all the nations under heaven, from clay into iron. Then he was thought to be mortal and corruptible like the rest of humankind. He was no different in appearance from other men. The formless and invisible God, without change or alteration, assumed a human form and showed himself to be a normal human being. He ate, he drank, he slept, he sweated, and he grew weary. He did everything other people do, except that he did not sin. For anyone to recognize him in that human body, and to believe that he was the God who made heaven and earth and everything in them was very exceptional.

This is why when Peter said: *You are the Son of the living God*, the Master called him blessed, saying: *Blessed are you, Simon Bar-Jonah, for flesh and blood has not revealed this to you* – you do not speak of something your eyes have seen – *but my Father who is in heaven*.

It is certain therefore that anyone who now hears Christ cry out daily through the holy gospels, and proclaim the will of his blessed Father, but does not obey him with fear and trembling and keep his commandments – it is certain that such a person would have refused to believe in him then, if he had been present, and seen him, and heard him teach. Indeed there is reason to fear that in his total incredulity he would have blasphemed by regarding Christ not as true God, but as an enemy of God.

St Symeon the New Theologian, *Catecheses*, 3.19: SC 113, 165–9

Fourteenth Sunday in Ordinary Time/Proper 9 Year C: Luke 10.1–12, 17–20 or 10.1–9

A READING FROM A SERMON BY ST AUGUSTINE

The gospel which has just been read raises a question. When the Lord told his disciples that the harvest was indeed abundant but labourers were scarce and urged them to ask the Lord of the harvest to send labourers to harvest his crop, which crop did he have in mind? That was the point at which he increased the group of twelve disciples whom he had named his apostles by the addition of another seventy-two, and his words make it clear that he sent all these out to gather in the right grain.

But which crop did he mean? Evidently not a crop of gentiles, from whom there was nothing to be reaped because as yet there had been no sowing among them. The conclusion must be that the crop in question consisted of Jews. The Jewish people were the harvest to which the Lord of the harvest came, and in which he dispatched his reapers. To the gentiles he could send no reapers at that time, only sowers. We may understand, then, that harvest time among the Jews coincided with sowing time among the gentiles, for out of the Jewish crop, sown by the prophets and now ripe for harvesting, the apostles were chosen.

Here we have the joy of observing the divine husbandry. How good it is to see God's gifts and watch the labourers in his field! Consider his twofold harvest, the one already reaped, the other still to come. That of the Jews is over and done, but there is a crop yet to be gathered in from the gentiles.

Now let us see if this can be demonstrated. And what better place to look for evidence than the holy Scriptures of the divine Lord of the harvest? Here in this very chapter of the gospel we have the saying: *The harvest is rich but the labourers are few; ask the Lord of the harvest to send labourers into his harvest.* This harvest is the people to whom the prophets preached, sowing the seed so that the apostles might gather in the sheaves. For the seed to sprout it was sufficient for the prophets to sow, but the ripe grain had to wait for the apostles' sickle.

Another time the Lord told his disciples: *You say that summer is still far off. Lift up your eyes and see that the fields are already white with ripe grain!* And he added: *Others have toiled over it, and you have entered into their labours.* Those others were Abraham, Isaac, Jacob, Moses, and the prophets. Because they worked hard at sowing, at the Lord's coming the grain was found to be ripe. Then the reapers were sent out, wielding the gospel as their sickle. They were to greet no one on the road, which meant they were to have no aim or activity apart from proclaiming the Good News in a spirit of brotherly love. When they arrived at the house they were to say: *Peace be to this house.* This greeting was no mere formula; being filled with peace themselves, the apostles spread it abroad, proclaiming peace and at the same time possessing it. Consequently when one of them, fully at peace with himself, pronounced the blessing: *Peace be to this house*, then if a lover of peace were in that house, the apostles' peace would rest upon him.

St Augustine, *Sermon* 101, 1–2, 11: PL 38, 605–7, 610

Fifteenth Sunday in Ordinary Time/Proper 10
Year A: Matthew 13.1–23 or 13.1–9

A READING FROM A HOMILY BY ST GREGORY THE GREAT

Dearly beloved, the reading from the holy gospel about the sower requires no explanation, but only a word of warning. In fact the explanation has been given by Truth himself, and it cannot be disputed by a frail human being. However, there is one point in our Lord's exposition which you ought to weigh well. It is this. If I told you that the seed represented the word, the field the world, the birds the demons, and the thorns riches, you would perhaps be in two minds as to whether to believe me. Therefore the Lord himself deigned to explain what he had said, so that you would know that a hidden meaning is to be sought also in those passages which he did not wish to interpret himself.

Would anyone have believed me if I had said that thorns stood for riches? After all, thorns are piercing and riches pleasurable. And yet riches are thorns because thoughts of them pierce the mind and torture it. When finally they lure a person into sin, it is as though they were drawing blood from the wound they have inflicted.

According to another Evangelist, the Lord spoke in this parable not simply of riches but of deceptive riches, and with good reason. Riches are deceptive because they cannot stay with us for long; they are deceptive because they are incapable of relieving our spiritual poverty. The only true riches are those that make us rich in virtue. Therefore, if you want to be rich, beloved, love true riches. If you aspire to the heights of real honour, strive to reach the kingdom of heaven. If you value rank and renown, hasten to be enrolled in the heavenly court of the angels.

Store up in your minds the Lord's words which you receive through your ears, for the word of the Lord is the nourishment of the mind. When his word is heard but not stored away in the memory, it is like food which has been eaten and then rejected by an upset stomach. A person's life is despaired of if he cannot retain his food; so if you receive the food of holy exhortations, but fail to store in your memory those words of life which nurture righteousness, you have good reason to fear the danger of everlasting death.

Be careful, then, that the seed received through your ears remains in your heart. Be careful that the seed does not fall along the path, for fear that the evil spirit may come and take it from your memory. Be careful that the seed is not received in stony ground, so that it produces a harvest of good works without the roots of perseverance. Many people are pleased with what they hear and resolve to undertake some good work, but as soon as difficulties begin to arise and hinder them they leave the work unfinished. The stony ground lacked the necessary moisture for the sprouting seed to yield the fruit of perseverance.

Good earth, on the other hand, brings forth fruit by patience. The reason for this is that nothing we do is good unless we also bear with equanimity the injuries done us by our neighbours. In fact, the more we progress, the more hardships we shall have to endure in this world; for when our love for this present world dies, its sufferings increase. This is why we see many people doing good works and at the same time struggling under a heavy burden of afflictions. They now shun earthly desires, and yet they are tormented by greater sufferings. But, as the Lord said, they bring forth fruit by patience, because, since they humbly endure misfortunes, they are welcomed when these are over into a place of rest in heaven.

St Gregory the Great, Forty Gospel Homilies, 1.15.1–2, 4

Fifteenth Sunday in Ordinary Time Year B (RL): Mark 6.7–13

A READING FROM THE COMMENTARY ON MARK BY ST THEOPHYLACT OF OHRID

Besides teaching himself the Lord also sent out the Twelve in pairs. The reason for sending them in pairs was so that they would go more readily, for they might not have been so willing to set out all alone, and, on the other hand, if he had sent more than two together, there would not have been enough apostles to cover all the villages. So he sent them out two by two: *two are better than one*, as Ecclesiastes says.

He commanded them to take nothing with them, neither bag, more money, nor bread, so as to teach them to despise riches, and to make people ashamed when they saw them preaching poverty by their own lack of possessions. For who would not blush for shame, strip himself of his possessions, and embrace a life of poverty when he saw an apostle carrying neither bag, nor even bread which is so very essential?

The Lord instructed them to stay in the same house so as not to give the appearance of restlessness, as though they moved from one family to another in order to satisfy their stomachs. On the other hand, he told them to shake the dust off their feet when people refused to receive them, to show that they had made a long journey for their sakes and they owed them nothing; they had received nothing from them, not even their dust, which they shook off as a testimony against them – a testimony of reproach. *Be sure of this, I tell you, Sodom and Gomorrah will fare better on the Day of judgement than those who will not receive you.* The Sodomites were punished in this world, so they will be punished less severely in the next. What is more, no apostles were sent to them. For those who refused to receive the apostles greater sufferings are in store.

So they set out to preach repentance. They cast out many demons, and anointed many sick people with oil and cured them. The fact that the apostles anointed the sick with oil is mentioned only by Mark, but the practice is also referred to in his general letter by James, the brother of the Lord, who says: *Are there any sick people amongst you? Let them send for the elders of the Church and let these pray over them anointing them with oil.* Oil is beneficial for the relief of suffering, and it also produces light and makes for cheerfulness. That symbolizes the mercy of God and the grace of the Spirit, through which we are freed from suffering and receive light, gladness, and spiritual joy.

St Theophylact of Ohrid, *On Mark*: PG 123, 548–9

Sunday of Proper 10B (RCL): Mark 6.14–29

A READING FROM A HOMILY ON MATTHEW BY ST JOHN CHRYSOSTOM

The whole work of the gospel-writers was to tell what related to Christ, and they would not have told this story were it not on Christ's account, that is because Herod said, *John is risen again.* But Mark said that Herod greatly honoured John the Baptist even though he had rebuked him, so great a thing is virtue.

Then the story carries on, *For Herod had seized John, and bound him in prison, for the sake of Herodias, his brother Philip's wife. For John said to Herod, 'It is not lawful for you to have your brother's wife?'* But on Herod's birthday the daughter of Herodias danced before them and pleased Herod. O diabolical revel! O satanic spectacle! O lawless dancing! and more lawless reward for the dancing! For a murder more impious than all murders was perpetrated, and he that was worthy to be crowned and publicly honoured was slain in prison and the trophy of the devils was set on the table.

So powerfully did Herod lust after that wretched girl just then, that he swore even to give her half of his kingdom, as Mark said, *He swore to her, 'Whatever you ask of me, I will give you, even half of my kingdom.'* Such was the value he set upon his royal power, that, made captive by his passion, he gave up his kingdom for a dance. But not so are the saints. They on the contrary mourn for such things as sin, rather than curse the sinner.

Let us then also do this, and let us weep for Herodias and for all those who imitate her. For many such revels take place even now, and, although John is not slain, the members of Christ are killed and in a far more grievous way. For it is not a head on a plate that the dancers of our time request, but they demand the souls of those who sit at the feast. When they make them slaves of their passions and lead them to unlawful loves they do not take off the head but slay the soul. Even though the daughter of Herodias is not present, the devil who danced in her even now holds his revels in the souls of the guests at such parties and carries them off captive.

St John Chrysostom, *Homilies on Matthew*, 48.2, 4, 8

Fifteenth Sunday in Ordinary Time/Proper 10 Year C: Luke 10.25–37

A READING FROM A HOMILY ON LUKE BY ORIGEN

To interpret the parable of the Good Samaritan, one of the Elders used to say that the man going down from Jerusalem to Jericho was Adam. He said Jerusalem was paradise, Jericho was the world, and the brigands were enemy powers. The priest was the law, the Levite the prophets, and the Samaritan Christ: Adam's wounds were his disobedience, the animal that carried him was the body of the Lord, and the '*pandochium*' or inn, open to all who wished to enter, was the Church. The two denarii represented the Father and the Son, and the innkeeper was the head of the Church, who was entrusted with its administration. The promised return of the Samaritan was a figure of the Second Coming of the Saviour.

The Samaritan was carrying oil – *oil to make his face shine*, as Scripture says, referring surely to the face of the man he cared for. He cleansed the man's wounds with oil to soothe the inflammation and with wine that made them smart, and then placed him on his own mount, that is, on his own body, since he had condescended to assume our humanity. This Samaritan bore our sins and suffered on our behalf; he carried the half dead man to the inn which takes in everyone, denying no one its help; in other words, to the Church. To this inn Jesus invites all when he says: *Come to me, all who labour and are overburdened, and I will give you new strength.*

After bringing in the man half dead the Samaritan did not immediately depart, but remained and dressed his wounds by night as well as by day, showing his concern and doing everything he could for him. In the morning when he wished to set out again he took from his own pure silver coins, from his own sterling money, two denarii to pay the innkeeper – clearly the angel of the Church – and ordered him to nurse with all diligence and restore to health the man whom for a short time he himself had personally tended.

I think the two denarii stand for knowledge of the Father and the Son, and of the mystery that the Father is in the Son and the Son in the Father. This was given to the angel as a recompense, so that he would care more diligently for the man entrusted to him. He was also promised that whatever he spent of his own in healing him would be repaid.

This guardian of souls *who showed mercy to the man who fell into the hands of brigands* was a better neighbour to him than were either the law or the prophets, and he proved this more by deeds than by words. Now the saying: *Be imitators of me as I am of Christ*, makes it clear that we can imitate Christ by showing mercy to those who have fallen into the hands of brigands. We can go to them, bandage their wounds after pouring in oil and wine, place them on our own mount, and bear their burdens. And so the Son of God exhorts us to do these things, in words addressed not only to the teacher of the law but to all of us: *Go and do likewise*. If we do, we shall gain eternal life in Christ Jesus, *to whom belongs glory power for ever and ever. Amen.*

Origen, *Homilies on Luke's Gospel*, 34.3, 7–9: SC 87, 402–10

Sixteenth Sunday in Ordinary Time/Proper 11 Year A: Matthew 13.24–43 or 13.24–30

A READING FROM A SERMON BY ST AUGUSTINE

The Lord has explained to us the parable he told. Consider what we choose to be in his field; consider what sort of people we are found to be at the harvest. The field, you see, which is the world, is the Church spread throughout the world. Let those who are wheat persevere until the harvest; let those who are weeds change themselves into wheat. This, you see, is the difference between people and real ears of wheat and real weeds, because with those things growing in a field whatever is wheat is wheat, and whatever are weeds are weeds. But in the Lord's field, which is the Church, what used to be grain sometimes changes into weeds, and what used to be weeds sometimes changes into grain; and nobody knows what's going to happen tomorrow.

Listen, dearest grains of Christ; listen, Christ's precious ears of wheat; listen, Christ's dearest corn. Take a look at yourselves, go back to your consciences, interrogate your faith, interrogate your love, stir up your consciences. And if you discover that you are good grain, let the thought occur to you, *Whoever perseveres to the end will be saved.* Any of you who on shaking up their consciences find themselves among the weeds must not be afraid to change. The command hasn't yet been given to cut, it isn't the harvest yet; don't be today what you were yesterday, or at least don't be tomorrow what you are today.

Is there anywhere, though, where that enemy has not sown weeds? Has he found any cornfields anywhere and not scattered weeds in them? Do you imagine he has sown them among the laity and not among the clergy, or the bishops? Or sown them among married men and not among those who have made profession of celibacy? Or sown them among married women and not among consecrated nuns? Or sown them in the houses of lay people and not in communities of monks? He's scattered them everywhere, sown them everywhere. Has he left anything unmixed?

But thanks be to God, who will be pleased in due course to sort things out, and who cannot be mistaken. It will not, I'm sure, have escaped the notice of your graces, that weeds are to be found in all kinds of harvests, even those in the most exalted and distinguished circles. They are to be found even among professed religious. And you say, 'Imagine, in that place, have bad people been found even there, have bad people been found even in that community?' But of course, bad people have been found everywhere, but the bad will not reign for ever with the good.

Why be surprised at finding bad people in a holy place? Don't you know that the first sin in paradise was disobedience, and that that was the sin by which the angels fell? Did they pollute the heavens? Adam fell; did he pollute paradise? One of Noah's sons fell; did he pollute the just man's house? Judas fell; did he pollute the band of the apostles? Sometimes, though, people are considered by human estimation to be grain, and in fact they are weeds; and others are reckoned to be weeds, but in fact are really grain.

It's because the truth is usually concealed in this way that the apostle says, *Do not judge before the time, until the Lord comes and lights up the things hidden in darkness; and he will make public the thoughts of the heart; and then each one will have praise from God.* Human praise is a passing thing; people sometimes praise someone bad without realizing it; people sometimes accuse someone holy without knowing it. May God pardon them for their ignorance, and come to their assistance in their difficulties.

St Augustine, *Sermon 73*A

Sixteenth Sunday in Ordinary Time/Proper 11 Year B: Mark 6.30–34 [53–56]

A READING FROM THE COMMENTARY ON ZECHARIAH BY DIDYMUS THE BLIND

In harmony with other texts on the raising up of a personage of great renown is the promise made by God in the book of Ezekiel the prophet. Addressing those to whom he wishes to show kindness and to save, God says: *I will raise up for you one shepherd, my servant David*; he, that is, who said in the gospel: *I am the good shepherd. The good shepherd lays down his life for his sheep.* As their leader and excellent protector, he exposes himself to danger for their sake. In fact he died, *by the grace of God tasting death for all*, so that by giving life to all he might glorify the Lord almighty. The holy prophet Micah foretold him when he prophesied in a canticle: *The Lord shall stand and watch over and feed his flock with strength, and they shall live in the name of God the almighty.* In other words, they shall have communion with him who said to Moses, the expounder of sacred truths: *I am who I am.*

And just as the true David, strong of hand and the best of shepherds, arose to tend the sheep who listen to the voice of Jesus, *the sheep led by his –* Jesus' *– hand, and the people of his pasture*, so also he who sprang from the stock spoken of in Scripture arose as an excellent general sent at the Father's good pleasure, and routed his terrified foes, striking their backs with his hands.

He is praised and glorified by his own brothers and sisters because he has been revealed as the firstborn among them, according to the Apostle's words: *Those whom he – God – foreknew and predestined to be conformed to the image of his Son, so that his Son might be the firstborn of many children.* Concerning these the firstborn says to God: *I will declare your name to my brothers and sisters; in the midst of the assembly I will praise you.*

Didymus the Blind, *Commentary on Zechariah*, 2.39–42:
SC 84, 446–9

Sixteenth Sunday in Ordinary Time/Proper 11 Year C: Luke 10.38–42

A READING FROM A HOMILY BY ST GREGORY THE GREAT

There are two lives in which Almighty God instructs us through his holy Word: that is, the active life and the contemplative life.

What is the active life? We live it when we give bread to the hungry; when we teach the ignorant God's words of wisdom; when we correct those who go astray, or recall to the path of humility some neighbour who has fallen into pride; when we look after the sick, dispense alms impartially according to need, and when we provide those entrusted to our care with all they need to live.

What is the contemplative life? We live that when, without in any way abandoning whole-hearted love of God and neighbour, we rest from exterior activity. In this rest all our energy is devoted to the single desire for our Creator. Here we are no longer concerned about our manifold active works. Treading all our cares under foot, our soul burns instead with desire to see the face of its Creator. Now we realize with grief how heavily the burden of our corruptible flesh weighs upon us, and we understand what it means to desire with ardent longing to join the Choirs of Angels as they praise God in song, to take our place among the citizens of heaven, and to rejoice over the eternal freedom from corruption enjoyed by those who never leave the presence of God.

These two lives are well symbolized by the two women Martha and Mary, the first of whom was busily occupied with her serving, while the second sat at the feet of the Lord and listened to his words. When Martha complained about her sister since she was doing nothing to help, the Lord answered her: *Martha, you are occupied and kept busy about many things, but only one is necessary. Mary has chosen the best part, and it shall not be taken away from her.* Note carefully that the part of Martha was not blamed, but that of Mary was praised. He didn't say that Mary had chosen the good part: he said it was the best, in order to show that Martha's part was still good. He made it clear what he meant by the 'best' part of Mary when he specified that it would not be taken away from her. For the active life comes to an end with the death of the body. Who will give bread to the hungry in our eternal homeland, where no one is hungry? Who will give drink to the thirsty, where no one thirsts? Who will bury the dead, where no one dies? Therefore the active life will be taken away along with this present age. The contemplative life, by contrast, begins here, but always directed towards its perfection in our heavenly homeland. For when the fire of love which begins to burn here, sees him whom it loves, it will burst out in much more ardent flames for love of him. The contemplative life is thus by no means to be taken away, for when the light of this present age comes to an end, it will then be perfected.

On the other hand, we must realize that although it is normal and good for the active life to pass over into the contemplative life, often the soul is driven from contemplation to active works of charity. Precisely the contemplative vision calls us back to activity, for it understands that the labour of good works must never be abandoned while we are in this life.

St Gregory the Great, *Homilies on Ezekiel*, 2.2.7–11:
SC 360, 105–13 (abridged)

Seventeenth Sunday in Ordinary Time/Proper 12 Year A: Matthew 13.[31–33] 44–52 or 13.44–46

A READING FROM THE COMMENTARY ON MATTHEW BY ORIGEN

To the seeker after fine pearls may be applied the words, *Seek and you will find*, and, *Everyone who seeks will find*. If you ask what is to be sought, and what will be found by everyone who seeks for it, I say with all confidence 'pearls' – especially that pearl which will be acquired by those who give their all, who sacrifice everything for it, the pearl Paul meant when he said: *I have accepted the loss of everything in order to gain Christ. Everything* means beautiful pearls; *to gain* Christ refers to the one pearl of great price.

Admittedly, a lamp is precious to people in darkness, and they need it until sunrise. Precious too was the radiance on the face of Moses – and I believe on the faces of the other prophets also. It was a sight of beauty leading us to the point of being able to see the glory of Christ, to whom the Father bore witness in the words: *This is my beloved Son, in whom I am well pleased.*

But *compared with this surpassing glory, what formerly was glorious now seems to have no glory at all.* We need at first a glory destined to be outshone by an all-surpassing glory, just as we need the partial knowledge which *will be superseded when that which is perfect has come.*

Thus everyone beginning to live a spiritual life and growing toward maturity needs tutors, guardians, and trustees until the fullness of time arrives for him, so that after all this, he who at first was *no different from a slave although he owned the whole estate*, may on his emancipation receive his patrimony from his tutor, guardians, and trustees.

This patrimony is the pearl of great price, and the coming of what is perfect to supersede what is imperfect when, after acquiring the forms of knowledge, if we may call them so, which are inferior to knowledge of Christ, one becomes able to understand the supreme value of knowing Christ. The law and the prophets fully comprehended are the preparation for the full comprehension of the gospel and the complete understanding of the acts and words of Christ Jesus.

Origen, *Commentary on Matthew*, 10.9–10: SC 162, 173–7

Seventeenth Sunday in Ordinary Time: Proper 12 Year B: John 6.1–15 [1–21]

A READING FROM THE *TRACTATES ON JOHN* BY ST AUGUSTINE

The miracles wrought by our Lord Jesus Christ are truly divine works, which lead the human mind through visible things to perception of the Godhead. God is not the kind of being that can be seen with the eyes, and more account is taken of the miracles than of the fact he rules the entire universe and governs all creation because it is so familiar. Scarcely anyone bothers to consider God's marvellous works, his amazing artistry in every tiny seed. And so certain works are excluded from the ordinary course of nature, works which God in his mercy has reserved for himself, so as to perform them at appropriate times. People who hold cheap what they see every day are dumbfounded at the sight of extraordinary works even though they are no more wonderful than the others.

Governing the entire universe is a greater miracle than feeding five thousand people with five loaves of bread, yet no one marvels at it. People marvel at the feeding of five thousand not because this miracle is greater, but because it is out of the ordinary.

Who is even now providing nourishment for the whole world if not the God who creates a field of wheat from a few seeds? Christ did what God does. Just as God multiplies a few seeds into a whole field of wheat, so Christ multiplied the five loaves in his hands. For there was power in the hands of Christ. Those five loaves were like seeds, not because they were cast on the earth but because they were multiplied by the one who made the earth.

This miracle was performed for the multitude to see; it was recorded for us to hear. Faith does for us what sight did for them. We behold with the mind what our eyes cannot see; and we are preferred to them because of us it was said: *Blessed are those who have not seen and yet believe.*

When the people saw the sign Jesus had performed they said, 'Surely this must be a prophet.' He was in fact the Lord of the prophets, the fulfiller of the prophets, the sanctifier of the prophets; yet he was still a prophet, for Moses had been told: *I will raise up for them a prophet like yourself.* The Lord is a prophet, and the Lord is the Word of God, and without the Word of God no prophet can prophesy. The Word of God is with the prophets, and the Word of God is a prophet. People of former times were deemed worthy to have prophets inspired and filled by the Word of God; we have been deemed worthy to have as our prophet the Word of God himself.

St Augustine, *Tractates on John,* 24.1, 6, 7: CCSL 36, 244, 247–8

Seventeenth Sunday in Ordinary Time/Proper 12 Year C: Luke 11.1–13

A READING FROM A HOMILY BY THE VENERABLE BEDE

Our Lord and Saviour wishes us to attain the joy of the heavenly kingdom, and so he taught us to pray for it, promising to give it to us if we did so. *Ask,* he said, *and you will receive, seek and you will find, knock and the door will be opened to you.*

We should consider most seriously and attentively what these words of the Lord may mean for us, for they warn that not the idle and feckless but those who ask, seek, and knock will receive, find, and have the door opened to them. We must therefore ask for entry into the kingdom by prayer, seek it by upright living, and knock at its door by perseverance. Merely to ask verbally is not enough; we must also diligently seek to discover how to live so as to be worthy of obtaining what we ask for. We know this from our Saviour's words: *Not everyone who says to me, 'Lord, Lord', will enter the kingdom of heaven, but only those who do the will of my heavenly Father.*

There is a need, then, for constant and unflagging prayer. Let us fall upon our knees with tears before our God and Maker; and that we may deserve a hearing, let us consider carefully how he who made us wishes us to live, and what he has commanded us to do. *Let us seek the Lord and his strength; let us constantly seek his face.* And in order to become worthy of finding him and gazing upon him, *let us cleanse ourselves from all defilement of body and spirit*, for only the chaste of body can be raised up to heaven on the day of resurrection; only the pure of heart can contemplate the glory of the divine Majesty.

If we would know what the Lord wishes us to ask for, let us listen to the gospel text: *Seek first the kingdom of God and its justice, and all these other things will be given you as well.* To seek the kingdom of God and its justice is to long for the graces of our heavenly homeland, and to give constant thought to the kind of upright living that will deserve to obtain them; for should we chance to stray from the path that leads there we shall never be able to reach our goal.

To ask God for the justice of his kingdom is to ask principally for faith, hope, and love. These virtues above all we should strive to obtain, for Scripture says: *The upright live by faith; mercy surrounds those who hope in the Lord*; and *To love is to fulfil the law, for the whole law is summed up in one word: You shall love your neighbour as yourself.* And so the Lord graciously promises that *the Father will give the good Spirit to those who ask him*, in order to show that those who of themselves are evil can become good by receiving the grace of the Spirit. He promises the good Spirit will be given by the Father because whether it is faith, hope, or any other virtue we desire to obtain, we shall do so only through the grace of the Holy Spirit.

As we do our best, then, to follow in our Lord's footsteps, let us ask God the Father for the grace of his Spirit to lead us along the path of that true faith which works through love. And that we may deserve to obtain our desire, let us strive to live in a way that will make us not unworthy of so great a Father; let us preserve inviolate in body and soul the sacramental rebirth of our baptism which made us children of God. Then, if we keep the almighty Father's commandments, he will certainly reward us with the eternal blessing which from the beginning he prepared as our heritage through Jesus Christ our Lord, who with the Holy Spirit lives and reigns with him, God for ever and ever. Amen.

Ven. Bede, *Homily 14*: CCSL 122, 272–3, 277–9

Eighteenth Sunday in Ordinary Time/Proper 13 Year A: Matthew 14.13–21

A READING FROM THE COMMENTARY ON THE DIATESSARON BY ST EPHREM THE SYRIAN

Our Lord in a desert place changed a few loaves into many, and at Cana turned water into wine. Thus before the time came to give men and women his own body and blood to feed on, he accustomed their palates to his bread and wine, giving them a taste of transitory bread and wine to teach them to delight in his life-giving body and blood. He gave them things of little value for nothing to make them understand that his supreme gift would be given yet more freely. He gave them for nothing what they could have bought from him, what in fact they wanted to buy, to teach them that he asked them for no payment. When it was not permitted them to give him the price of bread and wine, which they could have done, they certainly could not pay him for his body and blood.

Moreover, as well as giving freely he lovingly cajoled us, offering us these small things without charge to attract us and cause us to go and receive something greater and beyond all price. He awakened our desire by things pleasing to the palate in order to draw us to that which gives life to the soul. He gave a sweet taste to the wine he created to show how great is the treasure hidden in his life-giving blood.

Consider how his creative power penetrates everything. Our Lord took a little bread, and in the twinkling of an eye multiplied it. Work that would take us ten months to accomplish he did with his ten fingers in a moment. His hands were as earth beneath the bread and his voice was as thunder above it. The movement of his lips acted as dew, the breath of this month as sunlight, and in a brief moment he accomplished what normally takes much time. Thus the shortage was forgotten; many loaves came from few as in the first blessing: *Be fruitful and multiply and fill the earth*.

The Lord also showed those to whom he gave his precepts the power of his holy word, and how swiftly he would regard those who accepted it. Nevertheless, he did not increase the number of loaves as much as he could have done, but only enough to satisfy those who were to eat them.

His power was not the measure of his miracle, but the people's hunger. Had his miracle been measured by his power it would have been a victory beyond all measure. Measured by the hunger of thousands, there was a surplus of twelve baskets full. Humans who practise any craft always fall short of their customers' desires – they are unable to meet their requirements; but what God does goes beyond anyone's desire. The Lord said: *Gather up what remains so that nothing is wasted*, because he wanted to be sure they would not think they had seen a vision. When the fragments had been kept for a day or two they would believe the Lord had really done this, and they had not just imagined it.

When they had had enough to eat the people realized that they had been fed in the desert just as in former times at the prayer of Moses, and they began to cry out: *Surely this must be the prophet who was to come into the world.*

St Ephrem the Syrian, *Commentary on the Diatessaron*, 12.1.305:
CSCO 145 *Script. Arm.*, ii, 115–17

Eighteenth Sunday in Ordinary Time/Proper 13 Year B: John 6.24–35

A READING FROM THE COMMENTARY ON JOHN BY ST THEOPHYLACT OF OHRID

Our ancestors ate manna in the desert; as it is written, 'He gave them bread from heaven to eat.' Wishing to persuade Christ to perform the kind of miracle that would provide them with bodily nourishment, the people in their insatiable greed called to mind the manna. What was the reply of our Lord Jesus, the infinite wisdom of God? *It was not Moses who gave you bread.* In other words, 'Moses did not give you the true bread. On the contrary, everything that happened in his time was a prefiguration of what is happening now. Moses represented God, the real leader of the spiritual Israelites, while that bread typified myself, who has come down from heaven and who am the true bread which gives genuine nourishment.' Our Lord refers to himself as the true bread not because the manna was something illusory, but because it was only a type and a shadow, and not the reality it signified.

This bread, being the Son of the living Father, is life by its very nature, and accordingly gives life to all. Just as earthly bread sustains the fragile substance of the flesh and prevents it from falling into decay, so Christ quickens the soul through the power of the Spirit, and also preserves even the body for immortality. Through Christ, resurrection from the dead and bodily immortality have been gratuitously bestowed upon the human race.

Jesus said to the people: 'I am the bread of life. Whoever comes to me shall never hunger, and whoever believes in me shall never thirst.' He did not say 'the bread of bodily nourishment' but 'the bread of life'. For when everything had been reduced to a condition of spiritual death, the Lord gave us life through himself, who is bread because, as we believe, the leaven in the dough of our humanity was baked through and through by the fire of his divinity. He is the bread not of this ordinary life, but of a very different kind of life which death will never cut short.

Whoever believes in this bread will never hunger, will never be famished for want of hearing the word of God; nor will such a person be parched by spiritual thirst for lack of the waters of baptism and the consecration imparted by the Spirit. The unbaptized, deprived of the refreshment afforded by the sacred water, suffer thirst and great aridity. The baptized, on the other hand, being possessed of the Spirit, enjoy its continual consolation.

St Theophylact of Ohrid, *On John*: PG 123, 1297–1301

Eighteenth Sunday in Ordinary Time/Proper 13 Year C: Luke 12.13–21

A READING FROM A HOMILY BY ST BASIL THE GREAT

The land of a rich man produced abundant harvests, and he thought to himself: 'What am I to do? I will pull down my barns, and build larger ones.'

Now why did that land bear so well, when it belonged to a man who would make no good use of its fertility? It was to show more clearly the forbearance of God, whose kindness extends even to such people as this. *He sends rain on both the just and the unjust, and makes the sun rise on the wicked and the good alike.*

But what do we find in this man? A bitter disposition, hatred of other people, unwillingness to give. This is the return he made to his Benefactor. He forgot that we all share the same nature; he felt no obligation to distribute his surplus to the needy. His barns were full to bursting point, but still his miserly heart was not satisfied. Year by year he increased his wealth, always adding new crops to the old. The result was a hopeless impasse: greed would not permit him to part with anything he possessed, and yet because he had so much there was no place to store his latest harvest. And so he was incapable of making a decision and could find no escape from his anxiety. *What am I to do?*

Who would not pity a man so oppressed? His land yields him no profit but only sighs; it brings him no rich returns but only cares and distress and a terrible helplessness. He laments in the same way as the poor do. Is not his cry like that of one hard pressed by poverty? *What am I to do?* How can I find food and clothing?

You who have wealth, recognize who has given you the gifts you have received. Consider yourself, who you are, what has been committed to your charge, from whom you have received it, why you have been preferred to most other people. You're the servant of the good God, a steward on behalf of your fellow servants. Do not imagine that everything has been provided for your own stomach. Take decisions regarding your property as though it belonged to another. Possessions give you pleasure for a short time, but then they will slip through your fingers and be gone, and you will be required to give an exact account of them.

What am I to do? It would have been so easy to say: 'I will feed the hungry, I will open my barns and call in all the poor. I will imitate Joseph in proclaiming my good will toward everyone. I will issue the generous invitation. "Let anyone who lacks bread come to me. You shall share, each according to need, in the good things God has given me, just as though you were drawing from a common well."'

St Basil the Great, *Homélies sur la richesse*, ed. Courtonne, pp. 15–19

Nineteenth Sunday in Ordinary Time/Proper 14
Year A: Matthew 14.22–33
A READING FROM A SERMON BY ST AUGUSTINE

The gospel tells us how Christ the Lord walked upon the waters of the sea, and how the apostle Peter did the same until fear made him falter and lose confidence. Then he began to sink and emerged from the water only after calling on the Lord with renewed faith.

Now we must regard the sea as a symbol of the present world, and the apostle Peter as a symbol of the one and only Church. For Peter, who ranked first among the apostles and was always the most ready to declare his love for Christ, often acted as spokesman for them all. For instance, when the Lord Jesus Christ asked who people thought he was and the other disciples had cited various opinions, it was Peter who responded to the Lord's further question, *But who do you say I am?* with the affirmation: *You are the Christ, the Son of the living God.* One replied for all because all were united.

When we consider Peter as a representative member of the Church we should distinguish between what was due to God's action in him and what was attributable to himself. Then we ourselves shall not falter; then we shall be founded upon rock and remain firm and unmoved in the face of the wind, rain, and floods, which are the trials and temptations of this present world. Look at Peter, who in this episode is an image of ourselves; at one moment he is all confidence, at the next all uncertainty and doubt; now he professes faith in the immortal One, now he fears for his life.

Lord, if it is you, bid me come to you upon the water. When the Lord said *Come,* Peter climbed out of the boat and began to walk on the water. This is what he could do through the power of the Lord; what by himself? *Realizing how violently the wind was blowing, he lost his nerve, and as he began to sink he called out, 'Lord, I am drowning, save me!'* When he counted on the Lord's help it enabled him to walk on the water; when human frailty made him falter he turned once more to the Lord, who immediately stretched out his hand to help him, raised him up as he was sinking, and rebuked him for his lack of faith.

Think, then, of this world as a sea, whipped up to tempestuous heights by violent winds. A person's own private tempest will be his or her unruly desires. If you love God you will have power to walk upon the waters, and all the world's swell and turmoil will remain beneath your feet. But if you love the world it will surely engulf you, for it always devours its lovers, never sustains them. If you feel your foot slipping beneath you, if you become a prey to doubt or realize that you are losing control, if, in a word, you begin to sink, say: *Lord, I am drowning, save me!* Only he who for your sake died in your fallen nature can save you from the death inherent in that fallen nature.

St Augustine, Sermon 76.1, 4, 5, 8, 9: PL 38, 479–83

Nineteenth Sunday in Ordinary Time/Proper 14
Year B: John 6.[35] 41–51

A READING FROM A SERMON BY ST EUTYCHIUS OF CONSTANTINOPLE

I have greatly longed to eat this passover with you before I suffer. The Lord's eating of the passover before he suffered was clearly symbolic and sacramental, because but for the passion it would not have been called the passover. He immolated himself sacramentally when, after supper, he took bread into his own hands, gave thanks, held it up and broke it, mingling himself with the sacred element. In the same way he also mixed the cup containing fruit of the vine; he gave thanks, showed it to God the Father, and said: *Take, eat,* and, *Take, drink; This is my body,* and, *This is my blood.*

Everyone receives the Lord's sacred body and precious blood in their entirety, even though each receives only a portion, for the mingling enables them to be shared among all without division. A seal imparts its complete image to everything it is impressed upon, yet remains a single seal. It is not diminished by use, nor is it altered in any way no matter how many impressions are made. The sound produced by the human voice goes out on to the air, yet remains a single sound. Carried on the air, it reaches the ears of all in full strength. No one hears more or less of it than anyone else. The same complete and undiminished sound comes to all its hearers, however numerous they may be; and yet it is a physical phenomenon, for sound is nothing but the vibration of air.

No one, then, after the sacramental sacrifice and the holy resurrection, should have any doubt regarding the incorruptible, immortal, holy, and life-giving body and blood of the Lord. Once infused into the sacred elements through the liturgical rites, they communicate their own properties no less than do the aforementioned examples. They are wholly present in every part, for in the Lord's body dwells corporally, that is to say, substantially, all the fullness of the divine nature of the Word of God. The breaking of this precious bread signifies his sacrificial death, and so he spoke of the passover as something to be longed for because it was to bring us salvation, immortality, and perfect knowledge.

St Eutychius of Constantinople, *On Easter*, 2–3: PG 86/2, 2394–5

Nineteenth Sunday in Ordinary Time/Proper 14
Year C: Luke 12.32–48 [32–40]

A READING FROM A HOMILY ON THE SONG OF SONGS BY ST GREGORY OF NYSSA

When the Lord says: *Let your loins be girded and your lamps lit*, he is warning us to stay awake; for a light shining in one's eyes drives away sleep, and a tightly fastened belt also makes sleep difficult, as the discomfort prevents relaxation. But the real meaning of the parable is perfectly clear: a person girded with temperance lives in the light of a clear conscience before God. And so, with the light of truth shining, the soul stays awake and is not deceived. It does not dally with illusive dreams.

If following the guidance of the Word we attain this goal, our lives will in a way be like those of the angels, for we are compared with them in the divine command: *You must be like people waiting for their master to return from a wedding, ready to open the door immediately when he comes and knocks.* It was the angels who were awaiting the Master's return from the wedding. They sat with unsleeping eyes at the heavenly gates, so that when he returned the King of glory might pass through them once more into the heavenly bliss from which, as the psalm says, he had come forth like a bridegroom from his tent. He took us to himself as his virgin bride, our nature once prostituted to idols being restored by sacramental rebirth to virginal incorruptibility. After the marriage, when the Church had been wedded to the Word – as John says, *He who has the bride is the bridegroom* – and admitted to the bridal chamber of the sacred mysteries, the angels awaited the King of glory's return to the blessedness which is his by nature.

And so the Lord said our lives should be like theirs. Just as they, living lives far removed from sin and error, are ready to receive the Lord at his coming, so we also should keep watch at the entrance of our houses, and prepare ourselves to obey him when he comes to our door and knocks. *Blessed*, he says, *are those servants whom the master finds so doing when he comes.*

St Gregory of Nyssa, *Homilies on the Song of Songs*, 11:
Jaeger, vi, 317–19

Twentieth Sunday in Ordinary Time/Proper 15
Year A: Matthew 15.21–28 [10–28]

A READING FROM A HOMILY BY ST JOHN CHRYSOSTOM

The Canaanite woman whose daughter was tormented by a devil came to Christ begging his help. Most urgently she cried out: *Lord, have pity on me. My daughter is grievously tormented by a devil.* Notice that the woman was a foreigner, a gentile, a person from outside the Jewish community. What was she then but a dog, unworthy to obtain her request? *It is not fair, said the Lord, to take the children's bread and give it to the dogs.* Nevertheless, by perseverance she became worthy; for Christ not only admitted her to the same noble rank as the children, dog though she was, but he also sent her away with high praise, saying: *Woman, you have great faith. Let it be as you desire.* Now when Christ says: *You have great faith*, you need seek no further proof of the woman's greatness of soul. You see that an unworthy woman became worthy by perseverance.

Now would you like proof that we shall gain more by praying ourselves than by asking others to pray for us? The woman cried out and *the disciples went to Christ and said, 'Give her what she wants – she is shouting after us.'* And he said to them: *I was sent only to the lost sheep of the house of Israel.* But when the woman herself, still crying out, came to him and said: *That is true, sir, and yet the dogs eat what falls from their master's table*, then he granted her request, saying: *Let it be as you desire.*

Have you understood? When the disciples entreated him the Lord put them off, but when the woman herself cried out begging for this favour he granted it. And at the beginning when she first made her request, he did not answer, but after she had come to him once, twice, and a third time, he gave her what she desired. By this he was teaching us that he had withheld the gift not to drive her away, but to make that woman's patience an example for all of us.

Now that we have learned these lessons, let us not despair even if we are guilty of sin and unworthy of any favour. We know that we can make ourselves worthy by perseverance.

St John Chrysostom, *Homily on the words, 'That Christ be proclaimed'*,
12–13: Bareille, 5, 595–6.

Twentieth Sunday in Ordinary Time/Proper 15
Year B: John 6.51–58

A READING FROM THE COMMENTARY ON JOHN BY ST THEOPHYLACT OF OHRID

We have heard that unless we eat the flesh of the Son we shall not have life. We must have unwavering faith, then, when we partake of the sacred mysteries, and not enquire, 'How?' Unspiritual people, that is, those led by a natural, human way of thinking, are not open to spiritual realities surpassing the natural order, so lack understanding of the spiritual nourishment the Lord's flesh affords.

Those who do not share in this flesh will not share in eternal life because they reject Jesus, the true life. What is consumed is the flesh not of a mere man but of God, and being one with the Godhead, it has power to deify. This is real nourishment, its sustaining power does not last only for a time; it does not decompose like perishable food, but helps us to attain everlasting life. Likewise the cup of the Lord's blood is real drink, but it does not quench our thirst only for a time, but keeps those who drink it free from thirst for ever; as the Lord said to the Samaritan woman: *Whoever drinks of the water that I shall give will never thirst again.* Whoever receives the grace of the Holy Spirit by sharing in the divine mysteries will never suffer from spiritual hunger and thirst the way unbelievers do.

Those who would eat my flesh and drink my blood live in me, and I live in them. As I draw life from the living Father who sent me, so whoever eats me will draw life from me. From these words we can begin to understand the mystery of communion. Those who eat and drink the Lord's flesh and blood live in the Lord and the Lord lives in them. A marvellous and inexplicable union occurs by which God is in us, and we are in God. Does this not fill you with awe as you listen?

It is not God alone that we eat, for he is intangible and incorporeal; he can be apprehended neither by our eyes nor by our teeth; nor, on the other hand, is it simply the flesh of a man, which would avail us nothing. Rather, in a union defying explanation, God has made flesh one with himself, so that the flesh now has life-giving power. This is not because its nature is changed into the nature of God. Of course not! A comparison may be made with iron put into fire. It remains iron but displays the energy of fire. So also the Lord's flesh remains flesh, but it has life-giving power because it is the flesh of the Word of God.

And so Christ says: *As I draw life from the Father,* or in other words, as I was born of the Father who is life, *so those who eat me will draw life from me*, because they will be united to me and as it were transformed into me, who am possessed of life-giving power.

St Theophylact of Ohrid, *Commentary on John*: PG 123, 1309–12

Twentieth Sunday in Ordinary Time/Proper 15 Year C: Luke 12.49–53

A READING FROM A COMMENTARY ON LUKE BY BLESSED DENIS THE CARTHUSIAN

I have come to cast fire upon the earth. In other words, I have come down from the highest heaven and appeared to men and women through the mystery of the incarnation in order to light the fire of divine love in human hearts. *And how I wish it were already ablaze!* How I wish it were already kindled, fanned into flame by the Holy Spirit, and leaping forth in good works.

Christ foretells that he will suffer death on a cross before the human race is inflamed by the fire of this love; for it was by his most holy passion that he won so great a gift for humankind, and it is chiefly the recollection of his passion that kindles the flame of love in Christian hearts.

There is a baptism which I must undergo. By divine decree there remains for me the duty of receiving a baptism of blood, that is, of being bathed, soaked upon the cross not in water but in my own blood poured out to redeem the whole world. *And what constraint I am under until that has been achieved* – until my passion is over and I say: *It is accomplished*. For Christ was impelled incessantly by the love within him.

The way to attain the perfection of divine love is then stated. *Do you think that I have come to bring peace on earth?* In other words, do not imagine that I have come to offer people a sensual, worldly, and unruly peace that will enable them to be united in their vices and achieve earthly prosperity. *No, I tell you*, I have not come to offer that kind of peace, *but rather division* – a good, healthy kind of division, physical as well as spiritual. Love for God and desire for inner peace will set those who believe in me at odds with wicked men and women, and make them part company with those who would turn them from their course of spiritual progress and from the purity of divine love, or who attempt to hinder them.

Good, interior, spiritual peace consists in the repose of the mind in God, and in a rightly ordered harmony. To bestow this peace was the chief reason for Christ's coming. This inner peace flows from love. It is an unassailable joy of the mind in God, and it is called peace of heart. It is the beginning and a kind of foretaste of the peace of the saints in heaven – the peace of eternity.

Bd Denis the Carthusian, *Commentary on Luke*: Opera omnia, xii, 72–4

Twenty-First Sunday in Ordinary Time/Proper 16 Year A: Matthew 16.13–20

A READING FROM A HOMILY BY ST JOHN CHRYSOSTOM

Peter was to be entrusted with the keys of the Church, or rather, he was entrusted with the keys of heaven; to him would be committed the whole people of God. The Lord told him: *Whatever you bind on earth shall be bound in heaven, and whatever you loose on earth shall be loosed in heaven.* Now Peter was inclined to be severe, so if he had also been impeccable what forbearance would he have shown toward those he instructed? His falling into sin was thus a providential grace to teach him from experience to deal kindly with others.

Just think who it was whom God permitted to fall into sin – Peter himself, the head of the apostles, the firm foundation, the unbreakable rock, the most important member of the Church, the safe harbour, the strong tower; Peter, who had said to Christ, *Even if I have to die with you I will never deny you*; Peter, who by divine revelation had confessed the truth: *You are the Christ, the Son of the living God.*

The gospel relates that on the night that Christ was betrayed Peter went indoors and was standing by the fire warming himself when a girl accosted him, *You too were with that man yesterday*, she said. But Peter answered: *I do not know the man.*

Just now you said: *Even if I have to die with you*, and now you deny him and say: *I do not know the man.* Oh Peter, is this what you promised? You were not tortured or scourged; at the words of a mere slip of a girl you took refuge in denial.

Again the girl said to him: *You too were with that man yesterday.* Again he answered: *I have no idea what man you mean.*

Who was it that spoke to you, causing you to make this denial? Not some important person but a woman, a doorkeeper, an outcast, a slave, someone of no account whatever. She spoke to you and you answered with a denial. What a strange thing – a girl, a prostitute, accosted Peter himself and disturbed his faith! Peter, the pillar, the rampart, could not bear the threat of a girl! She had but to speak and the pillar swayed, the rampart itself was shaken.

A third time she repeated: *You too were with that man yesterday*, but a third time he denied it. Finally Jesus looked at him, reminding him of his previous assertion. Peter understood, repented of his sin, and began to weep. Mercifully, however, Jesus forgave him his sin, because he knew that Peter, being a man, was subject to human frailty.

Now, as I said before, the reason God's plan permitted Peter to sin was because he was to be entrusted with the whole people of God, and sinless-ness added to his severity might have made him unforgiving towards his brothers and sisters. He fell into sin so that remembering his own fault and the Lord's forgiveness, he also might forgive others out of love for them. This was God's providential dispensation. He to whom the Church was to be entrusted, he, the pillar of the churches, the harbour of faith, was allowed to sin; Peter, the teacher of the world, was permitted to sin, so that having been forgiven himself he would be merciful to others.

St John Chrysostom, *Homily on SS Peter and Elias*: PG 50, 727–8

Twenty-First Sunday in Ordinary Time/Proper 16 Year B: John 6.60–69 [56–69]

A READING FROM THE COMMENTARY ON JOHN BY ST CYRIL OF ALEXANDRIA

To whom shall we go? Peter asks. In other words, 'Who else will instruct us the way you do?' Or, 'To whom shall we go to find anything better?' *You have the words of eternal life*; not hard words, as those other disciples say, but words that will bring us to the loftiest goal, unceasing, endless life removed from all corruption. These words surely make quite obvious to us the necessity of sitting at the feet of Christ, taking him as our one and only teacher, and giving him our constant and undivided attention. He must be our guide who knows well how to lead us to everlasting life. Thus, thus shall we ascend to the divine court of heaven, and, entering the church of the first born, delight in blessings passing all human understand-ing.

That the desire to follow Christ alone and to be with him always is a good thing leading to our salvation is entirely self-evident; yet we may learn this from the Old Testament as well. When the Israelites had shaken off Egyptian tyranny and were hastening towards the promised land, God did not allow them to make disorderly marches; nor did the Lawgiver let each one go where he would, for without a guide they should undoubtedly have lost the way completely. They were ordered to follow: to set out with the cloud, to come to a halt again with it, and to rest with it. Keeping with their guide was the Israelites' salvation then, just as not leaving Christ is ours now. For he was with those people of old under the form of the tabernacle, the cloud, and the fire.

They were commanded to follow, and not undertake the journey on their own initiative. They were to halt with the cloud and to abide with it, that by this symbol you might understand Christ's words: *Whoever serves me must follow me, so as to be with me wherever I am.* For being always in his company means being steadfast in following him and constant in cleaving to him. But accompanying the Saviour Christ and following him is by no means to be thought of as something done by the body. It is accomplished rather by deeds springing from virtue. Upon such virtue the wisest disciples firmly fixed their minds and refused to depart with the unbelievers, which they saw would be fatal. With good reason they cried out, 'Where can we go?' It was as though they said: 'We will stay with you always and hold fast to your commandments. We will receive your words without finding fault or thinking your teaching hard as the ignorant do, but thinking rather, *How sweet are your words to my throat! Sweeter to my mouth are they than honey or the honeycomb.*

St Cyril of Alexandria, *Commentary on John*, 4.4: PG 73, 613–17

Twenty-First Sunday in Ordinary Time Year C (RL): Luke 13.22–30

A READING FROM A SERMON BY BLESSED JOHN HENRY NEWMAN

Nothing is more clearly brought out in Scripture, or more remarkable in itself than this, that in every age, out of the whole number of persons blessed with the means of grace, few only have duly availed them of this great benefit. So certain, so uniform is the fact, that it is almost stated as a doctrine. *Many are called, few are chosen.* Again, *Strive to enter into the strait gate; for many, I say unto you, shall seek to enter in, and shall not be able.* And again, *Wide is the gate, and broad is the way, that leads to destruction, and many there be which go in thereat. Strait is the gate, and narrow is the way that leads unto life, and few there be that find it.*

The very temptation you lie under to explain away the plain words of Scripture, shows you that your standard of good and evil, and the standard of all round you, must be very different from God's standard. It shows you, that if the chosen are few, there must be some particular belief necessary, or some particular line of conduct, or something else different from what the world supposes, in order to account for this solemn declaration. It suggests to you that perchance there must be a certain perfection, completeness, consistency, entireness of obedience, for a person to be chosen, which most people miss in one point or another. It suggests to you that there is a great difference between being a hearer of the word and a doer; a well-wisher of the truth, or an approver of good people or good actions, and a faithful servant of the truth. It suggests to you that it is one thing to be in earnest, another and higher to be *rooted and grounded in love*. It suggests to you the exceeding dangerousness of single sins, or particular bad habits. It suggests to you the peril of riches, cares of this life, station, and credit.

Of course we must not press the words of Scripture; we do not know the exact meaning of the word *chosen*; we do not know what is meant by being saved *so as by fire*; we do not know what is meant by *few*. But still the few can never mean the many; and to be called without being chosen cannot but be a misery. We know that the person, in the parable who came to the feast without a wedding garment, was *cast into outer darkness*. Let us then set at nought the judgement of the many, whether about truth and falsehood, or about ourselves, and let us go by the judgement of that line of Saints, from the Apostles' times downwards, who were ever spoken against in their generation, ever honoured afterwards, – singular in each point of time as it came, but continuous and the same in the line of their history – ever protesting against the many, ever agreeing with each other. And, in proportion as we attain to their judgement of things, let us pray God to make it live in us; so that at the Last Day, when all veils are removed, we may be found among those who are inwardly what they seem outwardly – who with Enoch, and Noah, and Abraham, and Moses, and Joshua, and Caleb, and Phineas, and Samuel, and Elijah, and Jeremiah, and Ezekiel, and the Baptist, and St Paul, have *borne and had patience, and for his name-sake laboured and not fainted*, watched in all things, done the work of an Evangelist, fought a good fight, finished their course, kept the faith.

Bd John Henry Newman, *Parochial & Plain Sermons*, v, 254–6, 267–9

Sunday of Proper 16 Year C (RCL): Luke 13.10–17

A READING FROM *AGAINST CELSUS* BY ORIGEN

Jesus himself, as Isaiah foretold, arose as a *light to those who sat in dark-ness and in the shadow of death*, so that we may therefore say, *Let us break their bonds asunder, and cast their cords from us.* If our enemies had been able to sound the depths of the Gospel narratives, they would not have counselled us to put our confidence in those demonic beings whom they call 'the keepers of the prison-house'. It is written in the Gospel that a woman was bowed down and could not lift up herself and when Jesus saw her, and perceived why she was bowed down, he said, *Ought not this woman, a daughter of Abraham whom Satan bound for eighteen long years, be set free from this bondage on the sabbath day?*

How many others are still bowed down and bound by Satan, who hinders them from looking up at all, and who would have us to look down also! No one can raise them up, except the Word which came by Jesus Christ and had previously inspired the prophets. Jesus came to release those who were under the dominion of the devil and, speaking of him, he said with that depth of meaning which characterized his words, *Now is the prince of this world judged.* We are, then, indulging in no baseless calumnies against demons, but are condemning their agency upon earth as destructive to humankind; we show that, under the cover of oracles and bodily cures, they are seeking to separate from God the soul which has descended to this *body of humiliation.*

All who feel this humiliation exclaim, *O wretched man that I am! who shall deliver me from the body of this death?* It is not in vain, therefore, that we expose our bodies to be beaten and tortured; for surely it is not in vain for a man to submit to such sufferings, if by that means he may avoid bestowing the name of gods on those earthly spirits that unite with their worshippers to bring him to destruction. Indeed, we think it both reason-able in itself and well-pleasing to God, to suffer pain for the sake of virtue, to undergo torture for the sake of piety, and even to suffer death for the sake of holiness; for *precious in the sight of God is the death of his saints.*

Origen, Against Celsus, 8.54

Twenty-Second Sunday in Ordinary Time/Proper 17 Year A: Matthew 16.21–27

A READING FROM A SERMON BY ST AUGUSTINE

If anyone wishes to be a follower of mine, let him renounce himself and take up his cross and come after me.

Our Lord's command seems hard and heavy, that anyone who wants to follow him must renounce himself. But no command is hard and heavy when it comes from one who helps to carry it out. That other saying of his is true: *My yoke is easy and my burden light.* Whatever is hard in his commands is made easy by love.

We know what great things love can accomplish, even though it is often base and sensual. We know what hardships people have endured, what intolerable indignities they have borne to attain the object of their love. What we love indicates the sort of people we are, and therefore making a decision about this should be our one concern in choosing a way of life. Why be surprised if people who set their hearts on Christ and want to follow him renounce themselves out of love? If we lose ourselves through self-love we must surely find ourselves through self-renunciation.

Who would not wish to follow Christ to supreme happiness, perfect peace, and lasting security? We shall do well to follow him there, but we need to know the way. The Lord Jesus had not yet risen from the dead when he gave this invitation. His passion was still before him; he had still to endure the cross, to face outrages, reproaches, scourging; to be pierced by thorns, wounded, insulted, taunted, and put to death. The road seems rough, you draw back, you do not want to follow Christ. Follow him just the same. The road we made for ourselves is rough, but Christ has levelled it by passing over it himself.

Who does not desire to be exalted? Everyone enjoys a high position. But self-abasement is the step that leads to it. Why take strides that are too big for you – do you want to fall instead of going up? Begin with this step and you will find yourself climbing. The two disciples who said: *Lord, command that one of us shall sit at your right hand in your kingdom and the other at your left*, had no wish to think about this step of self-abasement. They wanted to reach the top without noticing the step that led there. The Lord showed them the step, however, by his reply: *Can you drink the cup that I am to drink?* You who aim at the highest exaltation, can you drink the cup of humiliation? He did not simply give the general command: *Let him renounce himself and follow me*, but added: *Let him take up his cross and follow me.*

What does it mean to take up one's cross? It means bearing whatever is unpleasant – that is 'following me'. Once you begin to follow me by conforming your life to my commandments, you will find many to contradict you, forbid you, or dissuade you, and some of these will be people calling themselves followers of Christ. Therefore if you meet with threats, flattery, or opposition, let this be your cross; pick it up and carry it – do not collapse under it. These words of our Lord are like an exhortation to endure martyrdom. If you are persecuted you ought, surely, to make light of any suffering for the sake of Christ.

St Augustine, *Sermon* 96, 1–4: PL 38, 584–6

Twenty-Second Sunday in Ordinary Time/Proper 17 Year B: Mark 7.1–8, 14–15, 21–23

A READING FROM THE TREATISE *AGAINST THE HERESIES* BY ST IRENAEUS

The Pharisees claimed that the traditions of their elders safeguarded the law, but in fact it contravened the law Moses had given. By saying: *Your merchants mix water with the wine*, Isaiah shows that the elders mixed their watery tradition with God's strict commandment. In other words, they enjoined an adulterated law which went against the law, as the Lord also made clear when he asked them: *Why do you transgress God's commandment for the sake of your tradition?*

By their transgression they not only falsified God's law, mixing water with the wine, but they also set against it their own law, called to this day the Pharisaic law. In this their rabbis suppress some of the commandments, add new ones, and give others their own interpretation, thus making the law serve their own purposes.

Their desire to justify these traditions kept them from submitting to God's law that taught them about the coming of Christ. Instead, they even found fault with the Lord for healing on the sabbath, which was not forbidden by the law, for in a sense the law itself healed by causing circumcision to be performed on the sabbath. On the other hand, they found no fault with themselves for breaking God's commandment by their tradition and the Pharisaic law just mentioned, or for lacking the essence of the law, which is love for God.

That this is the first and greatest commandment, the second being love of our neighbour, the Lord taught by saying that the whole of the law and the prophets depend on these two commandments. He himself brought no greater commandment than this but he renewed this same commandment by bidding his disciples love God with their whole heart, and their neighbour as themselves.

Paul also says that *love is the fulfilment of the law.* When all other charisms fail, faith, hope, and love remain, but the greatest of all is love. Knowledge is of no avail without the love of God, nor is understanding of mysteries, faith, or prophecy. Without love all are vain and profitless. Love on the other hand perfects a person, and one who loves God is perfect both in this world and the next, for we shall never stop loving God – the longer we gaze upon him the more our love for him will grow.

St Irenaeus, *Against Heresies*, 4.12.1–2: SC 100, 508–14

Twenty-Second Sunday in Ordinary Time/Proper 17 Year C: Luke 14.1, 7–14

A READING FROM THE COMMENTARY ON LUKE BY ST BRUNO OF SEGNI

Invited to a wedding feast, the Lord looked round and noticed how all were choosing the first and most honourable places, each person wanting to take precedence of the others and to be raised above them. He then told them this parable, which even taken literally is most useful and appropriate for all who like to be honoured, and fear being put to shame. To those of lower station it affords courtesy, and to those of higher condition respect. However, since it is called a parable, it must have some other interpretation besides the literal one. Let us see then what this wedding feast is, and who are the people invited to it.

This wedding feast takes place in the Church every day. Every day the Lord makes a wedding feast, for every day he unites faithful souls to himself, some coming to be baptized, others leaving this world for the kingdom of heaven. We are all invited to this wedding feast – all of us who have received faith in Christ and the seal of baptism. This table set before us is that of which it is said: *You have prepared a table before me in the sight of those who trouble me.* Here is the showbread, here the fatted calf, here the lamb who takes away the sins of the world. He is the living bread come down from heaven, here placed before us is the chalice of the New Covenant, here are the gospels and the letters of the apostles, here the books of Moses and the prophets. It is as though a dish containing every delight was brought and set before us. What more then can we desire? What reason is there for choosing the first seats? There is plenty for all no matter where we sit. There is nothing we shall lack.

But whoever you may be who still desire the first place here – go and sit in the last place. Do not be lifted up by pride, inflated by knowledge, elated by nobility, but the greater you are the more you must humble yourself in every way, and you will find grace with God. In his own time he will say to you: *Friend, go up higher, and then you will be honoured by all who sit at table with you.* Moses sat in the last place whenever he had the choice. When the Lord, wishing to send him to the Israelites, invited him to take a higher place, his answer was: *I beg you, Lord, send someone else. I am not a good speaker.* It was the same as saying: 'I am not worthy of so great an office.' Saul, too, was of small account in his own eyes when the Lord made him king. And Jeremiah, similarly, was afraid of rising to the first place: *Ah, Lord God,* he said, *look, I cannot speak – I am only a child.*

In the Church, then, the first seat, or the highest place, is to be sought not by ambition but by humility; not by money but by holiness.

St Bruno of Segni, *Commentary on Luke*, 1.14: PL 165, 406–7

Twenty-Third Sunday in Ordinary Time/Proper 18 Year A: Matthew 18.15–20

A READING FROM A HOMILY BY ST JOHN CHRYSOSTOM

The Apostle says: *Whether you eat or drink, or whatever you do, do it all for the glory of God.*

You will be doing everything for the glory of God if, when you leave this place, you make yourselves responsible for saving a brother or sister, not just by accusing and rebuking him or her, but also by advising and encouraging, and by pointing out the harm done by worldly amusements, and the profit and help that come from our instruction. You will also be preparing for yourself a double reward, since as well as greatly furthering your own salvation, you will be endeavouring to heal a fellow member of Christ's body. It is the Church's pride, it is the Saviour's command, not to be concerned only about our own welfare, but about our neighbour's also.

Think to what high honour you raise yourself when you regard the salvation of a brother or sister as a matter of extreme importance. As far as is humanly possible you imitate God himself, for listen to what he says through the prophet: *Whoever leads another from wrong to right will be as my own mouth.* In other words, 'Whoever tries to save a negligent brother or sister, and to snatch him or her from the jaws of the devil, is imitating me as far as a human being can.' What other work could equal this? Of all good deeds this is the greatest; of all virtue this is the summit.

And this is perfectly reasonable. Christ shed his own blood for our salvation; and Paul, speaking of those who give scandal and wound the consciences of people seeing them, cried out: *Because of your knowledge a weak brother or sister is destroyed – someone for whom Christ died!* So if your Lord shed his blood for that person, surely it is right for each of us to offer at least some words of encouragement and to extend a helping hand to those who through laxity have fallen into the snares of the devil.

But I am quite certain that you will do this out of the tender love you bear your own members, and the two will make every effort to bring your brothers and sisters back to our common Mother, because I know that through the grace of God you are able to admonish others with wisdom.

St John Chrysostom, *Catecheses*, 6.18–20: SC 50, 224–5

Twenty-Third Sunday in Ordinary Time/Proper 18 Year B: Mark 7.31–37 [24–37]

A READING FROM *THE HOMILIES ON THE GOSPELS* BY THE VENERABLE BEDE

The deaf-mute, of whose marvellous cure by our Lord we have just now heard when the gospel was read, represents those members of the human race who merit being freed by divine grace from the error brought on by the devil's deceit. Man became deaf, unable to hear the word of life after, puffed up as he was against God, he listened to the serpent's deadly words; he was made mute and unable to declare the praises of his Maker from the time when he presumed to have a conversation with his seducer. Rightly did God close man's ears from hearing the praises of his Creator along with the angels – those ears which the unsuspecting enemy by his speech had opened to hearing denunciation of this same Creator; rightly did God close man's mouth from proclaiming the praises of his Creator along with the angels – that mouth which the proud deceiver had filled with his lies about the forbidden food, in order, as the devil said, to improve upon the work of this same Creator. And alas, the unfortunate rebellion of the human race, which sprouted in a corrupt manner at the root, began to spread in a much more corrupt way in shoots from the branches, so that when our Lord came in the flesh, with the exception of a few of the faithful from among the Jews, almost the entire world, now deaf and mute, was wandering away from the recognition and confessional of the truth.

When Christ said 'Effeta' (that is, 'be opened'), he did this in order to heal the ears which a longstanding deafness had closed up, but which this touch now opened that they might hear. Hence I believe a custom has prevailed in the Church that his priests, first among all the elementary stages of consecration that they perform for those whom they are preparing to receive the sacrament of baptism, touch their nostrils and ears with saliva from their mouth, while they say 'Effeta'. By the saliva from their mouth they symbolize the taste of heavenly wisdom to which they are being introduced. By touching the nostrils they indicate that, once they have cast aside all harmful delights, they should always embrace only the odour of Christ, about which the Apostle says, *We are the good odour of Christ to God in every place*, and they should remember that, following the example of blessed Job, they are not to speak falsehood with their lips, nor with their tongue meditate on lying, as long as breath is in them and the Spirit of God is in their nostrils. Moreover, by the touching of the ears they indicate that, once they have left off listening to wicked tongues, they are to listen to the words of Christ and do them, like the prudent man who built his house upon a rock.

Each one of us, dearly beloved brothers, who has received the baptism of Christ according to the sacred rites, has been consecrated in this way. All who are going to receive this healing and saving bath according to the sacred rites, either at the approaching time of Easter, or at some other time, will be consecrated in this way. Hence it is most necessary that we should fear to defile thoughtlessly what the Lord has propitiously deigned to cleanse and sanctify in us, and to profane it as though it were of little account; but if any of us has partaken of a meal of disgraceful wickedness, let us hurry to cleanse ourselves once more at the font of tears and repentance.

Ven. Bede, *Homilies on the Gospels*, 2.6

Twenty-Third Sunday in Ordinary Time/Proper 18
Year C: Luke 14.25–33

A READING FROM THE CONFERENCES OF
ST JOHN CASSIAN

The tradition of the Fathers and the authority of Holy Scripture both affirm that there were three renunciations which every one of us must strive to practise. To these let us turn our attention.

First, on the material level, we have to despise all worldly wealth and possessions; secondly, we must reject our former way of life with its vices and attachments, both physical and spiritual; and thirdly, we should withdraw our mind from all that is transitory and visible to contemplate solely what lies in the future and to desire what is unseen.

We read that the Lord commanded Abraham to make all three renunciations at once when he said to him: *Leave your country and your kindred and your father's house.* First he said, *your country,* meaning worldly wealth and possessions; secondly, *your kindred,* that is our former way of living, with its habits and vices which have grown up with us and are as familiar to us as kith and kin; thirdly, *your father's house,* in other words every secular memory aroused by what we see.

This forgetfulness will be achieved when, dead with Christ to the elemental spirits of this world, we contemplate as the Apostle says, *not the things that are seen but those that are unseen, for what is seen is temporal but what is unseen is eternal.* It will be achieved when in our hearts we leave this temporal and visible house and turn the eyes of our mind toward that in which we shall live for ever; when, though living in the world, we cease to follow the spirit of the world in order to fight for the Lord, proclaiming by our holy way of life that, as the Apostle says, *our homeland is in heaven.*

It avails little to undertake the first of these renunciations, even with wholehearted devotion inspired by faith, unless we carry out the second with the same zeal and fervour. Then having accomplished this as well we shall be able to go on to the third, whereby we leave the house of our former father, of him who fathered us as members of a fallen race, *children of wrath like everyone else,* and turn our inward gaze solely toward heavenly things.

We shall attain to the perfection of this third renunciation when our mind, no longer dulled by contact with a pampered body, has been cleansed by the most searching refinement from every worldly sentiment and attitude, and raised by constant meditation on divine things and spiritual contemplation to the realm of the invisible. It will then lose all awareness of the frail body enclosing it or of the place it occupies, so absorbed will it be by things divine and spiritual.

St John Cassian, *Conferences*, 3.6–7: SC 42, 145–7

Twenty-Fourth Sunday in Ordinary Time/Proper 19 Year A: Matthew 18.21–35

A READING FROM A HOMILY BY ST AUGUSTINE

The Lord puts the parable of the unforgiving debtor before us that we may learn from it. He has no desire for us to die, so he warns us: *This is how your heavenly Father will deal with you if you, any of you, fail to forgive your brother or sister from your heart.*

Take notice now, for clearly this is no idle warning. The fulfilment of this command calls for the most vigorous obedience. We are all in debt to God, just as other people are in debt to us. Is there anyone who is not God's debtor? Only a person in whom no sin can be found. And is there anyone who has no brother or sister in his debt? Only if there be someone who has never suffered any wrong. Do you think anyone can be found in the entire human race who has not in turn wronged another in some way, incurring a debt to that person? No, all are debtors, and have others in debt to them. Accordingly, God who is just has told you how to treat your debtor, because he means to treat his in the same way.

There are two works of mercy which will set us free. They are briefly set down in the gospel in the Lord's own words: *Forgive and you will be forgiven*, and, *Give and you will receive*. The former concerns pardon, the latter generosity. As regards pardon he says: 'Just as you want to be forgiven, so someone is in need of your forgiveness.' Again, as regards generosity, consider when a beggar asks you for something that you are a beggar too in relation to God. When we pray we are all beggars before God. We are standing at the door of a great householder, or rather, lying prostrate, and begging with tears. We are longing to receive a gift – the gift of God himself.

What does a beggar ask of you? Bread. And you, what do you ask of God, if not Christ who said: *I am the living bread that has come down from heaven*? Do you want to be pardoned? Then pardon others. Forgive and you will be forgiven. Do you want to receive? Give and you will receive.

If we think of our sins, reckoning those we have committed by sight, hearing, thought, and countless disorderly emotions, I do not know whether we can even sleep without falling into debt. And so, every day we pray; every day we beat upon God's ears with our pleas; every day we prostrate ourselves before him saying: *Forgive us our trespasses, as we also forgive those who trespass against us.* Which of our trespasses, all of them or only some? All, you will answer. Do likewise, therefore, with those who have offended you. This is the rule you have laid down for yourself, the condition you have stipulated. When you pray according to this pact and covenant you remember to say: *Forgive us, as we also forgive our debtors.*

St Augustine, *Sermon* 83.2, 4: PL 38, 515–16

Twenty-Fourth Sunday in Ordinary Time/Proper 19 Year B: Mark 8.27–35 [27–38]

A READING FROM A SERMON BY ST CAESARIUS OF ARLES

When the Lord tells us in the gospel that anyone who wants to be his follower must renounce himself, this injunction seems harsh; we think he is imposing a burden on us. But an order is no burden when it is given by one who helps in carrying it out.

To what place are we to follow Christ if not where he has already gone? We know that he has risen and ascended into heaven: there, then, we must follow him. There is no cause for despair – by ourselves we can do nothing, but we have Christ's promise. Heaven was beyond our reach before our Head ascended there, but now, if we are his members, why should we despair of arriving there ourselves? Is there any reason? True, many fears and afflictions confront us in this world; but if we follow Christ, we shall reach a place of perfect happiness, perfect peace, and everlasting freedom from fear.

Yet let me warn anyone bent on following Christ to listen to St Paul: *One who claims to abide in Christ ought to walk as he walked.* Would you follow Christ? Then be humble as he was humble; do not scorn his lowliness if you want to reach his exaltation. Human sin made the road rough but Christ's resurrection levelled it; by passing over it himself he transformed the narrowest of tracks into a royal highway.

Two feet are needed to run along this highway; they are humility and charity. Everyone wants to get to the top – well, the first step to take is humility. Why take strides that are too big for you – do you want to fall instead of going up? Begin with the first step, humility, and you will already be climbing.

As well as telling us to renounce ourselves, our Lord and Saviour said that we must take up our cross and follow him. What does it mean to take up one's cross? Bearing every annoyance patiently. That is following Christ. When someone begins to follow his way of life and his command-ments, that person will meet resistance on every side. He or she will be opposed, mocked, even persecuted, and this not only by unbelievers but also by people who to all appearances belong to the body of Christ, though they are really excluded from it by their wickedness; people who, being Christians only in name, never stop persecuting true Christians.

If you want to follow Christ, then, take up his cross without delay. Endure injuries, do not be overcome by them. If we would fulfil the Lord's command: *If anyone wants to be my disciple, let him take up his cross and follow me*, we must strive with God's help to do as the Apostle says: *As long as we have food and clothing, let this content us.* Otherwise, if we seek more material goods than we need and desire to become rich, we may fall prey to temptation. The devil may trick us into wanting the many useless and harmful things that plunge people into ruin and destruction. May we be free from this temptation to the protection of our Lord, lives and reigns with the Father and the Holy Spirit for ever and ever. Amen.

St Caesarius of Arles, *Sermon* 159.1, 4–6: CCSL 104, 650, 652–4

Twenty-Fourth Sunday in Ordinary Time/Proper 19 Year C: Luke 15.1–32 or 15.1–10 [RCL 15.1–10]

A READING FROM A HOMILY BY ST PETER CHRYSOLOGUS

Finding something we have lost gives us a fresh joy, and we are happier at having found the lost object than we should have been had we never lost it. This parable, however, is concerned more with divine tenderness and compassion than with human behaviour, and it expresses a great truth. Humans are too greedy to forsake things of value for love of anything inferior. That is something only God can do. For God not only brought what was not into being, but he also went after what was lost while still protecting what he left behind, and found what was lost without losing what he had in safe keeping.

This story, then, speaks of no earthly shepherd but of a heavenly one, and far from being a portrayal of human activity, this whole parable conceals divine mysteries, as becomes clear from the number mentioned when Christ says: *Which of you, if you had a hundred sheep and lost one of them ...* You see how the loss of a single sheep made the shepherd grieve as though the whole flock were no longer in safe keeping but had gone astray, and how this made him leave the ninety-nine to go after the lost one and search for it, so that its recovery might make the flock complete again.

But let us now unfold the hidden meaning of this heavenly parable. The man who owns the hundred sheep is Christ. He is the good shepherd, the loving shepherd, who in a single sheep, that is in Adam, fashioned the whole flock of humankind. He set this sheep in a place of rich pasturage amidst the pleasures of paradise, but heedless of the shepherd's voice it trusted in the howling of wolves, lost the protection of the sheepfold, and was pierced through by deadly wounds.

Christ therefore came into the world to look for it, and he found it in the Virgin's womb. He came in the body assumed at his human birth, and raising that body on the cross, he placed the lost sheep on his own shoulders by his passion. Then in the intense joy of the resurrection he brought it to his heavenly home. *And he called his friends and neighbours*, that is the angels, and said to them: *Rejoice with me, for I have found the sheep that was lost.*

The angels joined Christ in gladness and rejoicing at the return of the Lord's sheep. They did not take it amiss that he now reigned over them upon the throne of majesty, for the sin of envy had long since been banished from heaven together with the devil, and it could not gain entry there again through the Lamb who took away the sin of the world!

Brothers and sisters, Christ sought us on earth; let us seek him in heaven. He has borne us up to the glory of his divinity; let us bear him in our bodies by holiness. As the Apostle says: *Glorify and bear God in your bodies.* That person bears God in his body whose bodily activities are free from sin.

St Peter Chrysologus, *Homily* 168: PL 52, 639–41

Twenty-Fifth Sunday in Ordinary Time/Proper 20
Year A: Matthew 20.1–16

A READING FROM A HOMILY BY ST AUGUSTINE

The gospel story about the vineyard workers is appropriate to this time of year, the season of the earthly grape harvest. But there is also another harvest, the spiritual one, at which God rejoices in the fruits of *his* harvest.

The kingdom of heaven is like a householder who went out to hire men to work in his vineyard. In the evening he gave orders for all to be paid, beginning with the last comers and ending with the first. Now why did he pay the lastcomers first? Will not everyone be rewarded at the same time? We read in another gospel passage how the king will say to those placed on his right hand: *Come, you whom my Father has blessed: take possession of the kingdom prepared for you from the foundation of the world.* If all, then, are to receive their wages together, how should we understand this statement about those who arrived at the eleventh hour being paid first, and those who had been working since daybreak being paid last? If I can say anything to further your understanding, thanks be to God. Give thanks to him who teaches you through me, for my own knowledge is not the source of my teaching.

To take an example, then, ask which of two workers receives his wages sooner, one who is paid after an hour, or one who is paid after twelve hours? Anyone will answer: 'One who is paid after an hour.' So also in our parable. All the workmen were paid at the same time, but because some were paid after an hour and others after twelve hours, the former, having had a shorter time to wait, may be said to have received their wages first.

The earliest righteous people like Abel and Noah, called as it were at the first hour, will receive the joy of resurrection at the same time as we do. So also will others who came later, Abraham, Isaac, and Jacob, and those contemporary with them, called as we may say at the third hour; Moses and Aaron and those called with them at the sixth hour; and after them the holy prophets, called at the ninth hour. At the end of the world all Christians, called at the eleventh hour, will receive the joy of resurrection together with those who went before them. All will be rewarded at the same time, but the first comers will have had the longest to wait. Therefore, if they receive their reward after a longer period and we after a shorter one, the fact that our reward is not delayed will make it seem as though we were receiving it first, even though we all receive it together.

In that great reward, then, we shall all be equal – the first to the last and the last to the first. For the denarius stands for eternal life, in which all will have the same share. Although through diversity of merit some will shine more brilliantly than others, in the possession of eternal life there will be equality. What is endless for all will not be longer for one and shorter for another. What has no bounds will have none either for you or for me. Those who lived chastely in the married state will have one kind of splendour; virgins will have another. The reward for good works will differ from the crown of martyrdom; but where eternal life is concerned there can be no question of more or less for anyone. Whatever may be the individual's degree of glory, each one will live in it eternally. This is the meaning of the denarius.

St Augustine, *Sermon* 87.1, 4–6: PL 38, 530–3

Twenty-Fifth Sunday in Ordinary Time/Proper 20 Year B: Mark 9.30–37

A READING FROM THE COMMENTARY ON MARK BY ST THEOPHYLACT OF OHRID

The Lord always alternated prophecies of his passion with the performance of miracles, so that he would not be thought to have suffered through lack of power. Therefore, after imparting the grievous news that men would kill him, he added the joyful tidings that on the third day he would rise again. This was to teach us that joy always follows sorrow, and that we should not be uselessly distressed by painfully events, but should rather have hope that better times will come.

He came to Capernaum, and after entering the house he questioned the disciples: 'What were you arguing about on the way?' Now the disciples still saw things from a very human point of view, and they had been quarrelling amongst themselves about which of them was the greatest and the most esteemed by Christ. Yet the Lord did not restrain their desire for pre-eminent honour; indeed he wishes us to aspire to the most exalted rank. He does not however wish us to seize the first place, but rather to win the highest honour by humility.

He stood a child among them because he wants us to become childlike. A child has no desire for honour; it is not jealous, and it does not remember injuries. And he said: 'If you become like that, you will receive a great reward, and if, moreover, for my sake, you honour others who are like that, you will receive the kingdom of heaven; for you will be receiving me, and in receiving me you receive the one who sent me.'

You see then what great things humility, together with simplicity and guilelessness, can accomplish. It causes both the Son and the Father to dwell in us, and with them of course comes the Holy Spirit also.

St Theophylactof Ohrid, *Commentary on Mark*: PG 123, 588–9

Twenty-Fifth Sunday in Ordinary Time/Proper 20 Year C: Luke 16.1–13

A READING FROM A SERMON BY ST GAUDENTIUS OF BRESCIA

The Lord Jesus, true teacher of the precepts that lead to salvation, wished to urge upon the apostles in his own time and all believers today the Christian duty of almsgiving. He therefore related the parable of the steward to make us realize that nothing in this world really belongs to us. We have been entrusted with the administration of our Lord's property to use what we need with thanksgiving, and to distribute the rest among our fellow servants according to the needs of each one. We must not squander the wealth entrusted to us, nor use it on superfluities, for when the Lord comes we shall be required to account for our expenditure.

Finally, at the end of the parable, the Lord adds: *Use worldly wealth to make friends with the poor, so that when it fails you,* when you have spent all you possessed on the needs of the poor and have nothing left, *they may welcome you into eternal dwellings.*

In other words, these same poor people will befriend you by assuring your salvation, for Christ, the giver of the eternal rewards, will declare that he himself received the acts of kindness done to them. Not in their own name, then, will these poor folk welcome us, but in the name of him who is refreshed in their persons by the fruit of our faith and obedience. Those who exercised this ministry of love will be received into the eternal dwellings of the kingdom of heaven, for the King will say: *Come, blessed of my Father, take possession of the kingdom prepared for you from the beginning of the world; for I was hungry and you fed me, thirsty and you gave me a drink.*

But *if you have been untrustworthy in the administration of worldly wealth, who is going to trust you with true riches?* For if someone cannot be relied on to administer worldly possessions that provide the means for all sorts of wrongdoing, would anyone dream of trusting that person with the true heavenly riches rightly and deservedly enjoyed by those who have been faithful in giving to the poor?

The Lord's query above is immediately followed by another: *If you cannot be trusted with another's property, who will give you your own?* Nothing in this world really belongs to us. We who hope for a future reward are told to live in this world as strangers and pilgrims, so as to be able to say to the Lord without fear of contradiction: *I am a stranger and a pilgrim like all my ancestors.*

What believers can regard as their own is that eternal and heavenly possession where our heart is and our treasure, and where intense longing makes us dwell already through faith, for as St Paul teaches, *Our homeland is in heaven.*

St Gaudentius of Brescia, Sermon 18: PL 20, 973–5

Twenty-Sixth Sunday in Ordinary Time/Proper 21 Year A: Matthew 21.28–32 [23–32]

A READING FROM A HOMILY BY ST CLEMENT OF ALEXANDRIA

The doors are open for all who sincerely and wholeheartedly return to God; indeed, the Father is most willing to welcome back a truly repentant son or daughter. The result of true repentance, however, is that you do not fall into the same faults again, but utterly uproot from your souls the sins for which you consider yourself worthy of death. When these have been destroyed God will again dwell within you, since Scripture says that for the Father and his angels in heaven the festal joy and gladness at the return of one repentant sinner is great beyond compare. That is why the Lord cried out: *What I want is mercy, not sacrifice. I desire not the death of a sinner but his conversion. Even if your sins are like crimson I will make them as white as snow; even if they are blacker than night I will wash them as white as wool.*

Although only God has power to forgive sins and cancel transgressions, the Lord commands us also to forgive our repentant brothers and sisters every day. So if we who are evil know how to give good gifts, how much more generous must be the Father of mercies, the good Father of all consolation, who is full of compassion and mercy, and whose nature it is to be patient and await our conversion! Genuine conversion, however, means ceasing to sin without any backward glances.

God pardons what is past, then, but for the future we are each responsible for ourselves. By repenting we condemn our past misdeeds and beg forgiveness of the Father, the only one who can in his mercy undo what has been done, and wipe away our past sins with the dew of his Spirit. And so, if you are a thief and desire to be forgiven, steal no more. If you are a robber, return your gains with interest. If you have been a false witness, practise speaking the truth. If you are a perjurer, stop taking oaths. You must also curb all the other evil passions: anger, lust, grief, and fear. No doubt you will be unable all at once to root out passions habitually given way to, but this can be achieved by God's power, human prayers, the help of your brothers and sisters, sincere repentance, and constant practice.

St Clement of Alexandria, *Who is the rich person who shall be saved?*
39–40: PG 9, 644–5

Twenty-Sixth Sunday in Ordinary Time/Proper 21 Year B: Mark 9.38–43, 45, 47–48

A READING FROM A CONFERENCE BY ST SYMEON THE NEW THEOLOGIAN

Do you not tremble when you hear God saying to you day after day throughout the whole of divine Scripture: *Let no evil word come from your mouth. Indeed I tell you that you will have to answer for a single careless word*, and: *You will receive a reward for a cup of cold water.*

My brothers, do not deceive yourselves. God loves us, and he is merciful and compassionate. I myself testify and acknowledge that it is his compassion that makes me confident of being saved. Nevertheless you must understand that this will be of no avail to those who refuse to repent and to keep God's commandments in every detail and with great fear. On the contrary, God will punish them more severely than people who are unbelievers and unbaptized.

O brothers, do not deceive yourselves; let there be no sin that seems small in your eyes, and that you treat lightly, as though it did no great harm to our souls. Right-minded servants make no distinction between a small sin and a great; if they offend by so much as a glance, a thought, or a word, they feel as if they have fallen away from the love of God, and I believe this is true. In fact, whoever has the slightest thought contrary to the divine will, and does not immediately repent and repel the assault of such a thought, but welcomes it and consents to it – that person is counted guilty of sin, and this is so even if he is unaware that his thought is sinful.

Consequently we need to be extremely vigilant and zealous, and to give much time to searching the divine Scriptures. The Saviour's command, 'Search the Scriptures', shows how profitable they are for us. So search them, and hold fast to what they say with great exactitude and faith. Then, when the divine Scriptures have given you an accurate knowledge of God's will, you will be able to distinguish without error between good and evil, and will not listen to every spirit, or be carried away by harmful thoughts.

You may be certain, my brothers, that nothing is so conducive to our salvation as following the divine commandments of the Saviour. Nevertheless we shall have to shed many tears, and shall need great fear, great patience, and constant prayer before the import of even a word of the Master can be revealed to us. Only then shall we perceive the great mystery hidden in short sayings, and be ready to die for the smallest detail of the commandments of God. For the word of God is like a two-edged sword, cutting off and separating the soul from all bodily desire and sensation. More than that, it is like a blazing fire, because it stirs up zeal in our souls, and makes us disregard all the sorrows of life, consider every trial we encounter a joy, and desire and embrace death, so fearful to others, as life and the means of attaining life.

St Symeon the New Theologian, *Catecheses*, 1.3: SC 96, 299–305

Twenty-Sixth Sunday in Ordinary Time/Proper 21 Year C: Luke 16.19–31

A READING FROM A HOMILY BY ST JOHN CHRYSOSTOM

It is worthwhile enquiring why the rich man saw Lazarus in Abraham's arms, and not in the company of some other righteous person. The reason is that Abraham was hospitable, and so the sight of Lazarus with Abraham was meant to reproach the rich man for his own inhospitality. Abraham used to pursue even passers-by and drag them into his home, whereas the rich man disregarded someone lying in his own doorway. Although he had within his grasp so great a treasure, such an opportunity to win salvation, he ignored the poor man day after day. He could have helped him but he failed to do so. The patriarch was not like that but just the opposite. He would sit in his doorway and catch all who passed by. And just as a fisherman casting a net into the sea hauls up fish, yes, but also quite often gold and pearls, so Abraham whilst catching people in his net finished by catching angels, strangely enough without knowing it.

Even Paul marvels at this and gives the advice: *Remember to welcome strangers into your homes, for some by doing so have entertained angels without knowing it.* And he did well to say *without knowing it*, for if Abraham had welcomed his guests with such kindness because he knew who they were he would have done nothing remarkable. He is praiseworthy only because, without knowing who the passers-by were and taking them to be simply human wayfarers, he yet invited them in with so much good will.

And this is true of you also. If you show much eagerness in welcoming some famous and distinguished person you do nothing remarkable; often the high rank of a guest compels even reluctant hosts to show every sign of courtesy. But we do something truly great and admirable when we give a most courteous welcome to all, even the outcasts of society or people of humble condition. Hence Christ himself praised those who so acted, declaring: *Whatever you did for one of these very poor people you did to me.* He also said: *It is not your Father's will that one of these little ones should perish.* Indeed, throughout the gospel Christ speaks a great deal about the little people and those of the humblest condition.

And so Abraham also, knowing this, did not ask who travellers were or where they came from, as we do today, but simply welcomed them all. Anyone wishing to show kindness should not inquire into other people's lives, but has only to alleviate their poverty and supply their needs, as Christ commanded when he said: *Imitate your Father in heaven, who makes his sun rise on good and bad alike, and sends rain on the just and the unjust.*

St John Chrysostom, *Homily 2 on Lazarus*, 5: Bareille, 2, 582–3

Twenty-Seventh Sunday in Ordinary Time/Proper 22 Year A: Matthew 21.33–43 [33–46]

A READING FROM A HOMILY BY ST BASIL THE GREAT

You need only to look at the vine to be reminded of your own nature, that is, if you observe it intelligently. No doubt you remember the image used by the Lord in which he says that he is the vine and the Father the vinedresser. Each of us who have been grafted onto the Church by faith he calls branches, and he urges us to bear much fruit so as not to be rejected as useless and thrown onto the fire.

Throughout the Scriptures the Lord continually likens human souls to vines. He says for instance: *My beloved had a vineyard on a fertile hillside*; and again: *I planted a vineyard and put a hedge round it.* Clearly it is human souls that he calls his vineyard, and the hedge he has put round them is the security of his commandments and the protection of the angels; for *the angel of the Lord will encamp around those who fear him.* Moreover, by establishing in the Church apostles in the first place, prophets in the second, and teachers in the third, he has surrounded us as though by a firmly planted palisade.

In addition, the Lord has raised our thoughts to heaven by the examples of saints of past ages. He has kept them from sinking to the earth where they would deserve to be trampled on, and he wills that the bonds of love, like the tendrils of a vine, should attach us to our neighbours and make us rest on them, so that always climbing upward like vines growing on trees, we may reach the loftiest heights.

He also requires that we allow ourselves to be weeded. To be spiritually weeded means to have renounced the worldly ambitions that burdened our hearts. Anyone who has renounced the love of material things and attachment to possessions, or who has come to regard as despicable and deserving of contempt the poor, wretched glory of this world, is like a weeded vine. Freed from the profitless burden of profitless aspirations, that person can breathe again.

Finally, following the implications of the comparison, we must not run to wood, or, in other words, show off or seek the praise of outsiders. Instead, we must bear fruit by reserving the display of our good works for the true vinedresser.

St Basil the Great, *Homilies on the Hexameron*, 5: SC 27, 304–7

Twenty-Seventh Sunday in Ordinary Time/Proper 22 Year B: Mark 10.2–16

A READING FROM A HOMILY ON THE VEIL OF MOSES BY ST JACOB OF SERUGH

In his mysterious plans the Father had destined a bride for his only Son and presented her to him under the guise of prophetic images. Moses appeared and with deft hand sketched a picture of bridegroom and bride but immediately drew a veil over it. In his book he wrote that a man should leave father and mother so as to be joined to his wife, that the two might in very truth become one. The prophet Moses spoke of man and woman in this way in order to foretell Christ and his Church. With a prophet's penetrating gaze he contemplated Christ becoming one with the Church through the mystery of water. He saw Christ even from the Virgin's womb drawing the Church to himself, and the Church in the water of baptism drawing Christ to herself. Bridegroom and bride were thus wholly united in a mystical manner, which is why Moses wrote that the two should become one.

With veiled face Moses contemplated Christ and the Church: the one he called 'man' and the other 'woman' so as not to reveal the full splendour of the reality. After the marriage celebration came Paul. He saw the veil covering their splendour and lifted it, revealing Christ and his Church to the whole world, and showing that it was they whom Moses had described in his prophetic vision. In an outburst of inspired joy the Apostle exclaimed: *This is a great mystery!* He revealed the meaning of the veiled picture the prophet had called man and woman, declaring: *I know that it is Christ and his Church*, who were two before but have now become one.

Wives are not united to their husbands as closely as the Church is to the Son of God. What husband but our Lord ever died for his wife, and what bride ever chose a crucified man as her husband? Whoever gave his blood as a gift to his wife except the One who died on the cross and sealed the marriage bond with his wounds? Who was ever seen lying dead at his own wedding banquet with his wife at his side seeking to console herself by embracing him? At what other celebration, at what other feast is the bridegroom's body distributed to the guests in the form of bread?

Death separates wives from their husbands, but in this case it is death that unites the bride to her beloved. He died on the cross, bequeathed his body to his glorious spouse, and now every day she receives and consumes it at his table. She consumes it under the form of bread, and under the form of the wine that she drinks, so that the whole world may know that they are no longer two but one.

St Jacob of Serugh, Homily on the Veil of Moses: Guéranger, iii,
1023–5

Twenty-Seventh Sunday in Ordinary Time/Proper 22 Year C: Luke 17.5–10

A READING FROM A SERMON BY ST AUGUSTINE

Reading the holy gospel nourishes in us the habit of prayer, builds up our faith, and disposes us to trust in the Lord rather than in ourselves. What more powerful incentive to prayer could be proposed to us than the parable of the unjust judge? An unprincipled man, without fear of God or regard for other people, that judge nevertheless ended by granting the widow's petition. No kindly sentiment moved him to do so; he was rather worn down by her pestering. Now if a man can grant a request even when it is odious to him to be asked, how can we be refused by the one who urges us to ask?

Having persuaded us, therefore, by a comparison of opposites that *we ought always to pray and never lose heart*, the Lord goes on to put the question: *Nevertheless, when the Son of Man comes, do you think he will find faith on earth?* Where there is no faith, there is no prayer. Who would pray for something he did not believe in? So when the blessed Apostle exhorts us to pray he begins by declaring: *Whoever calls on the name of the Lord will be saved*; but to show that faith is the source of prayer and the stream will not flow if its springs are dried up, he continues: *But how can people call on him in whom they do not believe?*

We must believe, then, in order to pray; and we must ask God that the faith enabling us to pray may not fail. Faith gives rise to prayer, and this prayer obtains an increase of faith. Faith, I say, gives rise to prayer, and is in turn strengthened by prayer. It was to guard against their faith failing that the Lord told his disciples: *Watch and pray that you may not enter into temptation.*

Watch, he says; *and pray that you may not enter into temptation.* What does it mean to enter into temptation? It means to turn one's back on faith. Temptation grows stronger in proportion as faith weakens, and becomes weaker in proportion as faith grows strong. To convince you, beloved, that he was speaking of the weakening and loss of faith when he told his disciples to watch and pray that they might not enter into temptation, the Lord said in the same passage of the gospel: *This night Satan has demanded to sift you like wheat; but I have prayed for you, Peter, that your faith may not fail.* Is the protector to pray, while the person in danger has no need to do so?

But in asking whether the Son of Man would find faith on earth at his coming, the Lord was speaking of perfect faith. That kind of faith is indeed hardly to be found on earth. Look at God's Church: it is full of people. Who would come here if faith were non-existent? But who would not move mountains if that faith were present in full measure? Mark the apostles: they would never have left everything they possessed and spurned worldly ambition to follow the Lord unless their faith had been great; and yet that faith of theirs could not have been perfect, otherwise they would not have asked the Lord to increase it.

St Augustine, *Sermon* 115: PL 38, 655

Twenty-Eighth Sunday in Ordinary Time/Proper 23 Year A: Matthew 22.1–14

A READING FROM A SERMON BY ST AUGUSTINE

All believers are familiar with the story of the wedding of the king's son and the banquet that followed it, and of how the Lord's table was thrown open to all comers. When everyone was seated, *the master of the house came in to see his guests, and among them he noticed one without a wedding garment. So he said to him, 'My friend, how did you get in here without a wedding garment?'*

Now what precisely does this mean? Let us try to find out what it is that some believers have, but which the wicked lack, for that will be what the wedding garment is.

Can it be one of the sacraments? Hardly, for these, as we know, are common to good and bad alike. Take baptism for example. It is true that no one comes to God except through baptism, but not every baptized person comes to him. We cannot take the sacrament as the wedding garment, then, for it is a robe worn not only by good people but also by wicked people. Perhaps, then, it is our altar that is meant, or at least what we receive from it. But we know that many who approach the altar eat and drink to their own damnation. Well, then, maybe it is fasting? The wicked can fast too. What about going to church? Some bad people also go to church.

Whatever can this wedding garment be, then? For an answer we must go to the Apostle, who says: *The purpose of our command is to arouse the love that springs from a pure heart, a clear conscience, and a genuine faith.* There is your wedding garment. It is not love of just any kind. Many people of bad conscience appear to love one another, but you will not find in them *the love that springs from a pure heart, a clear conscience, and a genuine faith.* Only that kind of love is the wedding garment.

If I speak in the tongues of men and of angels, says the Apostle, *but have no love, I am nothing but a booming gong or a clashing cymbal. If I have the gift of prophecy, if I have all knowledge and understand all mysteries, if I have faith strong enough to move mountains, but have no love, I am nothing.* In other words, even with all these gifts I am nothing without Christ. Does that mean that prophecy has no value and that knowledge of mysteries is worthless? No, they are not worthless but I am, if I possess them but have no love. But can the lack of one good thing rob so many others of their value? Yes, without love my confession of the name of Christ even by shedding my blood or offering my body to be burnt will avail me nothing, if I may do this out of a desire for glory. That such things can be endured for the sake of empty show without any real love for God the Apostle also declares. Listen to him: *If I give away all I have to the poor, if I hand over my body to be burnt, but have no love, it will avail me nothing.* So this is what the wedding garment is. Examine yourselves to see whether you possess it. If you do, your place at the Lord's table is secure.

St Augustine, *Sermon* 90.1, 5–6: PL 38, 559, 561–3

Twenty-Eighth Sunday in Ordinary Time/Proper 23 Year B: Mark 10.17–30

A READING FROM A HOMILY BY ST CLEMENT OF ALEXANDRIA

There is nothing like listening again to the statements in the Gospels which, because you were listening to them without examination, were distressing you. These things are written in the Gospel according to Mark and are also found with slight variations in the other gospels, but in each they have the same meaning.

Our Lord and Saviour was asked a most appropriate question: the Life was asked about life, the Saviour about salvation, the Teacher about the chief doctrines taught, the Truth about true immortality, the Word about the word of the Father, the Perfect about perfect rest, the Immortal about immortality. He was asked about those things for which he descended, and having been called 'good', and starting from this, he begins his teaching by turning the pupil to God. God is the Good, the first and only dispenser of eternal life, which the Son, who received it of him, gives to us.

This man is persuaded that he does not lack righteousness but that he is entirely destitute of life, thus he asks it from him who alone is able to give it. He is confident in the law, but he addresses the Son of God in supplication and is transferred from faith to faith. Jesus, accordingly, does not charge him with not having fulfilled all things out of the law, but he loves him and fondly welcomes his obedience in what he had learned; but he tells him that he is not perfect as respects eternal life, because he had not fulfilled what is perfect. He is a doer of the law, but idle at what leads to true life. The law is good, who denies this? For *the commandment is holy*, but Christ is the fulfilment *of the law for righteousness to everyone that believes*; and not as a slave making slaves, but sons, and brethren, and fellow-heirs, who perform the Father's will.

He says, *If you will be perfect. ...*, and thus he was not yet perfect. The expression 'if you will' shows the self-determination of the soul conversing with Christ, for choice depends on the man being free; but the gift depends on God as the Lord. And God gives to those who are willing and passionately desire, to those who ask that their salvation may become their own. For God does not compel (for compulsion is repugnant to God), but he supplies to those who seek, and bestows on those who ask, and opens to those who knock. If you will, if you really will, and are not deceiving yourself, you can acquire what you lack. You only lack one thing, the one thing which abides, the Good, that which is now above the law, which the law does not give, which the law does not contain, which is the prerogative of those who live. But he departed displeased, annoyed at the commandment of the life for which he asked. For he did not truly wish life, as he claimed. He was capable of busying himself about many things; but the one thing, the work of life, he was powerless, disinclined, unable to accomplish.

This is the same as what the Lord said to Martha, who was occupied with many things and distracted and troubled with serving. Martha blamed her sister because, while she worked, her sister sat at Christ's feet devoting her time to learning: *Martha, you are troubled about many things, but Mary hath chosen the good part, which shall not be taken away from her.* Thus the Lord called the man to leave his busy life, and cleave to the One and adhere to the grace of him who offered everlasting life.

Clement of Alexandria, *Who is the rich person who shall be saved?*
4–6, 8–10

Twenty-Eighth Sunday in Ordinary Time/Proper 23 Year C: Luke 17.11–19

A READING FROM *QUESTIONS ON THE GOSPELS* BY ST AUGUSTINE

We can understand the lepers of this Gospel story to represent those whose Christian faith is all mixed up with various errors. These errors are like diseased spots disfiguring a healthy skin. The lepers stand far off from the divine Teacher, but still they call on him to cleanse away the spots of false doctrine by his word of truth. *Jesus, Teacher,* they cry, *have mercy on us!*

How though should we understand his command to go off at once, even though now cleansed, and show themselves to the Priests?

No faithful Christian can doubt that the Priesthood of the Jews represented or prefigured the Royal Priesthood we have in the Church. Into this Priesthood every member of the Body of Christ, the true and supreme High Priest, is consecrated. Among the Jews of old, only Kings and Priests were anointed; but now all receive that two-fold anointing, as St Peter says in his first Letter, when he calls the whole Christian people a *Royal Priesthood*. Our Saviour needs no intermediary, yet he wishes to act publicly through this Priesthood in teaching doctrine or administering the Sacraments. So Paul heard the voice of the Lord saying directly to him: *Why are you persecuting me?* But then he was sent to Ananias, so that by that Priesthood which is established in the Church he might learn the mystery of Christian doctrine, and his healthy appearance, now free from the leprosy of error, might be certified.

The varied colour of leprous skin is also a figure of disunity in the Church. When Paul and Barnabas went up to Jerusalem to explain the Gospel they'd been preaching to the Gentiles, James and Peter and John, reckoned to be pillars of the Church, gave their right hands in fellowship. This conference showed the Apostolic doctrine in its uniform healthy appearance, all discolouring of disunity excluded.

We see an example of someone going to show himself to the Priests when the angel ordered Cornelius to send for Peter. He and his companions came spiritually to the Priests in order to receive sacramental baptism: but we note they had already been cleansed, for even before their baptism they received the gift of the Holy Spirit and spoke in tongues.

The ingratitude of the nine cleansed lepers continues to be manifested in the Church. Some people may indeed through membership of the Church and acceptance of all her doctrine be free from spiritual leprosy: but they fail to recognize the one who cleansed them, and become inflated with pride. The Apostle speaks of such people: *they knew God, but did not worship him as God or give thanks to him.* In so far as they knew God, they were cleansed from leprosy, but in so far as they were ungrateful, they remained imperfect. The number nine, needing one to make it up to ten, signifies imperfection. The one who returned to give thanks signifies the unity of the Church, and of the Kingdom of Heaven: and he has this unity even without the other nine. *He was a Samaritan,* a word which means Guardian. Thus the Psalmist sings: I *will guard my strength for you, through thanksgiving.* Subject to the King, then, this Samaritan preserved the unity of the Kingdom by his humble devotion.

St Augustine, *Questions on the Gospels*, 2.40: CCSL 44B, 97–102

Twenty-Ninth Sunday in Ordinary Time/Proper 24 Year A: Matthew 22.15–21

A READING FROM THE COMMENTARY ON LUKE BY ST AMBROSE

In this passage the Lord is showing us how circumspect we have to be in replying to heretics or Jews. Somewhere else he says: *Be wise as serpents.* Many understand this verse in the following way: the serpent lifted up in the desert prefigured the Cross of Christ by which would be destroyed the venom of the evil spirit. So, we are being told to be wise and circumspect as Christ, but simple as the Spirit, the Dove. See, here is the Serpent who always protects his head and saves it from mortal injury. When the Jews asked Jesus if he had received his authority from heaven, he replied: *John's baptism, was it from heaven, or was it from men?* Since they dared not deny that John's baptism was from heaven, they would have appeared out of their minds if they had denied that their own Author was from heaven.

Our Lord asked for a coin and then enquired whose image was on it. For very different from the image of God is the image of the world. That is why Paul warns us: *Since we once bore the image of the earthly one, let us bear also the image of the heavenly one.*

Christ, being *God's image*, does not bear the image of Caesar. Peter does not bear Caesar's image, for he says: *We have left all things and followed you.* And you won't find Caesar's image with James or with John, for they are *Sons of Thunder.* But you will find that image in the sea where monsters swim, with their heads crushed under the waters; while the principal monster, once his head is crushed, is given as food to the people of Ethiopia.

But if Christ did not carry Caesar's image, why did he pay the tax? I reply that he did not pay it out of what was his, but simply gave back to the world what belonged to the world. And you, too, if you do not want to owe anything to Caesar, do not have possessions that pertain to this world. But in fact, you do have money, and you do owe tribute to Caesar. If truly you desire not to be under an obligation to any earthly king, give up all that you have and follow Christ.

It is well that the Lord first makes clear what is to be rendered to Caesar: for no one can belong to the Lord unless they renounce the world.

Yes, yes, we all renounce it in word; but in our heart we do not renounce it. In word we renounce it when we receive the sacred Mysteries. But what a heavy chain we drag if we do not honour a promise that we made to God! Remember what Scripture says: *Better not to make a vow, than to make a vow and break it.* A solemn promise to God is a more serious matter than a business contract. Keep your solemn promise so long as you are in this body, before your creditor comes and puts you in prison: *I tell you truly, you shall not get out till you have paid the last farthing.*

St Ambrose, *Commentary on Luke*, 9.34–6

Twenty-Ninth Sunday in Ordinary Time/Proper 24 Year B: Mark 10.35–45

A READING FROM A HOMILY BY ST JOHN CHRYSOSTOM

When the ten disciples were indignant with James and John for separating themselves from their company in the hope of obtaining the highest honour, Jesus corrected the disorderly passions of both groups. Notice how he did it.

He called them to him and said: 'Gentile rulers lord it over their people, and holders of high office make their authority felt. This must not happen among you. On the contrary, whoever wants to be first among you must be last of all.'

You see that what the two brothers wanted was to be first, greatest, and highest: rulers, one might almost say, of the others. So, revealing their secret thoughts, Jesus put a curb on this ambition, saying: *Whoever wants to be first among you must become the servant of all.* If you wish to take precedence and to have the highest honours, aim for whatever is lowest and worst: to be the most insignificant and humble of all, of less account than anyone else; to put yourselves after the others. It is virtue of this kind that wins the honour you aspire to, and you have an outstanding example of it near at hand. *For the Son of Man came not to be served but to serve, and to give his life as a ransom for many.* This is what will make you illustrious and far-famed. See what is happening in my case. I do not seek glory and honour, yet by acting in this way I am gaining innumerable blessings.

The fact is that before the incarnation and self-abasement of Christ the whole world was in a state of ruin and decay, but when he humbled himself he lifted the world up. He annulled the curse, put an end to death, opened paradise, destroyed sin, flung wide-open the gates of heaven, and introduced there the firstfruits of our race. He filled the world with faith in God, drove out error, restored truth, caused our firstfruits to ascend a royal throne, and gained innumerable blessings beyond the power of myself or anyone else to describe in words. Before he humbled himself he was known only to the angels, but after his self-abasement he was recognized by the whole human race.

St John Chrysostom, *Homily 8 against the Anomoeans*:
Bareille, 2, 253–4

Twenty-Ninth Sunday in Ordinary Time/Proper 24 Year C: Luke 18.1–8

A READING FROM A HOMILY ON THE LORD'S PRAYER BY ST GREGORY OF NYSSA

The divine Word teaches us how to pray, explaining to disciples worthy of him, and eagerly longing for knowledge of prayer, what words to use to gain a hearing from God.

Those who fail to unite themselves to God through prayer cut themselves off from God, so the first thing we have to learn from the Word is that we *need to pray continually and not lose heart*. Prayer brings us close to God, and when we are close to God we are far from the Enemy. Prayer safeguards chastity, controls anger, and restrains arrogance. It is the seal of virginity, the issuance of marital fidelity, the shield of travellers, the protection of sleepers, the encouragement of those who keep vigil, the cause of the farmer's good harvest and of the sailor's safety. Therefore I think that even if we spent the whole of our lives in communion with God through thanksgiving and prayer, we should still be as far from adequately repaying our benefactor as we should have been had we not even desired to pay him.

Time has three divisions: past, present, and future. In all three we experience the Lord's kindly dealings with us. If you consider the present, you live in him; if you consider the future, your hope of obtaining what to look forward to is in him; if you consider the past, you would not have existed had you not been created by him. Your birth is his kindly gift to you, and after birth his kindness toward you continued, since as the Apostle says you live and move in him. On this same kindness depend all your hopes for the future. Only over the present have you any control. Therefore, even if you give thanks to God unceasingly throughout your life you will hardly meet the measure of your debt for present blessings, and as for those of the past and future, you will never find a way of repaying what you owe.

And yet we, who are so far from being capable of showing due gratitude, do not even give thanks to the best of our ability. We fail to set aside, I say not the whole day, but even the smallest portion of the day, to be spent with God.

Who restored to its original beauty that divine image in me that was blurred by sin? Who draws me back to the blessedness I knew before I was driven out of paradise, deprived of the tree of life, and submerged in the abyss of worldliness? As Scripture says: *There is no one who understands.* If we realized these things we would give thanks continually, endlessly, throughout the whole of our lives.

St Gregory of Nyssa, *Homily on the Lord's Prayer*:
PG 44, 1119, 1123–6

Thirtieth Sunday in Ordinary Time/Proper 25
Year A: Matthew 22.34–40 [34–46]

A READING FROM A SERMON BY ST AUGUSTINE

I know, beloved, how well fed you are every day by the exhortations of Holy Scripture, and what nourishment your hearts find in the word of God. Nevertheless, the affection we have for one another compels me to say something to you, beloved, about love. What else is there to speak of apart from love? To speak about love there is no need to select some special passage of Scripture to serve as a text for the homily; open the Bible at any page and you will find it extolling love. We know this is so from the Lord himself, as the gospel reminds us, for when asked what were the most important commandments of the law he answered: *You shall love the Lord your God with all your heart, and with all your soul, and with all your mind; and you shall love your neighbour as yourself.* And then, just in case you might be tempted to search further through the pages of Holy Scripture for some commandments other than these two, he added: *The entire law and the prophets also depend upon these two commandments.* If the entire law and the prophets depend upon these two commandments, how much more must the gospel do so?

People are renewed by love. As sinful desire ages them, so love rejuvenates them. Enmeshed in the toils of his desires the psalmist laments: *I have grown old surrounded by my enemies.* Love, on the other hand, is the sign of our renewal as we know from the Lord's own words: *I gave you a new commandment – love one another.*

Even in former times there were people who loved God without thought of reward, and whose hearts were purified by their chaste longing for him. They drew back the veils obscuring the ancient promises, and caught a glimpse through these figures of a new covenant to come. They saw that all the precepts and promises of the old covenant, geared to the capacities of an unregenerate people, prefigured a new covenant which the Lord would bring to fulfilment in the last age. The Apostle says this quite clearly: *The things that happened to them were symbolic, and were recorded for us who are living in the last age.* When the time for it came the new covenant began to be openly proclaimed, and those ancient figures were expounded and explained so that all might understand that the old covenant promises pointed to the new covenant.

And so love was present under the old covenant just as it is under the new, though then it was more hidden and fear was more apparent, whereas now love is more clearly seen and fear is diminished. For as love grows stronger we feel more secure, and when our feeling of security is complete fear vanishes, since, as the apostle John declares: *Perfect love casts out fear.*

St Augustine, *Sermons*, Mai 14.1–2: PLS, 2, 449–50

Thirtieth Sunday in Ordinary Time/Proper 25 Year B: Mark 10.46–52

A READING FROM THE *EXHORTATION TO THE GREEKS* BY ST CLEMENT OF ALEXANDRIA

The commandment of the Lord shines clearly, enlightening the eyes. Receive Christ, receive power to see, receive your light, 'that you may plainly recognize both God and man'. *More delightful than gold and precious stones, more desirable than honey and the honeycomb* is the Word that has enlightened us. How could he not be desirable, he whom illumined minds buried in darkness, and endowed with clear vision 'the light-bearing eyes' of the soul?

'Despite the other stars, without the sun the whole world would be plunged in darkness.' So likewise we ourselves, had we not known the Word and been enlightened by him, should have been no better off than plump poultry fattened in the dark, simply reared for death. Let us open ourselves to the light, then, and so to God. Let us open ourselves to the light, and become disciples of the Lord. For he promised his Father: *I will make known your name to my brothers and sisters, and praise you where they are assembled.*

Sing his praises, then, Lord, and make known to me your Father, who is God. Your words will save me, your song instruct me. Hitherto I have gone astray in my search for God; but now that you light my path, Lord, and I find God through you, and receive the Father from you, I become co-heir with you, since you were not ashamed to own me as your brother.

Let us, then, shake off forgetfulness of truth, shake off the darkness that dims our eyes, and contemplate the true God, after first raising this song of praise to him: 'All hail, O Light!' For upon us buried in darkness, imprisoned in the shadow of death, a heavenly light has shone, a light of a clarity surpassing the sun's, and of a sweetness exceeding any this earthly life can offer. That light is eternal life, and those who receive it live. Night, on the other hand, is afraid of the light, and melting away in terror gives place to the day of the Lord. Unfailing light has penetrated everywhere, and sunset has turned into dawn. This is the meaning of the new creation; for the Sun of Righteousness, pursuing his course through the universe, visit all alike, in imitation of his Father, *who makes his sun rise upon all*, and bedews everyone with his truth.

He it is who has changed sunset into dawn and death into life by his crucifixion; he it is who has snatched the human race from perdition and exalted it to the skies. Transplanting what was corruptible to make it incorruptible, transforming earth into heaven, he, God's gardener, points the way to prosperity, prompts his people to good works, 'reminds them how to live' according to the truth, and bestows on us the truly great and divine heritage of the Father, which cannot be taken away from us. He deifies us by his heavenly teaching, instilling his laws into our minds, and writing them on our hearts. What are the laws he prescribes? That all, be they of high estate or low, shall know God: *And I will be merciful to them*, God says, *and I will remember their sin no more.*

St Clement of Alexandria, *Protrepticus*, 11: SC 2, 181–3

Thirtieth Sunday in Ordinary Time/Proper 25
Year C: Luke 18.9–14

A READING FROM A SERMON BY ST AUGUSTINE

The reading of the holy gospel encourages us to pray and to believe, and to rely not on ourselves but on God.

But because faith belongs not to the proud but to the humble, *he said to some, who considered themselves just and despised the rest, this parable: Two men went up into the temple to pray, one a Pharisee and the other a tax collector. The Pharisee was saying, Thank you, God, for my not being like other people.* He might at least have said 'like many other people'. What can 'like other people' mean, but everyone except himself? 'I', he said, 'am just, the rest are sinners.' *My not being like other people, unjust, extortioners, adulterers.* And here's this tax collector nearby providing you with a reason to grow more self-satisfied than ever: *like this tax collector here*, he says. 'I', he says, 'am in a class by myself; this fellow belongs to the rest. I am not', he says, 'in the least like this man, by reason of my just deeds, which ensure that I am not unjust. *I fast twice a week, I give tithes of everything I possess.*'

Search his words for anything he asked God for, and you won't find it. He went up to pray; he didn't want to ask God for anything, but to praise himself. Not satisfied with not asking God for anything but praising him-self instead, he must go on to insult a person who was really praying. *But the tax collector was standing a long way off*; and yet God himself was drawing near to him. His conscience kept him at a distance, his piety kept him at it. *But the tax collector was standing a long way off.* God, though, was watching him from close at hand, *for the Lord is on high, and he looks on the lowly.* The high and mighty, however, he knows from afar, people such as that Pharisee. God indeed knows the high and the mighty from afar, but he does not pardon them.

Listen to some more about the tax collector's humility. Not content with standing a long way off, *He would not even lift up his eyes to heaven.* In order to be looked at, he wasn't going to look. He hadn't the nerve to look up; conscience was weighing on him, hope was supporting him. Listen to some more still: *He was beating his breast.* He was exacting pun-ishment from himself; that's why the Lord spared him when he confessed. *He was beating his breast, saying, Lord, be gracious to me a sinner.* There you have a person actually asking for something. Why be surprised if God pardons him, when he himself acknowledges what he is?

You have heard the matter at issue between the Pharisee and the tax collector; listen now to the judgement. You have heard the proud accuser, you have heard the humble accused; now listen to the judge. *Amen, I tell you.* Truth says it, God says it, the judge says it. *Amen I tell you, that tax collector went down justified from the temple, rather than that Pharisee.* Tell us the reason, Lord. Look, I see the tax collector going down justified from the temple, rather than the Pharisee. I'm asking why. 'You're asking why? This is why. *Because everyone who exalts himself will be humbled, and whoever humbles himself will be exalted.*'

You have heard the judgement; beware of having such a bad case. I'll put it differently: you have heard the judgement; beware of pride.

Let them see now, let them hear all this, those people whoever they are, gabbling away about their impieties, and relying on their own pow-ers; let them listen, those who say, 'God made me a human being, I make myself just.' Why, you're worse and more detestable than the Pharisee! That Pharisee indeed proudly called himself just, but still he at least gave thanks to God for it. He called himself just; but still he gave thanks to God. *Thank you, God, for my not being like other people.* 'Thank you, God'; he gives thanks to God because he is not like other people; yet he is blamed as a proud and conceited man; not because he gave thanks to God, but because apparently he didn't desire to have anything else added to him.

Thank you for my not being like other men, unjust. So you, then, are just; so you don't ask for anything; so now you are full; so human life is not a trial and a temptation upon the earth; so now you're full; so now you have more than enough; so now there's no reason why you should say, *Forgive us our debts.* What, then, must a person be who impiously assails God's grace, if this man is condemned for pride in saying grace?

St Augustine, *Sermon* 115

Dedication Festival Year A (CWL alternative): Matthew 21.12–16

(First Sunday in October or Last Sunday after Trinity)

A READING FROM THE HOMILIES ON JOSHUA BY ORIGEN

All of us who believe in Christ Jesus are said to be living stones, according to the words of Scripture: *Like living stones, let yourselves be built into a spiritual house, to be a holy priesthood, to offer spiritual sacrifices accept-able to God through Jesus Christ.*

When we look at the construction of earthly buildings, we can see how the largest and strongest stones are always set in the foundations, so that the weight of the whole building can rest securely on them. In the same way you should understand how some of the living stones referred to by Scripture have become the foundations of a spiritual building. And who are those foundation stones? The apostles and the prophets. This is what Paul himself declares in his teaching: *You are built upon the foundation of the apostles and prophets, Christ Jesus himself being the cornerstone.*

You should learn that Christ himself is also the foundation of the building we are describing, so that you may more eagerly prepare your-selves for the construction, and be found to be one of those stones strong enough to be laid close to the foundation. For these are the words of Paul the Apostle, *No other foundation can anyone lay than that which is laid, namely Christ Jesus.* Blessed are those, therefore, who will be found to have constructed sacred and religious buildings upon such a glorious foundation!

But in this building of the Church there must also be an altar. From this I conclude that those of you who are ready and prepared to give up your time to prayer, to offer petitions and sacrifices of supplication to God day and night, such people I say will be the living stones out of which Jesus will build his altar.

Reflect upon the praise that is lavished upon these stones of the altar. *Moses the lawgiver*, Joshua said, *ordered that an altar be built out of unhewn stones, untouched by a chisel*. Who now are these unhewn stones? Perhaps these unhewn, undefiled stones could be said to be the holy apostles, who together make one altar by reason of their harmony and unity. For Scripture tells that, as the apostles prayed together with one accord they opened their mouths and said, *You, Lord, know the hearts of all*.

These then, who were able to pray with one mind, with one voice and in one spirit, are perhaps worthy of being employed together to form an altar upon which Jesus may offer his sacrifice to the Father.

But let us too strive to be of one mind among ourselves, and to speak with one heart and voice. Let us never act out of anger or vainglory, but united in belief and purpose, let us hope that God may find us stones fit for his altar.

Origen, *Homilies on Joshua*, 9.1–2: SC 71, 144–6

Dedication Festival Year B (CWL alternative): John 10.22–29

(First Sunday in October or Last Sunday after Trinity)

A READING FROM A SERMON BY ST AUGUSTINE

we are gathered together to celebrate the dedication of a house of prayer. This is our house of prayer, but we too are a house of God. If we are a house of God, its construction goes on in time so that it may be dedicated at the end of time. The house, in its construction, involved hard work, while its dedication is an occasion for rejoicing.

What was done when this church was being built is similar to what is done when believers are built up into Christ. When they first come to believe they are like timber and stone taken from woods and mountains. In their instruction, baptism and formation they are, so to speak, shaped, levelled and smoothed by the hands of carpenters and craftsmen.

But Christians do not make a house of God until they are one in charity. The timber and stone must fit together in an orderly plan, must be joined in perfect harmony, must give each other the support of love, or no one would enter the building. When you see the stones and beams of a building holding together securely, you enter the building with an easy mind; you are not afraid of it falling down around you in ruins.

Christ the Lord wants to come into us and dwell in us. Like a good builder he says: *A new commandment I give you: love one another.* He says: *I give you a commandment.* He means: Before, you were not engaged in building a house for me, but you lay in ruins. Therefore, to be raised up from your former state of ruin you must love one another.

Remember that this house is still in the process of being built in the whole world: this is the promise of prophecy. When God's house was being built after the Exile, it was prophesied in the words of a psalm: *Sing a new song to the Lord; sing to the Lord, all the earth.* For *a new song* our Lord speaks of a *new commandment.* A new song implies a new inspiration of love. To sing is a sign of love. The singer of this new song is full of the warmth of God's love.

The work we see complete in this building is physical; it should find its spiritual counterpart in your hearts. We see here the finished product of stone and wood; so too your lives should reveal the handiwork of God's grace.

Let us then offer our thanksgiving above all to the Lord our God, *from whom every best and perfect gift comes.* Let us praise his goodness with our whole heart. He it was who inspired in his faithful people the will to build this house of prayer; he stirred up their desire and gave them his help. He awakened enthusiasm among those who were at first unconvinced, and guided to a successful conclusion the efforts of people of goodwill. So God, *who gives to those of goodwill both the desire and the accomplishment* of the things that belong to him, is the one who began this work, and the one who has brought it to completion.

St Augustine, *Sermon* 336.1, 6: PL 38, 1471–5

Dedication Festival Year C (CWL alternative): John 2.13–22

(First Sunday in October or Last Sunday after Trinity)

SEE THE READING FOR LENT 3B BY ST AUGUSTINE, PAGE 106.

Thirty-First Sunday in Ordinary Time/Proper 26
Year A: Matthew 23.1–12

A READING FROM THE COMMENTARY ON MATTHEW BY ST PASCHASIUS RADBERTUS

Christ is called master, or teacher, by right of nature rather than by courtesy, for all things subsist through him. Through his incarnation and life upon earth we are taught the way to eternal life. Our reconciliation with God is dependent on the fact of his being greater than we are. Yet, having told his disciples not to allow themselves to be called master, or to love seats of honour and things of that kind, he himself set an example and was a model of humility. It is as though he said: Even as *I do not seek my own glory (though there is One who seeks it)*, so neither must you love to be honoured above others, or to be called master. Look at me: *The Son of Man did not come to be served but to serve, and to give his life for many.*

This was said not only for the instructions of his disciples, but also for those who are teachers in the Church. None of them must seek positions of honour; whoever wishes to be greater than the rest must first become the servant of all, as Christ himself did. If anyone wants a high office let him want the labour it entails, not the honour it will bring him. He should desire to serve and minister to everyone, and not expect everyone to serve and minister to him. For the desire to be served comes from the supercilious attitude of the Pharisees; the desire to serve from the teaching of Christ. Those who canvass for positions of honour are the ones who exalt themselves; those who delight in serving and caring for others are the ones who humble themselves so as to be exalted by God. Note that it is not those whom the Lord exalts who will be humbled, but those who exalt themselves, and similarly it is those who of their own accord humble themselves who will be exalted by the Lord.

After specifically reserving the office of teaching to himself, Christ immediately went on to give as the rule of his teaching that whoever wants to be greatest should be the servant of all. And he gave the same rule in other words when he said: *Learn of me, for I am meek and humble of heart.* Anyone therefore who wants to be Christ's disciple must hasten to learn the lesson he professes to teach, for a perfect disciple will be like his master. Otherwise, to learn the master's lesson, far from being a master himself, he will not even be a disciple.

St Paschasius Radbertus, *Commentary on Matthew*, 10.22: PL 120, 769–70

Sunday of Proper 26 Year A (CWL): Matthew 24.1–14

A READING FROM A HOMILY ON MATTHEW BY ST JOHN CHRYSOSTOM

Jesus had said to them, *Your house is left desolate*, and had warned them of many terrible things to come and so the disciples came to him, pointing out the beauty of the temple and wondering whether such beauty was to be destroyed. He now no longer merely talks to them of desolation but foretells total destruction, *There shall not remain one stone upon another*. And this is true, for there are parts of it destroyed unto the foundations.

The disciples were in agony to know the day of his coming, because they desired to behold that glory which is the cause of countless blessings. They asked him two things: when shall these things be? that is, the overthrow of the temple; and, what is the sign of your coming? Luke however says that the question only concerned Jerusalem, as though they were supposing that its destruction heralded his coming. And Mark says that only Peter, Andrew, James and John asked him concerning the end of Jerusalem because they had greater freedom of speech.

He said, *Take heed that no man deceive you. For many shall come in my name, saying, I am Christ, and they shall deceive many. You shall hear of wars and rumours of wars. Do not be troubled; for all these things must come to pass, but the end is not yet.* He again foretells to them grievous things, commanding them on two grounds to watch so that they will neither be seduced by the deceit of those who would beguile them, nor be overpowered by the violence of ills that shall overtake them. When he spoke of *wars and rumours of wars*, he meant the troubles that would come upon them and because they supposed that after that war the end would come, he warned them, saying, *But the end is not yet, for nation shall rise against nation, and kingdom against kingdom, all these are but the beginning of sorrows.*

At an appropriate time he introduced this talk of their ills, offering them a consolation from the common miseries because he said it is, *for my name's sake that you shall be hated. Then many shall be scandalized and shall betray each other, and many false Christs and false prophets shall arise, and they shall deceive many. Because iniquity shall abound, the love of many shall wax cold; but he that endures to the end shall be saved.*

Knowing these things, then, let us not be scandalized, neither let us be confounded at any of the things that happen, but making space for God's providence, let us give heed to virtue and flee vice, that we may also attain

to the good things to come, by the grace and love towards humanity of
our Lord Jesus Christ.

John Chrysostom, *Homilies on Matthew*, 75.1–2, 5

Thirty-First Sunday in Ordinary Time/Proper 26 Year B: Mark 12.28–34

A READING FROM *THE ASCETICON* OF ST BASIL THE GREAT

The Lord himself gave this order to his commandments: the commandment to love God is the first and greatest, and the commandment to love
one's neighbour is second in order and like the first, or rather it completes
the first and depends on it.

We possess the power to love implanted in us from the first moment
that we were formed. The proof of this is not external, but can be learnt
from within oneself because by nature we desire beautiful things and without being taught we have affection for those near to us and towards all
our benefactors. Now what is more marvellous than the divine beauty?
What desire is so keen and intolerable as that which comes from God
upon the soul cleansed from all evil and causes it to cry, *I am wounded by
love?* Wholly indescribable and inexplicable are the flashes of the divine
beauty: speech cannot express them, hearing cannot receive them. This
beauty is unseen by fleshly eyes, and comprehended only by the soul when
it has illumined one of the saints and left in them the sting of intolerable
desire. Oppressed by this life as if it were a prison. Those souls touched by
the divine desire could hardly restrain themselves, they had an insatiable
desire to behold the divine beauty and prayed that their contemplation of
the sweetness of the Lord might last on into life eternal. So then, humans
naturally desire beauty. But the good is properly beautiful and lovable.
Now God is good, and all things desire good. Therefore all things desire
God.

Children and even animals have a natural affection for their parents.
Shall we not seem more stupid than infants, even wilder than beasts, if we
do not love our Maker? Even if we have not known his nature from his
goodness, we ought to have an extraordinary love and affection for him
from the very fact of having been made by him, and to cling continually to
his memory as children cling to their mother.

As we have been commanded to love our neighbour as ourselves, we can also ask whether we have power from God to fulfil this commandment too. Now we all know that a human being is a tame and sociable animal, not a solitary and fierce one, for nothing is so characteristic of our nature as to associate with one another, to need one another and to love our kind. So the Lord himself first gave us the seeds of these things, and now demands their fruits, saying, A *new commandment I give to you, that you love one another*. He even links the commandments in such a way as to transfer to himself the good done to our neighbour, for he says, *I was hungry and you gave me food*, and adds: *As you did it to one of the least of these brothers or sisters of mine, you did it to me*. Therefore in keeping the first commandment one also keeps the second: and through the second one returns again to the first. The one who loves the Lord also loves his neighbour and the one who loves his neighbour also loves God, since God accepts the favour as conferred on himself.

St Basil of Caesarea, *Asceticon*, Longer Responses 1–3 (abridged)

Thirty-First Sunday in Ordinary Time/Proper 26 Year C: Luke 19.1–10

A READING FROM A HOMILY BY ST PHILOXENUS OF MABBUG

All who were called by the Lord obeyed his summons at once, provided love of earthly things did not weigh them down. For worldly ties are a weight upon the mind and understanding, and for those bound by them it is difficult to hear the sound of God's call.

But the apostles, and the righteous people and patriarchs before them, were not like this. They obeyed like people really alive, and set out lightly, because no worldly possessions held them bound as though by heavy fetters. Nothing can bind or impede the soul that is alive: it is open and ready, so that the light of the divine voice, each time it comes, finds the soul capable of receiving it.

Our Lord also called Zacchaeus from the sycamore he had climbed, and immediately Zacchaeus hastened to come down, and welcomed him into his house, for he had been hoping to see him and become his disciple even before he was called. And that is a marvellous thing – our Lord had not spoken to him, and Zacchaeus had not seen the Lord with the eyes of the body, and yet he believed in him simply on the word of others. This was because in him faith had been preserved in its natural life and health. He showed his faith by believing in our Lord as soon as he heard he was coming; and the simplicity of his faith was seen when he promised to give half his goods to the poor, and to restore fourfold what he had taken by fraud. For if Zacchaeus' spirit had not been filled at that moment with the simplicity proper to faith, he would not have made this promise to Jesus, and he would not have given out and distributed, in a brief space of time, what his labours had amassed over many years. Simplicity scattered on all sides what had been accumulated by cunning; purity of soul dispersed what had been obtained by guile; faith made a public renunciation of what had been found and appropriated by unrighteousness.

For faith's only possession is God, and it refuses to own anything else besides him. Faith sets no store by possessions of any kind, apart from God, its one lasting possession. Faith has been implanted in us so that we may find God and possess nothing but him, and so that we may recognize that everything that exists is harmful apart from him.

St Philoxenus of Mabbug, Homilies, 4.78: SC 44, 96–7

ORDINARY TIME BEFORE ADVENT

THEN suddenly upon Mount Zion a blaze of the sun, shining clear from the south-east, shall come forth from the Creator, gleaming more brightly than the mind of man can conceive, when the Son of God shall appear hither through the vault of heaven. All-glorious from the eastern skies shall come the presence of Christ, the aspect of the noble King, gentle in spirit toward his own, bitter toward the wicked, wondrously varied, diverse to the blessed and the forlorn.

Cynewulf

ETERNAL Father, whose Son Jesus Christ ascended to the throne of heaven that he might rule over all things as Lord and King: keep the Church in the unity of the Spirit and in the bond of peace, and bring the whole created order to worship at his feet; who is alive and reigns with you, in the unity of the Holy Spirit, one God, now and for ever. Amen.

Collect for Christ the King, *Common Worship*

BLESSED are you, Sovereign God, our light and our salvation, to you be glory and praise for ever. Now, as darkness is falling, wash away our transgressions, cleanse us by your refining fire and make us temples of your Holy Spirit. By the light of Christ, dispel the darkness of our hearts and make us ready to enter your Kingdom, where songs of praise for ever sound. Blessed be God, Father, Son and Holy Spirit.

From Evening Prayer from All Saints to Advent, *Common Worship*

O DAY of wrath, that day will dissolve the world in ashes just as David and the Sibyl have foretold! The trumpet, scattering a wondrous sound through the land of the dead, will summon all before the throne. Death and nature will marvel when the creature arises to respond to the Judge. O King of tremendous majesty, who freely saves those who must be saved, save me, source of mercy. Remember, merciful Jesus, that I am the cause of your way on earth: don't lose me on that day. You forgave Mary and heard the prayer of the crucified thief: give hope to me as well! Grant me a place among the sheep, separate me from the goats, set me on your right hand. O God of majesty, gracious splendour of the Trinity, join us with the blessed. Amen.

From the thirteenth-century Latin hymn, *Dies irae, dies illa*

'Now we give you thanks that Jesus Christ is the King of Glory, who over-comes the sting of death and opens the kingdom of heaven to all believers. He is seated at your right hand in glory and we believe that he will come to be our judge.'[8] In the Church of England calendar the Sundays after All Saints' Day, which may itself be kept on a Sunday, form a group of 'Sundays before Advent' in the period of Ordinary Time between Eastertide and Advent when red vestments may be worn instead of the usual green of Ordinary Time. This season from All Saints to Advent has a special emphasis on the saints and on the reign of Christ on earth and in heaven and it is a new development in the calendar, possibly related to the way that the secular Christmas has trespassed on Advent.

The Church of England *Alternative Service Book 1980* had a series of 'Sundays before Christmas' during this time and some Protestant Churches have observed a 'Kingdomtide' of varying lengths since the 1930s, a prac-tice reflected in the 'Season of the Kingdom' from All Saints to Advent proposed for the Church of England in the 1990s. These terms were not generally adopted by *Common Worship*, the General Synod having rejected a 'Kingdom Season', but they have clearly affected current prac-tice, which also has its roots in the broader Catholic tradition. Advent has been of variable lengths in the past and November, with its com-memoration of All Souls and Remembrance Sunday, is traditionally kept as a 'month of the dead' during which Christians visit graves, pray for the departed and consider their destiny. The 'Sundays before Advent' do thus have a particular traditional ambiance. This is less evident in the Lection-ary as the Gospels at the Sunday Eucharist during this period follow the three-year Ordinary Time cycle of continuous reading but, because of the shape of the three Gospels themselves, there are a number of eschatologi-cal themes.

The feast of All Saints on 1 November is important for this season. At Rome in the beginning of the seventh century Pope Boniface IV dedi-cated the Roman temple called the Pantheon to St Mary and all the Holy Martyrs and in the next century Pope Gregory III built a chapel in honour of 'all the holy martyrs and confessors'. There thus developed a desire to commemorate all the saints together and, perhaps beginning in England, this came to be celebrated on 1 November. The Gospel for the feast is the beatitudes from Matthew 5, but the *Revised Common Lectionary* also gives readings from John 11 and Luke 6 in years B and C. In the Byzantine East a feast of All Saints is kept on the Sunday after Pentecost.

---

8 Short preface from the day after All Saints' Day until the day before the First Sunday of Advent, *Common Worship*.

The Church's year ends on its last Sunday with the feast of Christ the King. This is a relatively recent celebration but its emphasis on the Kingship of Christ and on the Last Days is firmly rooted in the Gospel and picks up themes from the traditional liturgy of the last weeks of the Christian year. The feasts of Epiphany, Easter and Ascension have always been, in a sense, commemorations of the Kingship of Christ. The daily prayer of the Roman Catholic Church uses at this time the magnificent eschatological hymn which is traditionally sung at funerals, the *Dies irae*, with its emphasis on the Last Things: death, judgement, heaven and hell. The feast of Christ the King was instituted by Pope Pius XI in 1925 on the Sunday before All Saints. It offered a Christian response to the all-embracing totalitarianism of that age which sought to exclude Christianity from public life. The revision of the Roman Catholic liturgy in the 1960s emphasized the eschatological elements in the feast and moved it to its current date with the title, 'Our Lord Jesus Christ, King of the Universe'. The feast has been adopted by other Churches which use the *Revised Common Lectionary*.

All Saints' Day (RL and RCL Year A): Matthew 5.1–12

(The Feast of All Saints is celebrated on 1 November, or as All Saints Sunday on the Sunday between 30 October and 5 November)

A READING FROM THE *EXPLANATION OF THE SERMON ON THE MOUNT* BY ST AUGUSTINE

In Christ's teaching here, there are in all eight sayings. In what comes after he speaks directly to those who were present, saying: *Blessed are you when people revile and persecute you*. But in the earlier sayings he spoke generally, for he did not say, *Blessed are you poor in spirit*, but rather, *Blessed are the poor in spirit*.

Let us then look at the number of sayings, for the beatitudes begin with humility: *Blessed are the poor in spirit*, blessed are those who are not puffed up with pride, whose soul submits itself to divine authority, fearing punishment after death even though it may be happy in this life. After this the soul then comes to the knowledge of the divine Scriptures, where it must show itself meek in its piety, lest it should condemn that which seems absurd to the unlearned, and should become unteachable in its obstinacy. Then it comes to understand the entanglements of this world in which it is held by carnal custom and sin; and so in this third stage, in which there is knowledge, the loss of the highest good is mourned over because it sticks fast in what is lowest. Then, in the fourth stage there is labour and much effort that the mind may wrench itself away from those things in which, by reason of their pestilential sweetness, it is entangled: here therefore righteousness is hungered and thirsted after. Here fortitude is very necessary because what is retained with delight is not abandoned without pain.

Then, at the fifth stage, those persevering in labour are given counsel on how to escape the entanglement of miseries; for unless one is helped by a superior, one cannot extricate oneself. It is a just counsel, that he who wishes to be assisted by a stronger should assist him who is weaker in that in which he himself is stronger: therefore it is said, *Blessed are the merciful, for they shall obtain mercy*. At the sixth stage there is purity of heart and one is able from a good conscience to contemplate that highest good which can be discerned by the pure and tranquil intellect alone. Lastly comes the seventh, wisdom itself, a wisdom which is the contemplation of the truth making the whole man at peace and assuming the likeness of God. This is thus summed up, *Blessed are the peacemakers, for they shall be called the children of God*.

The eighth returns to the starting-point, because it shows and commends what is complete and perfect; therefore in the first and the eighth the kingdom of heaven is named, *Blessed are the poor in spirit, for theirs is the kingdom of heaven*; and, *Blessed are they which are persecuted for righteousness' sake, for theirs is the kingdom of heaven*. It is now said, *Who shall separate us from the love of Christ? shall tribulation, or distress, or persecution, or famine, or nakedness, or peril, or sword?* Seven in number, therefore, are the things which bring perfection: for the eighth brings into light and shows what is perfect, so that starting from the beginning again, all the others are perfected by means of these stages.

St Augustine, *Explanation of the Sermon on the Mount*, 3.10

All Saints' Day (RCL Year B): John 11.32–44

SEE THE READING FOR THE LENT 5A FROM ST
PETER CHRYSOLOGUS, PAGE 112.

All Saints' Day (RCL Year C): Luke 6.20–31

A READING FROM THE LETTER OF ST CLEMENT OF
ROME TO THE CORINTHIANS

My dear friends, it is the example of the righteous that we must make our own. It is written, *Seek the company of the saints, for those who seek their company shall be sanctified*. There is also another passage in Scripture which states, *With the innocent you will be innocent, and with the chosen you will also be chosen; likewise with the perverse you will deal perversely*. So let us take the innocent and the just as our companions, for they are God's chosen ones.

Why is there all this quarrelling and bad feeling, divisions and even war among you? Have we not all the same God, and the same Christ? Do we not possess the same Spirit of grace which was given to us? Have we not the same calling in Christ? Then why do we tear apart and divide the body of Christ? Why do we revolt against our own body? Why do we reach such a pitch of insanity that we forget that we are members one of another? Do not forget the words of Jesus our Lord, *Woe to that man, it would be better for him never to have been born rather than to scandalize one of my elect. Indeed it would be better for such a person to have a great millstone round the neck and be drowned in the sea rather than lead astray one of my chosen ones.* Your disunity has led many astray, has made many doubt, has made many despair, and has brought grief upon us all. And still your rebellion continues.

Read again the letter of blessed Paul the apostle. What did he write to you at the beginning of his ministry? Even then you had developed factions. So Paul, inspired by the Holy Spirit, wrote to you concerning himself and Cephas and Apollos. Perhaps that division was less culpable because you were supporting apostles of high reputation and a person approved by them.

We should put an end to this division immediately. Let us fall down before our Master and implore his mercy with our tears. Then he will be reconciled to us and restore us to the practice of loving one another as befits us who are Christians. For this is indeed the gate of righteousness that leads to life, as it is written, *Open to me the gates of righteousness. When I have entered there, I shall praise the Lord. This is the gate of the Lord; the righteous shall enter through it.*

There are many gates that stand open before you, but the gate of righteousness is the gateway of Christ. All who enter through this gate are blessed, pursuing their way in holiness and righteousness, performing all their tasks without discord. A Christian may be faithful, may have the power to utter hidden mysteries, may be discriminating in the evaluation of what is said and pure in his actions. But the greater a person seems to be, the more humbly they ought to act, and the more zealous for the common good they should be rather than for their own self-interest.

St Clement of Rome, *Letter to the Corinthians,* 46, 48

Thirty-Second Sunday in Ordinary Time/Proper 27 Year A: Matthew 25.1–13

A READING FROM THE ORATIONS OF ST GREGORY NAZIANZEN

The place before the great sanctuary in which you will stand immediately after your baptism symbolizes the glory of the world to come. The singing of psalms with which you will be received is a prelude to the hymns of heaven. The lamps you will light prefigure that great procession of lights in which we shall go to meet the Bridegroom with the bright lamps of faith, our souls radiant and pure. Very careful shall we be not to fall asleep, in case the awaited One should arrive unexpectedly. Nor shall we come without the oil of good works, for fear of being excluded from the bridal chamber.

I see with my mind's eye the misery of such a disaster. On the Bridegroom's arrival a loud cry will summon the wise, who will go forth to meet him with their lamps burning brightly, being amply supplied with fuel; while the others, in utter confusion, will belatedly go to the storekeepers for some oil. Swiftly the Bridegroom will enter and the wise will go in with him, but the foolish will be shut out because when it was time to enter they were still busy preparing themselves. They will lament bitterly when they learn too late the penalty for the carelessness, and find that, despite all their pleas, they are denied entry to the bridal chamber because of their own folly.

In another way, they resemble the guests who failed to attend the wedding feast a noble father gave for a noble bridegroom. One did not come because he had recently married, another because he had just bought a field, a third because he had bought a yoke of oxen. But these were costly acquisitions when for the sake of small gains they forfeited greater.

There is no place in heaven for the arrogant and careless, nor yet for one dressed in rags instead of a wedding garment, even though while on earth such a one may think himself fit for the resplendence of the world to come and, deceived by vain hopes, slip in among the faithful without their knowledge.

What will the next world be like? Once we are within, the Bridegroom knows what he will teach the souls that have entered with him, and how he will be united with them. I believe that he will live with them and teach them yet higher and holier mysteries. May we ourselves have a share in that life: both we who impart this teaching and you who receive it, in Christ himself, our Lord, to whom be glory and power for ever. Amen.

St Gregory Nazianzen, Oration 40.46: PG 36, 425

Thirty-Second Sunday in Ordinary Time/Proper 27 Year B: Mark 12.38–44

A READING FROM A LETTER BY ST PAULINUS OF NOLA

What have you, asks the Apostle, *that you have not received?* This means, beloved, that we should not be miserly, regarding possessions as our own, but should rather invest what has been entrusted to us. We have been entrusted with the administration and use of temporal wealth for the common good, not with the everlasting ownership of private property. If you accept the fact that ownership on earth is only for a time, you can earn eternal possessions in heaven.

Call to mind the widow who forgot herself in her concern for the poor, and, thinking only of the life to come, gave away all her means of subsistence, as the judge himself bears witness. Others, he says, have given of their superfluous wealth. But she, possessed of only two small coins and more needy perhaps than many of the poor – though in spiritual riches she surpassed all the wealthy – she thought only of the world to come, and had such a longing for heavenly treasure that she gave away, all at once, whatever she had that was derived from the earth and destined to return there.

Let us then invest with the Lord what he has given us, for we have nothing that does not come from him: we are dependent upon him for our very existence. And we ourselves particularly, who have a special and a greater debt, since God not only created us but purchased us as well – what can we regard as our own when we do not possess even ourselves?

But let us rejoice that we have been bought at a great price, the price of the Lord's own blood, and that because of this we are no longer worthless slaves. There is, however, freedom that is baser than slavery, namely, freedom from justice. Whoever has that kind of freedom is a slave of sin and a prisoner of death. So let us give back to the Lord the gifts he has given us; let us give to him who receives in the person of every poor man or woman. Let us give gladly, I say, and great joy will be ours when we receive his promised reward.

St Paulinus of Nola, Letter 34.2–4: CSEL 29, 305–6

Proper 27 Year B (CWL): Mark 1.14–20
SEE THE READING FOR SUNDAY 3B BY ST CAESARIUS OF ARLES

Thirty-Second Sunday in Ordinary Time/Proper 27 Year C: Luke 20.27–38

A READING FROM THE TREATISE *AGAINST HERESIES* BY ST IRENAEUS

Our Lord and Master answered the Sadducees, who say that there is no resurrection and therefore dishonour God and discredit the law, and he revealed both the resurrection and God when he said to them, *You err, not knowing the Scriptures, nor the power of God.* For, *touching the resurrection of the dead,* he says, *have you not read that which was spoken by God, saying, I am the God of Abraham, the God of Isaac, and the God of Jacob?* And he added, *He is not the God of the dead, but of the living; for all live to him.* By these arguments he made it clear that it was he who spoke to Moses out of the bush, and declared himself to be the God of the fathers. He is the God of the living. For who is the God of the living unless the one who is God, and above whom there is no other God? Daniel the prophet, when Cyrus king of the Persians said to him, *Why do you not worship Bel?* said, *Because I do not worship idols made with hands, but the living God, who established the heaven and the earth and has dominion over all flesh.* Daniel also said, *I will adore the Lord my God, because he is the living God.*

The one who was adored by the prophets as the living God is the God of the living. It is his Word who spoke to Moses, the same Word who also put the Sadducees to silence and revealed the gift of resurrection, thus revealing both truths to those who are blind. He revealed both the resurrection and the true God. For if he is not the God of the dead, but of the living, and he was also called the God of the fathers who were sleeping, it is quite clear that they live to God. They have not passed out of existence, since they are children of the resurrection. Our Lord himself is the resurrection, as he himself declares, *I am the resurrection and the life.* But the fathers are his children; for it is said by the prophet: *Instead of your fathers, you shall have sons.* Christ himself, therefore, together with the Father, is the God of the living, who spoke to Moses, and who was also manifested to the fathers.

And teaching this very thing, he said to the Jews: *Your father Abraham rejoiced that he should see my day; and he saw it, and was glad.* What does he mean? *Abraham believed God, and it was reckoned to him as righteousness.* In the first place, Abraham believed that he was the maker of heaven and earth, the only God; and in the next place, that he would make his seed as the stars of heaven. In righteousness, therefore, having left his earthly kindred, he followed the Word of God, walking as a pilgrim with the Word, that he might afterwards dwell with the Word.

In righteousness also the Apostles, being of the race of Abraham, left the ship and their father and followed the Word. In righteousness also we, possessing the same faith as Abraham and taking up the cross just as Isaac carried the wood, follow him. For in Abraham humanity had learned beforehand and had become accustomed to follow the Word of God. For Abraham, according to his faith, followed the command of the Word of God, and with a ready mind delivered up as a sacrifice to God his only-begotten and beloved son, in order that God also might be pleased to offer up for all Abraham's seed his own beloved and only-begotten Son, as a sacrifice for our redemption.

St Irenaeus, *Against Heresies*, 4.5.2–4

Thirty-Third Sunday in Ordinary Time/Proper 28 Year A: Matthew 25.14–30
A READING FROM A HOMILY ON MATTHEW BY ST JOHN CHRYSOSTOM

In the parable of the talents the Master entrusted money to his servants and then set out on a journey. This was to help us understand how patient he is, though in my view this story also refers to the resurrection. Here it is a question not of a vineyard and vine dressers, but of all workers. The Master is addressing everyone, not only rulers, or the Jews.

Those bringing him their profit acknowledge frankly what is their own, and what is their Master's. One says: *Sir, you gave me five talents*; another says: *You gave me two*, recognizing that they had received from him the means of making a profit. They are extremely grateful, and attribute to him all their success.

What does the Master say then? *Well done, good and faithful servant* (for goodness shows itself in concern for one's neighbour). *Because you have proved trustworthy in managing a small amount, I will give you charge of a greater sum: come and share your Master's joy.*

But one servant has a different answer. He says: *I knew you were a hard man, reaping where you have not sown and gathering where you have not winnowed; and I was afraid, and hid your talent. Here it is – you have back what belongs to you.*

What does the Master say to that? *You wicked servant! You should have put my money in the bank*, that is, 'You should have spoken out and given encouragement and advice.' 'But no one will pay attention.' 'That is not your concern. You should have deposited the money,' he says, 'and left me to reclaim it, which I should have done with interest', meaning by interest the good works that are seen to follow the hearing of the word. 'The easier part is all you were expected to do, leaving the harder part to me.' Because the servant failed to do this, the Master said: *Take the talent away from him, and give it to the servant who has the ten talents. For to everyone who has more will be given, and he will have enough and to spare; but the one who has not will forfeit even the little he has.*

What is the meaning of this? That whoever has received for the good of others the ability to preach and teach, and does not use it, will lose that ability, whereas the zealous servant will be given greater ability, even as the other forfeits what he had.

St John Chrysostom, *Homily* 78: Bareille, 12, 93–5

Thirty-Third Sunday in Ordinary Time Year B (RL): Mark 13.24–32

A READING FROM *THE CHRIST* BY CYNEWULF

Lo! At midnight, unawares, the great day of the Lord omnipotent shall mightily overtake the dwellers on earth, the bright creation; as oft a daring robber, a crafty thief, prowling about in darkness, in the murky night, suddenly comes upon careless men bound in sleep, and sorely assails them unprepared.

Then together unto Mount Zion shall ascend a great multitude, radiant and joyful, the faithful of the Lord; glory shall be theirs. Thereupon from the four corners of the world, from the uttermost regions of earth, angels all-shining shall with one accord blow their crashing trumpets; the earth shall tremble under them. Glorious and steadfast they shall sound together over against the course of the stars, chanting in harmony and making melody from south and from north, from east and from west, throughout the whole creation; all humankind shall they wake from the dead unto the last judgement; they shall rouse the children of men all aghast from the ancient earth, bidding them straightway arise from their deep sleep.

There one may hear a sorrowing people, sad of heart and greatly disquieted, sorely afraid and pitifully bewailing the deeds done in the body. This shall be the greatest forewarning ever shown unto humans before or since. There all the hosts of angels and of devils shall mingle, the fair and the swart; there shall be a coming of both the white and the black, according as an abode is prepared all alike, for saints and sinners.

Then suddenly upon Mount Zion a blaze of the sun, shining clear from the south-east, shall come forth from the Creator, gleaming more brightly than the human mind can conceive, when the Son of God shall appear hither through the vault of heaven. All-glorious from the eastern skies shall come the presence of Christ, the aspect of the noble King, gentle in spirit toward his own, bitter toward the wicked, wondrously varied, diverse to the blessed and the forlorn.

The vast creation shall resound, and the fiercest of raging fires shall sweep over the whole earth before the Lord; the fiery flame shall hurtle; the heavens shall burst asunder; all the firm-set flashing stars shall fall. The sun itself, which shone so brightly above the former world for the children of men, shall be turned dark, even to the hue of blood; the moon, also, which of old gave light for mortals in the night season, shall fall headlong; and the stars shall be hurled from heaven by the fury of the storm-vexed air.

Now shall the Almighty, the glorious Prince, Creator of great kings, come into the assembly with his angel band. An exultant host of his retainers shall be there also. The souls of the blest shall journey with their Lord, when the Protector of humankind shall visit the nations of earth with dread punishment.

Therefore whoever desires to have life with the Creator should bestir himself while body and spirit are joined together. Let him zealously foster the beauty of his soul according to God's will, and be careful in word and deed, in thought and conduct, while this world, speeding with its shadows, may still shine for him; so that he lose not in this fleeting time the blessedness of his joy and the fullness of his days, the beauty of his work and the reward of glory, which the righteous King of heaven shall give at that holy tide as a meed of victory to those who in spirit obey him with gladness.

Cynewulf, *The Christ*, Part 3, *Doomsday*: Whitman, 33–6, 59

Proper 28 Year B (RCL): Mark 13.1–8

SEE PROPER 26A (CWL) FROM ST JOHN
CHRYSOSTOM, PAGE 265.

Thirty-Third Sunday in Ordinary Time/Proper 28
Year C: Luke 21.5–19
A READING FROM A LETTER BY ST NILUS OF SINAI

In time of trial it is of great profit to us patiently to endure for God's sake, for the Lord says: *By patient endurance you will win life for yourselves.* He did not say by your fasting, or your solitude and silence, or your singing of psalms, although all of these are helpful in saving your soul. But he said: *By patient endurance* in every trial that overtakes you, and in every affliction, whether this be insolent and contemptuous treatment, or any kind of disgrace, either small or great; whether it be bodily weakness, or the belligerent attacks of Satan, or any trial whatsoever caused either by other people or by evil spirits.

By patient endurance you will win life for yourselves, although to this must be added wholehearted thanksgiving, and prayer, and humility. For you must be ready to bless and praise your benefactor, God the Saviour of the world, who disposes all things, good or otherwise, for your benefit.

The Apostle writes: *With patient endurance we run the race of faith set before us.* For what has more power than virtue? What more firmness or strength than patient endurance? Endurance, that is, for God's sake. This is the queen of virtues, the foundation of virtue, a haven of tranquillity. It is peace in time of war, calm in rough waters, safety amidst treachery and danger. It makes those who practise it stronger than steel. No weapons or brandished bows, no turbulent troops and advancing siege engines, no flying spears or arrows can shake it. Not even the host of evil spirits, nor the dark array of hostile powers, nor the devil himself standing by with all his armies and devices will have power to injure the man or woman who has acquired this virtue through Christ.

St Nilus of Sinai, *Letters*, 3.35: PG 79, 401–4

Christ the King Year A: Matthew 25.31–46
A READING FROM *ON CHRIST AND THE ANTICHRIST* BY ST HIPPOLYTUS

As the holy gospel clearly proclaims, the Son of Man will gather together all nations. *He will separate people one from another, as a shepherd separates sheep from goats. The sheep he will place at his right hand, the goats at his left. Then he will say to those at his right: Come, my Father's blessed ones, inherit the kingdom prepared for you from the foundation of the world.* Come, you lovers of poor people and strangers. Come, you who fostered my love, for I am love. Come, you who shared peace, for I am peace.

Come, my Father's blessed ones, inherit the kingdom prepared for you who did not make an idol of wealth, who gave alms to the poor, help to orphans and widows, drink to the thirsty, and food to the hungry. Come, you who welcomed strangers, clothed the naked, visited the sick, comforted prisoners, and assisted the blind. Come, you who kept the seal of faith unbroken, who were swift to assemble in the churches, who listened to my Scriptures, longed for my words, observed my law day and night, and like good soldiers shared in my suffering because you wanted to please me, your heavenly King. *Come, inherit the kingdom prepared for you from the foundation of the world.* Look, my kingdom is ready, paradise stands open, my immortality is displayed in all its beauty. Come now, all of you, *inherit the kingdom prepared for you from the foundation of the world.*

Then, astounded at so great a wonder – at being addressed as friends by him whom the angelic hosts are unable clearly to behold – the righteous will reply, exclaiming: *Lord, when did we see you hungry and feed you? Master, when did we see you thirsty and give you a drink? When did we see you,* whom we hold in awe, *naked and clothe you? When did we see you,* the immortal One, *a stranger and welcome you? When did we see you,* lover of our race, *sick or in prison and come to visit you?* You are the Eternal, without beginning like the Father, and co-eternal with the Spirit. You are the One who created all things from nothing; you are the King of angels; you make the depths tremble; you *are clothed in light as in a robe*; you are our Maker who fashioned us from the earth; you are the Creator of the world invisible. The whole earth flies from your presence. How could we possibly have received your Lordship, your royal Majesty, as our guest?

Then will the King of Kings say to them in reply: *Inasmuch as you did this to one of the least of these my brothers and sisters, you did it to me.* Inasmuch as you received, clothed, fed, and gave a drink to those members of mine about whom I have just spoken to you, that is, to the poor, you did it to me. So come, enter *the kingdom prepared for you from the foundation of the world*; enjoy forever the gifts of my heavenly Father, and of the most holy and life-giving Spirit. What tongue can describe those blessings? *Eye has not seen, nor ear heard, not human heart conceived what God has prepared for those who love him.*

St Hippolytus, *On Christ and the Antichrist*, 1–43: PG 10, 944–5

Christ the King Year B: John 18.33–37

A READING FROM THE *TRACTATES ON JOHN* BY ST AUGUSTINE

Listen, everyone, Jews and Gentiles, circumcised and uncircumcised. Listen, all kings of the earth. I am no hindrance to your rule in this world, for *my kingdom is not of this world*. Banish the groundless fear that filled Herod the Great on hearing that Christ was born. More cruel in his fear than in his anger, he put many children to death, so that Christ also would die. But *my kingdom is not of this world*, says Christ. What further reassurance do you seek? Come to the kingdom not of this world. Be not enraged by fear, but come by faith. In a prophecy Christ also said: *He*, that is, God the Father, *has made me King on Zion his holy mountain*. But that Zion and that mountain are not of this world.

What in fact is Christ's kingdom? It is simply those who believe in him, those to whom he said: *You are not of this world, even as I am not of this world*. He willed, nevertheless, that they should be in the world, which is why he prayed to the Father: *I ask you not to take them out of the world, but to protect them from the evil one*. So here also he did not say: *My kingdom is not in this world*, but is *not of this world*. And when he went on to prove this by declaring: *If my kingdom were of this world, my servants would have fought to save me from being handed over to the Jews*, he concluded by saying not 'my kingdom is not here', but *my kingdom is not from here*.

Indeed, his kingdom is here until the end of time, and until the harvest it will contain weeds. The harvest is the end of the world, when the reapers, who are the angels, will come *and gather out of his kingdom all causes of sin*; and this could not happen if his kingdom were not here. But even so, it is not from here, for it is in exile in the world. Christ says to his kingdom: *You are not of the world, but I have chosen you out of the world*. They were indeed of the world when they belonged to the prince of this world, before they became his kingdom. Though created by the true God, everyone born of the corrupt and accursed stock of Adam is of the world. On the other hand, everyone who is reborn in Christ becomes the kingdom which is no longer of the world. For so has God snatched us from the powers of darkness, and brought us into the kingdom of his beloved Son: that kingdom of which he said: *My kingdom is not of this world; my kingly power does not come from here*.

St Augustine, *Tractates on John*, 115.2: CCSL 36.644–5

Christ the King Year C: Luke 23.35–43

A READING FROM THE HOMILY ON THE CROSS AND THE THIEF BY ST JOHN CHRYSOSTOM

Lord, remember me in your kingdom. But before he had laid aside the burden of his sins by confessing them did the thief dare to say the words *Remember me in your kingdom*. Do you not see the value of that confession? It opened paradise! It gave the former brigand the confidence to seek admission to the kingdom!

That the cross brings us untold blessings is surely obvious. Have you set your heart upon a kingdom? Then tell me, can you see any such thing? All that meets the eye are nails and a cross, and yet this very cross, Christ says, is the symbol of the kingdom. I proclaim him King, therefore, because I see him crucified, for it becomes a king to die for his subjects. He himself said that *the good shepherd lays down his life for his sheep*, and so the good King too lays down his life for his subjects. Christ laid down his life, and that is why I proclaim him King: *Lord, remember me in your kingdom*.

Do you not see, then, how the cross symbolizes the kingdom? If you desire further proof, it lies in the fact that the cross did not leave Christ earthbound, but lifted him up and carried him back to heaven. We know this because at his glorious second coming the cross will be with him. He called it his glory to teach you how sacred it is. *When the Son of Man comes, the sun will be darkened and the moon will not give its light*. Such a blaze of light will there be that even the brightest stars will be eclipsed. *Then the stars will fall, and the sign of the Son of Man will appear in heaven*. So you see the power of the sign of the cross!

When a king is entering a city, his soldiers take up their standards, and, carrying them aloft across their shoulders, go before him to announce his coming. So also shall the armies of angels and archangels precede the Lord when he comes from heaven. Bearing his sign on their shoulders, they will proclaim the coming of the King.

St John Chrysostom, *Homily on the Cross and the Thief*, 1, 3–4:
PG 49, 403–4

BIOGRAPHICAL NOTES
ON THE AUTHORS

St Aelred of Rievaulx (1110–67) was born at Hexham, Northumbria and, after spending time at the court of King David I of Scotland, entered the Cistercian Abbey of Rievaulx in Yorkshire where he was elected Abbot in 1147. Under him the monastery flourished as a place of asceticism, prayer and fraternal charity. His writings include sermons and works of history and spirituality, of which the best known are his *Mirror of Charity* and *Spiritual Friendship*. He is one of the greatest teachers of Christian love and friendship.

St Ambrose (*c.*339–97) was born at Trier, the son of the Praetorian Pre-fect of Gaul. He became Governor of Aemilia-Liguria and was based in Milan. When he went to keep peace among warring factions at an episcopal election in the city in 374 he was himself acclaimed as Bishop, although he was still unbaptized. Having been baptized and ordained he devoted himself to the study of theology and became a famous preacher. He championed the freedom of the Church, and was willing to oppose the Emperor when he felt the gospel required it, for example he made Theodosius do penance for ordering his soldiers to fire on the crowd in the stadium at Thessalonica in 390 after a riot. He composed a number of hymns which were used in the liturgy and was influential in the conversion of St Augustine.

St Augustine (354–430) was born at Thagaste in Africa, the son of a pagan father and a Christian mother, St Monica. He received a Christian educa-tion, but joined the sect of the Manichaeans and was not baptized until 387. In 391 he was ordained priest and in 395 he became coadjutor bishop to Valerius of Hippo, whom he succeeded in 396. Augustine's theology was formulated in the course of his struggle with four heresies: Arianism, Donatism, Manichaeism and Pelagianism. His writings are voluminous and his influence on subsequent theology immense. He moulded the thought of the Middle Ages and from the sixteenth century was a major influence on both Catholic and Reformed theology. Yet he was above all a pastor and one of the greatest spiritual writers of the Church.

St Basil the Great (*c.*330–79) was one of the three great Cappadocian Fathers. He received an excellent education and began a career as a rhetorician before a spiritual awakening led him to receive baptism and become a monk. After visiting ascetics in Egypt, Palestine, Syria and Mesopotamia, he decided that it was better for monks to live together in monasteries than alone as hermits, and he had a great influence on monasticism in Cappadocia and Pontus. In 370 Basil became Bishop of Caesarea. His main concern was for the unity of the Church and ortho-dox doctrine, and he was deeply involved in church politics. His efforts for unity and orthodoxy bore fruit only after his death. Basil's writings include doctrinal, ascetic and educational treatises as well as letters and sermons, his monastic teaching or *Asketikon* influenced St Benedict and monasticism in the West.

St Basil of Seleucia (died *c.*458–60) was Bishop of Seleucia in Isauria and he took part in the great controversies around the Council of Chalcedon in 451. Forty-one sermons attributed to him on different portions of the Old Testament have survived, together with writings about St Thecla, a legendary female companion of St Paul.

St Bede the Venerable (673–735) was born on the monastic estates of the Northumbrian monastery of Wearmouth which he entered at the age of seven, transferring to the sister monastery of Jarrow after its foundation in 682. He spent the rest of his life there in prayer, teaching and writing. Many of his works survive, including *The Ecclesiastical History of the English People*, commentaries on the Bible and scientific and educational works. He is buried in Durham Cathedral and is the only Englishman in Dante's *Paradiso*.

St Bernard of Clairvaulx (1090–1153) was born of noble parents and entered the monastic order of Cîteaux. He was soon made Abbot of Clairvaulx which he built up into a model austere monastic community following the rule of St Benedict. His spiritual reputation was such that he had great influence in the Church, influencing papal elections, preaching a crusade and writing a rule for the Knights Templar. His main legacy to the Church is found in his Cistercian order and in his writings, such as his treatise *On Loving God* and his sermons on the Song of Songs.

St Bruno of Segni (*c.*1047–1123), Bishop of Segni and Abbot of Monte-cassino, was born at Solero in Piedmont, educated at Bologna, and became a canon at Sienna. He came to Rome in 1079 and was closely involved in attempts to reform the Church. While retaining his bishopric he entered the monastery of Monte Cassino in 1099, continuing to work for reform and becoming Abbot in 1107, although he was later forced to return to Segni where he died. He wrote on church reform and produced a number of exegetical works.

St Caesarius of Arles (468/70–542) was born at Chalon-sur-Saône to Roman Burgundian parents. He became a monk at the island monastery of Lérins, where he was excessively ascetic, but then moved on to the pastoral life at Arles where he became Bishop and worked for the poor and sick. He was greatly influenced by St Augustine both in his theology and preaching and he encouraged the laity to study the Scriptures. Many of his sermons have survived; he wrote the first monastic rule specifically for women and he presided over the Council of Orange in 529 which promulgated important Christian teaching on grace and free-will.

St Chromatius of Aquileia (died *c.*406) was from Aquileia where he was ordained and eventually became Bishop. He was a friend of SS Ambrose and Jerome and mediated in the famous quarrel between Jerome and Rufinus. He also supported St John Chrysostom when he was persecuted. A *Commentary on Matthew* and a number of his sermons survive.

St Clement of Alexandria (*c.*150–215) was born at Athens of pagan parents. Nothing is known of his early life nor of the reasons for his conversion. He was the pupil and the assistant of Pantaenus, the director of the catechetical school of Alexandria, whom he succeeded about the year 200. In 202 Clement left Alexandria because of the persecution of Septimus Severus, and resided in Cappadocia with his pupil Alexander, later Bishop of Jerusalem. Clement may be considered the founder of speculative theology. He strove to protect and deepen faith by the use of Greek philosophy. Central in his teaching is his doctrine of the Logos, who as divine reason is the teacher of the world and its lawgiver. Clement's chief work is the trilogy, *Exhortation to the Greeks*, *The Teacher* and *Miscellanies*.

St Clement of Rome (first century) wrote a letter AD *c.*96 in the name of the Roman Church to the Church of Corinth which is a precious witness to apostolic faith and ministry and one of the earliest Christian writings outside the New Testament. He was said to have been one of the early

Bishops of Rome and many legends and later writings have been attached to his name.

Cynewulf (ninth century?) was an Anglo-Saxon poet, literate in Latin and probably a cleric. Nothing certain is known of him outside that which can be discerned from his writings. Four poems are certainly by him as they contain his name woven into the text in runic signatures, *Juliana* (on a martyr), *Elene* (on St Helena), *Christ II: The Ascension* and *Fates of the Apostles*.

St Cyril of Alexandria (*c*.376–444) was born near Alexandria and succeeded his uncle Theophilus as Pope and Patriarch of Alexandria in 412. He played a prominent role in the turbulent life of the city, in conflict with the civil authorities, Jews and pagans. In the wider Church he defended the personal unity of Christ and opposed the theology of Nestorius, Patriarch of Constantinople, who denied that Mary could be called Theotokos (mother of God). Cyril's views were accepted at the Council of Ephesus in 431, not without a certain amount of manipulation. He was an outstanding theologian in the Alexandria tradition who advanced the Church's knowledge of Christ and his works include letters, exegetical works, some sermons and a number of theological treatises.

Blessed Denis the Carthusian (1402–71), Denys van Leeuwen or Denis Ryckel, was born in the province of Limburg and after studies at the university of Cologne entered the Carthusian monastery at Roermond in 1423. He accompanied Nicholas of Cusa on his mission to reform the Church in Germany and was involved in the foundation of the Charterhouse at Hertogenbosch but his main legacy to the Church are his voluminous writings. He wrote commentaries on the whole Bible as well as many theological and spiritual works, all of which were summaries of the teaching of others. He was consulted by many and campaigned for the reform of the Church.

Didymus the Blind (*c*.313–98) was blind from his youth and, because of his great learning, was made director of the catechetical school of Alexandria by Athanasius where he taught Rufinus and Jerome. He wrote many commentaries on Scripture and theological works including a treatise on the Holy Spirit. He was posthumously condemned as an Origenist but there has been a revival of interest in his teaching aided by the rediscovery of some of his works in Egypt in 1941.

St Ephrem the Syrian (*c*.306–73) was a theologian and deacon who lived in Nisibis but settled in Edessa after the Persian invasion of 363 (these are modern Nusaybin and Urfa in South-East Turkey). He composed many works in Syriac, mainly in verse but also prose commentaries on the Bible, and his hymns have retained their place in the liturgy. He is popularly known as the 'Harp of the Spirit' and is one of the greatest of the Syriac Fathers. It is said that he died ministering to plague victims.

St Eutychius of Constantinople (*c*.512–82) was the son of a Byzantine general, became a monk and was Patriarch of Constantinople from 552 to 565 and from 577 to 582. He presided over the Council of Constantinople in 553 and consecrated the rebuilt church of Haghia Sophia in Constantinople in 562. He was deposed and exiled by the Emperor Justinian for opposing imperial religious policy but was restored under Justin II. His extant works include a letter to Pope Vigilius of Rome and a discourse on the resurrection.

St Gaudentius of Brescia (died 410) was elected Bishop of Brescia and consecrated by St Ambrose in 387. He had lived for a time in the Christian East, was a friend of St John Chrysostom and defended him when he was persecuted by the Emperor. Some letters and several of his sermons survive, including a set preached at Easter.

Godfrey of Admont (died 1165) became Abbot of the Benedictine Abbey of Admont in 1137 and is said to have fostered monastic studies and built up the Abbey library. He supported church reform and many exegetical homilies are attributed to him.

St Gregory of Antioch (died 593) was a Byzantine monk at Jerusalem who became Abbot of Sinai and then *c*.570 Patriarch of Antioch. He promoted orthodox doctrine and was said to have been a fine preacher; some of his sermons have survived.

St Gregory Nazianzen (329–89), one of the three great Cappadocian Fathers, was born to a landowning family near Nazianzus, of which his father was Bishop. He received a fine education at Caesarea, Alexandria and Athens, where he became close friends with St Basil of Caesarea. He was ordained priest by his father but fled to live the monastic life with Basil. With Basil he studied the Scriptures and the writings of Origen. Gregory reluctantly became Bishop of Sasima but then administered the see of Nazianzus before retiring to a monastery. In 379 he was called to Constantinople where he preached his powerful Theological Orations, which helped define Christian faith in the Holy Trinity, and was made Bishop of the city. He presided over the Ecumenical Council of Constantinople in 381 but, after many attacks on him, he returned to Cappadocia, administering the diocese of Nazianzus and then spending his final years on a family estate in prayer and the writing of poetry. His theological writings led to him being given the title 'the Theologian', which he shares with St John the Apostle, and his relics are now preserved in the Patriarchate at Constantinople (Istanbul).

St Gregory of Nyssa (*c.335–c.395*), one of the three great Cappadocian Fathers, was the younger brother of SS Basil of Caesarea and Macrina. His sister had a great influence on his intellectual and spiritual development and he wrote of her in his *Life of Macrina* and *On the Soul and Resurrection*. Gregory married and pursued a secular career but was later ordained, became Bishop of Nyssa and played a central role in defining and defending the orthodox faith in the Holy Trinity. His writings include theological treatises on the Trinity, commentaries on Ecclesiastes and the Lord's Prayer and other spiritual works of great insight such as his *Life of Moses* and *Commentary on the Song of Songs*.

St Gregory Palamas (1296–1359) was born in Constantinople, the son of a courtier, and became a monk on Mount Athos. After living in monastic communities he withdrew to a skete (a monastery that combines solitary and community life) and practised hesychasm (the prayer of the heart). Gregory was ordained priest at Thessaloniki and defended hesychasm, later becoming Archbishop of Thessaloniki. He has been canonized by the Eastern Orthodox Church and is commemorated in the Byzantine rite on the second Sunday of Lent.

St Gregory the Great (540–604) was born into a wealthy Roman family and became Prefect of Rome. He later converted the family villa on the Caelian hill into a monastery and adopted the monastic life. He was sent by the Pope as an ambassador to Constantinople and was himself elected Bishop of Rome in 590. He sent missionaries to convert the pagan Anglo-Saxons in England and his many letters show him as an outstanding Bishop and an able administrator. His works include the *Pastoral Rule* (a guide for bishops), the *Dialogues* in which he tells the stories of Italian saints such as Benedict, a commentary on Job, and forty homilies on the Gospels. He is traditionally associated with the reform of the liturgy and of liturgical chant which is called 'Gregorian chant' after him.

St Gregory the Wonderworker (c.213–c.270) was born in Neocaesarea in Pontus (in modern Turkey) and was probably a pupil of Origen at Caesarea in Palestine. On his return home he was consecrated Bishop of his native city and built up the Christian community attracting a reputation for miracle-working and missionary zeal. He composed a panegyric on Origen and an *Exposition of the Faith* based on what he taught new Christians. Other works are attributed to him, not all of which are genuine.

Blessed Guerric of Igny (1070s–1157) was born at Tournai and educated at its cathedral school. Under the influence of St Bernard he became a Cistercian monk at Clairvaux and then became Abbot of Clairvaux's daughter house at Igny near Rheims. The monastery flourished under his guidance and his spiritual teaching may be seen in his extant sermons preached to his monks gathered in chapter on the feasts and seasons of the year.

St Hilary of Poitiers (c.300–68) was born at Poitiers into a pagan family and received a good education in Greek as well as Latin. After studying the Bible he, his wife and his daughter all became Christians. He became Bishop of his native city and worked hard to defend the orthodox faith against the Arians, for which he was banished to Phrygia where he spent four years in exile. He was influenced by the theology of Tertullian and possibly by that of Irenaeus and Origen. He wrote many works including *On the Trinity* and commentaries on the Gospel of Matthew and on the Psalms.

St Hippolytus (c.170–236) was a Roman priest who probably came originally from the East. When Callistus, Bishop of Rome, relaxed the penitential discipline of the Church, Hippolytus opposed him and became a rival bishop, the first 'anti-pope'. The schism continued into the episcopate of Pontianus, but when Pontianus and Hippolytus were both exiled to the mines of Sardinia they were reconciled before dying as martyrs for the faith. Not all writings attributed to his name are actually by him and he has been associated with a number of early liturgical texts including the *Apostolic Tradition*. The title of this and other works supposedly by Hippolytus have been discovered in Rome inscribed on an ancient statue of a woman which was given a bearded head in the sixteenth century.

St Irenaeus of Lyons (c.130–200) was born to a Christian family, probably in Smyrna because as a boy he had heard St Polycarp, the Bishop of Smyrna who knew people who had seen Jesus. He moved to Gaul and became a priest and then Bishop of Lyons in 177 when his predecessor was martyred. He opposed the mythological speculations of the Gnostics and taught the importance of the full humanity of Jesus and the apostolic succession of bishops. His greatest work is his *Against Heresies* in five books which is one of the first great theological syntheses.

St Jacob of Serugh (*c*.451–521), born in a village on the Euphrates, was one of the greatest of the Syriac poet-theologians. He was educated at the Christian School of Edessa and lived through times of persecution by the Persians and schism within the Christian community when his Syriac community separated from the Imperial Church. He wrote hundreds of homilies in verse (*memre*) and in 519 he was elected Bishop of Batnan da-Serugh.

St Jerome (*c*.342–420) was born at Stridon (near the modern Ljubljana) in Dalmatia and studied in Rome where he was baptized. He travelled to Syria where he studied the Bible, began to learn Hebrew, lived as a hermit near Antioch and was ordained priest. He continued his theological studies in Constantinople under St Gregory Nazianzen and then came to Rome where he worked for Pope Damasus I, began his translation of the Bible into Latin, known as the Vulgate, and was the spiritual director of many noble women. Accusations of improper conduct and the death of one of his devout women caused him to withdraw to the East where he heard Didymus the Blind lecture at Alexandria. He settled at Bethlehem with various friends and disciples and, funded by the aristocrat Paula, spent his last 34 years writing and studying. His many works include commentaries on the Bible, translations of Origen's homilies, many letters, historical polemical and theological works. He was a passionate man, involved in many controversies and fierce in debate.

St John Chrysostom (*c*.347–407) was born at Antioch and studied under Diodore of Tarsus, the leader of the Antiochene school of theology. After a period of great austerity as a hermit, he returned to Antioch where he was ordained deacon in 381 and priest in 386. From 386 to 397 it was his duty to preach in the principal church of the city, and his best homilies, which earned him the title 'Chrysostomos' or 'the golden–mouthed', were preached at this time. In 397 Chrysostom became patriarch of Constantinople, where his efforts to reform the court, clergy and people led to his exile in 404 and finally to his death from the hardships imposed on him. Chrysostom stressed the divinity of Christ against the Arians and his full humanity against the Apollinarians.

St John Cassian (*c.*360–435), born in South-Eastern Europe. He and his friend Germanus went to Palestine as young men and entered a hermitage near Bethlehem. Three years later they stayed with the monks of Egypt for fifteen years until, with other followers of Origen, they were persecuted and went to appeal to St John Chrysostom at Constantinople, where Cassian was ordained deacon. He then moved, via Rome, to found a monastery on the Egyptian model near Marseilles. His *Conferences* and *Institutes*, celebrated for their spiritual teaching, presented the doctrine of the monks of the East adapted for the monks of the West and influenced St Benedict who ordered them to be read to his monks each evening.

Blessed John Henry Newman (1801–90) was brought up in the Church of England under Evangelical influence. He was a leader of the Anglican Oxford Movement and he joined the Roman Catholic Church in 1845. He founded an Oratorian community which settled in Birmingham, was engaged in many controversies and was made a cardinal in 1879. A sensitive man capable of deep friendships, he was a famous preacher and writer and his thought was nourished by the Fathers of the early Church. His influence has been great on both Anglicanism and Roman Catholicism and he is commemorated in both the Roman and English church calendars.

John Justus Landsberg (1489/90–1539) was born at Landsberg am Lech in Bavaria, studied at Cologne and entered the Carthusian monastery of St Barbara at Cologne in 1509. He was made novice master, in 1530 he became prior of the Charterhouse of Cantave near Jülich, and four years later he returned to Cologne where he remained sub-Prior until his death. He wrote much, including homilies on the epistles and gospels of the liturgical year, always emphasizing the love of God.

John Scotus Eriugena (*c.*815–77) was born and educated in Ireland. A competent Greek scholar, he travelled to France where he became Master of the Palace School under the Emperor Charles the Bald, introduced Greek thought to the Latin West and was one of the leading figures of the Carolingian Renaissance. He was a Christian Platonist and was also influenced by St Augustine, the Cappadocian Fathers, and Pseudo-Dionysius whom he translated into Latin. He defended free will and opposed predestination, and wrote commentaries on the Gospel of John, but some of his writings were later condemned as heretical.

Julian of Vézelay (*c*.1080–1165) was a Benedictine monk of the Abbey of Vézelay in Burgundy. His collection of sermons were preached to his brethren in their chapter meetings.

St Leo the Great (*c*.395–461) was an influential Italian cleric in contact with Cyril of Alexandria and John Cassian when he was elected Bishop of Rome in 440. He asserted the authority of the Bishop of Rome as successor of St Peter and defended Rome against Attila the Hun (although it was sacked by the Vandals in 455). His 'tome' or letter on the true doctrine about Christ was accepted as authoritative, along with some doctrinal letters of St Cyril of Alexandria, by the Council of Chalcedon in 451 and his sermons are well-crafted statements of Christian doctrine.

St Maximus of Turin (died *c*.408–23) was Bishop of Turin and died during the reign of Honorius and Theodorius the younger. Little more is known about him but over a hundred of his sermons survive which reveal a popular preacher with an interest in the liturgy.

St Nicholas Cabasilas (*c*.1322–after 1391) was educated at Constantinople and became an imperial official and friend of the Byzantine Emperor John VI Cantacuzenos. When the Emperor was deposed in 1354 he retired from political life and devoted himself to theology, serving as a priest in a monastery near Constantinople. Many of his works survive and the best known are his *Life in Christ* and *Commentary on the Divine Liturgy*, which are marked by a profoundly sacramental spirituality. He is venerated as a saint in the Eastern Orthodox Church and his writings are widely read in the West.

St Nilus of Sinai (died after 430), also known as Nilus of Ancyra, was a disciple of St John Chrysostom at the Imperial court who is said to have agreed with his wife to separate so that he could become a monk on Mount Sinai with one of his sons. He was well known as a theologian and spiritual father and many sought his advice. He wrote many treatises on the ascetic life and a large corpus of letters has survived, not all of them genuine. Many of the works of the great Christian spiritual teacher Evagrius of Pontus were preserved under his name. Nilus is widely venerated in the Christian East.

St Odilo of Cluny (*c*.962–1048) entered the Benedictine Abbey of Cluny in 991 and became Abbot and was ordained priest in 994. He refused to become a bishop and under his leadership the congregation of Cluny grew and spread into Spain. He worked hard to establish the 'Peace of God' (the use of spiritual sanctions to protect non-combatants, such as peasants and clergy, from violence), assisted many during the famines of his time and was responsible for the feast of All Souls on 2 November. Only a few of his writings, including some sermons, have survived.

Origen of Alexandria (184/5–253/4), the son of a Christian martyr, was one of the greatest theologians and biblical scholars of the Christian Church who was learned in contemporary Greek philosophy and had a profound influence on later writers. He was educated in Alexandria, where he became head of the catechetical school, and later taught in Ceasarea in Palestine where he was ordained priest. He was imprisoned and tortured for his faith during the Decian persecution and died shortly after. He wrote many works including commentaries on almost all the books of the Bible but most of these have been lost, partly because some of his theological speculations were condemned at church councils after his death.

St Paschasius Radbertus (c.785–860) was brought up by the nuns of Notre Dame at Soissons, after being left abandoned on their doorstep. He received the monastic habit at Corbie, and was the confidant of two successive abbots. On the death of Abbot Wala, Paschasius himself became abbot, but he found the office uncongenial and resigned after seven years. He always refused to be raised to the priesthood. Paschasius, who was a prolific writer, is noted especially for the part he played in establishing Catholic doctrine on the Eucharist. He also wrote lengthy commentaries on Matthew and on the forty-fourth psalm.

St Paulinus of Nola (354–431) was from a noble senatorial family and educated by the poet Ausonius but after a short secular career married a Christian called Therasia and became a Christian himself. Their first child died soon after birth and they retired to their Spanish estates to live an intense Christian ascetic life. He was ordained priest and moved with his wife to Nola in Campagna, where he was consecrated Bishop, and they lived by the tomb of St Felix to whom he credited his conversion. He was in touch with many of the Christian leaders of his age such as SS Jerome, Martin and Augustine and he wrote many letters and poems.

St Peter Chrysologus (c.380–450) was born in Imola and became Bishop of Ravenna c.433. He was famous for his short but profound sermons, which caused him to be called 'Chrysologus' or 'golden-worded', and he was supported in his ministry by the Empress Galla Placidia.

St Philoxenus of Mabbug (died 523) was born in the village of Tahal, east of the Tigris, and was educated at Edessa. With many other Syriac

Christians he opposed the Council of Chalcedon and was ordained Bishop of Mabbug in 485. He was exiled by the Emperor Justin I and murdered at Gangra in Paphlagonia. A noted theologian, he revised the Syriac version of the Bible and his surviving works, noted for their elegant style and spiritual insight, include sermons, letters, liturgical texts, commentaries on the Gospels and theological works.

Rupert of Deutz (c.1075–1129) entered the Benedictine Abbey of St Lawrence, Liège, as a boy oblate and became Abbot of St Heribert, Deutz, in 1120. He composed commentaries on the Scriptures, a treatise on the liturgy and many other works. He made significant contributions to the theology of the Incarnation, the problem of evil, devotion to the Virgin Mary and to contemporary debates on the Eucharist.

St Symeon the New Theologian (949–1022) was born into the Byzantine nobility, became a monk under the guidance of Symeon the Studite and for twenty-five years was Abbot of the Monastery of St Mammas. His teaching that one could experience God directly led to controversy and he was sent into exile. He, together with John the Apostle and Gregory Nazianzen, is one of only three saints to be given the title 'Theologian' by the Byzantine Church, meaning one who taught from their own experience of God. His writings include the hymns of Divine Love, the ethical discourses and the catecheses.

Theodotus of Ancyra (died c.445) was Bishop of Ancyra (modern Ankara in Turkey). At first a supporter of Nestorius, he later transferred his allegiance to Cyril of Alexandria whom he supported at the Council of Ephesus in 431. Among his writings are sermons for the feasts of Christmas (one of which was read at the Council of Ephesus) and the Presentation, which are important early witnesses to the celebration of these two feasts.

St Theophylact of Ohrid (1055–1107) was born in Greece, became tutor to the son of the Emperor at Constantinople and, in his early twenties, was elected archbishop of Achrida in Bulgaria (modern Ohrid in Macedonia). He was a notable pastor and defended the interests of the Bulgarian Church from the Patriarchate of Constantinople. Influenced by the writings of St John Chrysostom, he composed fine commentaries on the Gospels, Acts, the letters of Paul and the minor prophets, and many of his letters and sermons also survive. His commentaries influenced Erasmus and are popular among modern Eastern Orthodox Christians.

St Thomas More (1478–1535) was a married man, a Humanist scholar with a European reputation and lawyer who became Chancellor of England. A complex person, he wrote theological works and opposed Lutheranism. His conscience would not allow him to accept King Henry VIII's divorce from Catherine of Aragon and he opposed the King's rejection of papal supremacy and so he was executed for treason on Tower Hill. He is commemorated in the calendars of the Roman Catholic Church and the Church of England.

FURTHER READING

A selection of books on the Fathers of the Church and their world, the Christian way to read the Bible, the Lectionary and the sacred liturgy.

Adolf Adam, *The Liturgical Year: Its History and its Meaning after the Reform of the Liturgy* (Pueblo Publishing Co., 1990).

Mike Aquilina, *The Fathers of the Church: An Introduction to the First Christian Teachers* (Our Sunday Visitor Inc., 1999).

Pope Benedict XVI, *Church Fathers from Clement of Rome to Augustine* (Ignatius Press, 2008).

Pope Benedict XVI, *Church Fathers and Teachers from Leo the Great to Peter Lombard* (Ignatius Press, 2010).

Normand Bonneau, *The Sunday Lectionary: Ritual, Word, Paschal Shape* (Liturgical Press, 1998).

Peter C. Bower, ed., *Handbook for the Revised Common Lectionary* (Westminster/John Knox Press, 1996).

Raniero Cantalamessa, *Easter in the Early Church* (Liturgical Press, 1993).

Michael Casey, *Sacred Reading: The Ancient Art of Lectio Divina* (Liguori, 1995).

Henry Chadwick, *The Early Church* (Penguin, 1993).

Consultation on Common Texts, *The Revised Common Lectionary* (Nashville, 1992).

Jean Corbon, *The Wellspring of Worship* (Paulist Press, 1988).

Jean Daniélou, *From Shadows to Reality: Studies in the Biblical Typology of the Fathers* (Burns & Oates, 1960).

Jean Daniélou, *The Bible and the Liturgy* (Darton, Longman & Todd, 1956).

Ivor J. Davidson, *The Birth of the Church*, Monarch History of the Church (Monarch, 2005).

Ivor J. Davidson, *A Public Faith: From Constantine to the Medieval World AD 312–600*, Monarch History of the Church (Monarch, 2005).

Henri de Lubac, *Medieval Exegesis: The Four Senses of Scripture*, 4 volumes (Eerdmans, 1998–).

Bertrand de Margerie, *An Introduction to the History of Exegesis, Volume 1, Greek Fathers* (Saint Bede's Publications, 1993).

Bertrand de Margerie, *An Introduction to the History of Exegesis, Volume 2, Latin Fathers* (Saint Bede's Publications, 1995).

Bertrand de Margerie, *An Introduction to the History of Exegesis, Volume 3, Saint Augustine* (Saint Bede's Publications, 1991).

Jeremy Driscoll, *Theology at the Eucharistic Table: Master Themes in the Theological Tradition* (Gracewing, 2003).

Christopher A. Hall, *Reading Scripture with the Church Fathers* (Intervarsity Press, 1998).

William Harmless, ed., *Augustine in his Own Words* (Catholic University of America Press, 2010).

Maxwell Johnson, ed., *Between Memory and Hope: Readings on the Liturgical Year* (Liturgical Press, 2000).

Morwenna Ludlow, *The Early Church* (Tauris, 2009).

Morwenna Ludlow and Scot Douglass, *Reading the Church Fathers* (T. & T. Clark, 2011).

Mariano Magrassi, *Praying the Bible: An Introduction to Lectio Divina* (Liturgical Press, 1998).

Adrian Nocent, *The Liturgical Year*, 4 volumes (Liturgical Press, 1977).

Thomas C. Oden and Christopher H. Hall, eds, *The Ancient Christian Commentary on Scripture*, 26 volumes to date (Intervarsity Press, 1998–).

Boniface Ramsey, *Beginning to Read the Fathers* (SCM Press, 1985).

Roman Lectionary, Study lectionary, 3 volumes (London, 1983).

Manlio Simonetti, *Biblical Interpretation in the Early Church: An Historical Introduction to Patristic Exegesis* (T. & T. Clark, 1994).

Thomas J. Talley, *The Origins of the Liturgical Year* (Liturgical Press, 1986).

Constantine Tsirpanlis, *Eastern Patristic Thought and Orthodox Theology* (Liturgical Press, 1991).

Robert L. Wilken, *The Spirit of Early Christian Thought: Seeking the Face of God* (Yale University Press, 2003).

Frances Young, Lewis Ayres and Andrew Louth, eds, *The Cambridge History of Early Christian Literature* (Cambridge University Press, 2004).

The Fathers of the Church in English

There are a number of series of English translations of the Fathers, for example:

Ancient Christian Texts (Intervarsity Press, 2009–).

Ancient Christian Writers (Paulist Press, 1946–).

Ante-Nicene Fathers, 10 volumes (reprint, Peabody Hendrickson, 1995).

Classics of Western Spirituality, includes some patristic authors, ed. Bernard McGinn (Paulist Press, 1978–).

Fathers of the Church (Catholic University of America Press, 1948–).

Nicene and Post-Nicene Fathers, 28 volumes (reprint, Peabody Hendrickson, 1995).

Popular Patristics Series, ed. John Behr (St Vladimir's Seminary Press, 1979–).

The Works of St Augustine: A Translation for the 21st Century, ed. John E. Rotelle and Boniface Ramsey (New City Press, 1990–).

INDEX OF GOSPEL PASSAGES

INDEX OF AUTHORS